Traditional
Chinese Penal Law

Traditional
Chinese Penal Law

Geoffrey MacCormack

EDINBURGH UNIVERSITY PRESS

© Geoffrey MacCormack 1990

Edinburgh University Press 1990
22 George Square, Edinburgh

Set in Monotype Perpetua
by Koinonia, Bury, and
printed in Great Britain by
Page Bros Ltd, Norwich

British Library Cataloguing
  in Publication Data
MacCormack, Geoffrey
  Traditional Chinese penal law.
  1. China. Criminal, history
  345.10509
ISBN 0 7486 0211 9

Contents

Preface

This is a book about the penal codes of imperial China, in particular those enacted by the T'ang, Sung, Ming and Ch'ing dynasties. It does not touch on the administrative law of these dynasties nor, except in passing, on the customary law relating to matters such as contract or property. Nor does it examine the rich case law of the Ch'ing period which formed the basis of Alabaster's Notes and Commentaries on Chinese Criminal Law and Bodde and Morris's Law in Imperial China. Hence the book deals not with traditional Chinese law as such but only with that component represented by the penal codes.

The primary sources are the texts of the penal codes themselves. The first part of the T'ang code, the section entitled 'General Principles', has been translated into English by Johnson (see list of abbreviations); otherwise I have used the excellent, punctuated edition of the code published in Beijing in 1983. Sometimes one can find a translation of a specific T'ang article in the French translations (Deloustal and Lê Code) of the early Vietnamese code derived from the T'ang code. In discussing the T'ang law I have often given a reference to these two translations (see list of abbreviations). The Sung Code is virtually identical with the T'ang, the Ming code has not as yet been translated into a Western language (for the edition used see list of abbreviations), although it closely resembles the Ch'ing code of which there are three partial translations available. The earliest (from the first part of the 19th century) is Staunton's translation into English. This gives a rendering of all the articles of the code (without distinguishing between text and official commentary), omitting sub-statutes and commentaries, but is not always accurate. Preferable are the two French translations by Boulais and Philastre both from the early part of the 20th century. Boulais omits some articles but includes a translation of many sub-statutes and fragments of commentary. Usefully it prints the Chinese text at the foot of the page. However it is neither as full nor as accurate as Philastre which is a translation of a Vietnamese code that more or less copied the Ch'ing. This translation not only gives a full and generally accurate translation of the articles of the code (distinguishing between text and official commentary) but includes many sub-statutes and (particularly helpful) translations of all of the general commentary and much of the 'upper commentary' of the code. It omits only the occasional article which was not adopted by the Vietnamese code. For bibliographical details of these translations see the list of abbreviations. Although the Yuan dynasty produced no penal code as such some of the legal collections promulgated in that period have been translated by Ratchnevsky (Un Code des Yüan) and Ch'en (Chinese Legal Tradition under the Mongols).

Other important primary sources are the Legal Treatises contained in the official Standard History of each dynasty. These are chapters which explain the history of legislation throughout the dynasty, discuss the utility of the punishments and offer much information on the working of the judicial system. All (apart from that of the Ch'ing) have been translated at least in part into a western language. There is a full translation of the two T'ang Legal Treatises by Bünger (Quellen zur Rechtsgeschichte der T'ang-Zeit) and of the Yuan by Ratchnevsky (Un Code des Yüan I-IV). Partial translations of the Sung and Ming Legal Treatises are available in Seidel, Studien zur Rechtsgeschichte der Sung-Zeit and Munzel, Strafecht im alten China (Ming).

I have sought to give a clear exposition of what I have taken to be the main branches of the law contained in the penal codes, with occasional references to pre-T'ang law, and in addition to provide some information on the social and intellectual milieu from which the codes emerged. The emphasis in the book is on the T'ang law and the extent to which it came to be modified in the Ming/Ch'ing period. It has seemed worthwhile to say quite a lot about T'ang law both because of the intrinsic importance and excellence of the T'ang code itself and because of the fact that much of the later law still closely follows the T'ang provisions. I have said only a little about the general historical background. Readers who come to the topic of traditional Chinese law for the first time may find it helpful to consult some recent general book on Chinese history such as Gernet's History of Chinese Civilization. A great deal of information is now being made available in the volumes of the Cambridge History of China in course of publication.

Since I started to learn classical Chinese some years ago I have received help from numerous people. First and foremost I thank Professor Wang Feng-xin of the Department of Western Languages in the University of Peking who spent countless hours helping me in my initial struggles with the T'ang code. I would also particularly like to thank Dr. P. Baker, Dr. I Burns, Prof. P. Ch'en, Dr. W. Dolby, Prof. A.F.P. Hulsewé, Mr. Liao Kang, Dr. W. Liu, Dr. M.J. Meijer and Prof. P. Stein for their help in different aspects of my work. I am grateful to Prof. F. Lyall for very kindly reading over the text and giving me his comments. None of these scholars is, of course, responsible for any errors or deficiencies in the work.

The skill of Ms Susan Kilpatrick, Mrs Maureen Mercer and Mrs Amanda Walton in the Law Faculty Secretariat ensured a smooth transition from typed draft to product of word processor. I thank them for their willingness to perform what at times must have seemed an endless task.

List of Abbreviations

Boulais: G. Boulais, Manuel du code chinois. Ch'eng Wen Publishing Co. Taipei, 1966 (reprint of 1924 edition). References are to the numbered paragraphs of the text unless prefixed with p. in which case the reference is to the page.

Deloustal: R. Deloustal, La justice dans l'ancien Annam, Bulletin de l'école française d'extrême orient 8 (1908), 177-220; 9 (1909), 91-122, 471-491, 765-796; 10 (1910), 1-60, 349-392, 461-505; 11 (1911), 25-66, 313-317; 12 (1912), 1-33; 13 (1913), 1-59; 19 (1919), 1-88; 22 (1922), 1-40. References are to the article number prefixing the paragraphs of Deloustal's translation.

Johnson: W. Johnson, The T'ang Code I. General Principles. Princeton U.P. Princeton. 1979.

Lê Code: Nguyen Ngoc Huy & Ta Van Tai with the cooperation of Tran Van Liem, The Lê Code. Law in Traditional Vietnam, 3 vols. Ohio U.P. Ohio. 1987. The references are to the article number prefixing the paragraphs of the translation and commentary in volumes I & II.

MLCCFL: Ming lü chi chieh fu li, 5 vols (Ming Code with Sub-statutes and Commentary). Ch'eng Wen Publishing Co. Taipei. n.d.

PHILASTRE: P.L.F. Philastre, Le code annamite, 2 vols, 2nd ed. Ch'eng Wen Publishing Co. Taipei. 1967 (reprint of 1909 edition).

TCLLHCPL: Ta Ch'ing lü li hui chi pien lang, 15 vols (Ch'ing Code with Sub-statutes and Commentaries). Ch'eng Wen Publishing Co. Taipei. n.d.

Note on Ch'ing Punishments

Throughout the book I have given the number of blows with the light or heavy stick according to that specified in the text of the code. In fact it has to be remembered that in practice the number was considerably less. See chapter 5 at note 30.

Chronological Table of Chinese Dynasties

SHANG (Yin)	c. 16th - 11th century B.C.
CHOU	c. 11th century -221 B.C.
Spring and Autumn period	770 - 475 B.C.
Warring States Period	475 - 221 B.C.
CH'IN	221 - 206 B.C.
HAN	206 B.C. - A.D. 220
Former (or Western) Han	206 B.C. - A.D. 24
Later (or Eastern) Han	25 - 220
THREE KINGDOMS	220 - 280
TSIN	265 - 420
SOUTHERN AND NORTHERN DYNASTIES	420 - 589
SUI	581 - 618
T'ANG	618 - 907
FIVE DYNASTIES	907 - 960
SUNG	960 - 1279
Northern Sung	960 - 1127
Southern Sung	1127 - 1279
YÜAN (Mongol)	1279 - 1368
MING	1368 - 1644
CHING (Manchu)	1644 - 1911

1

Historical Background

This chapter offers an overview of the main points in the development of traditional Chinese legal history taking as its focus the principal periods into which Chinese history is divided. If one starts with the earliest dynasty about which anything much is known, the Western Chou founded around 1100 B.C., and ends with the fall of the Ch'ing dynasty in 1911 (the close of the imperial age), one is covering a span of approximately 3000 years. On the whole little is known of the penal law prior to the T'ang dynasty, founded in the 7th century A.D., from which emanates the first code to have survived in its entirety. The account of the law given in the following chapters is based on the codes of the T'ang and later dynasties, with occasional references to earlier material. Consequently in my introductory survey I have discussed the legal developments of the pre-T'ang period more fully than those of the post-T'ang, in particular making only a few general remarks on the penal law of the Ming and Ch'ing dynasties.

The Archaic Period: Shang and Western Chou

Little can be said of the law applied in these early dynasties, the Shang being traditionally dated to the 16th-11th centuries BC and the Chou to the 11th-8th centuries. The main sources are literary but the problem is that a number of documents purporting to emanate from the Shang or early Chou dynasties, included in the Book of Documents (*Shu-ching*), in fact were written some hundreds of years later.[1] Nevertheless one document, The Announcement of K'ang (*K'ang kao*), generally held to be authentic, does permit one to establish some conclusions on the law of the early Chou dynasty, and even permits a little insight into the law of the previous Shang dynasty. The Announcement contains the instructions issued by king Wu, the first ruler of Western Chou, to a younger prince (K'ang) on the occasion of the latter's appointment to a fief. It offers advice on the way the prince is to administer justice within his territory, and provides the modern investigator with valuable information on the law of the archaic period.

First, it appears clear that the Chou conquerors continued to apply rules established by the Shang for the infliction of punishments for offences. The king urges K'ang 'to set forth those items of the law and take for punishments and verdicts the norms of the Yin (another name of the Shang). Use their just punishments and just killings'.[2] There is an implication here that the Shang, whether or not they applied them, had a set of rules, held to be just, specifying offences and their punishments. Knowledge of these rules appears to have been generally diffused at least among the ruling and official classes. It is difficult to see how this could have been so unless the Shang archives had contained written versions of the rules. One may note, even at this archaic period, the presence of a feature which characterised traditional Chinese law throughout its history, an ineradicable association of punishment with law.

Emphasis is also placed upon punishment in the rules of the Chou dynasty itself. On several occasions the king refers to, or urges caution in, the application of the rules imposing punishments.[3] These statements show a strong concern with substantive and procedural justice. The rules themselves should be designed to promote virtue and repress evil doing[4] and they should be applied in a fair manner after due and proper consideration of the facts of the case by the judge.[5] In particular the ruler should not punish purely in accordance with his personal wishes, and he should ensure that his officials apply the existing law and not on their own initiative introduce innovations.[6]

The sources of the rules may have been varied. Undoubtedly the king himself might introduce rules. The *K'ang kao* itself mentions King Wen's rules prescribing punishments for those who were unfilial or unbrotherly.[7] From another set of instructions on the dangers of drinking given by King Wu to Prince K'ang, it appears that the king had himself prohibited drinking by people in groups and prescribed the death penalty for this offence.[8] Even subordinate rulers such as prince K'ang may have had a limited discretion for the determination of which conduct should entail punishment. However one receives the impression that the 'just norms' which the prince is to apply are those which are accepted generally by the society, or at any rate by its ruling elite, and are not necessarily the enactments of any particular ruler. Perhaps the position was that such 'customary' rules received the imprimatur of the ruler, and that special importance was accorded to the fact that they had been accepted by the founder of the dynasty. Thus the reference to King Wen's rules prescribing punishments for the unfilial and the unbrotherly may mean not that the king introduced these rules for the first time, but that he inaugurated the dynasty on their basis. Nevertheless the early Chou kings do seem to have possessed the power to introduce new rules of law, though one cannot be sure what constraints might have operated to control the exercise of this power.

With respect to the content of the law, one has some sparse information. The existence of rules on unfilial and unbrotherly conduct, and the drinking of intoxicating liquor has already been noted. In addition there is evidenced the existence of rules punishing traitors, thieves, murderers and those who use force against others.[9] King Wu instructs the prince to punish the persistent and deliberate offender with death even though his offence be small, but not to kill one who errs by mischance even though his offence be great.[10] One may perhaps infer from this that the rules themselves differentiated punishment according to whether the offence was committed intentionally or not. It is worth remembering that rules on all these matters, with the exception of that prohibiting drinking, appear in the codes of the later imperial dynasties. Unfilial conduct, for example, until the end of the Ch'ing dynasty, was treated as one of the most serious offences in the code.

The only punishments mentioned in the *K'ang kao* are physical: putting to death, cutting off the nose, cutting of the legs.[11] The fine was also known.[12] One may conjecture that fines were imposed in cases of non-intentional offences, though it remains possible that these attracted a physical mutilating punishment short of death.

We may conclude that the early Chou, and probably also the Shang, dynasty possessed written collections of rules imposing punishments. To a settled core handed down from one king to the next, and indeed passing from the Shang to the Chou, would be added from time to time rules introducing new offences or modifying the punishments for established ones. Two further points may be made. There is nothing in the *K'ang kao* to suggest that the penal rules applied only to a certain class of the population, for example those who did not rank as noble. Nor, equally, is there any evidence that the noble and official class were given special privileges or exempted from the normal punishments. Indeed the evidence, admittedly fragmentary, points the other way. Prince K'ang is told to punish with death officials who do not themselves keep the laws or introduce new offences on their own authority.[13]

Secondly, it seems that the content of the penal rules was made available to the people. On two occasions king Wu refers to the need to 'set forth' the laws which are to apply within the fief.[14] How was this done? Oral explanation is one possibility. This is implied in the instruction to the prince to 'set forth' the law when he is acting as a judge.[15] Another possibility is visual representation. Sources from a later period attribute to the earliest Chinese rulers the practice of suspending 'representations' (*hsiang*) of the penal laws outside their palaces for the information of the public.[16] It is no longer thought, as previously,[17] that *hsiang* simply means 'pictures of the punishments', but rather is to be understood as a 'full description' in the sense of a full written version.[18] Nevertheless in view of the general illiteracy pictures of the punishments may have been included in the written 'representation'. Although the documents from the early Chou period do not evidence this practice of suspending 'representations' of the penal laws, there may well have been some such method of acquainting the people with the offences and their punishments.[19]

The Spring and Autumn (770-475 B.C.) and Warring States (475-221 B.C.) Periods

From the *K'ang kao* one catches a glimpse of law in the early years of the Chou dynasty. How it was actually applied we do not know. For the four centuries or so in which the Western Chou empire endured the precepts of king Wu no doubt remained the aspiration; the extent to which they were actually applied is probably impossible to determine. With the dissolution of the empire at the beginning of the eighth century B.C. and the onset of the turbulent and confused period known as that of the Spring and Autumn uncertainty increases. The content of the law and the official attitude to punishments no doubt varied considerably in the different states at different periods of time. Fragments of information can be obtained from the *Tso-chuan*. This is a history of the political fortunes of the various states that emerged as autonomous units after the collapse of the centralised Western Chou government, dealing with events from the end of the 8th to the middle of the 5th B.C. It is thought to have been compiled during the Warring States period but to have been based on earlier records.[20] Used with caution it may be taken as evidence of the thought and practices of rules and statesmen in the Spring and Autumn period.

Passages in the *Tso-chuan* show that statesmen, when speaking of the role of punishments in the government of the state, advocated much the same approach as that taken by king Wu. The punishments themselves should be moderate and reasonable; they should be applied only in accordance with the law, and not to gratify a ruler's whim; and they should be applied to high ranking officials as well as to ordinary people. Inadvertent offences should be pardoned in the sense that death or the mutilating punishments should not be imposed.[21] Practice, however, might well be different. Two stories from the *Tso-chuan* illustrate the predilection of rulers or powerful ministers for the arbitrary exercise of power.

In 538 B.C. the ruler of the state of Ch'i asked his minister Yen Ying why he wished to live in an uncomfortable house next to the market. Yen replied that it was convenient for him to purchase goods. When asked by the ruler what things were cheap, and what dear he said 'shoes for people whose toes have been cut off are dear and other shoes are cheap', the point being that the ruler 'punished so many that there were people who sold shoes for those whose toes had been cut off'. As a result of his minister's implied criticism the ruler thereafter punished more rarely.[22] This anecdote shows that in practice there might be little restraint upon a ruler's power to inflict mutilating punishments as he wished.

In 563 B.C. the minister Tzu K'ung came to supreme power in the state of Cheng. He made a 'writing' requiring those of all ranks to accept the rules which he established. When they refused to obey he threatened them with punishment. Tzu Ch'an remonstrated with him and by appealing to considerations of political expediency persuaded him to burn the 'writing' publicly. Although Tzu K'ung bowed to pressure and changed his intention, the very fact that he should have formally drafted such a rule shows that in practice a ruler or powerful minister had considerable freedom in the exercise of legislative power.[23]

The most important events in the legal history of the Spring and Autumn period were attempts at codification of the law, a process that occurred in several states throughout the 7th and 6th centuries B.C. The *Tso-chuan* records that in 621 B.C. the minister Hsüan Tzu of Chin 'established regular rules for the conduct of government affairs, adjusted the laws and the definitions of crimes, codified penal matters ... restored to their original form the distinctions of rank... When all these regulations were completed he delivered them to the appropriate officials so that they might be carried into practice throughout the state of Chin, and to serve as its regular laws'.[24] In 536 B.C. the government of Cheng under its first minister Tzu Ch'an (referred to above) inscribed on bronze its code of laws, establishing the punishments for specific offences.[25] Likewise in 513 B.C. the state of Chin had inscribed on tripods the penal code prepared by Hsüan Tzu nearly a century earlier.[26] In 501 B.C., according to the *Tso-chuan*, the state of Cheng put to death Teng Hsi but continued to use a code written by Teng on bamboo tablets.[27] This is a particularly interesting piece of information since, if accurate, it suggests that within the same state during a comparatively short space of time different codes were drawn up and operated. If the code inscribed on bronze in 536 B.C. had still been in force it is difficult to see the need for a further code written on bamboo. Of course it is possible that the bamboo code was merely a modified version of the bronze.

No direct evidence is supplied by the *Tso-chuan* on the content of these various codes, other than their preoccupation with the imposition of punishments. But there is one possibly significant piece of indirect evidence. A speech critical of the code of 513 B.C. is put into the mouth of Confucius.[28] He is made to say that the people in concentrating on the penal laws will no longer honour the noble and thus the distinction between noble and base will be eroded.[29] It is possible that the ground of the objection here is the fact that the laws did not give the noble and official class a privileged position. One has, however, to be wary of reading too much into the remarks attributed to Confucius since the original code on which the 513 redaction was based had established rules on the 'distinction between ranks'.

What were the reasons for the production of these (and almost certainly other) codes? Probably the driving thrust was the wish of rulers and ministers to intensify central control over their subjects. H.G. Creel has drawn attention to the transition from a 'feudal' to a 'bureaucratic' system of government, the former characterised by a delegation of power to the holders of fiefs, the latter by the retention of power at the centre and its exercise at the local level by strictly accountable professional administrators.[30] The transition to bureaucratic, centralised administration as it developed in various states during the course of the Spring and Autumn period would have been helped by the enactment and consolidation, in a systematic fashion, of laws which both defined the functions and powers of officials and established in clear terms the range of offences for which punishments were to be imposed. It would certainly be necessary for the officials themselves to know the details of the laws. But it seems also that one reason for inscribing the codes on metal was to facilitate knowledge of the law by the people as a whole. Indeed the fact that the people would come to know the laws and so regulate their behaviour by them and not out of respect for their superiors is advanced by Shu-hsiang of Chin in a letter to the responsible minister in Cheng as a criticism of the codification of 536 B.C.[31]

During the even more turbulent period (the Warring States) that succeeded the Spring and Autumn in which the principal states fought constant battles for survival and supremacy, in some states at least there came to be an increasing resort to detailed penal and administrative rules by the central government. The best known, and indeed most notorious, advocate of a reliance upon law was Lord Shang, chief minister of the state of Ch'in in the middle of the 4th century B.C. He prevailed upon the ruling duke to introduce a wide ranging and severe set of laws applicable to nobles as well as commoners, designed to strengthen the agricultural productivity and military capacity of the state.[32] Precise details of these laws have not survived

However in 1975 a tomb excavated in the province of Hupei was found to contain a large number of bamboo slips inscribed with details of the laws of the state of Ch'in current in the 3rd century B.C.[33] Although themselves numerous these laws represent only a part of the code then in force in Ch'in. They are those which a relatively low ranking official found necessary for the conduct of local administration especially with regard to the management of labour and grain. Their complexity and sophistication show that Ch'in law, both administrative and penal, had reached a high degree of development by the 3rd century B.C. This in turn suggests that, although they may owe much to Lord Shang's initiatives, there had been a long period of evolution perhaps extending over several centuries in which the government of Ch'in had been experimenting with, and increasingly relying upon, detailed administrative and penal rules. The process of codification may thus have had a longer history than has sometimes been supposed.[34]

If we were able to rely upon the authenticity of the documents contained in the *Shu-ching* we would have evidence of the existence of elaborate and comprehensive penal codes even before the collapse of the Western Chou empire. One such document entitled *The Punishments of Lü (Lü Hsing)* purports to give the instructions of King Mu (traditional reign dates: 1001-947 B.C.) to the prince of Lu on the subject of the punishments.[35] The main theme of the king's charge to the prince, bolstered by frequent appeals to the lessons of antiquity, is that, while there is need for punishments, great care should be taken in their application. This was all the more important because the punishments meant were corporal, ranging from death to the branding of the body. Once inflicted they could not be undone. Hence the prince is urged to see that merciful and discriminatory persons are appointed as judges, that only those properly found guilty should be punished and that in cases of doubt fines should be imposed instead of physical punishment.[36]

The complexity of the code to which the king refers is indicated by the fact that there are stated to be 200 offences punishable by death, 300 by castration, 500 by leg-cutting, 1000 by nose-cutting and 1000 by branding. From the injunction laid upon judges in determining a case 'publicly to open the law codex'[37] it appears that the penal rules were stated in the form of a written code. However modern scholarship is divided on the date of the *Lü Hsing*. H.G. Creel categorically holds that it emanated from the period of the Warring States and therefore expresses a conception and development of law characteristic of this period.[38] Other scholars, however, while not necessarily holding that king Mu himself wrote the document, attribute it to the end of the Western Chou period around 800 B.C.[39]

The Ch'in (221-206 B.C.) and Han (206 B.C. - 220 A.D.) Empires

In 221 B.C. the state of Ch'in completed the conquest of the other states and attained supremacy in China. Its laws now constituted the code of the newly constituted Ch'in empire.[40] Later tradition stigmatised the Ch'in code as a harsh and cruel instrument of tyrannical government. Undoubtedly the comprehensiveness and precision of the administrative and penal rules created by the Ch'in rulers and ministers had helped to create a powerful military state efficiently controlled by a central bureaucracy, and so had contributed to the eventual triumph of Ch'in in the struggles of the states. But so far as one can judge from the text of the laws discovered in 1975 the penal measures applied by the Ch'in code do not appear to have been unduly draconian or oppressive. Certainly mutilating punishments were used, but so they had been in earlier centuries by other states, and so they continued to be for a time even under the Han. Noticeable is the frequent use of fines, especially for breach of duty by officials, and forced labour (often but not always combined with mutilation).

Two points may be made with respect to the content of the Ch'in penal rules. In view of the fact that Lord Shang in the fourth century had insisted that the law should apply to all equally, irrespective of rank, it is interesting to observe that privileged status entailed a diminution in punishment. For example where an individual falsely accused another of an offence, his punishment should be mutilation and forced labour. But where the false accuser possessed high status, perhaps belonging to an official or aristocratic family, the mutilation was omitted from the punishment.[41] The second point is that one can already see a resemblance between the content of some of the Ch'in laws and that of the later imperial codes. For example the rules regulate the punishment for the infliction of injuries in a fight according to the nature of the injury and the type of weapon used.[42]

The Ch'in empire barely survived the death of its founder in 210 B.C. Little more than a year passed before the first rebellions broke out and in 207 Liu Pang, the future emperor Kao-ti and founder of the Han dynasty, occupied the Ch'in capital and captured the second Ch'in emperor, thus effectively putting an end to the dynasty. On this occasion two events significant for legal history occurred. Hsiao Ho, a companion of Liu Pang and the future chancellor of Han, 'gathered up completely from the courts of the Lieutenant Chancellor of Ch'in the charts, registers, the documents and the writings.'[43] These archives must have included the text of the Ch'in laws. A little later Liu Pang summoned the important men of the region and said to them 'Fathers and Elders you have suffered long enough from the cruel laws of the Ch'in dynasty: those who spoke ill or criticised the government have been cruelly executed with their relatives, those who talked in private (i.e. plotted against the government) have been publicly executed in the market place... I am merely going to agree with you, Fathers and Elders, upon a code of laws in three articles: he who kills anyone will be put to death; he who wounds anyone or robs will be punished according to his offence; as to the remainder, I am repealing and doing away with all the laws of the Ch'in dynasty'.[44]

Of these two events it was the first which proved to have lasting importance. Once Liu Pang had overcome his rivals and assumed the title of emperor in 202 he found it expedient to continue the legal regime of the Ch'in and never implemented his agreement to reduce the laws to three. Pan Ku, the official historian of the Han dynasty, states 'At the beginning of his reign he conformed to the people's wishes when he made an agreement with them in three articles; when the empire had been subjugated he commanded Hsiao Ho to set in order the criminal laws and orders'.[45] This is where Hsiao Ho must have found his appropriation of the Ch'in archives useful. We are told that 'the Law of Three Sections proved insufficient to restrain villainy, so at that stage the Chancellor of State Hsiao Ho gathered together the laws of Ch'in and choosing those which were suitable for those times, he made Statutes in nine sections'.[46] The laws multiplied further until 'writings and documents filled tables and cupboards and the officials in charge were unable to look at them all. Due to this, those who had to apply them in the commandeers and feudal states were at variance; sometimes the crimes were the same and the verdicts different'.[47]

All in all it is difficult to see that the position reached under the Han with respect to the penal law was very different from that which obtained under the Ch'n. Perhaps there were less executions, particularly those ordered at the discretion of the emperor. Certainly the mutilating punishments (with the exception of castration) were abolished in 167 B.C. and replaced with floggings. But these were so severe that in practice they amounted to capital punishment and steps had to be taken to reduce the number of blows and regulate the size of the stick with which they were administered.[48]

Although the actual structure and organisation of the Han penal code are not known it is clear that it contained a version of many of the rules that appeared in the 'General Principles' and 'Specific Offences' sections of the later dynastic codes. Thus Han law knew rules relating to the ten abominations, the privileges of nobles and officials, the mitigation in punishment to be accorded the old or the young, and the mutual concealment by close relatives of each other's offences. These are all matters dealt with in the 'General Principles' sections of the later codes. Furthermore many of the subjects which A.F.P. Hulsewé has listed as dealt with by the Han statutes and ordinances are found in the 'Specific Offences' sections of the later codes. One may instance specifically the material falling under the Statutes on Robbery and the Statutes on Banditry.[49]

The Three Kingdoms - Sui Dynasty (220 - 618 A.D.)

From the dissolution of the Later Han empire in the beginning of the 3rd century A.D. until the reunification of China under the Sui at the beginning of the 7th intervened a period of disunity and upheaval. It was marked by a basic division between the South and the North. The Chinese successors of the Han with their capital in the north were driven to the south by barbarian invaders who established themselves as the rulers of the northern provinces. Thereafter a multitude of dynasties, often short lived, ruled in the north and south. Although the centre of civilization had now shifted to the south, Chinese culture retained its hold in the north and indeed, as has been the case throughout Chinese history, triumphed over the invaders. The northern conquerors became thoroughly sinicised, adopting not just Chinese culture in general but also the Chinese law inherited from the Han.

Despite its political and military chaos this period was of great importance for the development of the law.[50] There were numerous attempts at codification by the various dynasties and experiments with different kinds and degrees of punishment. The broad result was the production under the Sui of a concise, well balanced code imposing punishments that had managed to strike the middle ground between the excessively severe and the unduly lenient. It was in this period that some of the principal features of traditional Chinese penal law were cast into a form that endured until the twentieth century: for example the five punishments, the ten abominations, the eight deliberations and the other privileges, the rules on collective prosecution and the liability of officials.

The essence of the process of codification may be chartered as follows. During the epoch of the Three Kingdoms the most important kingdom, that of Wei, produced a code in 234. Its successor state Tsin, which for a very brief time managed to secure control of all China, in turn produced a code in 268. Both these codes were greatly influenced by that of Han, the Tsin code in fact adopting the nine chapters of the Han code and adding a further eleven sections, showing the influence of the Wei code.[51] With the expulsion of the Tsin from the north by the barbarians at the beginning of the 4th century, their code also went south. Lost in the 5th century it was reconstructed from oral memory during a later southern dynasty, the Liang by whom it was promulgated in 503 A.D. This version was revised and extended by the succeeding Ch'en dynasty in the latter part of the 6th century. Being too large and confused this final product of codification in the south had no influence on the later development of the law.

The line of codification which ultimately proved to be significant was established in the north. The Northern Wei (Toba) dynasty adopted the Han/Tsin code as the basis of its own codification at the end of the 5th century. The Northern Ch'i dynasty, taking as its model the Wei and Tsin codes, produced in 564 an important code in twelve sections, conspicuous for its clarity and simplicity. The ruling house attached great importance to the dissemination of the code and all prospective officials were ordered to study it as part of their education. From the perspective of legal history this code was considerably more influential than the much longer code produced about the same time by another northern dynasty, the Northern Chou. After the reunification of the empire by the Sui it was the code of the Northern Ch'i that provided the main model for the code of the new dynasty first promulgated in 581, revised in 583. This code, like the 564 code, was in twelve sections but contained almost half the number of articles, 500 instead of 949. Although a later Sui code in 18 sections was promulgated in 607 it was the 583 code that endured for posterity through its incorporation as the basis of the T'ang code.

The T'ang Dynasty 618-967

Despite the collapse of the Sui dynasty through the misgovernment and extravagance of its second ruler, China, after a few years of renewed civil war, remained united under the T'ang dynasty, one of the most important in the country's history. The first decades of this dynasty saw perfected a system of law and administration that in essentials survived until the end of the imperial period. One of the achievements of the age, perhaps not sufficiently appreciated by the Chinese themselves, was the T'ang penal code which provided an admirably clear and precise statement of offences entailing punishment and of the conditions under which punishment would be imposed.[52]

The first T'ang emperor Kao-tsu, like Liu Pang the founder of the Han dynasty, upon his occupation of the Sui capital in 617 proclaimed a 'fundamental law' in twelve articles restricting the death penalty to murder, robbery, desertion from the army and treason. Issued for political reasons to attract support from a populace suffering under the harsh punishments of the last years of the Sui, this law was rapidly replaced by a code founded upon the Sui code of 583. The earliest version promulgated in 619 contained only 53 articles; this was expanded to 500 in 624. The code was revised in 637 with a decrease in the number of offences entailing death or life exile, and thereafter there were frequent revisions until the final redaction of the code in 737. The most important change was the incorporation in 653 of an authoritative commentary drafted by a commission of legal experts headed by the emperor's brother-in-law, Chang-sun Wu-chi. This not only provided a lucid explanation of the highly elliptic articles of the code, but frequently introduced further rules not in the text of the code. It is the 737 redaction of the code which survives today.

In 755 commenced the rebellion of An Lu-shan. Although finally put down eleven years later the rebellion destroyed the administrative units of the empire. The dislocation was such that the central.government under the T'ang never again recovered full control over the more remote provinces whose governors had become accustomed to considerable autonomy during the course of the rebellion. The code remained in theory the law of the empire but was not in fact fully applied except in those areas under the direct control of the court.[53] It is perhaps for this reason that no major revision of the code was completed after the rebellion. Changes in the law continued to be made but these were introduced by imperial decrees which were never incorporated into the code. One sees here the beginning of the shift in emphasis away from the code and towards individual imperial decrees which became more marked under the Sung.

In its final form the T'ang code contained 502 articles organised into twelve books, the first setting out the 'General Principles'of the law, and the others the multitude of 'Specific Offences'.[54] Among the 'General Principles' are the rules defining the five punishments (beating with the light or heavy stick, penal servitude, life exile and death), the ten abominations (being the most serious offences, those directed against the state, the person of the emperor or the family), the various privileges of the nobles and officials, the collegiate liability of officials, the mitigation in punishment accorded the young, the old and the infirm, the treatment of offences involving 'illicit goods'(*tsang*), the entitlement of relatives to mutual concealment of offences and the circumstances under which confession entailed immunity from punishment.

The 'Specific Offences' section deals with the following matters, defining each individual offence and establishing the punishment for it. First is the book on 'The Imperial Guard and Prohibitions', setting out the offences concerned with unauthorised entry of imperial property, failure by guardsmen to carry out their duties and the illegal passing through boundary gates. The next book on 'Administrative Regulations' defines the duties of officials and imposes punishments for their breach. Among them are detailed rules on the composition and transmission of official documents, corruption and abuse of power. In the 'Household and Marriage' book are contained the rules requiring the registration of members of a household (for taxation and labour purposes), those regulating the use and disposition of family land, and those defining the circumstances under which marriage and divorce are permissible.

The book on 'The Public Stables and Granaries', apart from regulating the duties of those in charge of government animals or property, contains an important set of articles on liability for damage or injury caused by animals. 'Unauthorised Levy' is concerned with offences in the raising or use of troops or public labour. 'Violence and Robbery' covers some grave offences against the state or the individual, namely treason, plotting to kill, theft, arson and kidnapping. 'Assaults and Accusations' covers other offences against the person, namely beating, physical injury, killing and making false accusations. 'Fraud and Counterfeit' lists offences relating to the forging or falsification of imperial or official documents, or involving other kinds of deception such as procuring a person's death through deceit.

A lengthy book on 'Miscellaneous Offences' deals *inter alia* with illicit sexual intercourse, failure to repay debts, improper practices in the sale of goods in the market, accidental fires and destruction of property. In this book is found the 'catch all' article which confers power on officials to order beatings for acts which should not have been done. The last two books 'Arrest and Flight' and 'Judgment and Prison' deal with a variety of procedural matters involving the arrest of criminals, desertion of military or civil posts, imprisonment, the conduct of trials, sentencing in general and the imposition of the death penalty in particular.

From the historical perspective the T'ang code is the most important penal code to have been produced in China. It survived virtually unchanged until the end of the Sung dynasty. When the Ming dynasty recast the law the T'ang code was still preserved as the basis of the new code. Indeed many of its provisions appeared almost verbatim in the Ming code and from there passed into the Ch'ing. Outside China the T'ang code had a great influence on legal development in South East Asia being adopted at different times in Vietnam, Korea and Japan.[55] Its success both internally and abroad was not due just to the fact that it was the only code to have survived intact from the mediaeval period. Its intrinsic excellence was undoubtedly the main element in its continuing influence. One may instance the conciseness of the language, the mathematical precision in the allocation of the punishments, the systematic ordering of the material and the success with which the legislators were able, with the help of relatively few technical notions, to provide rules for a vast number of different situations. To this one may add the fact that its solutions, reached after many centuries of experimentation, were generally equitable and in harmony with the fundamental morality of the Chinese.

The Sung Dynasty (960-1279)

A military revolt brought to an end the T'ang dynasty at the end of the ninth century and ushered in a short period of disunity known as the Five Dynasties. During this period several short-lived military dictatorships ruled the northern provinces. Despite the anarchic conditions the T'ang code was re-issued with additions at least by some of these dynasties. It was the version used by the last of them, the Later Chou, published in 958, that was taken as a model by the general who succeeded in re-establishing a unified empire in 960, and assumed the throne. The first

Sung emperor, T'ai-tsu, followed tradition in establishing a commission to undertake a revision of the laws. But the penal code produced by the commission in 963 and adopted as the law of the empire under the name *Sung hsing t'ung* presented some interesting features. Whereas the Han and Sui/T'ang empires had drafted codes that were new in form and substance even though they borrowed a great deal from previous codes, the Sung code took over the T'ang code virtually without modification and simply inserted at appropriate places edicts or other rules which had come into force since 737 but had never been incorporated in the code.

A striking example occurs right at the beginning of the code. Its first articles reproduce the articles and commentary of the T'ang code which establish and define the five punishments: capital punishment (decapitation and strangulation), life exile to distances ranging from 3000 to 2000 *li*,[56] penal servitude for periods ranging from three years to one, beating with the heavy stick ranging from 100 to 60 blows and beatings with the light stick ranging from 50 to 10 blows. However when he ascended the throne T'ai-tsu, putting into practice the Confucian principle of humanity, reduced the severity of the T'ang punishments. For example 100 blows with the heavy stick was now to be 20, and life exile to 3000 *li* was now to be hard labour for one year together with a beating of 20 blows.[57] No alterations to the articles or commentary of the code were made. The new rules were simply inserted as an appendix after the article on life exile and before that on the death penalty (where there were no changes).

The Sung code also incorporated from the T'ang code articles which had become obsolete even during the T'ang period itself, for example, those designed to implement the *ch'ün tien* system of land tenure under which land was granted to families by the emperor upon various conditions precluding the right of alienation. Although in practice under both the T'ang and Sung dynasties land granted by the state was bought and sold by families, the rules in the codes forbidding such alienations were retained. Thus the Sung code in this respect adopted rules which for some centuries before had not been applied.[58]

Clearly demonstrated in the Sung code are two interesting and related phenomena. On the one hand the new dynasty took over almost verbatim the T'ang code even to the extent of retaining completely obsolete articles. On the other even very important amendments did not entail modification of its actual articles; they were inserted merely as appendices to the articles which they affected. On the face of it articles which had become obsolete or rendered ineffective remained in force as the law. Yet it is difficult to say exactly in what sense they counted as law. Possibly one can go no further than to say they were still regarded as the law, just as any other provisions of the code, and yet were not applied in practice.

What explains these phenomena? The crucial point is the unwillingness of the Sung and even late T'ang legislators to alter the text of the 737 version of the code. Previously founders of dynasties who had borrowed much from the law codes of their predecessors at least rewrote the existing codes to the extent necessary to accommodate them to the changed times. The fact that the founder of the Sung dynasty did not adopt this method appears to be explicable only by the particular veneration in which the T'ang code was held. This would have been induced not only by general respect for a great dynasty but also by admiration for the intrinsic excellence of the code itself.

Another unusual feature of Sung legislative practice was the reluctance to alter or revise the penal code once it had been promulgated in 963. Many changes in the law occurred throughout the succeeding centuries. They were frequently promulgated in the form of an imperial edict. Past practice had been to incorporate the terms of relevant edicts into the code at one of the periodic revisions or at least to insert the text of the edict after the article to which it related. Neither practice was adopted under the Sung. Edicts were not incorporated into the penal code but published in separate collections. So extensive did these collections become that they tended to supplant the code as the main source of law. This tendency was accelerated by a decision of the emperor Shen-tsung in 1079. He expressly provided that criminal cases not covered by the code were to be decided in accordance with the relevant edict and altered the title of the whole corpus of legislation from 'code, statutes, decrees and regulations' to 'edicts, statutes, decrees and regulations'[59]. The substitution of 'edict' for 'code' expresses the fact that for practical purposes the latter had been supplanted by the former. The great neo-Confucian philosopher Chu Hsi (1130-1200) is credited with the observation that the code had been replaced by imperial edicts.[60]

The Yüan Dynasty (1279-1368)

The Mongolian domination of China led to a break in legal tradition, particularly in the failure of the Mongolian dynasty to produce a penal code of the kind that had appeared under the T'ang and Sung. Such a failure appears to have been the result of the deliberate policy of the Mongol rulers who, despite the strong urging of their Chinese officials for a code of the traditional type, did not consider this to be suitable for a multi-national empire in which the Mongols retained their own customary law. Nevertheless Chinese law, after an initial set back, continued to flourish and, indeed, in the latter part of the dynasty Chinese officials began to take a greater interest in the law than had been the case under earlier dynasties.

The strength of the native Chinese legal tradition was seen even before the Mongolian invasion. At the beginning of the 12th century the Sung had already lost control of the northern provinces to a nomadic people who founded a new dynasty with the capital at Peking, known as the Chin or Northern Sung. The Chin rulers and their people rapidly became sinicised and adopted a law code modelled on that of the T'ang (the *T'ai ho lü*).[61] The Mongols who destroyed the Chin dynasty and established themselves in the north before proceeding to the final conquest of the south kept in force the *T'ai ho lü* until their supremacy over the whole of China was effectively secured. In 1271 Kublai Khan abrogated the *T'ai ho lü* and no code of like nature was reinstated until the Ming.

After the abrogation of the *T'ai ho lü* Mongolian customary law was the dominant element in the system of official law until the emperor bowed to the pressure of the Chinese and consented to the issue of a 'code' in 1291. This was an important collection of laws (the *Chih-yüan hsin-ko*) applicable to the Chinese population. Although arranged systematically according to subject matter it was not a penal code in the traditional sense since many of the rules contained in it were not rules prescribing punishments for offences. It contained both administrative and penal measures.[62] Later in the dynasty the pressure for Chinese laws increased and several important codifications or surveys of legal material were issued, all again combining the administrative with the penal and none following the format of the T'ang/Sung penal code. Nevertheless to judge from the account of Yuan law, preserved in the official history of the dynasty, which was drawn from one of these vast collections (the *Ching-shih ta-tien* of 1331), the substance of the penal law was similar to that of the T'ang.[63] Indeed the emperor who had commissioned the *Ching-shih ta-tien* is said to have remarked of the section entitled *Hsien-tien* (Judicial Institutions) 'Is it not the T'ang code!'.[64]

Generally speaking there is no decline in the study and development of the law under the Yüan. In fact the interest of the Chinese officials and literati in law appears to have been considerable and to have marked a change from the attitude typified by the remark of the ninth century poet Su Shih, 'One does not read the codes!'.[65] Recent studies have shown that the old view according to which the Mongolian conquest was merely a barbaric and depressing interlude between two great Chinese epochs of civilization, the Sung and the Ming, should be revised, at least with respect to legal institutions. Working in partnership the Mongolian rulers and their Chinese ministers and advisers constantly sought to improve the administration of justice and, in particular, to tackle the problems posed by the considerable ethnic diversity of the empire as well as the existence of powerful professional groups such as the military and the priests. The result was the production of a rather more lenient system of punishments than that in force under the Ming and Ch'ing, the development of new and efficient legal procedures especially for the determination of cases involving persons belonging to different ethnic groups or to the military or priestly castes, and the incorporation into Chinese law of some rules of Mongolian customary law. One of these Mongolian additions that survived into the later law was the obligation placed on the offender to supply 'funeral' or 'nourishment' expenses to the family of the victim in cases of killing or injury.[66]

The Ming Dynasty (1368-1644)

In the latter part of the 14th century the Chinese reasserted themselves and secured the expulsion of the Mongols. A new, native dynasty – the Ming – was established on the throne. Its founder, the emperor T'ai-tsu, reverted to the traditional pre-Yüan pattern of codification and in particular looked to the T'ang code as his model. At the same time he was concerned to counter what was perceived as the laxity of the Yüan regime in matters of punishment.[67] Initially T'ai-tsu adopted the example of the first Han and Sung emperors in issuing a simple statement of the rules which were to be applied by his government. The *Ta Ming Ling* (Great Ming Ordinance) dates from the first year of his reign (1368). This contained both administrative and penal rules, in all 145 articles, and was intended to provide a clear and simple statement of the law for the guidance of the people. An important feature was the arrangement of the material. The rules were grouped according to the main areas of activity for which the government assumed responsibility. These were placed under the control of six ministries or boards, namely those of Civil Office, Revenue and Population, Rites, War, Punishments and Public Works.[68]

In 1374 the first regular penal code of the new dynasty was promulgated. According to the Ming Legal Treatise it followed the T'ang code in its division of the material. Of its 606 articles only 31 were fully new; the rest were taken directly from the T'ang code or from other legislation (also probably based on the T'ang code).[69] In subsequent years this code - the *Ta Ming Lü*- was revised, the process of revision culminating in the promulgation of a major new penal code in 1397, near the end of T'ai-tsu's reign. Although in substance much was still owed to the T'ang code, many of its articles reappearing in virtually identical language, the organisation of the new code was quite different. The model may have been the *Ta Ming Ling* since in the penal code of 1397 the material is arranged by subject matter according to the divisions of governmental authority represented by the six ministries or boards. The first part is constituted by the 'General Principles' section, then follow six main 'Specific Offences' sections. Under 'Administrative Law' are comprised the rules specifying punishments for breach of duty by officials. Under 'Civil Law' are comprised the rules on family and marriage, land, government storehouses, taxes, money lending and public markets. Under 'Ritual Law' are comprised the penal rules dealing with sacrifices and ceremonies. Under 'Military Law' are the rules on imperial palaces, imperial guards, the frontier, horses and cattle and postal services. The section on 'Penal Law' comprises offences against the person such as killing, physical injury, insult, various offences against property, in particular theft, sexual offences, miscellaneous offences and offences committed by those responsible for the administration of justice. Finally the section on 'Public Works' deals with public construction and the conservation of rivers.[70]

This reorganisation of the material in the penal code can be seen as an improvement upon the arrangement found in the T'ang code and its successors. It brings the penal code into line with the principal classification adopted for the conduct and regulation of government business. The Ming code also exhibits a further formal improvement over the T'ang code, in that its arrangement of the specific articles in the seven sections is more systematic; there is a better grouping of articles dealing with the same subject matter. For example book 19 of the Ming code (falling within the section on 'Penal Law') is headed 'Homicide' (*jen ming*). It contains twenty articles dealing with different cases of killing, though incorporating as well some injuries falling short of death and one or two other offences. The T'ang code contains no such book devoted to homicide. Instead the various provisions that contemplate acts resulting in a person's death are mainly to be found scattered through three books, those on 'Violence and Robbery', Assaults and Accusations' and 'Miscellaneous Articles'.

One sees that the compilers of the Ming code in rethinking the basic classification of the material treated the fact of killing and the offences related to it more systematically than the compilers of the T'ang. Furthermore the grouping of the rules in a book headed 'Homicide' evidences the importance attached to killing as an offence. When the T'ang code was compiled the emphasis was not upon killing as such but upon violent acts in general, on fights, assaults and beatings. In the Ming code there is a shift in focus evidenced in the grouping of the specific rules under the head of 'Homicide'. It is the fact that someone was killed that now emerges as the most important element which a number of rules have in common and so provides the basis for their membership of the same group.[71]

The T'ang code itself had contained 502 articles. The Ming code of 1374 increased the number to 606, and the code of 1397 made what appears to be a considerable reduction to 460. However, the mere citation of the number of the articles is misleading in comparing the comparative extent of the codes. What frequently happened was that the Ming legislators in their process of re-ordering the material of the T'ang code simply combined into one article what had been two or more separate articles.

An important step took place during the Ming dynasty to facilitate the adjustment of the penal code to changing circumstances and the requirements of the time. Prior to the Ming, changes to the formal law had been accomplished essentially by imperial edict. Such edicts might be introduced into the code at one of its periodic revisions in the form of an article or, as occurred in the Sung code, added as an appendix to the article. Generally however the Sung and Yüan dynasties saw the proliferation of large quantities of legal decisions or rules emanating from the emperor or the highest judicial bodies, sometimes assembled in vast collections, but never integrated into the penal code. In the Yüan dynasty of course this would have been impossible since no formal code as such was promulgated. In the Ming dynasty there also proliferated rules on cases not covered by the code, emanating from the courts or the emperor. In 1500 a collection of such rules (known as *li*, an expression normally translated in this context as 'sub-statute') containing 297 items was issued. The intention was to make clear which of the specific decisions on penal matters made since the enactment of the *Ta Ming Lü* might still be used; and equally to affirm the role of the *li* as a support, not a contradiction, of the penal statutes.[72] Further *li* were subsequently added to this collection which constituted a separate supplement to the penal code. In 1585 the code and the collection of *li* were combined into one text. After each article there followed any *li* relating to the same subject matter. It was the code of 1585, incorporating both lü and li, that provided the model for the penal code of the Ch'ing dynasty.[73]

The Ch'ing Dynasty (1644-1911)

Internal troubles and revolts in the 17th century gave another non-Chinese people, the Manchus, the opportunity of invading and taking control first of Peking and the north (by consent of the Chinese themselves) and then of the south (by military conquest). Unlike the Mongols the Manchus were ready to provide a penal code for their Chinese subjects and took as their model the Ming code in its redaction of 1585. The fact that the new rulers were prepared to promulgate a penal code modelled on that of the Ming within two years of their occupation of the capital - the first Ch'ing code was issued in 1646 - may be due to the fact that, before the occupation, the Ming code and other Chinese legal collections had already been translated into Manchu.[74] Hence the Manchu court was not only familiar with the Ming code but may even have utilised it in its own country (Manchuria).

The code of 1646 adopted most of the articles (lü) and sub-statutes (li) of the Ming code. Thereafter changes of the penal law were effected mainly by means of li. On the whole the prevailing theory was that the lü, the articles, represented the fundamental laws that should not be changed, whereas the li were the means by which the law could be adapted to new situations. Although subsequent editions of the code did make some changes in lü, most changes were accomplished by the addition of li.[75] After the promulgation of the first code li subsequently approved were not incorporated into its text but issued in separate collections. Not until the promulgation of the second edition in 1725 were the new li added to the code. Subsequent revisions saw a great increase in the number of li, and by the latter part of the 19th century their total was not much short of 2000.[76]

From the edicts of the first three emperors of the Ch'ing dynasty introducing the codes issued in their name one can learn something of the official attitude to the penal code.[77] The Shuh-chih emperor in 1647 declared the necessity for the existence of a fixed set of laws to act as a guide to the magistrates and so prevent a multitude of erroneous decisions requiring subsequent change by the emperor himself. In 1679 the K'ang-hsi emperor deplored the fact that the conduct of the people had become increasingly wicked and violent, so leading to the need for severer punishments and expressed the wish that the efficacy of the punishments should be carefully examined. The Yung-cheng emperor in

1725 declared his compassion for the fate of criminals and emphasised
the need to see that the infliction of punishment was fair. He ordered
a revision of the laws 'so as most effectively to fulfil our design of adapting
the penalties of the laws in a just proportion to the crimes against which
they are denounced'.[78]

Its content settled in the first part of the 18th century, the Ch'ing code
was not subject to further major change until the 20th century, and this
time the impetus came from Western influence. A concrete result of this
was seen in 1905 with the removal from the code of the punishments seen
to be the most cruel or barbaric, the replacement of beatings with fines,
the abolition of the wholesale punishment of innocent persons for the
crime of a relative, and of the use of torture in judicial proceedings. A
revision of the code was published in 1910 which incorporated these
improvements. This version of the code survived the fall of the dynasty
in 1911 and remained in force until 1928.[79]

Notes

1. The Book of Documents, one of the main Confucian classics, purports to
   be a collection of documents from the archives of the Shang and early
   Chou rulers. Many of these are now considered to be forgeries from a
   much later date (see generally Creel, The Origins of Statecraft in China,
   447ff). For a fuller account of the earliest Chinese law see MacCormack,
   Law and Punishment in the Earliest Chinese Thought.
2. Para 13. The best translation of the *K'ang kao* is that of Karlgren, The Book
   of Documents, 39f. Here and in the following notes I cite it according
   to the numbered paragraphs of his translation. Other translations are by
   Legge, The Shou King, 381ff and Couvreur, Chou King, 232ff.
3. Para. 3,8,10,16,21.
4. Especially para. 4,16,22.
5. Para. 10,12.
6. Para. 13,17
7. Para. 16. King Wen was the father of king Wu.
8. These instructions are in a document entitled *Chiu kao* (on which see Creel,
   op.cit., 451), translated by Karlgren, op.cit., 43f (see para. 14), Legge,
   op.cit., 399 ff and Couvreur, op.cit., 245 ff.
9. *K'ang kao* para. 15
10. Para. 8
11. Para. 10.
12. Cf. Creel, op.cit., 189.
13. Para. 17.
14. Para. 11, 13.
15. Para. 11
16. These are writings thought to have been compiled in the period of the
    Warring States: *Chou-li* (purporting to describe the administrative and
    legal system of Western Chou, translated by Biot, Le Tcheou-li II, 314

(on it see Creel, op.cit., 478f); *Tso-chuan* (see below at note 20), translated Legge, The Ch'un Ts'ew with the Tso Chuen, 802, Couvreur, La chronique de la principaute de Lou III, 613ff. See also The Bamboo Annals (on which Creel, op.cit., 483f), translated by Legge, The Annals of the Bamboo Books, 147, 149.

17. Legge, Shou King, 38; Couvreur, Chou King, 21.
18. Karlgren, Glosses on the Book of Documents, 87 (gl. 1267).
19. Cf., however, the cautious remarks of Bodde, The State and the Empire of Ch'in, 27 nll.
20. See Creel, op.cit., 475f.
21. Legge, Ch'un Ts'ew, 86, 102, 186, 212, 213, 420, 440 448f, 589, 656.
22. Legge, op.cit., 589.
23. Legge, op.cit., 448.
24. Legge, op.cit., 243f; cf. also Hsiao, A History of Chinese Political Thought, 377n. Nothing is said in the text about the *Fa ching*, a code of laws reputedly drafted by Li K'uei, minister of the state of Wei around 400 B.C. Some scholars have taken this to be the ancestor of all the later codes (cf. Escarra, Le droit chinois, 33, 91; Needham, Science and Civilisation in China II, 523), but almost certainly the tradition crediting Li K'uei with a code of laws cannot be taken as correct (cf. Hulsewé, Remnants of Han Law, 28f, and Legalists and the Laws of Ch'in, 8; Pokora, The Canon of Laws by Li K'uei).
25. Legge, op.cit., 609f.
26. Legge, op.cit., 732.
27. Legge, op.cit., 772, and cf. Creel, Legal Institutions and Procedures during the Chou Dynasty, 41.
28. Legge, op.cit., 732.
29. Cf. Creel, op.cit., 37.
30. Creel, The Beginning of Bureaucracy in China, 132.
31. Legge, op.cit., 609f.
32. See Duyendak, The Book of Lord Shang, 14f.
33. Generally see Hulsewé, Remnants of Ch'in Law.
34. Cf. the remarks of Hulsewé, op.cit., 12.
35. Translated Karlgren, Book of Documents, 74f; Legge, Shoo King, 588ff; Couvreur, Chou king 375ff. See also MacCormack, The *Lü Hsing*: Problems of Legal Interpretation.
36. Much of this is reminiscent of the views expressed in the *K'ang kao*.
37. *Lü hsing* para. 20 (Karlgren).
38. Creel, Origin of Statecraft in China, 161, 463.
39. Hulsewé, Legalists and Laws of Ch'in, 3 and note 7.
40. Generally on the Ch'in law see the work of Hulsewe, cited note 33, and the same author's Ch'in and Han Law.
41. Hulsewé, Remnants of Ch'in Law, 16, 149 (D89).
42. Hulsewé, op.cit., 142 (D67f).
43. Dubs, History of the Former Han Dynasty I, 58.
44. id.
45. Dubs, op.cit., 146.
46. The Former Han Legal Treatise, translated by Hulsewé, Remnants of Han

Law, 333.

47. Former Han Legal Treatise, op.cit., 338.

48. Former Han Legal Treatise, op.cit., 336f.

49. Hulsewé, Remnants of Han Law, 32ff.

50. See especially Balazs's introduction to, and translation of, the Sui Legal Treatise (Traité juridique du 'Souei-Chou'); also Ch'ü, Law and Society in Traditional China, 276 n295.

51. Heuser, Das Rechtskapitel im Jin-Shu, 28f.

52. Generally on the T'ang code see Johnson (Introduction); MacCormack, The T'ang Code: Early Chinese Law.

53. See Twitchett, Implementation of Law in Early T'ang China.

54. I have adopted the terminology used by Johnson, 275ff.

55. For the versions adopted in Vietnam see Deloustal and Lê Code.

56. One *li* roughly equals one third of a mile.

57. For further details of the Sung reductions see chapter 5, at note 14.

58. See Twitchett, Financial Administration under the T'ang Dunasty, 1f, 10, and further below in chapter 10, 236f.

59. See Seidel, Studien zur Rechtsgeschichte der Sung-Zeit (containing a translation of the first part of the Sung Legal Treatise), 13f, 67.

60. Miyazaki, Administration of Justice during the Sung dynasty, 57. See also Seidel, op.cit., 21ff and Das Zurücktreten des Gesetzesbuches zugunsten der Erlasse in Recht der Sung-Zeit. Not all scholars go as far in holding that a peculiarity of Sung legal practice was the replacement of the penal code by imperial edicts. Cf. Langlois, 'Living Law' in Sung and Yüan Juriprudence, 169; McKnight, From Statute to Precedent, 114f.

61. Generally see Franke, Jurchen Customary Law and the Chinese Law of the Chin Dynasty.

62. A reconstruction of a portion of this code can be found in Ch'en, Chinese Legal Tradition under the Mongols, 107ff.

63. See Ch'en, op.cit., 33ff. The Yüan Legal Trestise has been translated by Ratchnesvsky, Un Code des Yüan.

64. Ch'en, op.cit., 35.

65. Pelliot, Notes de bibliographie chinoise, 123.

66. Ch'en, op.cit., 52ff.

67. Cf. Munzel, Strafrecht im alten China, 67. This contains a translation of the first part of the Ming Legal Treatise.

68. This adopts the terminology used by Bodde and Morris, Law in Imperial China, 61.

69. Munzel, op.cit., 37.

70. See Bodde and Morris, op.cit., 60f; Weggel, Chinesische Rechtsgeschichte, 91f.

71. Cf. MacCormack, The T'ang and Ming Law of Homicide, and chapter 8 below, 181ff.

72. Munzel, op.cit., 46; Bodde and Morris, op.cit., 65.

73. For an example of the history of a particular sub-statute originating in the late Ming period see Meijer, An Aspect of Retribution in Traditional Chinese Law.

74. Pelliot, op.cit., 139.

75. See Metzger, The Internal Organization of Ch'ing Bureaucracy, 84 ff.
76. Bodde and Morris, op.cit., 66. For a general description of the Ch'ing code see Jones, Studying the Ch'ing Code.
77. These are translated in Staunton, lxvff.
78. Staunton, lxix.
79. Ichiko, Political and Institutional Reform, 1901-11, 408f.

2

The Social and Intellectual Background

This chapter considers certain broad aspects of the organisation of society in traditional China, as well as the attitudes to law and punishment held by the educated class. Without a preliminary understanding of these matters it is difficult to understand the assumptions upon which the composition of the penal codes has been based. The most significant aspect of Chinese social organisation has been the emphasis upon the family and kinship relationships. By 'family' I mean in this context the typical household consisting of grandparents, their sons with their wives and children, and their unmarried daughters.

The early Confucians had singled out the five fundamental relationships as being those of ruler and subject, father and son, elder and younger brother, husband and wife and friend and friend.[1] Of these only one, that of friend and friend, presupposed a horizontal relationship of equality. The other four are all vertical relationships in which one member is the senior and the other the junior. Thus within the family the father, elder brother and husband are all senior with respect to the son, younger brother and wife. The hallmark of the relationship between senior and junior is the duty of respect and submission owed by the latter to the former. Reflected here is the Confucian, and even pre-Confucian belief, of the necessity for the maintenance of what were seen to be natural distinctions. Their maintenance was held to be fundamental to the well-being of society.

Outside what I have termed the 'family', kinship and affinal relationships were of great importance in an individual's life. Much of his or her day-to-day activity involved contact with relatives or in-laws. Within the whole circle of kin and affines it was relatives on the father's side who mattered most. Traditional Chinese society was essentially patrilineal, based on a clan and lineage system, membership of which was determined through the male line only. Relatives through the mother were not discounted altogether, but the range within which they were important was much less. The same obtained with respect to relatives acquired through marriage.

Relationships between kin, like whose within the family, were structured according to the principles of generation and age. Those belonging to a higher generation, for example brothers of a father or grandfather, were the senior and entitled to respect from those of a junior generation. Equally relatives who belonged to the same generation, for example the children of brothers, classified themselves as senior or junior according to age, the latter again showing respect to the former.

The social requirements dictated by family, kin and affinal relationships were to a very considerable extent built into the penal codes in a number of different ways. Sometimes the codes used the ordinary terminology of kinship, referring, for example, to parents, paternal or maternal grandparents, or father's brothers. At other times this could not conveniently be done. Where large numbers of kin were involved some short hand method had to be found to describe them. It was not convenient to refer constantly to brothers of grandfather, paternal cousins twice removed and so on. The obvious alternative was to refer collectively to kin in groups according to the nearness or remoteness of the relationship. For example, reference could be made to all those related in the first degree, or the second degree. The mode of reference actually adopted by the codes was similar, though not identical, to the classification of kin by degrees.

What the codes did was to utilise the terminology associated with mourning. A fundamental requirement of kinship was the obligation to mourn, in a striking and obvious fashion, the death of a relative. This obligation pertained more to patrilineal than to other relatives in the sense that the class of patrilineal kin for whom mourning was worn was far greater than the class of matrilineal or affinal kin. Both the period of mourning and the kind of mourning attire varied according, on the one hand, to the nearness or remoteness of the relationship and, on the other, to the relationship of seniority between the deceased and mourner. For example a son and a father stood in the same degree of relationship to each other, yet one was the senior and the other the junior. Consequently the son as junior was required to mourn for the maximum period of three years, whereas the father as senior was required to mourn merely for one year. On the other hand seniority was disregarded (for mourning purposes) in the relationship between brothers, each mourning the other, irrespective of age, for the same period (one year).

There were five main degrees of mourning (the *wu fu*). A large number of patrilineal, and a much smaller number of matrilineal or affinal relatives, were divided into these five categories. Thus the codes by referring to relatives of the first degree of mourning or of the fifth degree were able to designate collectively, without specifying in detail, which precise relatives were meant.[2] For the first degree the time of mourning was three years (in fact 27 months), for the second, one year (though there were variations of time within this degree), for the third, nine months, for the fourth, five months and for the fifth, three months.[3]

Also reflected in the codes is the division between the three main social classes, the nobles and officials, the ordinary free people and the slaves and other 'mean' groups.[4] The rules in the codes which treat these classes in different ways allow one to speak of a legal as well as a social division between them. To a considerable extent membership of these groups was hereditary in the sense that an individual normally kept the same social status as his father. But both upward and downward 'social mobility' were possible. Someone from a non-official family might, through education and the passing of the appropriate examinations, elevate himself to the official class, and equally a person born into the free, commoner class might voluntarily or involuntarily descend into one of the 'mean' groups. A boy or a girl might be sold as a slave or choose to become an entertainer or prostitute (both 'mean' occupations). The criterion for membership of the class of officials seems to have been fairly uniform in the centuries from the Han to the Ch'ing, that is, employment by the emperor in a regular civil service post ranging from district magistrate upwards. On the other hand the criteria for membership of the lowest social class appear to have varied. The T'ang had a number of statuses akin to that of the slave not recognised in Ch'ing law, and the Ch'ing recognised a number of 'mean' groups, for example, entertainers, prostitutes and constables, not identified as such in T'ang law.

Generally speaking one can say that the officials were legally in a more favourable position than the commoners, and slaves and 'mean' people in a less favourable position. However even within the classes of officials and servile persons further distinctions were drawn. The precise privileges accorded an official by the law depended upon his rank, and the degree of disability or disadvantage imposed upon 'mean' persons depended upon whether they were actually slaves or not (T'ang law, for example, distinguishing between 'slaves' and 'personal retainers').

Particularly to be noted is the fact that in all dynasties marriage between the 'free' and the 'unfree' was either prohibited altogther or very severely restricted. Finally one may note briefly that conquest of the Chinese by foreign peoples led to legal and other distinctions between the conqueror and the conquered. Both the Mongols (Yüan dynasty) and the Manchu (Ch'ing dynasty) were to some extent segregated from the mass of Chinese. Cases involving them were dealt with by special tribunals; they enjoyed certain legal rights denied to the Chinese, and the punishment they incurred for offences was not always the same as that incurred by a Chinese for the same offence.[5]

What I have termed the 'intellectual background' refers to the attitudes of the educated and official class, on the one hand, to the proper place of law in government, where law is understood primarily in the sense of rules imposing punishments, and, on the other, to the relationship between man, particularly the ruler, and the universe. The opinions held on these matters, often showing a remarkable consistency over many centuries, influenced the content of the penal codes, though the precise nature and extent of the influence is sometimes a matter of controversy.

From the beginning of recorded Chinese history at the time of the early Chou until the end of the Ch'ing dynasty discussions of law concentrated on the extent to which the ruler should make use of punishments in conducting his government, and the nature of the punishments which it was permissible to use. The line of thought dominant for the whole of this immense period of time was that rules imposing punishments should be employed only where necessary to preserve the proper functioning of the fundamental social relationships, namely those between ruler and subject, father and son and husband and wife. Of course maintenance of these relationships required a wide apparatus of rules punishing *inter alia* offences threatening the good order of the state, failure by officials to play their part in the securing of good order, and breaches of the moral code defining proper behaviour between kin.

On this view of the role of law it was usually unnecessary for the state to intervene in the conduct of affairs by individuals except in so far as their behaviour threatened the fundamental social and family relationships. This approach was in line with the broad tenets of Confucian belief, and probably also with the pre-Confucian thinking from which Confucius and his followers drew their inspiration. But it had not gone unchallenged and for a brief period in the fourth and third centuries B.C. was supplanted by a rather different school of thought generally known as 'legalism'.

Although ultimately legalism was displaced from dominance with the establishment of the Han empire, some of its characteristic beliefs continued to influence the development of the law. Briefly one may chart the 'history of ideas' on the role of law as follows.[6]

At the very beginning of the Chou dynasty around 1100 B.C. one already finds a clear appreciation of the need for the ruler to govern with the help of rules imposing punishments. King Wu in his instructions to prince K'ang takes for granted the fact that the prince will have to apply punishments. His main concern is that the prince should exercise benevolence and virtue in his rule and in particular make moderate and reasonable use of the punishments. The king stresses that the continuance of Heaven's favour and therefore of the authority to rule is contingent upon the ruler's virtuous exercise of power.[7] Similar themes are found in the speeches ascribed to rulers, ministers or officials in the Spring and Autumn period during which China effectively (though nominally still under the Chou ruler) was fragmented into a number of independent states. There is a constant refrain of the need for punishments, but at the same time the need for virtue in the ruler and the moderate use of punishment are also stressed.[8] Official thought at this time does not appear to have regarded law (punishment) as inferior to moral example in the government of the people. Equally it does not give any primacy to law. Law is tolerable only if combined with virtue. The ruler must himself set a good example, formulate good laws and apply them justly.

During the Spring and Autumn period itself, from the latter part of the 6th century B.C., the thesis that law and moral example occupied equal positions in the ruler's plan of government came under attack in the teaching of Confucius and his followers. Both Confucius (551-479 B.C.) and his chief follower Mencius (373-289 B.C.) clearly placed the primacy upon virtue and moral example. In their surviving writings they say a great deal about the necessity for the ruler to set a good example in his personal life. Should the ruler in his relationship with his minsiters and subjects and with the members of his family conduct himself according to the moral and ritual code (*li*), his good example will spread throughout the country and ensure that the people also will learn right behaviour. Hence there will be no need for punishments. In fact even the most extreme adherents of Confucius probably allowed a limited place in government to rules imposing punishments on the ground that the nature of some people was irreparably bad. The only way such persons could be induced to behave properly was through fear of punishment. However the role of law, in the general context of government, would still be minimal, provided the ruler possessed sufficient virtue.

The promulgation of penal codes by some states in the sixth century attracted criticism by officials or statesmen who advocated Confucian views. One such criticism is even attributed in the *Tso-chuan* to Confucius himself.[9] From the language used it is difficult to be sure of the exact grounds of the criticism. Four possible grounds may be identified. First it is fairly clear that the opponents of the laws saw their promulgation to the public as improperly shifting the emphasis in government. Instead of relying upon the laws, a reliance manifested through their inscription on bronze tripods, the ruler should rely upon his own virtue and good example and those of his ministers. Second, the very promulgation of specific offences and their punishments may have been thought to constitute a 'corruption of morality' in the sense that people were now induced to determine their conduct according to a calculus of the likelihood of punishment. Instead of reflecting upon the morality of their behaviour they would merely consider whether they could 'get away with it' or not.[10] Related to this and the following ground is a third, namely that a specific description of offences for each of which an exact punishment is prescribed debarred the judge from taking into account the full circumstances of the affair, including the character and worth of the accused, and any particular mitigating factors. The fourth possible ground is that the laws offended the Confucian conception of status. This point requires a little elaboration.

Confucian, and possible also pre-Confucian, thought not only emphasised the importance of what were seen as natural hierarchies in social and family relationships: ruler and subject, father and son, husband and wife, but also accepted a hierarchy constituted by the distinction between the 'superior man' (*chün tzu*) and the 'low, mean people' (*hsiao jen*). This hierarchy had always been accepted in Chinese social life, the class of the 'superior man' being constituted by the nobles, that of the 'low people' by the ordinary commoners. Confucius himself adopted the distinction but argued for a redefinition. For him the 'superior man' was a person who, through education and self-cultivation, had learnt the proper way to behave and so was competent to assist the ruler in the government of the people. The 'low' or 'inferior man' was a person who had not acquired knowledge of the *li* and therefore could not be expected spontaneously to regulate his conduct in accordance with them. Confucian thought favoured the view that punishments, understood at this time in the physical sense of death or mutilation, should not be imposed on the 'superior man' who was expected to conduct himself according to *li*. If he transgressed seriously the appropriate course would be for him to take his own life. Punishments as such, if applied at all, should be reserved for the 'inferior man' who was unacquainted with *li*. This viewpoint is expressed in a famous and much quoted sentence in one of the writings contained in the Confucian ritual classic, the Book of Rites or *Li Chi*, where it is said '*Li* do not extend down to the common people; punishments do not extend up to the officials'.[11] Consequently the Confucians may have objected to the 6th century law codes also on the ground that the punishments were made to apply to all alike.

The opposition of the early Confucians to the promulgation of penal codes and their advocacy of the primacy of moral example over punishment had little practical effect. Both Confucius and Mencius had a dispiriting time visiting the courts of rulers and attempting in vain to persuade them to listen to their advice. Rulers were interested in practical expedients by which they might save themselves and their states from conquest by a powerful neighbour or, alternatively, by which they might themselves successfully conduct a campaign of aggrandizement at the expense of other states. In the increasingly turbulent and unstable times of the late Spring and Autumn and Warring States periods rulers and their ministers found more appealing the advice of political theorists who took a position diametrically opposed to that of the Confucians. These were the thinkers who have come to be called 'legalists'. Although they differed in the details of what they advocated, some laying the stress on the use of punishment itself, some preferring to stress other techniques of government, they all firmly discounted the relevance of morality to government.

The best known representatives of the legalist school are Lord Shang and Han Fei Tzu. Lord Shang was the chief minister of the state of Ch'in (which ultimately founded the Ch'in empire) in the early 4th century B.C. He was remarkable in his own time and in after ages for the harshness with which he applied in practice the main tenets of his philosophy. These are found in the book which bears his name, and even if there is little of this work that Lord Shang himself composed, much in it reflects his thought.[12] His principal reforms may be summarised as follows. The most important activities for the people to engage in were agriculture and war, prowess in these activities being rewarded, their neglect and the pursuit of other activities (such as literature or learning) penalised. Family solidarity was held to be detrimental to the state. Hence married sons were required to leave the parental home and cultivate land as a separate household. Units of ten and five individuals were established for the purpose of controlling crime. The crime of one member would ensure the punishment of the others; failure to denounce the crime of a member itself entailed capital punishment. The result was to destroy the relationship of trust and cooperation within the family and induce family members to inform upon each other. A passage from the Book of Lord Shang vividly expresses his intention:

> If penalties are made heavy and relations are involved in the punishments, petty and irascible people will not quarrel, intractable and stubborn people will not litigate, slothful and lazy people will not idle, those who waste their substance will not thrive, and those of evil heart, given to flattery, will bring about no change. If these five kinds of people do not appear within the territory, then it is certain waste lands will be brought under cultivation.[13]

Punishments for offences were to be draconian. The lightest offence was to be punished with the greatest severity on the ground that if the punishments were made severe enough, the ruler in the end would be able to dispense with punishment altogether. Finally all should be treated alike by the law. There should be no distinction in terms of treatment between the 'superior' and the 'inferior'. Lord Shang secured his own downfall by insisting that even the crown prince should be punished for an offence. On the prince's accession to the throne Lord Shang was compelled to flee from court.

Lord Shang realised that in order for his new rules to be effective, it was necessary that their terms be made intelligible to the people. Hence he insisted on the need for simplicity, clarity and precision in the drafting of the laws. Paragraph 26 of the Book of Lord Shang reports a supposed conversation between the minister and his ruler on the best method of introducing a set of laws that would be clearly understood and capable of immediate application. In this context Lord Shang urges that the legal title to property must be clear and fixed, in order to ensure security of possession and, more generally, that everyone's rights and duties as established by the law must be fixed and clear, not open to discussion, in order to prevent wickedness and confusion spreading throughout the country. He remarks, 'Therefore did the sages, in creating laws, make them clear and easy to understand and the terminology correct, so that stupid and wise without exception, could understand them'.[14]

Han Fei Tzu was a scholar of the early third century B.C. who belonged to the princely house of the minor state of Han. Without political influence, he achieved the most thorough balanced and mature statement of the legalist position. Although Han Fei Tzu's approach is more sophisticated than Lord Shang's the same basic themes recur. Law is conceived as a system of rewards and punishments designed to promote conduct beneficial to the state. The fact that punishments should be definite and heavy is stressed. Their deterrent function is seen as the most important, although Han Fei Tzu does seem to admit that those who do not obey the laws themselves deserve to be punished.[15] The flavour of his views on law can best be gathered from some quotations taken from his writings:

> The ruler makes laws so as to establish the standard of right (i.e. it is the laws themselves that are the sole determinants of what is right and wrong).[16]

> It is the duty of the sovereign to make clear the distinction between public and private interests, enact laws and statutes openly and forbid private favours.[17]

> If laws are distinct and clear, the worthy cannot over-run the unworthy, the strong cannot outrage the weak, and the many cannot violate the few.[18]

> Suppose you cast laws and institutions aside and get angry blindly, then though you slaughter many, the culprits would not be afraid of you. If the crime is committed by A but the consequent disaster befalls B, then hidden resentment will grow.[19]

> The law is codified in books kept in government offices, and promulgated among the people... Law wants nothing more than publicity.[20]

> Law includes mandates and ordinances that are manifest in the official bureaux, penalties that are definite in the mind of the people, rewards that are due to the careful observers of law, and punishments that are inflicted on the offenders against orders. It is what the subjects and ministers take as model.[21]

> The enlightened sovereign in governing the state would increase custodians and intensify penalties and make the people stop vices according to law but not owing to their own sense of integrity. For illustration, mothers love children twice as much as fathers do, but a father enforces orders among children ten times better than a mother does.[22]

> Heavy penalties are not for the sole purpose of punishing criminals. The law of the intelligent sovereign is not disciplining only those who are being suppressed, for to discipline only the suppressed is

the same as to discipline dead men only... For the heavily punished are robbers, but the terrified and trembling are good people. Therefore, why should those who want order doubt the efficacy of heavy penalties.[23]

Clarifying laws and statutes by forbidding literary learning and concentrating on meritorious services by suppressing private advantages, are public benefits. To enact the law is to lead the people, whereas if the superior esteems literary learning, the people will become sceptical in following the law.[24]

When laws are too vague, vagabonds dispute. For this reason... the laws of the intelligent ruler always penetrate the minute details of fact.[25]

To shed bitter tears and dislike penalties, is benevolence; to see the necessity of inflicting penalties, is law. Since the early kings held to the law and never listened to weeping, it is clear enough that benevolence cannot be applied to the attainment of political order.[26]

Legalist ideas as exhibited in the career of Lord Shang and set forth in the writings of Han Fei Tzu show several marked differences from the early Confucian conception of government. First, a much greater scope was accorded the law. Indeed precisely because it was necessary to compel people to undertake the activities of agriculture and warfare, discourage them from engaging in other pursuits such as education and generally to harness them thoroughly to the service of the state, there is little in their lives that might escape legal regulation. Professor Hulsewe has commented that the surviving fragments of the Ch'in law of the 3rd century B.C. 'show how the Ch'in state tried to extend its influence over all spheres of life of its inhabitants. This may well be, at least partly, the result of the ideas and activities of the School of Law'.[27] By contrast the Confucian approach was to give to the penal law as minimal a role as possible in the regulation of the behaviour of the people.

For the legalists the effectiveness of the laws was directly related to the heaviness of the punishments imposed. Their view of human nature was pessimistic. People would only serve the state loyally, in ways beneficial to it, if they were induced by fear or perhaps sometimes encouraged by rewards. Hence punishments must be sufficiently ferocious to act as deterrents. Again this contrasts with the early Confucian expectations of man. For Mencius human nature was intrinsically good. People therefore should be taught the right way to behave, particularly through the example of their superiors. They should not be terrorised into submission. One may conjecture that both Confucius and Mencius looked upon punishment, when it was necessary, as more retributive and reformative than deterrent.

The legalists not only distrusted the traditional virtues of the Confucians; they considered them positively harmful to the successful ordering of the state. Lord Shang actively tried to destroy or weaken the bonds between family members. He labelled as 'lice' or 'evils' care for old age, filial piety, brotherly duty, benevolence and virtuous conduct in general.[28] Han Fei Tzu, without perhaps going as far as Lord Shang, regarded benevolence and righteousness as detrimental to the strength and good order of a state; they set up standards of behaviour other than those prescribed by the law itself.[29] For both legalists the sole measure of what was right and wrong should be the law. Only in this way could disputes divisive of society be avoided. It was imperative that the laws should be clear and certain giving no scope for conflicting interpretations. In particular they should not be applied in a benevolent or lenient fashion or in such a way as to take account of mitigating circumstances. All this was anathema to the Confucians.

A corollary of strictness in the application of the laws was impartiality. All - with the possible exception of the ruler himself - were to be equal before the law. This entailed not only that all who broke the law should be punished but that the same offences should receive the same punishments, irrespective of the status of the offender. An official or person of high rank was not permitted to have a lesser punishment than an ordinary person received for the same offence. This again did not accord with the Confucian conception of punishment being more appropriate to the ordinary person than to the official or noble. It is interesting to see that Lord Shang's ideas on equality before the law did not represent the practice in his own state a century later. Professor Hulsewé notes 'that position in the hierarchy continued to count, with the result that superiors were often punished more lightly than their subordinates and in particular that the possessors of aristrocratic rank suffered less than ordinary commoners or slaves'.[30]

Lord Shang's vision was more than fulfilled with the rise to supremacy of the state which he had served for so long, and the assumption by the king of Ch'in of the imperial title. Undoubtedly Lord Shang's ruthless policies had contributed to the efficiency with which Ch'in built up the military power that enabled it to triumph over its rivals. Despite the fact that the new imperial dynasty was short lived and gave way to a dynasty

(Han) which re-established Confucianism firmly as the official doctrine of the state, certain of the tenets of legalism continued to exercise a subterranean influence - not acknowledged as such - and were in effect adopted by Confucian officials.

The process of absorption can already be seen in the writings of one of the greatest Confucian thinkers, Hsün Tzu who lived during the period in which Ch'in was rising to supremacy. Little is known of his life. For a while he was a prominent scholar at the court of Ch'i, then the leading intellectual centre in China, and later held a post as magistrate in the state of Ch'u. Among his disciples were two prominent legalists, Han Fei Tzu[31] and Li Ssu, the prime minister of the first Ch'in emperor. Hence it appears likely that Hsun Tzu was not entirely unsympathetic to all aspects of legalist doctrine, even though, as a Confucian, there was much that he could not accept.

Hsün Tzu shows the influence of legalist thought most clearly in his acceptance of law as a necessary part of government. On the other hand he differed from the legalists in refusing to treat moral example as irrelevant to government. For him the best solution was to combine the two techniques, moral example and law. The ruler himself should be virtuous and should see that the laws enshrined and enforced moral principle. Hsün Tzu made an interesting and cogent point, possibly intended to be a reply to the conviction of some legalists that a set of laws was all that was needed for the control of the people.[32] The legalist assumption was that law should be self-sufficient in that all situations should be forseen and covered by it. Its exactness and clarity should be such that the judge is left in no doubt as to the correct sentence to be imposed. Hsün Tzu realised that this was not a situation that would ever fully obtain in practice. There would always be some cases that were not covered exactly by the laws. Hence he argued that where the laws existed they should be carried out, but where they did not exist, where there were 'gaps' in the law, then the judge (or the ruler) was 'to act in the spirit of precedent and analogy'.[33] What is implied here is that the judge and the ruler should draw upon the principles of morality in dealing with situations for which there is no legal rule exactly in point. Hence it is necessary that those entrusted with the administration of justice should be virtuous or superior persons (*chün tzu*).

With respect to the use of punishment Hsun Tzu advocates a doctrine that again seems to combine legalist and Confucian elements. The following passage taken from a discussion in his writings on punishment gives the essence of his thought: 'When punishment fits the crime there is good government; when it does not fit the crime there is bad government. Hence in good governments the punishments are severe; in bad governments the punishments are light'.[34] The last sentence could well have been written by Lord Shang. However the first expresses more a retributive function of punishment. The legalists on the whole had emphasised its deterrent function. This is also of concern to Hsün Tzu. Elsewhere in his writings he defines the duties of the minister of justice as 'to forestall violence and cruelty, prevent licentiousness and wipe out evil, employ the five punishments as a warning, causing the violent and cruel to change their ways and the wicked to desist from wickedness'.[35] Yet Hsün Tzu would not have accepted that heavy punishments should be imposed for light offences. The punishment should be in proportion to the degree of wickedness exhibited.

Hsün Tzu's thinking about law and punishment represents what was portrayed as the ideal system of government virtually throughout the whole of Chinese royal and imperial history. His views are not dissimilar from those of king Wu expressed in his instructions to prince K'ang. Equally they were shared by the Confucian administrators of the Han and the later dynasties who generally urged the imposition of severe punishments for severe offences, but also advocated the infusion of benevolence and compassion into law.

What has been called 'the Confucianisation of the law'[36], a process in effect reflecting a perception of law of the kind held by Hsün Tzu, took place throughout the Han and culminated in the T'ang dynasty. Its most conspicuous aspect was the firm entrenchment of the family and the behaviour expected of family members towards each other. The principal duties imposed by the moral code on relatives were incorporated in the penal codes and punishments, often heavy, prescribed for their breach. It is noticeable, as will be seen, how many of the offences falling under the 'ten abominations' were constituted by breach of proper behaviour within the family or between kin. The codes regulated family and kinship behaviour in two rather different ways. On the one hand they enforced certain fundamental duties arising out of the fact of kin or affinal relationships, in particular those of mourning, filial piety, concealment of offences and marriage. On the other hand the punishment for offences which did not arise specifically from family or kin relationships was varied where these offences were committed by relatives. In this way the law was able to take account of the hierarchical structure of the family, and the dominant position of 'senior' with respect to 'junior' relatives. Consequently the general principle implemented by the codes was that offences committed by 'junior' against 'senior' relatives were punished more heavily than those committed by 'senior' against 'junior' relatives. Examples will be given in succeeding chapters.

Other prominent features of the codes were also inspired by the wish of the legislator to preserve and enforce Confucian values. The privileged status accorded to nobles and officials with respect to punishment may possibly reflect the Confucian view that the 'superior man' should not be subjected to legal punishments in the same way as the 'low' or 'mean man'. This is a matter on which there is some dispute.[37] In other matters, as in the mitigation of punishment allowed to the old, young and the mentally or physically disabled, or the exemption from punishment entailed under certain circumstances by confession, one can see obvious traces of the Confucian emphasis on the virtues of benevolence, compassion and regeneration through repentance.

In their content the penal codes thus give effect to the Confucian system of values. It is in their form that one finds evidence of legalist influence. By this I mean that the drafting techniques employed in the codes were those developed principally by the legalist officials of the state of Ch'in. These were inherited by the Han and from there passed to later dynasties, no doubt with further refinements. Above all one sees exhibited in the codes the legalist virtues of comprehensiveness, clarity and precision. Within the general subject areas which they covered the codes attempted to legislate comprehensively. Just as the legalist had argued that the judge should have no doubt as to the correct law to be applied, so the framers of the codes attempted to ensure that for any situation intended to be covered there should be a rule either specifically stated or clearly inferable. Judicial discretion should be kept to a minimum since otherwise there was the likelihood of divergent and contradictory applications of the law. One may even suggest with some plausibility that the strict liability of officials and judges for mistakes imposed by the codes arose from legalist insistence that the law as stated in the codes should be correctly applied.

To achieve the objective of correct application of law by the judge it was necessary that the rules should be not only comprehensive but also clear and precise. The emphasis on precision sometimes led to a brevity of formulation that might cause misunderstanding except to those most expert in the details of the law. However, starting with the T'ang code, if not earlier, official commentaries were added to clarify, expand and make more simple what was stated in the articles. The result is that on the whole the codes - if one discounts the accretion of sub-statutes, especially under the Ch'ing - can be regarded as models of lucidity.

In one other important respect there may be legalist influence. This is in the law of procedure. It is likely that the detailed rules on the conduct of proceedings in court, the use of torture in the initial investigations, and the provisions for the review of sentences owe much to the practices of the state of Ch'in. The law of Ch'in in the third century B.C. provided for the utmost care to be exercised in the investigation of the facts, defined the way in which suspected criminals were to be interrogated, and probably also contained detailed provisions on the review of cases, though these have not survived.[38]

A final question concerns the extent to which the content of the penal codes has been influenced by the traditional Chinese beliefs on the relationship between man and the universe. This is a matter upon which there is some controversy. Western discussions of the Chinese view of the relationship between man and the universe are focused generally upon the notions of 'cosmic harmony' and 'natural law', the differences and similarities between these two notions not always being made entirely clear. One aspect arising from this discussion may be clarified at the outset, namely the extent to, and the sense in, which the codes constitute a natural law.[39]

The great dynastic penal codes from the T'ang to the Ch'ing were embodiments of *li* in the sense that they incorporated and enforced the fundamental values of Confucian society. Since the behaviour required by *li* was deemed to hold good at all times and for all societies - in that it provided a standard of behaviour by which other nations were judged - it constituted an absolute morality. Consequently the traditional Chinese penal codes can be said to constitute a natural law in the sense that they were concerned to ensure the legal enforcement of absolute moral duties. The same can be said of the law enforced by the early Chou dynasty and is probably true of Han law as well. No doubt there were some periods of Chinese history, in some states or dynasties, when it would be misleading or quite untrue to describe the positive law as natural law in the above sense. The law enforced in Ch'in at the time of Lord Shang and later provides an example. Nevertheless throughout most of its long history traditional Chinese penal law can effectively be described as a natural law in the sense of a law designed to enforce an absolute morality.

There is a further sense in which one can speak of the codified law as a natural law. It constitutes natural law because it forms part of the natural order of things and so accords with the will of Heaven. Again a notion of this kind is characteristic of the educated and official thinking about law virtually throughout Chinese royal and imperial history, with the possible exceptions already mentioned. What varies is the conception held of Heaven. For the early Chou it is fairly clear that Heaven was conceived as a personal God. In later thought Heaven often appears more as an 'impersonal principle' or just as the 'sky' to which sacrifices and prayers might be offered.[40] What one has to avoid is the imputation of Western notions foreign to Chinese thought. Thus it is a mistake to treat the Chinese conception of natural law as identical with that of St Thomas Aquinas or to analyse it as the product of a non-human agency disclosed to man through the exercise of his reason.

In this second sense of 'that which forms part of the natural order of things', natural law is an aspect of the general thesis on the structure of the universe widely diffused in Western literature under the head of 'cosmic harmony'. According to this thesis the phemonena making up the universe are believed in traditional China to have pre-ordained patterns of behaviour in the sense that they have a fixed place in the general scheme of things and interact with other phenomena in a deliberate and regular fashion. When all the phenomena of the universe are behaving as they should there is 'equilibrium', 'balance' or 'harmony'. Among the phenomena of the universe are man and his actions. These also have their natural, regular and proper modes of behaviour, namely that which is required by, and fits into, the general scheme of things. Man's behaviour is a potent source of disharmony within the universe. Should he not behave in the natural and regular fashion - and this meant behave in accordance with the Confucian *li* - the universe would become 'imbalanced'; man's misbehaviour would disturb also the regular behaviour of other phenomena.

Of particular relevance to the good ordering of the universe is the behaviour of the ruler - the chief representative of man. Should he conduct himself properly in his private life and govern well, the universe will remain in harmony and the seasons behave in harmony. But should he be profligate, licentious or excessively cruel and misgovern, the natural phenomena of the universe will react adversely. The seasons will not behave as they should; there will be excessive rain or drought; prodigies and omens will appear and so on. Indeed should the ruler's conduct prove irredeemably wicked the 'mandate of Heaven' will be withdrawn and the dynasty come to an end.

From this general thesis of 'cosmic harmony' some Western scholars have extracted specific propositions on the relationship believed to exist in traditional China between crime and natural phenomena. For example Bodde and Morris state:

> What really concerned the law - though this is to be surmised rather than explicitly read in the Chinese legal literature - were all acts of moral or ritual impropriety or of criminal violence which seemed in Chinese eyes to be violations or disruptions of the total social order. The existence of the norms of propriety was intended to deter the commission of such acts, but since they occurred, the restoration of social harmony required that punishment be inflicted to exact retribution from their doer. In the final analysis, a disturbance of the social order really meant, in Chinese thinking, a violation of the total cosmic order because, according to the Chinese world-view, the spheres of man and nature were inextricably interwoven to form an unbroken continuum.[41]

In his most recent general account of Han law Professor Hulsewé adopts a similar view and indeed implies that it was current before and after as well as during the Han.[42] This contrasts with the opinion expressed in his earlier work on Han law when he refers to 'the archaic idea that punishment is an act to redress the harmony of nature which has been disturbed by the crime' and adds 'I do not think that in Han times the idea was still active or alive, except where crimes qualified as impious or nefarious were concerned, but this fundamental concept continued to live in the terminology'.[43]

Elsewhere I have tried to argue that the general thesis of 'cosmic harmony' as stated in the West may be somewhat overdrawn, and indeed misleading, if it is taken to represent the thought of most educated Chinese at all periods of history.[44] It is clear that many Confucian literati subscribed to some kind of view that might be given the generic label of 'cosmic harmony', the best known example being the Han Confucian Tung Chung-shu.[45] But there were many variations in the details of the views held; some literati did not subscribe to the thesis at all, and many, particularly in the later dynasties, probably paid no more than lipservice to it.

Particularly questionable is the notion - in so far as it is represented as a prevalent characteristic of Chinese thought - that each crime committed by an individual was believed to disturb 'cosmic harmony', and thus entail the malfunctioning of natural phenomena, unless it was 'requited' with exactly the appropriate punishment. It is worth emphasising the reservation made by Bodde and Morris, that such a view of the relationship between crime and punishment is nowhere explicitly stated in the legal sources. This, so far as I can determine, is correct. Neither the codes nor the case reports from the Ch'ing period provide direct evidence for this view. What Ch'ing legal officials frequently stress is the need for the punishment to match the crime. But the idea expressed here is merely that the degree of wickedness of the deed should receive a corresponding degree of punishment. In other words the Chinese judges, as frequently judges in other societies, advocated the retributive function of punishment.

Some evidence (other than the general assertion of a belief in 'cosmic harmony') is of course advanced for the proposition that legal punishment is believed to restore the disruption in the harmony of the universe caused by a crime. Many statements can be found in historical and literary sources to the effect that excessive cruelty in punishment, or the failure to punish those responsible for outrageous crimes, leads to adverse manifestations of nature, such as excessive rain or drought.[46] Undoubtedly such statements reflect a widespread belief, current at different periods of time, that gross cases of injustice are likely to lead to the visitation of an evil on the part of Heaven. But one should not, on the basis of this position, draw the conclusion that every crime was thought (both by the ordinary people and those responsible for the administration of justice) to disturb the harmony of nature unless the appropriate punishment was imposed on the offender.

Two other pieces of evidence, more closely related to legal practice, are often cited. These are the rules in the penal codes which specify the times of the years in which criminals might lawfully be executed, and the reasons for the grant of amnesties. All the penal codes, drawing upon a much earlier tradition, in principle provided that criminals should be executed in the seasons of autumn and winter, not those of spring and summer. The Ch'ing code which was the least restrictive in this respect, prohibited executions during the first month of spring and the last month of summer.[47] Since spring and summer are the seasons of growth, whereas autumn and winter are the seasons of decay, it has been argued that the reason for the rule is the belief that acts of destruction of human life committed in the season of growth will disturb the harmony of nature and so prevent the seasons of spring and summer from properly fulfilling their rule. Even if this explanation were correct it would be rash to draw any inference as to the belief underlying the relationship between crime and punishment in general. But in fact it is doubtful whether the explanation can be accepted as adequate, certainly for the later periods of Chinese history. For this time the explanation for the retention of the rules may simply be an 'innate conservatism', the practice of adopting a set of rules from one reign to the next and indeed from one dynasty to the next. This explanation will not do for the earlier period. Some other reason must be advanced for the introduction of the rules in the first place.

One knows that the early Chinese were acutely conscious of the processes of nature and sharply differentiated betwen the seasons of growth and those of decay. To assign executions to the latter and forbid them for the former would have been an entirely appropriate procedure in the sense that it was fitting for executions to take place when nature itself was dying. Once this practice had become established, it is highly probable that people from time to time might argue that a particular seasonal oddity was caused by the execution of criminals in spring and summer. But one is not necessarily justified in explaining the origin of the institution in terms of a belief that the harmony of nature will be disturbed, with a consequent occurrence of abnormalities, should criminals be executed in the spring or summer. Still less would one be justified in drawing the conclusion that the failure to punish appropriately any crime was believed to lead to a similar disharmony.

Throughout the imperial period amnesties were frequently issued. These granted to offenders or certain classes of offenders a reprieve and cancellation or mitigation of punishment.[48] The reason for the issue of an amnesty might be stated to be the benevolence of the emperor and his compassion for his subjects. In addition it was sometimes said that the reason was the emperor's conviction, induced by some natural disaster, that there had been errors in the administration of justice. For example Thomas Metzger cites a shift to a more lenient policy of law enforcement (not strictly an amnesty) around 1792 prompted at least in part by the emperor's concern that the harshness with which piracy had been suppressed in the Taiwan area had caused a drought.[49] However one should again be wary of drawing too sweeping a conclusion from highly fragmentary evidence. The amnesties that do invoke a formula connecting error in the administration of justice with the occurrence of some natural disaster may be merely repeating a traditional set form of words, not in fact believed to be true, if they are thought about at all.[50] Furthermore no consistent connection between the issue of an amnesty and the belief of the emperor that there has been a serious miscarriage of justice can be demonstrated. Consequently there is little justification for construing amnesties collectively as a mechanism by which the balance of the universe, disturbed through the failure to convict the guilty or the conviction of the innocent, was restored to harmony.[51]

What one may credibly assert with respect to the relationship between the doctrine of cosmic harmoney and the penal codes is this. One may accept that by and large many people in all dynasties held that the acts of the ruler should accord with the 'will of Heaven'. Among these acts was the promulgation of the penal codes. Just as the 'will of Heaven' determined the course of natural phenomena so it determined the way in which humans should behave. Hence the ruler should ensure that the rules of behaviour enforced by means of the penal code accorded with the 'will of Heaven'. The essence of such beliefs and no doubt the source of their strength and persistency is their vagueness. They can be held without committing one to a manifestly absurd position or to specific beliefs that are too plainly contradicted by the evidence of the ordinary senses.

On the other hand the belief that each act contrary to the code (each 'crime') disturbs the 'harmony of the universe' in the sense of its physical (not its social) composition and calls forth a response on the part of nature unless it is met with a corresponding act of requital does carry a flavour of the absurd. It is very difficult to accept on the basis of such evidence as is presented that any such belief was prevalent in traditional China, or at least was genuinely held. This does not exclude the possibility, as already said, that glaring or repeated acts of injustice or maladminstration on the part of the ruler or his officials might genuinely be believed to prompt some manifestations of Heaven~s displeasure in the form of a natural disaster or prodigy. Even here one still has to bear in mind the fact that no more than lip-service may be paid to beliefs formally stated.[52]

Notes

1. See, for example, Mencius (translated Lau), 102.
2. The introductory material published in editions of the later codes (Ming and Ch'ing) includes the tables of mourning. See (for the Ch'ing code) Boulais p 17f; Philastre I, 71ff.
3. See especially Baker, Chinese Family and Kinship, 107ff; also cf. Freedman, Lineage Organization in Southeastern China, 40ff; Bodde and Morris, Law in Imperial China, 35f;; Ch'ü, Law and Society in Traditional China, 16f.
4. See especially Ch'ü, chapter 3.
5. For details see Ch'ü, 201 ff.
6. See especially Lee, The Legalist School and Legal Positivism, and cf. MacCormack, Law and Punishment: the Western and the Traditional Chinese 'Legal Mind'.
7. Para. 21ff (Karlgren). See chapter 1 note 2.
8. See chapter 1 at note 21.

9. See chapter 1 at note 28.

10. For the point see Lee, op.cit., 40. Cf. also Analects II.3 (Soothill, Analects of Confucius 8).

11. Slightly adapted from Creel's translation in Legal Institutions and Procedures during the Chou Dynasty, 39.

12. See Duyvendak, Book of Lord Shang, 141ff.

13. Duyvendak, op.cit., 179f.

14. Duyvendak, op.cit., 334. Cf. MacCormack, Rectification of Names in Early Chinese Legal and Political Thought, 385f.

15. Liao, Han Fei Tzu II, 242f.

16. Liao, op.cit., I, 166.

17. Liao I, 167.

18. Liao I, 267.

19. Liao I, 273.

20. Liao II, 188 (slightly amended).

21. Liao II, 212.

22. Liao II, 241.

23. Liao II, 243

24. Liao II, 251

25. Liao II, 256.

26. Liao II, 281.

27. Legalists and Laws of Ch'in, 22.

28. Duyvendak, op.cit., 85.

29. Liao II, 275.

30. Legalists and Laws of Ch'in 12.

31. This corrects an error in my paper cited note 6, 247 n 23.

32. I leave aside here other elements of legalist thinking such as the importance of 'methods' in government. For this see Creel, The *Fa-chia:* 'Legalists' or 'Administrators'?

33. Watson, Hsün Tzu, 35.

34. Dubs, Works of Hsuntze.

35. Watson, op.cit., 49.

36. Ch'ü op.cit., 267.

37. Cf. the remarks of Creel, Legal Institutions and Procedures during the Chou Dynasty, 39. See further chapter 6 at notes 87 and following.

38. See Hulsewé, Legalists and Law of Ch'in, llf; Remnants of Ch'in Law, 6f.

39. I draw here upon two previous studies, Natural Law and Chinese Philosophy, and Natural Law and Cosmic Harmony in Traditional Chinese Legal Thought (giving references to the sources and literature).

40. Cf. Fung, History of Chinese Philosophy I, 30f; Eichhorn, Die alte chinesische Religion und das Staatskultwesen, 23, 37f, 71f, 248.

41. Law in Imperial China, 4 and cf. 43ff. Cf. also the remarks of Ocko, I'll Take It All the Way to Beijing: Capital Appeals in the Qing, 291, 292.

42. Ch'in and Han Law, 522.

43. Remnants of Han Law I, 81. This view seems to me closer to the truth.

44. See the articles cited note 39. For an example of the 'lip service' approach see Liu, Ou-yang Hsiu, 157.

45. A glimpse of his thought can be obtained from the portion of his writings

translated by Fung, History of Chinese Philosophy II, chapter 2.

46. For examples see Williams, The Middle Kingdom I, 465f; Ch'ü, op.cit., 213ff.

47. Bodde and Morris, Law in Imperial China, 561. For the provisions of the code see Philastre I, 112 Decree IV; Boulais 35, 1694.

48. On amnesties see chapter 5, p. 125f.

49. The Internal Organization of Ch'ing Bureaucracy, 51, 52 n26.

50. Contra, however, Metzger, op.cit., 51.

51. See generally McKnight, The Quality of Mercy, chapter 6 and cf. his note 2 at 153.

52. See chapter 12 for further remarks on theses which link the understanding of the traditional Chinese penal law to a doctrine of cosmic harmony.

3

Sources of Law

Throughout the imperial period the emperor was accepted as the sole source of law. One may say that law was an expression of the emperor's will, although not all expressions of the imperial will consituted law. If one takes law for present purposes as rules which regulate behaviour by defining the conditions under which punishment will be imposed, then such rules were promulgated or made public by imperial edict.[1] An edict might introduce just a single rule for a particular case, or it might bring into effect a whole code, either when initially established or when subsequently revised. In the case of a code neither the emperor nor his advisers have personally introduced all the rules of which it is composed. Many are carried on automatically from one reign to the next, or have even been inherited from previous dynasties. Hence the imperial will in this respect is confirmatory rather than innovatory.

One might say that decisions of judges in criminal cases constituted sources of law in the sense that the judge as an official of the imperial civil service acted with the authority of the emperor. However it is perhaps better to regard judicial decisions as an indirect rather than a direct source. This is because, at least in the later period, situations brought to the attention of the central government through the judicial process might result in the issue of an edict establishing a new rule. Such a rule is derived from, and is based upon, the content of a judicial decision or series of such decisions but it is introduced as a specific rule of law through express enactment by the emperor.

Within the context of 'sources of law' and subject to the reservations made above one may distinguish basically between codes, edicts and judicial decisions. Before these are discussed a preliminary point deserves attention. Penal law is essentially a set of rules emanating from the emperor which imposes punishments on officials or ordinary people who behave, or fail to behave, in certain ways. It is not (at least directly) concerned with the establishment of the rights of the individual or with the protection of individual freedom. For this reason it has been asserted that the content of the imperial codes and edicts does not constitute law in the Western sense but rather should be regarded as 'administrative regulations'.[2] Although, of course, any attempt to define law is notoriously hazardous, this seems an overly restrictive approach. The penal codes issued by the emperor have those characteristics of positive law identified in textbooks of jurisprudence in their sections on the Austinian theory of law. They are commands addressed by the sovereign to his subjects backed by the threat of sanction. They can also be regarded as a natural law, although not necessarily in the sense in which this expression is understood in the Western legal and moral tradition. For example the traditional Chinese law is not held to be a law derived from reason or a mechanism for the safeguarding of the natural rights of man.

The penal codes are collections of rules, the precise composition of which varied from dynasty to dynasty. Common to all are the core articles (*lü*) which established both the essential ingredients of each offence and the circumstances which were to be taken into account for the determination of the punishment. Again common to all is the addition of a commentary on the articles, but the range and authority of the commentaries varied. One of the great dynastic codes, that of the Sung, contains imperial edicts establishing rules additional to those contained in the articles. The Ming and Ch'ing codes do not contain edicts as such but they do have, in addition to the articles, numerous further rules designated *li* (sub-statutes). After describing the components of each of the main codes I shall make some remarks on the relative ranking of both the codes themselves and their components as sources of law.

The T'ang code consists of 502 articles arranged according to subject matter in 12 books. Interspersed in the text of the articles and written in smaller characters is a series of 'notes' or, as is sometimes said, commentaries. These notes may clarify a difficult expression in the article or add supplementary points. Originally the code consisted just of the articles and the notes inserted in them. Both are phrased very elliptically and often they are extremely difficult to understand. Therefore in 653 A.D. a commentary was added to each article. Known as the *shu-i*, this commentary explained the meaning of both the article and the notes and often included important rules not expressed in the articles themselves or the notes. Part of the commentary was composed in the form of a question and answer in which hypothetical cases - ones not apparently covered by the article to which the commentary related - were raised and answered. The *shu-i* commentary forms an integral part of the T'ang code and is as authoritative as the articles and notes.

The Sung code reproduces the articles, notes and commentary of the T'ang code. But it also incorporates further material. At the time of its promulgation in 963 A.D. the punishments of the T'ang code were considered too harsh and hence a section was added to the article detailing the five punishments. This establishes the reduced scale of punishments to be applied under the Sung. Furthermore one finds scattered throughout the code the text of imperial edicts introducing a particular rule different from, or additional to, those stated in the articles, notes or commentary. These edicts were inserted after the article to which their content was most closely related. They cover the period from the final reduction of the T'ang code in 737 to the promulgation of the Sung code.[3] Penal rules enacted after 963 were not incorporated into the code since it was never revised and, indeed, during the course of the dynasty came to be used with increasing infrequency.

With the Ming and Ch'ing codes one has a change of format. Their core is still constituted by the *lü*, many taken directly from the T'ang code although rearranged and regrouped. But the later Ming codes and the Ch'ing codes are characterised by the inclusion of sub-statutes specifically denominated *li*. Relatively sparse in the final version of the Ming code they proliferate under the Ch'ing, constituting by the latter part of the 19th century a very considerable portion of the Ch'ing code. In a sense the Ming and Ch'ing *li* can be seen as successors to the imperial edicts incorporated into the Sung code. Like the latter they are specific decisions on legal points formally made by the emperor in an edict with the effect of introducing a new penal rule. They may originate in edicts promulgated by the emperor with the advice of his officials, or even just on his own initiative, or as decisions of the Board of Punishment to which imperial approval is given. In all cases the new rule can only function as part of the penal system and provide a basis for future judicial decision provided the permission of the emperor has been received for its incorporation into the code. The *li* differ from their T'ang or Sung prototypes in their function. They are specifically designed as supplements to the penal code, to be incorporated in its body after the article to which they are most relevant. They constitute the main means by which the codes at regular intervals were systematically brought up to date.[4]

With respect to the commentaries found in the codes, an important distinction has to be drawn between 'official' and 'private'.[5] Official commentaries were those compiled on the instructions of the government, ultimately of the emperor, and inserted in the text of the code at the time of its promulgation. They were deemed to have an authority equal to that of the articles themselves. The notes inserted in the articles of the T'ang and Sung codes and the *shu-i* explanation are both official commentaries. Neither reappears in the Ming and Ch'ing codes. The official commentary in these codes is termed the *hsiao chu* or 'small commentary'. As in the T'ang and Sung codes it is inserted in appropriate places in the body of, or immediately following, the articles, being in smaller characters. This allows the respective portions of the block of text constituting article and commentary to be distinguished at a glance.

The official commentary of the Ming and Ch'ing codes is much fuller than that supplied by the notes in the T'ang and Sung codes, some of which have been incorporated into the text of a Ming or Ch'ing article. Consequently the Ming and Ch'ing 'small commentary' provides a more comprehensive explanation of the terms of the article than do the T'ang and Sung notes. Sometimes very important modifications to the law are made by this commentary.[6] In the course of time the official Ming/Ch'ing commentary itself became considerably more elaborate. That found in the later editions of the Ch'ing code is lengthier than that of the final version of the Ming code.

Private commentaries, as the name suggests, were those written by private scholars without official authority or standing. A number were written during the Ming dynasty and became the basis for more elaborate commentaries prepared during the Ch'ing. Publishers often included one or more of these commentaries in the editions of the code they produced. For example the edition of the Ming code produced in 1907 under the auspices of the Commission for the Reform of the Laws contains a private commentary entitled *tsuan chu* ('incorporated commentary').[7] It is printed in the same size characters as the article and is inserted between this and any *li* that might be added. The 'incorporated commentary' offers brief and simple observations on the meaning of the article.[8] The most important of the Ming commentaries appears to have been the *chien-shih* ('explanatory notes') written by Wang K'en-t'ang at the beginning of the 17th century.[9] It is still quoted occasionally in 19th century cases and passages from it are included in the commentaries to late Ch'ing editions of the code.

Of the numerous Ch'ing commentaries that which proved most popular and successful was Shen Chih-ch'i's *chi-chu* ('collected commentaries'), the first edition of which appeared in 1715. Although a private commentary this appears to have become the standard work, included by the latter part of the 19th century in all the main editions of the Ch'ing code. It is sometimes explicitly quoted in judicial decisions and was certainly consulted by officials much more frequently than is evident from their actual citations of it. The *chi-chu* was divided into two parts which may be termed the 'general' and the 'special'. In order to understand their role in the editions of the Ch'ing code, one has to have a visual impression of the layout adopted for the printing of the articles, sub-statutes and various commentaries.

I have taken for my example the edition of the code entitled *Ta Ch'ing lü-li hui-chi pien-lan*.[10] Each page is horizontally divided into four layers, the bottom being the largest and the top the smallest. In the bottom layer appear in columns from right to left, first the text of the article interspersed with the official commentary (*hsiao-chu*) in smaller characters, then the general commmentary of Shen Chih-ch'i, also in smaller characters, which provides a comprehensive explanation of the article and official commentary, and then, in larger characters again, the text of the various *li* subjoined to the article. The *li* have no official commentary probably because they could readily be revised or deleted if found to be obscure or difficult to interpret.[11] The next layer up contains extracts from Shen's 'special' or 'upper' commentary and occasionally from some other commentary such as the *chien-shih*, already mentioned, as well as summaries of relevant cases. Further explanatory material may be included in the third layer and the fourth layer at the top has brief references to other sections of the code.[12]

The authoritative components of the Ming and Ch'ing codes were the *lü* (including the official or 'small' commentary) and the *li*. The general and upper commentaries were clearly helpful aids in the interpretation of the *lü* and the *li* and were sometimes, though rarely, cited in cases,[13] but they were not binding on officials entrusted with the decision or review of cases. On the other hand the *lü* and the *li* were binding, and indeed the official deciding a case was required to cite in his proposed judgment the particular *lü* or *li* upon which he relied for his sentence.[14] Hence the critical question to be determined is the relative authority possessed respectively by the *lü* and *li*.

One might have expected the *lü* to have the greater authority. This is because they possessed a 'sanctity' not wholly bestowed on the *li*. A considerable number of the Ch'ing *lü* could be traced back to the T'ang code. They were inherited from past dynasties and there was the most extreme reluctance on the part of Ch'ing officials to recommend that they be changed.[15] The same attitude came to be attached to any rule once it had acquired the status of a *lü*. Although some changes were made during the Ch'ing period, particularly at the time of the revision of the code in 1725-7, the general opinion that prevailed was that 'the *lü* are completed laws which once fixed do not change'.[16]

As a result of the official reluctance to modify the *lü*, most major changes made necessary by altered circumstances were effected through the making and incorporation of a *li*. In 1689 the Board of Punishments declared the relationship between *lü* and *li* to be: 'The text of the *lü* is a completed book transmitted from the past; the *li* are fixed after deliberation according to the circumstances of the case'.[17] The fact that the making of a *li* was prompted by new circumstances, especially as brought to light in recommendations of the Board of Punishments, meant that it dealt with a specific state of affairs that could not be assimilated under the general wording of a *lü*. The *lü* thus tended to be statements of the general position, in that they established the broad elements of an offence, whereas the *li* provided solutions for particular combinations of facts that had not been taken into account in the formulation of the *lü*.

Once a *li* had been inserted in the code it also acquired a certain 'sanctity' in that there appears to have been a reluctance to delete it. Quite frequently, however, the *li* were revised and substantial changes introduced. The edition of the code from 1871, cited above,[18] notes at the end of each *li* the date of its introduction and the dates of any revision to which it had been subjected. Given the facts that the *li* partook of something of the 'sanctity' of the *lü*, it is not surprising that the Board of Punishments often determined cases with reference primarily to the *li*. Indeed it can be said that for practical purposes the *li* had the greater authority.[19] An official late Ch'ing source states: 'Those who sentence ought to take the revised penal regulations (*li*) as the standard; they should not stick blindly to the text of the statutes'.[20]

Individual imperial edicts as sources of law are more important in T'ang and Sung times than in Ming and Ch'ing. By this I am referring to edicts which establish particular rules of law and as such are cited in legal treatises, compilations or judicial decisions. During the later dynasties the process of fairly regular revision of the codes and the practice of compiling and inserting *li* meant that changes in the law (which, of course, had to receive imperial approval) were no longer cited in terms of a specific edict. During the T'ang and Sung dynasties the position was different. After the final revision of the T'ang code in 737 changes in the law were effected by separate edicts. A well known example is supplied by the memorial of the poet Po Chu-i in 822 on the correct interpretation of an important section of the *shu-i* commentary dealing with the distinction between intentional killing and killing in the course of a fight. This was endorsed by imperial edict.[21] As has been seen the text of decisions on points of law was inserted where appropriate in the Sung code. During the Sung, edicts became the most important source of penal law. The code, after its initial promulgation, gradually fell into the background. Collections of edicts were issued and in effect took the place of the code itself.[22] Such collections continued to be important as sources of law in the Yuan period, when they were combined with other material to form massive compilations of regulations.[23]

Judicial decisions, especially those pronounced by the highest tribunals, the Supreme Court of Justice or the Board of Punishments, or given with the personal endorsement of the emperor, can be said to constitute sources of law in the sense that such precedents were regularly followed by other tribunals in similar cases. However one cannot speak of a doctrine of precedent of the kind known to the English common law. There do not appear to have been clear rules requiring the officials exercising judicial functions to follow cases emanating from certain sources. Indeed to an extent the evidence goes the other way. The central government was sometimes concerned that provincial courts were too often following precedents at the cost of subverting or bypassing the penal rules established by that government.

Under the T'ang no authoritative collections of judicial decisions from the Supreme Court of Justice or the Board of Punishments (Ministry of Justice) are known to have been compiled or circulated.[24] However the emperor himself was frequently concerned with judicial cases and promulgated his decision in an edict. As such the edict was intended to settle only the immediate question brought to the emperor for decision and not to lay down a rule applicable to future cases. However some of these rulings were deemed sufficiently important to merit their establishment as general rules of law. In this case the edict was transferred into a 'decree' or 'regulation' (*ko*) and its content included in the collections of 'decrees' periodically issued. These were authoritative, and established emendments to the penal code itself or to other rules of law.[25] The process by which the individual ruling of the edict was transferred into the general rules of the decree, reminds one of the process by which in the Ming and Ching dynasties judicial decisions, endorsed by the emperor, might become transferred into *li*. However as Karl Bunger has remarked, the T'ang decrees were not authoritative interpretations of the law emanating from the highest courts but rather new rules, changing or adding to the law, made by the emperor.[26]

There was an important distinction between an imperial edict which merely established a precedent for a special case and a decree which was intended to have lasting validity. This distinction is enshrined in an article of the T'ang code itself which provides that judges were not to be allowed to cite as a precedent an imperial decision on a specific case that had not yet been promulgated as a permanent ruling (*ko*).[27] The concern expressed here that judges should be controlled in their use of 'precedents' is also underlined in a series of rules and edicts from the post 737 period which one finds appended to the equivalent article in the Sung code. These show that it cannot have been easy for a judge to observe the distinction made in the code between edicts dealing with a special case and decrees laying down a general rule. They are instructed not to use 'precedents' (*li*)[28] in such a way as to subvert or abrogate the general law as established by the emperor. In dealing with criminal cases for which no clear ruling can be found in the text, first, of the latest relevant edict, then of the regulations, and finally of the code, judges may resort to analogy. Again they should start by considering first the terms of the latest edict and then look at the regulations (*ko*) and code. If they still remain in doubt they should memorialise the throne for a decision.[29] The whole thrust of these rules is directed at minimising the possibility that judges might arrive at decisions not in accordance with the imperial will.[30]

Some information on the process of judicial interpretation and the authority possessed by judicial decisions under the T'ang can be gathered from the memorial of Po Chu-i referred to above. A case of homicide involving the construction of a phrase in the *shu-i* commentary was remitted for consideration to Po as Grand Secretary of the Grand Secretariate. This post entailed the responsibility of advising the emperor on legal matters.[31] The first interesting point is that both the Supreme Court of Justice and the Ministry of Justice, the two highest tribunals concerned with legal matters, had agreed on the meaning to be given to the clause in question. Their interpretation in fact accorded with that adopted in previous decisions. However Po in a well argued opinion sustained a different interpretation and prevailed upon the emperor to accept it. His opinion was taken as authoritative in the later law.[32] Here we have an instance in which the interpretation affirmed by the entire judicial system was overruled by a government official acting on behalf of the emperor.

In the course of his memorial Po refers to certain earlier decisions of the Supreme Court upon which it had relied in the present case. He holds that these earlier cases should be distinguished on their facts, but adds that, even if they were sufficiently similar to be apt analogies, they were wrong in law. Why, he asks, should this matter? It matters, he concludes, because they then become 'precedents' (*li*) which cannot be relied upon.[33] There is a clear implication in Po's remarks that decisions of the Supreme Court of Justice were cited as precedents and followed not only by lower courts but by the Supreme Court itself. Yet the exact way in which such precedents were binding cannot be determined.

Evidence for the regular compilation and publication of precedents (*li*)[34] for criminal cases is first apparent in the Sung dynasty.[35] These were decisions of the highest judicial tribunals which had received imperial approval and were intended to furnish guides for the decision of future cases. One problem with their use was the extent to which they proliferated, so creating the same difficulties as those posed by the abundance of decrees or edicts: distinguishing the relevant from the obsolete, finding the appropriate punishments, and deciding between conflicting rules. Brian McKnight instances the problem confronting the compilers of a new collection of precedents in 1099. They were faced with an existing compilation containing more than 10,000 decisions. After excising those that were superfluous because the law was sufficiently clear, those that should never have been used beyond the case from which they arose and those that had been overruled, the compilers were left with a mere 141 decisions.[36] A second (related) problem in the use of precedents was the extent to which decisions, especially those given or endorsed by the emperor, could legitimately be applied to the determination of other cases. The fact that a number of such decisions were specifically ordered not to be available as *li* seems to have done little to alleviate the problem. Two instructive passages from the Sung Legal Treatise illustrate these problems. At the beginning of the 12th century leading court officials demonstrated that the use of precedents (*li*) by judges was becoming excessive and indeed beginning to subvert the law (*fa*). The emperor thereupon ordered the various ministeries to go through the collections of *li* in use and remove any that were opposed to the law.[37] What is evident here is a concern that the extension of decisions given for particular cases beyond the facts of those cases was leading to a nullification of the regular law intended by the emperor to be applied generally, and perhaps also that a legislative power properly held by the emperor alone was in fact being exercised by subordinate officals.[38]

A further passage explains the position obtaining at the time of, and indeed partly responsible for, the redaction of the edicts, statutes, regulations and ordinances (not judicial decisions) promulgated in 1172. It is said that even where the statutory rules have been established, officials still decide matters by reference to precedents, and conversely, where there is no precedent, then even though a statutory rule is clearly applicable, the matter is left undecided. The position may be so bad that the obscurity caused by the wholesale application of precedents harms the general law (*fa*), or that their application is in effect determined by the taking of bribes.[39]

The impression which one receives from passages of the kind quoted is that precedents were regarded during the Sung in an ambivalent fashion. Clearly their use was encouraged, as evidenced by the collections that were made, and by the frequent recourse to the emperor for decisions in particular cases that subsequently were treated as precedents. Yet they were also, at least at times during the Sung, regarded not so much as part of the regular law (*fa*) but as contrary to it.[40] Precedents subverted or nullified the statutory law. There may also have been an ambivalence on the part of the imperial court to what it saw as abuses of precedents. From one point of view this detracted from the authority of the statutory enacted law and hence from the law as established by the emperor, but from another the constant recourse to the emperor for special decisions with the likely result of increasing the number of precedents may have been encouraged since it left the final decision in the hands of the central government.[41]

The Yüan experience seems to have been not too dissimilar from that of the Sung. Paul Ch'en observes that 'collections of legal cases with decisions were also compiled and made readily available to the Yüan officials so as to provide them with the proper judicial guidance'.[42] The Yüan legal compilations regularly appear to have included collections of precedents or rules established by decided cases (*tuan-li*). Thus, a collective text of laws and precedents was compiled during the Ta-te reign (1297-1307)'.[43] According to the official Yüan history (*Yüan Shih*) the emperor Ying-tsung (1321-24) ordered the compilation of an immense collection of legal materials entitled Comprehensive Institutions of the Great Yuan (*Ta Yüan t'ung-chih*). This contained three categories of law: (i) edicts (decrees), (ii) articles and codes, and (iii) decided precedents (*tuan-li*)[44]. The number of precedents included is said to be 717, organised according to the divisions of the T'ang and Sung codes.[45] Another major legal compilation, the *Yuan tien-cheng*, also promulgated during the reign of Ying-tsung, likewise contained a large number of precedents.[46] As these compilations became outdated so the number of new precedents and other laws grew with the result that a further compilation of legal materials promulgated in 1346 with the title *Chih-cheng t'iao-ko* contained 1050 precedents.[47]

When one reads through the Ming Legal Treatise one frequently comes across references to 'precedents' (*li*)[48]. Furthermore one comes across statements reminiscent of those found in the Sung Legal Treatise to the effect that the statutory rules (*lü*) have fallen into decay and been overtaken by *li*. The profusion of *li* is so great that abuses arise in the administration of justice.[49] As under the Sung there is a clearly demonstrated concern that the indiscriminate use of rules made for particular cases is damaging the regular statutory law. Yet the sense of *li* does not seem to be quite the same as that of the term in the Sung Legal Treatise. While it is possible that the *li* mentioned in the Ming Legal Treatise include judicial decisions used as precedents, on the whole the expression seems to denote what have been described above as 'sub-statutes'. Of course many sub-statutes originated in the decisions of the highest judicial bodies, but the emphasis in the Ming discussions seems to be on the rules once they have been extracted from the judicial decision and been specifically designated as a *li*, a sub-statute which was to constitute an authority for future cases falling within its scope. Requests to the throne for the promulgation of collections of *li* also seem to refer to sub-statutes rather than just judicial decisions.[50] Perhaps what is reflected here is the accelerated process under the Ming by which judicial decisions were elevated to the status of a *li* in the sense of a sub-statute. For this reason it is possible that collections of pure judicial decisions were more rare and less important than under the Sung or Yüan.

Nevertheless judicial decisions in particular cases, when endorsed by the emperor, constituted the same kind of problem as that experienced in earlier dynasties. Like the T'ang and Sung codes the Ming contained a rule seeking to prevent the improper utilisation by judges of imperial decisions intended to deal with particular cases only. According to article 21 of book 28[51] such decisions cannot be cited or applied by analogy as though they belonged to the penal code itself. The word *lü* used here probably refers to both the statutes (strictly *lü*) and the sub-statutes (*li*) of the code. The general commentary of the Ch'ing code[52], which certainly expresses also the position of the Ming legislators, states that the unchanging and enduring law of the code should not be affected or modified by decisions which vary the normal punishment according to the special circumstances of a particular case.

Attempts by the government to control the extent to which officials, especially those acting as judges in the provinces, might randomly resort to 'precedent' were continued throughout the Ch'ing dynasty. During this period a further dimension of the problem receives more explicit attention in the sources. There was not just the difficulty posed by the improper use on the part of subordinate officials of decisions in legal cases handed down by the emperor. A further, more general difficulty was caused by the proliferation, within the Ch'ing judicial system, of actual decisions in criminal cases with the resultant temptation for provincial judges to rely too heavily upon them and so pay insufficient attention to the limits imposed by the statutory law (*lü* and *li*). The Ch'ing code contains a statute identical to that of the Ming on the need for judges to refrain from citing or relying upon imperial decisions, intended to settle special cases, as though they were a general rule of the code.[53] An important sub-statute was added to this statute in 1738. In Metzger's translation (slightly modified) it runs:

(Officials, except those at the three offices of penal law at the capital) may only quote the penal statutes (*lü*) and regulations or precedents (*li*) proper. It is wholly and severely prohibited that they drag in anything of the nature of *ch'eng an* (established cases) which have not yet been authorised as *t'ung-hsing* (general circulars) and established as *ting-li* (fully established precedents or regulations), with the result that the sentence is too severe or lenient. If the governors-general or governors in handling a penal mattter really find an old case which is closely similar (to the matter in hand) and can be adduced as a precedent *(li)* they are permitted to report it in their memorial and append a request that it be established as a *ting-li,* the Board of Punishments then closely examining the matter.[54]

Two early 19th century edicts also illustrate the problem of judicial precedent. An edict of 1804 addressed itself to the improper use by officials of conflicting cases (*an*) as precedents with a consequent 'corrupt manipulation' of the law. Apparently officials of the Boards in the capital had been resorting to previously decided cases even where there was a relevant statute or sub-statute; hence they are instructed only to bring in cases by way of analogy where there is no directly relevant *ting-li* (fully established precedent, i.e. sub-statute). The Boards were ordered to delete conflicting *an* from their records and review those which should be made into sub-statutes at the next revision of the code. The same problems were still experienced in 1811 when a further edict commanded the removal of *an* which conflicted with sub-statutes, and the insertion of rules established by appropriate *an* among the sub-statutes[55].

Several important concepts are mentioned in these sources: *an, ch'eng an, t'ung-hsing, ting-li and li*. *An* is the general term for a legal case, whatever its particular standing or provenance.[56] *Ch'eng an*, where the phrase is used in the context of penal law, are 'leading cases' which have a special relevance because they involve a decision by analogy. They are not direct applications of a statute or sub-statute, but indirect applications through analogy. Hence they introduce something new into the law and become important as precedents.[57] *T'ung-hsing* are cases which have reached the Board of Punishments, been revised and deemed by the Board and the emperor to be sufficiently important for circulation to the provincial authorities throughout the penal system. The fact that they are to be circulated already implies that by authority of the Board and the emperor they are to be followed at lower levels.[58] *Ting-li* is an expression which appears to be synonomous with *li* when used to designate a sub-statute. *Li* itself is the most difficult expression to understand because of the range of 'standards' to which it can refer.[59] While in Ch'ing legal contexts it frequently means 'sub-statute', it may also be used just in the sense of a judicial decision which is utilised as a precedent. In the sub-statute quoted above it appears to be used in both senses. In the phrase 'penal statutes and regulations or precedents' it means 'sub-statutes', whereas in the phrase 'old case which... can be addressed as a precedent' it means a judicial decision.

Ting-li, as regular sub-statutes, were clearly binding on all courts and, indeed, it was a punishable offence for a judge to decide a case either in defiance of, or without regard to, a relevant *li* (sub-statute).[60] More difficult to determine is the precise degree of authority possessed under the Ch'ing system by *an* or *ch'eng-an* and *t'ung hsing*. In both cases one is dealing with decisions of the Board of Punishments, often given greater weight through imperial endorsement. It is likely that *t'ung-hsing*, at least for lower courts, possessed equivalent authority to a sub-statute in cases where the facts under consideration could be subsumed neither under a *lü* nor a *li*. *T'ung-hsing* established the punishment appropriate for the offence arising from such facts, where the matter was deemed important enough for the Board to request imperial permission for the circulation of the decision throughout the penal system. Furthermore *t'ung-hsing* appear to have been the main source from which the body charged with the revision of the laws, the Statutes Commission, selected the new *li* to be added to the code.[61] The sub-statute of 1738 places *t'ung-hsing* on the same level as *ting-li*.

Most trouble is caused by *an* or *ch'eng-an*, as can be seen from the terms of the sub-statute and the edicts of 1804 and 1811. Clearly the authorities in the capital considered that subordinate jurisdictions were relying too heavily upon previous cases, with the result that the *lü* and the *li* were not being properly applied, and decisions were being given that imposed the wrong degree of punishment. They may have realised that it was impossible to forbid altogether the reliance by provincial officials upon cases previously decided by the Board. Hence a compromise was adopted in the sub-statute of 1738. Lower courts were permitted to cite *ch'eng-an* where no relevant *lü* or *li* (including perhaps *t'ung-hsing*) could be found to govern the case. However they were required merely to indicate the relevance to the present circumstances of the previously decided *ch'eng-an* and to request the throne, after review by the Board, to consent to the elevation of the *ch'eng an* to a *ting-li*. From this it is clear that *ch'eng-an* themselves possessed no binding force.[62]

The restrictions on the citing of *ch'eng-an* did not apply to the judicial authorities in the capital, and in particular to the Board of Punishments. One finds the Board citing from time to time by way of precedent two or three earlier cases. It does so purely in order to provide support for a ruling which it proposes in the given case, and not because it treats such previous decisions as binding upon it.

So far I have described the sources of official law, and indeed within that area have taken into account only penal, excluding public (constitutional and administrative) law. Unofficial law is also of relevance in the present context because there existed a variety of rules, emanating from a source other than the emperor, which touched upon topics contained in the penal codes. These rules can be classified both according to their origin and the relation which they bear to the official, codified rules. I shall examine them here within the framework constituted by their origin: that is, they are created either by kinship groups (clans) or commercial associations of unrelated persons (guilds), or they arise from custom. But it is useful to bear in mind the other possible classification since it enables one to grasp the overall effect of the official and unofficial rules in criminal law. From this point of view the unofficial rules may be classified either as reinforcing the official rules (by imposing sanctions for behaviour already punished by the code), or as supplementing them (by dealing with matters left untouched by the code), or as conflicting with, and prevailing over, the codified rules.

Clans were composed of all persons regarded as being descended patrilineally from a designated (remote) ancestor. These persons bore the same surname, might live in the same village or locality or be more widely dispersed. Visible features of the existence of a clan were clan leaders, land reserved for clan purposes and an ancestral hall in which sacrifices were made to the founding ancestor and matters of concern to the whole clan discussed and settled. Clan organisation was developed particularly under the Sung and later dynasties and came to be marked by the production of formal written rules, appended to the clan genealogy, intended to inspire clan members with the Confucian ethic and ensure that they behaved in the morally right way.[63] The content of these rules appears to have become settled mainly during the 18th century. Generally clan organisation was strong in south and central China, but less effective in the north.[64]

While the clan rules to some extent concern themselves with general injunctions to inculcate virtuous behaviour and refrain from vice and profligancy they also establish quite specific offences for which definite punishments are imposed. Sometimes these offences concern behaviour which is already made punishable by the penal code, for example unfilial behaviour, adoption as legal successor of an individual not belonging to the clan, fighting and beating, theft and felling trees in the ancestral graveyard. The punishments are lighter than those imposed by the code. One suspects that normally, once the offence had been detected and punished by the clan, that would be the end of the matter. The culprit would not in addition be referred to the authorities for trial. Occasionally the rules provide that he is to receive the official punishment as well, but this would normally apply only in the case of repeated offences where the individual came to be regarded by the clan as incorrigible and unmanageable. Other rules are concerned with misdemeanours that were not made criminal offences by the state (for example, drinking, quarrelling, lack of respect for elders, failure to maintain proper segregation between the sexes, or improper use of clan property). Finally one notes the occasional rule which prescribes or permits an act prohibited by the penal code (for example the divorce of a wife who has made a general nuisance of herself but has not committed one of the faults for which the code authorises repudaition, or the adoption of a person as heir from outside the clan). Some examples of actual rules follow.[65]

> Anyone in the *tsu* (clan) who becomes a thief, when his crime has been discovered, is to be put in chains. He is to be given forty hard blows and is to be driven out of the ancestral hall. If there is one who becomes a bandit, once his crime is proved true, the whole *tsu* is to join in beating him to death. Should he escape he is to be

denounced to the authorities.

If a real case of manslaughter occurs in the *tsu*, the whole *tsu* is to join in denouncing the criminal to the authorities, so that the crime may be judged according to the law. In case of a suicide through hanging or drowning, it is only permitted to go to the ancestral hall, so that the affair may be settled by group action, and the body buried....Should anyone make a false accusation (that is, pretend a relative had been driven to suicide by someone) in order to harm another person, he is to be punished with 30 strokes.[66]

If there should occur in the *tsu* any attempts at oppression of the young by relying on one's age, at bullying the weak by relying on one's strength, or, worse, should quarrels and fights take place, these cases should be brought before the the head of *tsu*. He is to convene the whole *tsu* to discuss the matter publicly and to settle the matter so that injuries between 'bone and flesh' (near relatives) or lawsuits that ruin the family may be avoided.[67]

I. Anyone who commits one of the ten abominations according to the criminal code is to be 'expelled'...

II. A woman who, aside from the seven offences that lead to divorce, disregards the *li-fa* (rules of *li* or morality, proper behaviour), that is, if she troubles and annoys the elders, maltreats the young, sows discord between 'bone and flesh', and starts quarrels with the neighbours, should be divorced. But if she does not misbehave too flagrangtly, it is all right to leave her name.[68] If she has no son she should be 'expelled'.[69]

1. Unfilial sons are to be administered 40 strokes with the big bamboo board.

2. Anyone insulting the older generation is to be administered 30 strokes with the same.

3. Gambling, drinking and the appropriation of another's property by violence are to be punished with 40 strokes.[70]

The government had probably always been in favour of the clan exercising, within certain limits, jurisdiction over the behaviour of its members. It no doubt recognised that the inculcation of the Confucian virtues which it sought to enforce through the penal codes was best effected by the training and instruction an individual received through the family and clan. Furthermore by dealing with minor offences committed by, and settling disputes between, members, the clan relieved the central authorities of task which otherwise would have fallen to them. As it was many matters which should under the code have been dealt with by the local magistrate never came to court; clan intervention and, where necessary, punishment were deemed to be sufficient. At the same time the government in the course of the 18th century came to see the possible value of the clan as a means of keeping the peace and maintaining the population under control. Imperials orders were issued requiring clan leaders to report to the authorities those members who were following evil courses.[71] The government's general strategy appears to have been to leave minor offences to be dealt with entirely by the clan, to reserve to itself jurisdiction over serious offences, but to use the clan for the detection, apprehension and surrender to the magistrate of serious or incorrigible offenders.[72]

Guilds shared some of the characteristics of clans. They again had a long history, although they appear in their most developed form under the Ch'ing.[73] The principle of association between non-related persons was common interest, derived either from the fact of engagement in the same trade or business, or from the fact of being a foreigner from the same place of origin. Thus within a particular town the carpenters, barbers, silk-weavers and millers might have their own association or guild. Likewise merchants and traders from a particular locality, conducting their enterprises in another area, formed associations for mutual protection. For example at the end of the 18th century traders from Ningpo established in Wenchow to earn their living declared:

> Here at Wenchow we find ourselves isolated; mountains and sea separate us from Ningpo, and when in trade we excite envy on the part of the Wenchowese, and suffer insult and injury we have no adequate redress. Mercantile firms, each caring only for itself, experience disgrace and loss - the natural outcome of isolated and individual resistance. It is this which imposes on us the duty of establishing a guild.[74]

Although guilds, (whether of local traders or non-indigenous merchants)[75] appear in origin to have been inspired by the need for protection either against the authorities or against local residents, they came to acquire large powers for the regulation of trade and commerce. Thus the guilds responsible for particular trades enacted and published rules governing such matters as working conditions within the trade, price levels and quality of goods. The merchant guilds also regulated the terms upon which the commodities in which they dealt were bought and sold. In both kinds of guild punishments (usually a fine) were imposed on members who did not comply with the rules; disputes between members were, where possible, to be settled by arbitration within the guild. Here are some examples of particular rules (current in the latter part of the 19th century).

> General Regulations of the Amoy-Fukien Sub-Guild of Ningpo: All dealing shall be in dollars. Promises to pay are to be from ten, twenty or thirty days (according to commodities particularised). Five days after sale, goods to be taken delivery of from godowns; if not taken by that time risks of fire and robbery to be borne by the purchaser.[76]

> Amoy Sub-Guild at Ningpo: Purchasers are to bring their own steelyards to the godowns. The weighing is to be in the presence of the parties concerned. When goods leave godowns or vessels, no corrections in weight are admissible, nor allowance made for breakages or leakages of enclosures of merchandise. No allowance for dried fruits that become damaged after the day of sale. Goods not taken delivery of five days after sale are subject to charge for storage. Three kinds of steelyards are recognised, and the commodities for the weighing of which one or other of these instruments is used are specifically named; each article to be weighed by the steelyard that has been fixed by custom.[77]

> Ningpo Fishmongers' Union Regulations: First - It is agreed that boatmen conveying fish from fishing stations, who place sand in the bottom of hampers, fraudulently increasing the weight, shall be mulcted to pay for a theatrical performance. Second. - It is agreed that we keep standard steelyards, and inflict the same fine on any of the Union who keep fraudulent instruments.[78]

> Wenchow Silk-Weavers' Union: It is agreed that members of the association shall work carefully and with their best skill, and pay for silk that has been damaged by bungling.[79]

Some of the guild rules can be regarded as more detailed applications of the few general rules contained in the penal code (for example, those on weights and measures and the quality of goods).[80] Many others regulate aspects of manufacture and commerce not touched on by the code at all. Even where the code did have a general provision it is likely that cases falling within its scope were left by and large to be dealt with by the relevant guilds. Magistrates requested to deal with commercial cases relied upon the guild regulations as authoritatively determining the conditions under which a transaction had been concluded.[81]

The rules written down and applied by clans and guilds can perhaps be regarded, at least in part, as crystallised and institutionalised custom. Some may represent innovations but many will have simply put into written form what was already accepted within the clan or guild as the proper way to do things. At a particular point in time certain practices or modes of behaviour deemed of especial importance or significance have been formally cast into rules governing the conduct of members of an institution (clan or guild). Aspects of customary behaviour singled out in this way may even have become fossilised; once they had become the subject of a written regulation further change might have been difficult. Indeed they may in time have come to be supplanted by contrary (unwritten) custom.

Falling outside the ambit of clan or guild rules is a further extensive area of custom or what has been called customary law.[82] This covers actual practices prevalent in localities followed with a degree of consistency that yields a claim of right or legitimate grievance should there not on a particular occasion be compliance with them. Such practices cover an infinite number of situations. Generally they are of particular importance in the fields of what modern lawyers would call property, contract and family law. Although it was the post-imperial period which saw the main attempts to collect and analyse material held to constitute customary law, the results obtained almost certainly give the position that obtained under the late Ch'ing.[83]

Customary practices were 'enforced' in a number of ways: by clans or guilds, by village headmen and elders and by the official courts themselves. Many disputes that broke out between families in a village, relating, for example, to customary rights to the use of land or water, were settled by arbitration or mediation within the village and did not reach the magistrate's court. Equally disputes arising from contractual relationships were settled either within the village or through the help of the guilds. However some cases did reach the magistrates. He apppears to have viewed his task simply as the ascertainment and application of the relevant customary rules, possibly remitting the matter to appropriate and experienced persons for settlement in accordance with those rules.[84]

The fact that a magistrate might be required to apply customary law raises the question of the relationship between the 'unofficial' and the 'official law'. What were the respective weights given to rules of customary or statute law? No problem, of course, would arise in cases where the subject matter was not covered by the code. But cases of direct conflict might arise. How was a magistrate to respond to them? An interesting statement on this point is to be found in a book written for the guidance of magistrates and their secretaries by Wang Hui-tsu (1731-1807), entitled Precepts for Local Administrative Officials.[85] In this influential work Wang in a paragraph headed 'you must respect local customs', urges the magistrate's legal secretary to ascertain the customs of the district and adds 'If you never act on a penal law or an edict without first seeing that it does not conflict with what local custom values, then there will be harmony between yamen and people, the magistrate's fame will spread, and his secretary's prestige will increase accordingly'.[86]

One might infer from Wang's language that where a local custom directly conflicted with a rule established by the penal code, the former was to be given precedence. There is evidence that in commercial, property and family matters customs contrary to what was prescribed in the code were at least tolerated by the authorities.[87] On the basis of this evidence one may be prepared to generalise and argue that in 'civil' questions the courts preferred to give effect to a local custom despite a contrary ruling on the specific issue to be found in the code. Whether the same latitude was extended to 'criminal' matters may be more doubtful, although Wang's remarks were probably intended to refer primarily to such issues. Whereas he certainly held that the code should be interpreted, where possible, so as to confirm to local custom, he may not have gone so far as to hold that the latter in a criminal matter prevailed over a directly contrary customary rule. To have taken up this position might have nullified the operation of the penal law altogether.

Notes

1. For the sake of simplicity I use the single term 'edict' to designate the act by which the legislative will of the emperor is manifested. Sometimes, however, it is convenient to make a distinction between 'edict' and 'decree' as in the discussion of the T'ang sources. In fact many different terms were used (not necessarily the same in all dynasties) for the emperor's formal legislative acts. See Vandermeersch, An Enquiry into the Chinese Conception of Law, 6ff.

2. Vandermeersch, op.cit.m, 12ff. Something further is said on this point in chapter 12.

3. Examples will be found below in chapters 10 and 11.

4. Many examples can be found in the first part of the Ming Legal Treatise, translated by Munzel (Strafrecht im alten China).

5. See Bodde and Morris, Law in Imperial China, 68 ff; Chen, The Influence of Shen Chih-ch'i's *Chi-chu* Commentary upon Ch'ing Judicial Decisions.

6. Cf. Bodde and Morris, op.cit., 70 (on the phrase 'after the assizes').

7. See Meijer, The Concept of *Ku-sha* in the Ch'ing Code, 91 n21, 93.

8. Examples can also be found in Meijer, op.cit., 93f; it is cited from time

to time in the course of this book.

9. Chen, op.cit., 173 and n20; Bodde and Morris, op.cit., 71f.

10. The Taiwan reprint is in 15 volumes consecutively paginated. Meijer, Abuse of Power and Coercion, 184 n1 translates the title as Convenient Survey of the *Lü* and *li* of the Great Ch'ing Dynasty with Commentary, and gives the orirgnal date of publication as 1871.

11. For this suggestion see Chen, op.cit., 171.

12. For an example of the layout taken from another edition of the code see van der Sprenkel, Legal Institutions in Manchu China, 131f.

13. See Chen, op.cit., 172.

14. See chapter 4 at note 82.

15. See generally Metzger, Internal Organisation of Ch'ing Bureaucracy, 84ff, 423ff. For a similar attitude under the Ming see Munzel, op.cit., 34f, 41, 48.

16. Quoted from a 1736 memorial by Metzger, op.cit., 84 n13.

17. Metzger id, and cf Alabaster, Notes and Commentaries on Chinese Criminal Law, XLIIIf, and generally Bodde and Morris, op.cit., 63f.

18. See note 10.

19. This was not always the case. For a Ming example where the authority of the *lü* was preferred to that of the *li* see Munzel, op.cit., 49 (on P'ang An). See also the pertinent remarks of Meijer, Criminal Responsibility for the Suicide of Parents, 111.

20. Metzger, op.cit. 86 n23. See also the remarks of McKnight, From Statute to Precedent, 122 (for Sung practice).

21. See Wallacker, The Poet as Jurist: Po Chu-i and a Case of Conjugal Homicide.

22. See chapter 1 at n59.

23. For examples see Ch'en, Chinese Legal Tradition under the Mongols, 31, 38.

24. See especially Bunger, Quellen zur Rechtsgeschichte der T'ang-Zeit, 51ff.

25. For 'decrees' (*ko*) see Bünger, op.cit., 36ff, and Twitchett, Fragment of the T'ang Ordinances of the Department of Waterways, 30ff (translating *ko* as 'regulation'). Under the Sung *ko* has a different sense (McKnight, From Statute to Precedent, 112f).

26. Bünger, op.cit., 54.

27. Article 486. Cf. Le Code 685; Deloustal, 684; Bunger, op.cit., 46 n65.

28. This is the same character as that which denotes the Ming or Ch'ing 'sub-statute' but is used in a different, though related sense. The general meaning of the term is defined in one of the great Chinese dictionaries as 'a standard which can be applied through comparison' (cited by Metzger, op.cit., 185). This points to the fact that a rule described as *li* may be cited in support of a decision given in a case similar to, though not identical with, that which gave rise to the rule itself (cf. the remarks of McKnight, op.cit., 115). The source of such rules is always the emperor's will but the particular context in which it is manifested varies. Although manifestations of the imperial will establishing rules may be termed 'edicts', the particular context may be the establishment of a general rule to govern a future class of case (described as 'edict' or sub-

statute') or the rendering of a decision for a particular legal case submitted to the throne (described as 'judicial decision' or 'precedent').

29. This rule is established in an edict of 931 A.D.

30. Cf. the remarks of Vandermeersch, Enquiry into the Chinese Conception of Law, 20.

31. See Wallacker, op.cit., 520.

32. Cf. Wallacker, op.cit. 518. One finds the text of Po's memorial included in Hsüeh Yun-sheng's parallel edition of the T'ang and Ming Codes (T'ang Ming Lü Ho Pien).

33. Wallacker, op.cit., 520.

34. See note 28 above. Sometimes the phrase *tuan-li* is used to describe such precedents.

35. See generally McKnight, op.cit., 114ff, 125; Miyazaki, Administration of Justice during the Sung Dynasty, 56, 57f; Burns, Private Law in Traditional China (Sung Dynasty), 38; Seidel, Studien zur Rechtsgeschichte der Sung-Zeit, 43f.

36. McKnight, op.cit., 116.

37. Seidel, op.cit., 71f.

38. Cf. here the remarks of McKnight, op.cit., 124f, pointing to the reluctance of subordinate officials to take decisions on their own initiative, with a consequent referral of problem cases to their superiors and ultimately to the emperor. Although the practice led to an even further increase in the number of 'precedents', the central government, McKnight suggests, may (somewhat paradoxically since it was also concerned to check the profusion of 'precedents') in fact have welcomed it precisely because the decision making was left firmly in its hands.

39. Seidel, op.cit., 76 (slightly modified).

40. Ratchnevsky, Code des Yüan II, 79 nl, writing of Yüan material points out that *li* ('precedent', in the sense of 'loi écrite', 'code') is often opposed to *fa* (in the sense of 'une norme qui est conforme au sentiment général de l'humanité et de la morale'). If he is right one has to say that it does not seem that the Sung officials understood the contrast between *li* and *fa* in the same way; for them the problem was that recourse to individual precedents led to a failure to apply properly the statutory law.

41. See note 38 above.

42. Chinese Legal Tradition under the Mongols, XVI.

43. Ch'en, op.cit., 21.

44. Ratchnevsky (Code des Yüan I, xvii n5) quotes from a Yüan source a definition of *tuan-li* as: 'les règles de jurisprudence sont des règles etablies en raison d'une affaire; en tranchant en affaire on crée une règle de jurisprudentce (*li*)'.

45. Ch'en, op.cit., 25, 29.

46. Ch'en, 31.

47. Ch'en 38.

48. See Munzel, Strafrecht im altem China, index under 'Präzendenzfalle'.

49. Munzel, 34f, 46.

50. Munzel, 47.

51. MLCCFL, 2026.
52. Philastre II, 711.
53. Article 370, Philastre II, 710, Staunton 456.
54. Metzger, Internal Organization of Ch'ing Bureaucracy, 201 n43 and see also the translation (requiring some modification) of Philastre II, 712.
55. The content of these edicts has been summarised by Metzger, op.cit., 202.
56. See in particular Metzger, 194ff.
57. Bodde and Morris, op.cit., 151f.
58. Bodde and Morris, 152.
59. See note 28 above.
60. See chapter 4 at notes 82, 83.
61. Bodde and Morris, op.cit., 152.
62. Metzger, op.cit., 204 makes the point that an exception is made in the case of *ch'eng an* that were shortly to acquire the status of a *ting-li*.
63. Clan rules in fact antedate the Sung, the earliest surviving set being that of the Yen family from the 6th century A.D. See Yen Chih-tui, Family Instructions for the Yen Clan.
64. On clans I have consulted the following accounts: Hu, The Common Descent Group in China and its Functions; van der Sprenkel, op.cit., 80ff; Liu, The Traditional Chinese Clan Rules, and the same author's An Analysis of Chinese Clan Rules: Confucian Theories in Action; Twitchett, The Fan Clan's Charitable Estate, 1050-1760; Hsiao, Rural China, chapter 8; also relevant are Dardess, The Cheng Communal Family, and Langlois, Authority in Family Legislation: the Cheng Family Rules.
65. See also the general remarks in Liu, Clan Rules, 172ff, and the detailed information summarised in her appendices.
66. The Wang clan of Kiangsu province, Hu, op.cit., 132.
67. The Hsü clan of Kiangsu province, Hu, 133.
68. The reason is to enable her son still to know his descent.
69. The I clan of Hupei province, Hu, 134, 135.
70. The T'an clan of Kiangsu province, Hu 135.
71. The duty to report evil doers to the government, placed on the clans, thus complemented the elaborate (and not altogether successful) *pao chia* system under which households, through persons appointed for the purpose, were to notify the magistrate of suspicious characters and report those who had committed serious offences (especially robbers and brigands). See Hsiao, op.cit., 43ff and cf. Boulais 343.
72. See Hsiao, op.cit., 348ff. He points out that in fact the government policy which encouraged strong clan organisation had dangers since clans, relying upon their local power, tended to engage in lawless practices and feuds. One also has to remember the rules on accusations brought against relatives contained in the code (see chapter 7) which made it a punishable offence for certain categories of relatives to accuse each other to the authorities of having committed an offence (with some exceptions).
73. See generally MacGowan, Chinese Guilds or Chambers of Commerce and Trade Unions; van der Sprenkel, op.cit., 89ff; Burgess, The Guilds of Peking; Golas, Early Ch'ing Guilds.
74. MacGowan, op.cit., 136.

75. See van der Sprenkel, op.cit., for the point that there was no necessary sharp distinction between these two kinds of association.

76. MacGowan, 146.

77. MacGowan, 148.

78. MacGowan, 171.

79. MacGowan, 174 (from whose essay many further examples and details can be gathered). Burgess, op.cit., 193f notes that the Peking guilds had far fewer formal rules than the guilds of south and central China; he suggests that unwritten custom played a greater part in Peking.

80. See chapter 10 at n43f.

81. Cf. van der Sprenkel, op.cit., 95; Brockman, Commercial Contract Law in Late Nineteenth-Century Taiwan, 106.

82. Van der Sprenkel, op.cit., 103. Cf. also her discussion in Urban Social Control, 620f.

83. In the early part of the twentieth century, commencing even before the collapse of the Ch'ing, the task of collecting and recording the different customs relating to legal matters in the Chinese provinces was instituted. The result was eventually published in 1930 under the title *Min shang shih hsi-kuan t'iao-ch'a pao-kao lu* (Collected Reports of an Investigation into Civil and Commercial Legal Customs). There is a German translation by E. Kroker in three volumes published in 1965 under the title Die amtliche Sammlung chinesischer Rechtsgewohnheiten (not seen). Generally see van der Sprenkel, op.cit., 103f, 161; Kroker, Concept of Property in Chinese Customary Law, 124f. Examples of custom, especially relating to property and contract, can be found in these works and also in Kroker, Dienst-und Werkvertrage im chinesischen Gewohnheitsrecht; Haas, Gewohnheitsrechtliche Vertragstypen in China; Wilkinson, Landlord and Labour in Late Imperial China; Zelin, The Rights of Tenants in Mid-Qing Sichuan. With respect to Taiwan, the cession of the island to the Japanese at the end of the 19th century led to a survey of the customary law there obtaining, the first results of which were published in 1900 (Oyamatsu, Laws and Customs of the Island of Formosa).

84. See especially the account given by Brockman, op.cit., of the magistrate's treatment of commercial cases in 19th century Taiwan. See also chapter 4, note 47.

85. See van der Sprenkel, op.cit., appendix 4.

86. Op.cit., 150.

87. For examples see McAleavy, Chinese Law, 112ff; Brockman, op.cit., 88f.

4

The Administration of Justice: Courts and Judicial Procedure

The Courts

Traditional China did not possess a separate system of courts staffed by professional judges of the kind known in the west. The root cause was probably that the doctrine of the separation of powers was never accepted or developed in China. Legislative, judicial and executive power ultimately rested exclusively in the person of the emperor. On his behalf and subject to his control power was exercised throughout the country by his officials. Such officials did not have the power to legislate but, like the emperor, they combined in their own persons executive and judicial power. Hence district magistrates, prefects or provincial governors to whom the task of determining criminal cases was delegated, carried out their judicial function only as one of the multifarious functions of subordinate government with which they were entrusted.[1]

An important consequence of the fact that those responsible for judicial decisions were the senior officials of a particular administrative unit (whether district, prefecture or province) is that they were primarily career administrators and not trained lawyers. Since they were liable to punishment themselves for proposing sentences which were mistaken in law it was necessary that they have expert advice on the applicable provisions of the code or other legal enactments. Hence presiding officials, even at district level, had on their staff persons who had made a special study of the law. But it was not until one reached the highest levels in the capital that those in charge of determining sentences were regularly experts in the law.

It is probable that the concentration of legal expertise in the capital was the outcome (whether consciously designed or not) of the practice adopted in virtually all dynasties for the handling of serious offences or cases where there was a legal doubt. This was the arrangement of bodies with judicial functions in a hierarchy of ascending importance from district courts at the bottom through prefectural and provincial courts in the middle to the central judicial organs in the capital at the top. The principle adopted is that the more serious the offence, the more important the body with the power of final disposition. For example, at the district level magistrates had the power to make final decisions only in cases where the appropriate punishment was a beating. At the other end of the scale all cases entailing capital punishment were finally determined by the highest judicial organs in the capital and still required the concurrence of the emperor before the sentence could actually be executed.

Great care was taken in the investigation of serious cases. All cases started at the lowest level, in the magistrate's district court or its equivalent in the capital. All were investigated in the first instance by the magistrate himself and he proposed the sentence appropriate to the offence. However where the sentence was beyond his competence for final decision the record of the case was sent to the next level - prefecture or province - together with the accused and the witnesses, and there fully re-investigated. Some cases were finally decided at this intermediate level. Those which were not, especially offences entailing the death penalty, were sent to the capital (normally only the record itself) and a further investigation was held. Thus the process of automatic review ensured that the magistrate's initial findings and proposed sentence were subject to careful, and in some cases repeated, revision. A further check on the soundness of decisions in criminal cases was constituted by the periodic reviews conducted by high ranking officials, such as censors, sent out from the capital to ensure that the administration of the districts, prefectures and provinces was proceeding smoothly.

From the review of criminal cases, whether conducted automatically or from time to time by inspecting officials, one has to distinguish appeals. It was open to the accused himself or members of his family, or indeed any member of the public, to assert that an injustice had occurred in his trial or conviction. The proper procedure was for the person asserting that an injustice had occurred through the decision of a particular tribunal to appeal to that tribunal's presiding officer and if that had no effect to the tribunal superior to it in the hierarchy. Once local remedies had been exhausted in the sense that an appeal had been taken through the hierarchy of tribunals without success, it was possible to appeal finally to the emperor himself. Grant of the appeal led to a reopening and re-investigation of the case.[2]

It is worth stressing the special concern shown in the infliction of the death penalty since this demonstrates the principle of compassion that characterised the traditional system of justice in a variety of ways. The essence of the matter was put by the founding emperor of the T'ang dynasty when in 631 he ordered that a sentence of death should be executed only after repeated memorials to the throne had each received an affirmative reply, declaring 'once the sentence has been executed a man cannot again come to life'.³ One finds the same sentiment expressed in the recommendations made by the Board of Punishments of the Ch'ing dynasty. Indeed the procedures of this dynasty were expressly designed to save a large number of persons convicted of capital offences from the actual fate of death. Not only might persons sentenced to die be given a reprieve through the normal procedure by which the sentence was reviewed, but special amnesties also ensured that persons under sentence of death often escaped with their lives.

Some detail on the way these general principles were applied in the various dynasties will make their operation clearer. The way justice was administered in Han times is known only imperfectly. Its most distinctive characteristic, in contrast to the practice of later dynasties, appears to have been that the emperor's judicial power was fully devolved in the sense that prefects at the local level had the authority to impose and carry out sentences of any degree of severity including death. Only cases in which the law was doubtful were to be referred to the capital.⁴

An important change in policy occurred during the Sui dynasty. In 592 the emperor Wen issued an edict providing that for the future prefectures were not to put into effect a sentence of death immediately after judgment, but were to send the record of the case to the capital for review by the Supreme Court of Justice. The Court in turn after completing its review was to send the papers to the Department of State from which they were transmitted to the throne for final decision.⁵ With modifications this rule was observed in all later dynasties.

The T'ang, prior to the disruption of the empire through the rebellion of An Lu-shan (755-762) which led to greater provincial autonomy,⁶ operated a system of justice at the local level, carefully controlled by the central authorities. Each level of the administrative hierarchy in relation to its judicial function possessed a clearly defined sphere of competence. The district court might pass final judgment only in cases involving a beating with the light or heavy stick. Other cases were investigated by the magistrate but then remitted with his recommendation to the prefecture. The prefect re-investigated all cases referred from the district but might give a final judgment only in those entailing a sentence of penal servitude. Those entailing a sentence of exile or death were referred to the capital for review by the Board of Punishments which might dispose finally of the former category. For offences entailing the death penalty there was a further elaborate process of review by the officials of the three highest ministries (Censorate, Secretariat and Chancery) with a final recommendation to the throne. The T'ang code itself by article 497 imposed a heavy punishment on officials who inflicted a death sentence before three memorials had been submitted to the throne and each approved. Even after this procedure had been completed three further days were to elapse before the execution took place.[7] The point was to allow the greatest possible opportunity for reflection on the need to take a human life.[8] In the metropolitan area the procedure was similar, with the Supreme Court of Justice having the role of the prefecture in the provinces.[9]

Under the Sung the system of justice was similar, the major modification concerning the handling of offences entailing a punishment of death or exile. Prefectures were placed into circuits and the activities of the prefects were reviewed by the supervisor of the circuit in which the prefecture was placed. The prefect was required to send all exile and death cases to the supervisor for review. The latter might give final judgment not only in all cases of exile but also in some cases of death. A distinction was drawn between sentences of death which should be memorialised and those which should not. When the facts and the law were clear and the offender consented to the sentence the case stopped at the circuit level. Only in cases of doubt or at the request of the offender was a referral made to the capital. Of course the fact that the accused might himself insist on referral suggests that all cases could have been submitted to the Supreme Court and Board of Punishments and ultimately to the emperor for review. But one does not know what pressure was brought on offenders, in clear cases at the circuit level, to accept the sentence.[10]

The Yüan dynasty established a complex series of administrative levels in the provinces at which all cases involving beating or penal servitude might be finally sentenced. With respect to cases involving exile or death it restored the T'ang rules that they should be submitted to the capital for review, the appropriate body being the Board of Punishments. Particularly difficult or important cases were transmitted further to the emperor and his advisers. Both the Ming and Ch'ing dynasties operated with four basic administrative levels: the district, prefecture, province and capital. Under the Ming the power of final judgment, in cases of beating, was vested in the district court and, in cases of penal servitude and exile, in the various prefectural or provincial courts. Offences entailing the death penalty were sent for review to the capital.[12]

Article 17, book 28, of the Ming code[13] provided that the district (*hsien*), sub-prefectural (*chou*) and prefectural (*fu*) courts might dispose of all cases involving punishments short of death, the cases all starting in the district court and proceeding where necessary through the hierarchy. Offences entailing the death penalty were to be referred to the Board of Punishments which was to check the recommended sentences and, if the death penalty was imposed, memorialise the throne for permission to execute it. The 'incorporated commentary' makes a distinction between 'light' punishments (those short of death) which might suitably be left for determination by the various authorities and the 'heavy' punishments (death) which should only be carried out after permission had been obtained from the throne. The reason again given is that once the execution has been carried out, the offender cannot be restored to life. A further article (book 28, article 27)[14] imposes a punishment on officials who carry out a sentence of death without waiting for the reply to the memorial requesting permission, or who fail to wait for three days after receiving permission.

In the Ch'ing dynasty less authority was accorded the provincial level.[15] The provincial court might give a final judgment only in cases of penal servitude provided no homicide was involved. All cases in which someone had been killed or which entailed a punishment of exile or death were referred to the Board of Punishments, the emperor being required to ratify all sentences of death.[16] Equally doubtful cases - those in which the decision was by way of analogy - were submitted to the Board for consideration. I have followed here the account given by Bodde and Morris.[17] It should however be noted that the rules stated in the code itself seem to be different. These follow the Ming rules in allowing the final judgment in offences entirely of exile to be given at the provincial level.[18] The general commentary to the Ch'ing article states that at the end of the year a report of all the cases in which the accused has been sentenced to penal servitude or exile is to be sent to the Board of Punishments.[19] Boulais attributes to the commentary the statement that the provincial authorities are to submit such sentences to the Board for its examination.[20] The matter is confused, and there appear to have been changes introduced in practice, although not incorporated in the text of the code.[21]

As has been seen concern at the taking of a human life had been a characteristic of the law at least from the T'ang period. During the Ming and Ch'ing dynasties this concern led to the creation of a further set of procedures by which a sentence of death once given and even confirmed by the emperor might nevertheless ultimately be commuted to a lesser punishment. This set of procedures is known as the Autumn Assizes, the origin of which goes back to Ming times although the full development of the institution occurred under the Ch'ing.[22] The text of the articles in the penal code simply specified for capital offences that the offender was to be put to death. However on numerous occasions after the specification of the type of death penalty in the article, the official 'small' commentary adds the words 'after the assizes'. This means that the sentence of death, once found to be appropriate in a particular case and confirmed by the emperor, is still to be reviewed at a special autumn meeting of the highest officials of the country. In effect two kinds of sentence of death were established by the code: that in which execution was to be immediate, in the sense that no further review was possible, and that in which execution was to be deferred until confirmation of the sentence had been obtained at the autumn meeting. Where a sentence of immediate execution was passed, the offender, after confirmation of the penalty by the emperor, was put to death as soon thereafter as possible.

What is called review of the sentence at the Autumn Assizes was in reality a complex process of re-investigation of the case. Once the Board's initial confirmation of the death sentence as one to be applied 'after the Assizes' had been ratified by the emperor, the case was referred back to its originating province for reconsideration by the Judicial Commissioner and other officials. Their task was not to re-open the question of the convicted offender's liability but to decide whether the case should now be classified as one in which the circumstances warranted the implementation of the death penalty, as one in which it should be postponed with eventual commutation to a lesser punishment (for example in a case of homicide where there had been no intention to kill), or as one in which there were circumstances worthy of imperial compassion (for example where the offender was old or young or a woman).[23] The preliminary classifications reached by the Judicial Commissioner were then submitted to the Board of Punishments for review. After a careful investigation by the Board's officials the results were announced at the autumn assembly of high dignitaries convoked to make the final recommendations to the throne.

Even at this stage a reprieve or at least a delay of execution was possible for those who had been placed in the 'deserving of death' category. The emperor held a ceremony in which he personally checked off with a vermilion brush the names of those on the assize lists presented to him who were to die. Should a name not be checked off execution was deferred until the next year when the list was again presented to the emperor. If a name escaped the vermilion brush a certain number of times the death penalty was commuted.[24] It should be emphasised that this was a rational and not an arbitrary or 'magical' proceeding. The emperor and his advisers would have considered prior to the actual ceremony which names should be checked off and which should escape.

Legal Personnel

As is well known traditional China never developed a legal profession. In the Confucian scheme of values knowledge of, or interest in, the law occupied a low place. Furthermore the government on more practical grounds distrusted the activities of those with legal skills unless they were used in the interests of the state and kept firmly under its control. Two particular consequences followed from such attitudes. In the first place the literati intending to make a career as an official did not attach importance to legal studies, even where these were available, and hence those in charge of the various provincial units of administration had little knowledge of the law despite the fact that one of their main responsibilities was the handling of judicial affairs.

In the second place the activities of members of the public who professed legal skills were to some extent repressed by the law. Both the Ming[25] and the Ch'ing codes[26] contained an article imposing a heavy punishment on those who encouraged others to initiate legal actions and drafted for them the appropriate complaint. This was intended to discourage the promotion of unnecessary litigation marked by a distortion or exaggeration of the facts. A proviso in the article exempts from liability those who help the ignorant and illiterate to begin a legal action where they have been wronged. Again an important sub-statute dealt with cases in which 'litigation tricksters' conspired with government clerks and tricked ignorant country people or practiced intimidation or fraud.[27] Although these measures were not in themselves unduly repressive they were interpreted in a way that made any offer to help or promote litigation hazardous.[28]

Except at the highest level in the capital those who investigated or reviewed criminal cases were not experts in the law. Under the Ch'ing the Judicial Commissioners (*an-ch'a chih*) who presided over the highest provincial court were trained in the law.[29] However in all dynasties the courts of the magistrates and prefects which investigated or processed criminal cases and gave final decisions in all but the most serious were not staffed by lawyers. Nor were the accused or their families represented by lawyers. Hence there was no legal advice formally available to the court. This constituted a problem. Not only were magistrates and prefects liable to punishment if they gave a wrong decision in law, but they were required to identify and quote in their judgments the statute or sub-statute of the penal code upon which they based their proposed sentence. Failure to do so was in itself a punishable offence.[30] Consequently it was necessary for the presiding official either himself to possess knowledge of the code or to have access to the advice of someone who did.

The government, at least in the later dynasties, was aware of the need for officials to have some legal knowledge. Both the Ming and the Ch'ing codes attempted to ensure that officials and their subordinate clerks (*li*) had an adequate knowledge of the law. It was enacted that each year they should be examined by their superiors in order to ascertain that they understood the sense of the laws and could explain them clearly. An official who failed to satisfy his superiors in this test was to be fined one month's salary, and a clerk found deficient in knowledge was to be given a beating of 40 blows with the light stick. A further provision of the same article (in a somewhat astonishing way) testifies to the importance which the Ming and Ch'ing governments attached to knowledge of the law. Any private individual (not in government employment) who was capable of reading, understanding and clearly explaining the laws was to be exempt from punishment for such first offence as had been committed inadvertently or had been imputed to him through the fault of another, provided the matter did not involve plotting rebellion, great sedition or treason.[31]

Although one does not know the extent to which the article was enforced, it does not seem that on the whole the ordinary official, even in Ming and Ch'ing times, possessed much detailed knowledge of the law. An exceptional magistrate might be well informed,[32] but most relied upon the advice of others. They might obtain it either from the clerks skilled in law attached to the office or from their private secretaries. Clerks were known in all dynasties from the T'ang to the Ch'ing, but private secretaries although known in the Ming really flourished only in the Ch'ing. Denis Twitchett has argued that the locally recruited clerks, often holding permanent and even hereditary appointments, in early T'ang times played a considerable part in the administration of justice. They handled the drafting of documents, including the judgment proposed by a magistrate or prefect, and were the main repository within the office of legal precedents. The regular, transferable officials hence relied heavily upon the practical experience and knowledge of their clerks.[33] Under the Sung the legal training of clerks was encouraged,[34] a process that continued under the Yüan where, indeed, because of the unusual circumstances brought about by the Mongolian conquest, many experienced clerks were appointed to regular official positions.[35] Although under the Ch'ing magistrates relied mainly upon their private secretaries for legal advice, the clerks in the office were still influential in legal matters because of their role in drafting and checking documents and their knowledge of legal precedent.[36]

On the whole in all dynasties the clerks employed in the offices of the magistrate or prefect were unpaid. For their livelihood they relied upon customary fees and 'gifts'. They were drawn from the locality and tended to serve for a longer period than any given magistrate or prefect who was always liable to transfer and in any case was never appointed to his native place. Their advantages to the administration were their experience and their knowledge of local conditions. Their disadvantages were their susceptibility to local pressures and openness to bribery. They were in a good position to manipulate a lawsuit in favour of a person who had treated them generously or who, through local connections, was in a position to put pressure upon them.[37] Consequently one finds a constant distrust expressed by the government with respect to their influence in distorting the law. For example, in 1831 an edict was issued instructing the officials themselves to see to the preliminary acceptance or rejection of petitions in legal matters and not leave the decision to their clerks or private secretaries whereby the door was opened to 'subterfuges, deceptions and irregularities'.[38] Despite detailed governmental regulations on the conduct of clerks and the possibility of severe punishment for misbehaviour it seems that little could be done to prevent abuses of the type described in the 1831 edict.[39]

Private secretaries are a phenomenon of the Ming and Ch'ing dynasties.[40] It seems that they evolved in response to two main factors, one, that there was even less opportunity for officials to acquire a training in law under these dynasties than in earlier times, and, two, that the subordinate regular officials of the Ming and Ch'ing were of a calibre inferior to that of their T'ang and Sung counterparts. Consequently Ming and Ch'ing officials in charge of units with judicial functions began to employ at their personal expense men of ability and learning, sometimes with previous experience as subordinate officials or clerks. These private secretaries were specialists in certain areas of administration, in particular taxation and law. In fact both the secretary for taxation and the secretary for law handled legal matters, but all criminal and the more important civil cases were within the province of the secretary for law.

The secretary for law did not participate in the actual trial of the case but advised the magistrate after its conclusion on the appropriate judgment and was responsible for drafting the submissions to go further to the next tribunal in the hierarchy. It would generally be the private secretary who advised the magistrate on the law applicable to a particular case. Although the division of function between private secretary and clerk is not entirely clear, it seems that clerks may have had more influence on the question of which legal actions were to be heard in the first place[41] than on the form taken by the magistrate's judgment once the case had been heard. Furthermore it is possible that the private secretaries were entrusted with the review of documents originally drafted by the clerks.

Despite the problems experienced through the manipulation by clerks of lawsuits for their own profit, the dual system under which the magistrate or senior official conducted legal proceedings and signed the record of the case, and the private secretary contributed the legal expertise seems to have worked tolerably well, at least for the handling of serious criminal cases. These were automatically reviewed by the Board of Punishments and its staff, that is by officials who had made a special study of law. A reading of the cases on homicide collected in the *Hsing-an hui-lan* suggests that many decisions forwarded from the provinces were found satisfactory by the Board. Where they did send back a case for further consideration the reason often is not that the provincial or local court had made a pure mistake of law, but that the Board was not satisfied that the full facts had been elicited.

Judicial Procedure

A preliminary point concerns the extent to which the traditional law distinguished between criminal and civil actions and, if so, the extent to which the procedure in civil cases differed from that in criminal. There is some difference of opinion in the modern literature on this point. A common approach is to hold that all actions brought before a magistrate's court are strictly criminal in the sense that they all involve an alleged breach of the criminal code and ought therefore to lead to the imposition of punishment.[42] Yet it is conceded that from T'ang times a practical distinction was drawn between serious criminal cases and minor cases involving claims to property, disputes over debts, breaches of the marriage laws and the like. The latter, often classed as civil, involved criminal offences usually entailing a relatively light punishment. They were not to be heard in the farming season, extending, roughly, from the fourth to the seventh months of the year. A sub-statute to this effect appears in the Ch'ing code,[43] and the practice is known from at least the time of the early T'ang.[44] Such cases were dealt with entirely at the level of the magistrate's court or, where they did go on appeal, at that of the prefectural or provincial court. They did not go, as did serious criminal cases, to the capital.[45] Apart from these differences, according to this approach, what are called criminal and civil cases were handled basically in the same way.

Recently, however, research conducted in the archives of a district magistrate's court from the years 1789-1895 has cast some doubt on this interpretation, at least for Ch'ing law. It appears that civil cases, defined as those governed by the provisions of the penal code on property, taxation and marriage, were handled differently as a separate category within the court. More importantly in cases such as those concerned with the recovery of loans and the mortgage of property as security the magistrate dealt with the issues and secured a settlement without ruling that a provision of the penal code had been broken or imposing a punishment.[46] This suggests that a wide range of civil disputes, not necessarily referring to, or arising from breaches of, the penal code were brought before the magistrate and that in dealing with them he looked not so much to the code as to local practice and custom.[47] In what follows I confine myself to the procedure of criminal cases.

While it is not possible to give an account of all aspects of the procedure that obtained in traditional courts - indeed much is still imperfectly known - attention should be drawn to some of its most characteristic features. These are the use of torture in the interrogation of the accused and others involved in the case, the importance attached to eliciting a confession from the accused, and the opportunities available to the accused or members of his family to seek a rehearing. Proceedings were inquisitorial in the sense that the presiding official attempted to elicit the truth from both the accused and the accuser. To some extent both were in the same position. If the magistrate disbelieved the accuser, the latter might find himself severely questioned and subject to liability under the law relating to false accusations.[48]

The principal difficulty facing the magistrate was the ascertainment of the facts of the case. Once this had been done he had the further task of establishing or proposing the appropriate sentence. As we have seen he was greatly assisted in this by those of his subordinates or staff who possessed some training in, and knowledge of, the law. Hence especially in serious cases where the punishments were heavy the major problem was to penetrate the exaggerations, deceits or lies of the parties and their supporters. In order to assist him to obtain the truth the magistrate was permitted to order the application of torture, usually in the form of beatings, but other methods, especially in the later dynasties, were also available. At the same time the law placed limits upon his use of torture and prescribed punishments which he himself incurred if he exceeded those limits. On the whole the law of the earlier dynasties seems to have been more careful in this regard than that of the later.

As early as the first century A.D. there were rules prescribing the manner in which torture should be applied but the extent to which it was legally limited under the Han is not known.[49] In the T'ang code there are clear rules. Article 476 provides that the judicial officers responsible for the questioning of a detainee (whether accused or accuser) must first very carefully and repeatedly examine his written submissions and other statements. If they are unable to discover the facts in this way they might then jointly agree to proceed to the application of legal torture.[50] Article 477 further provides that judicial torture should not be applied to a detainee more than three times, the commentary adding that the hearings should be 20 days apart; nor should the number of blows inflicted with the heavy stick in all exceed 200. When the punishment for the offence under examination is itself a beating with the heavy or light stick, the beating(s) ordered by way of torture should not exceed the number of blows prescribed as punishment. The only instruments permitted were the heavy and (by implication) the light stick. Should the person to be beaten have boils or sores on the skin, the application of the torture must be deferred until he is cured. Punishments are prescribed for the failure to observe these various rules. A stark note is sounded at the conclusion of the article. Should the torture be inflicted according to the rules and yet the person undergoing it unexpectedly dies there is to be no liability on the part of the magistrate or other officials concerned. One has the impression that death under torture - despite the legal safeguards - might not have been an uncommon occurrence.[51]

The same rules appear in the Sung code; the legal position on the application of torture appears to have been similar to the T'ang.[52] Yüan law perhaps went even further in protecting the position of the accused who was the most obvious recipient of torture. A rule contained in the collection of laws promulgated in 1291 provided that the official in charge of the proceedings should not apply torture unless the case looked suspicious and, although there was clear evidence of the commission of an offence, the accused still refused to acknowledge his guilt and tried to conceal the truth.[53] When one comes to the Ming and Ch'ing dynasties one finds that the legal position appears to have changed, somewhat to the detriment of the accused or others involved in criminal proceedings.

In Ming law much more latitude than was possible in T'ang times seems to have been accorded officials in the use of torture while conducting criminal proceedings. The law appears mainly to have been concerned to prevent abuses that stemmed from personal enmity or corruption. Article 28.2 establishes a heavy punishment for officials who deliberately torture innocent persons in the course of their investigation. Should it in fact be necessary to apply torture to persons appearing as witnesses, as where they refuse to disclose the truth although the guilt of a person accused is clear, torture may be authorised by a written order. Should a person tortured in these circumstances die the officials responsible are not liable.[54] A sub-statute following the article states that where tribunals investigate capital offences, cases of theft or plunder or other serious matters, severe torture may be necessary; in other cases only the regular punishments - beatings appear to be meant - are to be used. Punishments are imposed on officials who, in such circumstances, use instruments of torture such as pressing sticks, head bands or branding irons.[55]

Considerably more information is available for the Ch'ing period from both legal and lay sources. Apart from containing an article similar to the Ming[56] the Ch'ing code contains a number of sub-statutes regulating the use of torture. These prescribe the nature of the instruments which may be legitimately used, a wider variety being available than under T'ang law.[57] They also impose punishments on officials who cause, through torture, the death of persons who are only indirectly involved in an affair, or should not be subject to torture at all (because they are too old or young or are immune for some other reason), or of two or more persons accused of non-capital offences.[58] Torture by 'pressing sticks' (for squeezing fingers or ankles) should only be used in the investigation of capital or other very serious offences, provided that there was clear evidence of the offence and yet the accused refused to confess or retracted a confession originally made.[59] Lay accounts contain vivid descriptions both of the tortures permitted by the law and those alleged to be frequently, although illegally, applied.[60] The general impression one obtains is that in Ming and Ch'ing times the possible range of tortures led to greater cruelty than under the earlier dynasties, and that the safeguards for those subjected to torture, especially in the investigation of serious offences, were minimal.[61] With some exceptions[62] no clear limits on the amount of torture to be inflicted appear to have been prescribed.

The use of torture derives primarily from the importance attached to confession on the part of the person accused. In this context 'confession' means an acknowledgment that he committed the offence of which he is charged, that the facts alleged against him are true. It is to be distinguished from 'confession' in the sense of a voluntary disclosure of the offence made before it has been discovered.[63] The expectation that the accused should confess before finally being found guilty is doubtless grounded upon a conviction, shared by many peoples, that very often one cannot be sure that a person has done something unless he himself acknowledges the fact. That such acknowledgment was an expectation rather than a rule of Chinese law is shown by the fact that no article or sub-statute requires a confession before conviction. Nonetheless the expectation was strong as can be seen from the reference to confession in the rules about torture.

In T'ang law[64] it was expressly provided that where the circumstances of the offence were clear and yet the accused still refused to confess, sentence could be passed on the basis of the facts proved. Where the facts were not clear and the accused (or other detainee) was tortured but had not confessed after receiving the maximum allowable number of beatings he was to be released upon provision of security (article 477). Underlying these rules is the requirement that one of two conditions must be satisfied before the accused can properly be sentenced. Either the facts necessary to establish the offence must be clearly proved independently of his evidence or he must acknowledge their truth. Torture was permissible to induce acknowledgment in difficult cases. Finally one may note the precarious position of the accuser. Where the accused has not confessed despite receiving the maximum permitted beating, the accuser in turn is to receive the equivalent number of blows, unless he acknowledges that he has made a false accusation for which he will suffer the prescribed punishment.[65] If he endures the beating without making the acknowledgment he also is to be released on bail.[66]

In Yüan law the expectation that the accused should confess appears to have been taken more seriously than in T'ang/Sung law. According to the article from the compilation of 1291, already discussed, torture was permissible only where the evidence was clear or at least there was some indication of guilt and yet the accused refused to confess. Here there is an implication that confession was a prerequisite of conviction. This may also have been the standpoint of the Ming and Ch'ing law.[67] The T'ang rule permitting sentence on clear evidence despite the absence of confession does not reappear in these codes. Rather one may deduce from the sub-statute of the Ch'ing code already mentioned that confession was required for conviction at least in serious cases. Severe torture is authorised where the accused does not confess, although the evidence against him is clear, or where he retracts a confession made at an earlier hearing. Huang Liu-hung in his book advising magistrates on the best way to carry out their duties certainly gives the impression that a magistrate should obtain the confession of the accused. He lists a number of techniques which a magistrate may employ to obtain the truth. Torture is included as a last resort by which confession is to be obtained, though the unreliability of a confession obtained only through the infliction of pain is emphasised.[68]

From confession of the kind just described has to be distinguished the procedure by which the accused in serious cases was required to submit to the verdict of the court. Confession itself relates to the ascertainment and proof of the facts. Once these have been satisfactorily proved, as by the accused's own acknowledgment, the law is considered and applied to the case. This yields a judgment in which the nature of the offence is specified and the punishment appropriate to it declared. All the main penal codes contain a rule requiring the presiding official to secure acceptance by the accused of his sentence. The T'ang and Sung codes provide that at the conclusion of the trial in cases which entail a punishment of penal servitude, exile or death, the accused or members of his family are to be summoned to hear the verdict and the reasons for the sentence. The accused, if present, should either submit (*fu pien*)[69] or state the reasons why he does not. In the latter event these reasons provide the basis for a retrial. The commentary explains that where only relatives are present it is merely necessary to communicate to them the verdict; they need not submit.[70] The Ming and Ch'ing codes contain similar articles,[71] the main difference being the inclusion of a proviso that members of the accused's family need not be summoned to hear the verdict where they live a certain distance away. From the fuller versions of the Ming and Ch'ing articles and the commentaries on them it is clear that the main purpose of the accused's submission was to secure his acceptance that the matter was now over and need not be re-opened. In fact, despite submission, it seems that even at a later stage it was possible for the accused or a member of his family to claim that an injustice had occurred and ask for a further hearing. On the other hand should the accused claim that the full facts had not come to light or that his original acknowledgment of guilt was untrue the court at this stage was bound to order a re-hearing.

The point last made is a convenient introduction to the topic of 'appeal' by the accused or his family[72]. Appeal, as already noted, must be distinguished from the automatic review of serious cases provided by the successive examinations conducted by the tribunals through which it passed, possibly as far as the Board of Punishments, and from reviews periodically conducted by supervisory officials. Whereas such reviews might pick up inconsistencies in the facts or omissions in the scrutiny of the evidence they were particularly concerned with questions of law and made sure that the lower tribunals had correctly identified and applied the relevant law. Appeals on the other hand were concerned not primarily with questions of law but with alleged injustice or oppression in the hearings held to determine the facts. Two particularly important grounds of complaint were that the full facts had not been brought out or that previous acknowledgment of guilt by the accused was untrue and had been extracted only through torture.[73] In all dynasties the accused or his family were given frequent opportunities to demand rehearings.

From the Han dynasty there is evidence that an accused who did not accept the verdict at his trial might demand a retrial at the same level; in serious cases members of his family could also apply for a fresh enquiry at the same level. There is no evidence of appeals from a lower to a higher tribunal.[74] The T'ang code likewise provided for serious cases that an accused who did not submit to the sentence might advance reasons for reconsideration. Even where he had submitted it is likely that he or his family could raise the matter afresh, either at a regular hearing before a higher tribunal or by special appeal to such tribunal. Even in cases not covered by this provision appeal to a higher tribunal on the ground of alleged injustice is likely to have been allowed, as it was in later dynasties. If the case entailed the death penalty the accused or his family could either persuade the highest review body to memorialise the emperor for a rehearing, or personally draw the emperor's attention to the case by striking the Petitioner's Drum or standing on the Petitioner's Stone.[75] Similar possibilities, with differences in detail, were available in Sung[76]

Yüan,[77] Ming[78] and Ch'ing[79] times.

Both the Ming and Ch'ing codes contained special rules applicable to capital cases. These probably formalised, in the context of the assizes, practices that had existed in previous dynasties. In the case of capital offences, when the sentences are revised at the assizes, the person sentenced to die may claim that his earlier admissions were incorrect, or members of his family may assert that there has been an injustice. Those in charge of the assizes are then bound to hold a fresh inquiry. Where such an inquiry discloses that an injustice has been done the officials responsible for conducting the previous hearings will be summoned and together with the officials presiding at the assizes will be required to rectify the judgment.[80] One notes again the special care taken to ensure that there should be no miscarriage of justice.

Judicial Discretion

In all dynasties the policy of the imperial court and government was to leave as little discretion as possible in the hands of officials acting as judges. The codes themselves by and large were designed to cover every eventuality at least with respect to serious offences. This means that the codes either explicitly isolated the specific acts or omissions for which punishment was to be imposed, or provided a procedure for the resolution of 'doubtful' cases. The legislators realised that it was not possible to define in advance every act (however trivial) which ought to receive punishment. Hence they introduced an article which is found in virtually identical form in all the codes from the T'ang to the Ch'ing on 'doing what ought not to be done'.[81] This provided that magistrates might impose 40 blows with the light stick for misconduct in general; where the misconduct was grave a beating of 80 blows with the heavy stick was authorised. A whole host of matters relating to public order or infringements of moral rules could be punished under this head. One notes that, although judges have unfettered discretion with respect to what constitutes misconduct and its gravity, their option with respect to punishment was severely circumscribed. Shen's 'upper commentary' stresses the fact that this 'catch-all' article itself was designed to impose limits on a judge's discretion. Without the guidelines that it provided there was a danger that judges might prove to be too severe or too lenient in particular cases.[82]

Two important techniques employed to ensure that judges kept within the limits of the penal code and did not on their own initiative effectively create new offences or apply disproportionate punishment were the rules providing for the review of decisions and those requiring judges to cite in their judgments the provision of the code upon which they relied. As has already been seen an elaborate mechanism of review was practised for all serious cases, frequently involving a final consideration by the legal authorities in the capital. Furthermore judicial decisions were subject to periodic scrutinies by supervisory officials. The reviewing officials would be concerned to see that the judge had correctly applied the law as set out in the penal code or other authoritative source to the facts. In this lies the significance of the citation in the judgment of the relevant statutory provision. All the codes again contained an article specifying that the judge must give a full citation of the provision of the code or other legislative source upon which his judgment was based.[83] The reviewing body was then able to determine whether the facts and the sentence were in accord with the rule cited by the judge. If they were not the latter in theory made himself liable to the punishment for giving a wrong judgment.[84]

One is still left with the problem of doubtful cases. What was a judge to do where there was a doubt either as to the facts or as to which statutory offence governed the facts. The T'ang code has an interesting rule on cases of doubt as to the facts.[85] This provided that in cases of doubt the statutory punishment for the offence charged should not be imposed but redemption by payment of copper allowed.[86] 'Doubt' was defined as arising in a case where the witnesses testifying to the truth of the facts alleged by the accused were balanced by those testifying to their falsity or the other evidence was evenly balanced, where the facts raised a presumption of guilt but there were no actual witnesses, or where witnesses were available but there was no concrete proof. The elaborate definition of 'doubt' again seems to rest upon an attempt to minimise the discretion open to the judge. He is not to be allowed lightly to determine that there is a doubt and consequently allow redemption. This provision does not appear in the Ming and Ch'ing codes. The reason is probably that doubt as to the facts was not seen in the later period as constituting a difficulty requiring resolution by a special article of the code. The presiding official was expected either to determine the facts or, if there was doubt, secure an admission by the accused, if necessary through the application of torture. Some of the homicide cases reviewed by the Board of Punishments specify the need for severe interrogation of those involved to ascertain the truth of the matter.

Cases in which there was doubt as to the law were covered by a rule, again contained in all codes, prescribing the duty of the judge where no formal article could be discovered in the code which exactly governed the circumstances before him. The content of the rule changed in the course of time. The T'ang code in the General Principles part provided:

> All cases involving sentencing of crimes that have no formal article, bring up a heavier offence in order to make clear a lighter punishment, if the punishment should be decreased. If the punishment should be increased then a lighter offence is brought up to make clear a heavier punishment.[87]

What is meant is illustrated by the commentary. Thus the code provides that there is no liability were a householder kills an intruder who enters his house at night without good reason; it follows, under this article, that should the intruder merely be wounded there is also no liability. Another provision states that where a person steals from a relative the punishment decreases proportionately to the closeness of the relationship.[88] If the offence is one of obtaining property by deceit or in some other unlawful way it is also to be governed by this rule. The article providing that a person who plots to kill a close 'senior' relative should be sentenced to beheading is held to apply where he actually wounded or killed in consequence of the plot. Likewise a rule excluding 'protection' for the beating or accusing to the court a 'senior' relative for whom mourning is worn for nine months is held to apply where such an offence is committed against a 'senior' relative for whom mourning is worn for one year.[89]

What strikes one with respect to the T'ang rules is that they appear to cover mainly cases which are logically within the ambit of a stated rule, even though they have not been separately articulated. Of the examples given in the commentary only that relating to theft suggests an extension of a rule beyond a case that would normally be taken to be implied already in its formulation. Even here one might argue that the extension is small since obtaining property by deceit or in some other unlawful way from a relative is very similar to theft. However these are only examples and it may have been that judges had a wider discretion in subsuming new situations under a given provision than the examples of the commentary suggest. Yet one suspects that in any case of real doubt as to the application of the law the matter would have been referred to higher authority for a ruling and ultimately to the emperor and his advisors.

The corresponding article of the Ming and Ch'ing codes is phrased differently and appears to give a judge somewhat wider scope in reaching decisions by analogy. It states that the code does not give an explicit prescription for every situation. If an offence falls to be decided and the code lacks a formal article that clearly governs the situation, an article is to be cited by analogy (*pi chao*) and a decision taken as to whether the punishment in the case under consideration should be lighter or heavier than (or the same as) that prescribed by the article. The decision once taken is to be submitted to the authorities in the capital and ultimately to the throne for confirmation[90]. The example given in the 'upper commentary' shows more latitude in the use of analogy than that revealed by the examples in the T'ang commentary. There is no rule in the Ch'ing code prescribing the punishment for the loss of the keys of the town gates. This is to be assimilated to the rule punishing the loss of an official seal, the reason, according to the commentary, being that in both cases the object lost is a kind of seal.[91] A number of decisions taken by analogy eventually came to be attached as an appendix to the code.[92]

The intention of the Ming and Ch'ing legislators was probably to give judges some scope in cases where the facts clearly disclosed criminal conduct but at the same time yielded some peculiarity which prevented their automatic subsumption under the description of a specific offence. Judges were instructed to look for the article or sub-statute in the code which dealt with the situation most similar to that before them and, once they had identified it, consider whether there should or not be a variation in the punishment to be imposed in the instant case. The extent to which they could broaden the range of the rules in this way was carefully monitored through the requirement that all decision by analogy should be submitted for review to higher authority.[93] From a number of them would eventually emerge new sub-statutes.[94]

Liability of the Judge for Wrong Judgments

The specific liability of judges has to be set in the general context of liability of officials for their decisions. Two general rules broadly applied throughout the period from the T'ang to the Ch'ing. The first is that officials were liable if they made a wrong decision, the nature of the punishment depending upon a variety of circumstances. This rule appears to stem from the fact that the administrative code clearly and in detail defined their duties. Failure in any respect to carry out a duty, or to carry it out properly, *ipso facto* ought to entail liability. The second rule is that all those officials concerned in the making of a decision incur a liability if it is wrong, though they are not all liable to the same degree. This rule stems from the hierarchical ordering of officials in any given adminis-trative unit and the practice of decision making that there obtained. A junior official perhaps one with the greatest expertise in the subject -

would prepare a draft decision; this would be reviewed by his immediate superior, pass through the hierarchy within the unit and finally be approved or rejected by its head, the senior official. Consequently all those associated with the process were deemed to take some responsibility for the decision.[95]

These rules applied to officials taking judicial decisions, just as to those taking administrative ones, the difference lying in the nature of the punishment imposed for error. All codes draw a distinction between the case where a judge deliberately gave a wrong decision and that where he did so merely through inadvertence. Where he had acted deliberately, induced thereby through the receipt of a bribe or personal enmity or favouritism, the extent of his liability depends upon the degree of injustice that results. If the judge has completely fabricated or distorted the evidence and secured the conviction of the accused for an offence which he had not committed, the judge is himself liable to the punishment prescribed for the offence of which he has wrongly convicted the accused. Conversely if he deliberately procures the acquittal of the accused for an offence which he has in fact committed he is still subject to the punishment for that offence.[96]

Should the accused have committed an offence entailing a certain punishment, but deliberately have been sentenced to a higher punishment the judge is himself sentenced to the difference. If the punishment should have been a beating of 60 blows with the heavy stick but the judge deliberately imposes a beating of 100 blows, he is to be sentenced to a beating of 40 blows. The same principle applies if he deliberately reduces the sentence which should be imposed. At this point a difference should be noted between the T'ang and Ming/Ch'ing rules. In T'ang law the judge was responsible for the automatic difference between the prescribed and the actual sentence. If the sentence should have been 3 years penal servitude and he imposed only 1 year he incurred a punishment of 2 years penal servitude. However the later law operated a complex system of conversions under which the difference between the prescribed and the actual punishment, if expressed in terms of penal servitude, was converted to a given number of blows with the heavy stick, and, if expressed in terms of exile, was converted to a given number of blows and a given period of penal servitude. Should the final result yield a beating in excess of 100 blows, a further conversion back to penal servitude was operated. Hence in cases of serious discrepancy between prescribed and actual punishment the most likely punishment for the judge was a combination of a beating and penal servitude. These rules on conversion did not apply where an innocent person was wrongfully convicted or a guilty person wrongfully acquitted.[97]

Where the wrong sentence was imposed through inadvertence and not deliberately a distinction was drawn between the case where the offender was wrongfully convicted or sentenced to a heavier punishment than his offence warranted and that in which he was wrongfully acquitted or sentenced to a lesser punishment than his offence warranted. In the former case the judge was sentenced to a punishment 3 degrees less than he would have incurred had he acted deliberately, and in the latter to punishment 5 degrees less. Presumably the difference in punishment reflects the kind of harm caused by the mistake. The consequences in the case of wrongful aggravation of punishment were more serious to the accused than in the case of wrongful reduction.98 This attention to consequences is also reflected in a further rule. Should no harm have been done by the mistaken sentence, that is, should in a case of aggravation the punishment not have been carried out, or in a case of reduction the accused not have been freed or, if freed, have been recaptured, or should in either case the accused have died from natural causes there will be a further reduction in punishment for the judge of one degree. This benefit applies whether the judge has acted deliberately or not.

The rule making liable all members of the administrative unit who had been concerned with the decision was common to the T'ang, Sung, Ming and Ch'ing dynasties, but the details of its application were different in the two later dynasties. In cases of mistaken judgement (not made deliberately) the T'ang code held that the prime responsibility rested with the official from whom the mistake had originated, whether this be the clerk who initially proposed the judgment or his superior in the hierarchy.[99] The Ming and Ch'ing codes apportion responsibility on a different basis. The official deemed to be principal in the offence and therefore liable to the full punishment is the *li-ts'ao*, that is, the clerk involved in the preparation and checking of the judgment. To be punished one degree less is his immediate superior, the *shou-ling kuan,* an official responsible for the supervision of the work of the clerks. To be punished one degree less again is the *tso-erh* official, the second-in-command of the administrative unit, and finally the head of the unit, the senior official in whose name the judgment is made, also receives a further reduction in punishment of one degree.

These rules appear to reflect a change in the organisation of work in the offices. Under the T'ang there is a greater degree of flexibility in the composition of judgments, so that errors might arise at different stages of the consideration of the record within the administrative unit. Under the Ming and Ch'ing the main responsibility for the determination of the law was placed upon a clerk who had had specialist training or experience.[100] The general commentary of the Ch'ing code says that 'the clerk ought to be versed in knowledge of the penal laws; he ought to examine, verify and point out the mistakes, and that is why he is considered as the most culpable'.[101] As has been seen, in Ch'ing times the individual primarily responsible for the draft of a judgment was the presiding official's private secretary. However he is not a member of the regular civil service but a private employee. Hence in allocating liability for a mistaken judgment the code singled out the clerk within the administrative office who was primarily concerned with legal matters.[102] Finally one should note that where only one of those involved in the decision has acted deliberately in making a wrong judgment and the others have not noticed, the one who commits the wrong is to be punished according to the law on deliberately giving a wrong judgment, but the others are still, according to their position in the hierarchy, to be punished according to the law on mistakenly giving a wrong judgment.[103]

The Ming and Ch'ing codes extend the concept of 'liability for a wrong judgment' to the case in which unauthorised torture has been used, though the formulation of the respective articles is different. In the Ming article after the opening clause establishing the liability of officials in charge for the case where there has been a deliberate and wrongful conviction of an innocent person or acquittal of a guilty person, the official commentary adds in small characters: 'this refers to the case where officials or their subordinates accept another's property (i.e. take a bribe) or use punishments not authorised by the law' and defines the latter as 'using fire or branding irons to burn a person or in winter months throwing cold water over him and the like'.[104] The corresponding article in the Ch'ing code has a briefer interlinear commentary which merely refers to the two cases of taking property and using unauthorised torture without giving examples.[105] What appears to be meant is that if the judge employs torture not authorised by the law either on the accused or on other persons involved and as a result procures an admission of guilt or evidence of guilt or innocence and on the basis of this convicts or acquits he is to be liable on the ground of deliberately giving a wrong judgment. One infers that where unauthorised torture is used to procure an aggravation or a reduction of a sentence the judge correspondingly will be liable. The 'upper commentary' states that where the judge would also be liable under the law forbidding the deliberate torturing of innocent persons,[106] he is to incur whichever would be the greater punishment, either that prescribed by the law on wrongful judgment or that by the law on deliberately torturing.

The rules in the T'ang code were different. Where a judge in employing torture exceeded the permitted amount of blows or used instruments not authorised by the law he was subject to specific penalties which varied according to the circumstances of the case (article 477). The law on liability for a wrong judgment was involved only where the judge was under an obligation to put the accuser to the same torture as the accused. Should he fail to do this, or should he torture the accuser where he was not allowed to do so, he was to be punished according to the law on deliberately or mistakenly giving a wrong judgment (article 478).

Notes

1. See the general observations in Shiga, Some Remarks on the Judicial System in China.
2. This is considered further below in the section on 'judicial procedure'.
3. Bünger, Quellen der Rechtsgeschichte der T'ang-Seit, 96 (translating the Old T'ang Legal Treatise).
4. For details see Hulsewé, Remnants of Han Law, 71ff.
5. Balazs, Traité juridique du 'Souei-chou', 83.
6. See especially Twitchett, Varied Patterns of Provincial Autonomy in the T'ang Dynasty.
7. For a more detailed account see Johnson 60 n.74.
8. Bünger, op. cit. 96.
9. Full details are given in Twitchett, Implementation of Law in Early T'ang China.
10. See Miyazaki, Administration of Justice during the Sung Dynasty, 59ff.
11. For details see Ch'en, Chinese Legal Tradition under the Mongols, 69ff.
12. No full study of the Ming judicial system is available. There are some useful observations in Hucker, The Censorial System of Ming China, 98f, 237ff.
13. MLCCFL, 2005f.
14. Op. cit. 2037.
15. Bodde and Morris state that the prefecture often functioned as a means of transmitting cases from the district to the provincial capital where they were re-investigated (Law in Imperial China, 115). But the detailed account of a case of homicide given by Alford, Of Arsenic and Old Laws, shows that a rigorous investigation at prefectural level was expected although not always accomplished (1206f). See also Shiga, Criminal Procedure in the Ch'ing Dynasty I, 17 and Ocko, I'll Take It all the Way to Beijing, 293 n4.
16. The Ch'ing code contained an article identical to Ming 28.27 (article 386, Philastre II, 724, Staunton, 460).
17. Op. cit., 115f. Shiga, op. cit., 17f is similar. A fuller account of the procedure applied in capital cases at the provincial level is given by Meijer,

Autumn Assizes in Ch'ing Law, 2f. For an example see Alford, op. cit., 1207f.

18. Boulais 1692 (translating the relevant rule from the administrative code). For the penal code see article 376, Philastre II, 692; Boulais 1693; Staunton 451.

19. Philastre II, 693. A sub-statute (694, Decree III) states that the report for each case should be complete and detailed.

20. p.721 n.2.

21. Cf. also the remarks of Philastre II, 696, 697.

22. Generally see Bodde and Morris, op.cit., 134ff; McKnight, Quality of Mercy, 98ff; Meijer, op.cit.

23. See especially Meijer, op.cit., 4; also see Bodde and Morris, op.cit., 138f; Shiga, op.cit 20f. The relevant sub-statutes are translated by Philastre II, 693ff.

24. For full details see Meijer, op.cit., 7ff.

25. Ming 22.9 (MLCCFL, 1727).

26. Ch'ing article 309, Philastre II, 447; Boulais, 1512; Staunton, 375.

27. Bodde and Morris, op.cit., 415.

28. id., case 203.5 and 526f. Nevertheless the services of 'litigation tricksters' appear to have been in great demand. See Ocko, op.cit., 292, 294f, 296, 297f, 302.

29. id.

30. See the section on 'judicial discretion' below.

31. Ming 3.1 (MLCCFL, 469); Ch'ing article 59, Philastre I, 321; Boulais 272 (incomplete); Staunton, 64.

32. Cf. the book written by Huang Liu-hung (a former magistrate) in the 17th century as a guide to magistrates on the conduct of their duties. This, entitled A Complete Book Concerning Happiness and Benevolence, contains a lengthy section on the law.

33. Varied Patterns of Provincial Autonomy in the T'ang Dynasty, 92f; Implementation of Law in Early T'ang China, 70ff.

34. Miyazaki, 69ff, and for their important role in advising magistrates and prefects see 61f, 64f.

35. Ch'en, op.cit., 88ff.

36. Ch'ü, Local Government in China under the Ch'ing, 36ff.

37. For examples see Ch'ü, op.cit., 49f.

38. Bodde and Morris, op.cit., 476f.

39. See further the section below on 'the liability of the judge for wrong judgments'.

40. See Ch'ü, op.cit., chapter 4. Wang Hui-tui (see chapter 3, at n.85) in a paragraph of his book headed 'Studying the Laws' emphasised the need for magistrates' secretaries to have a thorough understanding of the code (van der Sprenkel, Legal Institutions in Manchu China, 143).

41. Cf. the edict of 1831 above.

42. See especially Twitchett, Implementation of Law in Early T'ang China, 65f; Bodde and Morris, op.cit., 118f. Cf. also van der Sprenkel, op.cit., 69; Cohen, Chinese Mediation on the Eve of Modernization, 1206 n.28; Shiga, op.cit., 3f.

43. Boulais, 1470 (summarised by Philastre II, 404f). The relevant administrative provision is translated in Buxbaum, Some Aspects of Civil Procedure and Practice at the Trial Level in Tanshui and Hsinchu from 1789-1895, 261f. Cf. also Ch'ü, op.cit., 118f.

44. See Twitchett, Implementation of Law in T'ang China, 66; and for Sung practice Miyazaki, op.cit., 59, and for Yüan practice, Ch'en, op.cit., 72f.

45. See however the remarks of Ocko, op.cit., 297.

46. Buxbaum, op.cit., 259f, 263ff. However reservations as to Buxbaum's findings have been expressed by Brockman, Commercial Contract Law in late Nineteenth-Century Taiwan, 82, 89.

47. See also the remarks of Huang Liu-hung, Complete Book Concerning Happiness and Benevolence, 446 n.2; Jamieson, Chinese Family and Commercial Law, 113f. It may also be appropriate to cite in this context the interesting preface (missing in the corresponding article of the T'ang code) to the article of the Ming and Ch'ing codes on intimidation and coercion. This states that where persons quarrel they should submit the dispute to the magistrate and abide by his decision, not have recourse to violent self-help (Ming 20.11 (MLCCFL, 1580); Ch'ing article 281, Philastre II, 304; Bonlais, 1380; Staunton, 335). How far villagers did choose to submit their disputes to the local magistrate for his adjudication is uncertain, but clearly the central government in Ming and Ch'ing China (if not earlier) looked upon the district magistrate as an arbiter available for the solution of disputes within the community. In carrying out this role he would have needed to be familiar with customary practices and adept at judging the facts of the dispute in the light of these practices. On custom generally see chapter 3.

48. See chapter 7, 167f, 172f.

49. Hulsewé, Remnants of Han Law, 76.

50. Translated in Lê Code 668, Deloustal 667. For the procedure generally cf. Twitchett, Implementation of Law in Early T'ang China, 66f.

51. Cf. Lê Code, 669; Deloustal, 668n.

52. Cf. the brief remarks of Miyazaki, op.cit., 61.

53. Ch'en, op.cit., 76f and article 10.2 translated at 153f.

54. MLCCFL, 1940.

55. There is an implication that these instruments might legitimately be used for the extraction of the truth in serious criminal cases.

56. Article 361, Philastre II, 623; Boulais, 1672; Staunton, 433.

57. Boulais, 1673 and cf. p.6; Staunton, 488.

58. Philastre II, 625f.

59. TCLLLHCPL, 4957f (summarised in Philastre II, 630f).

60. See Doolittle, Social Life of the Chinese I, 335f, 341f; Huang, op.cit., 273ff; Ch'ü, op.cit., 125.

61. For the Ming cf. the remarks of Münzel, Strafrecht im alten China, 18. In the Ch'ing case reported at length by Alford excessive torture is applied in order to extract a confession (op.cit., 1204, 1206, 1209). Cf. also the observations in a memorial of the Board of Punishments submitted to the throne in 1906, translated by Meijer, Introduction to Modern Criminal Law in China, 160. For a discussion of decisions of the Board in cases of

death resulting from an illegal application of torture see Harrison, Wrongful Treatment of Prisoners.

62. Staunton, 488f, translates a sub-statute providing that the severe methods of torture applicable in cases of robbery or homicide should not be used more than twice (also summarised Philastre I, 119). Bodde and Morris, op.cit., 98 quote the Ch'ing Legal Treatise as stating that the maximum beating for any prisoner was 30 blows of the heavy stick daily.

63. On this see chapter 7.

64. Article 476 (cf. note 50 above; Shiga, Criminal Procedure in the Ch'ing Dynasty II, 120 n.124). For the position in Sung law see Miyazaki, op.cit., 61 and n.23 at 73.

65. I am inferring this from the wording of the article which is not explicit on the point.

66. Article 478. See note 51 above. In cases of theft or homicide, where the accusation has been brought by a relative of the victim and the accused does not confess under torture, there is no reciprocal torture of the accused because, so it is said, of his initial difficulty in ascertaining the correctness of the facts.

67. Shiga, op.cit., 120 says, 'It was a basic principle throughout the imperial era in China that responsibility for an offence must be confirmed by the offender's own confession. Yet the principle was never proclaimed explicitly in law, since it was held to be self-evident'.

68. Op.cit., 278. For an example of the danger see Alford, cited note 61.

69. On this expression see Yang, Excursions in Sinology, 80.

70. Article 490. Cf. Lê Code, 691. For abuses of the procedure in Sung times see Miyazaki, op.cit., 64.

71. Ming 28.22 (MLCCFL, 2028); Ch'ing article 381, Philastre II, 713; Boulais, 1697, Staunton, 456.

72. Generally for the Ch'ing see Shiga, Criminal Procedure in the Ch'ing Dynasty I, 30ff; Ocko, op.cit.

73. A good example is in Alford, cited n.61 above.

74. Hulsewé, Remnants of Han Law, 79f, 90f.

75. Twitchett, Implementation of Law in Early T'ang China, 67.

76. Miyazaki, op.cit. 62ff.

77. Ch'en, op.cit., 79.

78. Hucker, Censorial System of Ming China, 98f.

79. Ch'ü, op.cit., 118 and n.ll at 273-4; Bodde and Morris, op.cit., 646f; Shiga, op.cit., 33; Alford, op.cit., 1208f, 1228; Ocko, op.cit., 294.

80. Ming 28.17 (MLCCFL, 2005f); Ch'ing article 376, Philastre II, 692 and commentary; Staunton, 451.

81. T'ang article 450 (cf. Lê Code, 642; Deloustal, 641); Ming 26.11 (op.cit., 1889); Ch'ing article 351, Philastre II, 571; Boulais, 1656; Staunton, 419.

82. Philastre II, 572.

83. T'ang article 484 (cf. Lê Code 683; Deloustal, 682 and n.2); Ming 28.21 (op.cit., 2026); Ch'ing article 380, Philastre II, 710; Staunton, 455. Cf. chapter 3 at notes 27, 53 for the related rule prohibiting the judge from relying upon imperial decisions intended to deal only with one particular case.

84. See the section below on 'the liability of the judge for wrong judgments'.
85. Article 502 (cf. Lê Code 708; Deloustal, 707 and n.l). There is a translation of the article and part of the *shu-i* commentary in Johnson, The Concept of Doubt in T'ang Criminal Law, 273f, although his translation of the definition of 'doubtful' differs from my understanding of the text.
86. On redemption see chapter 5, 105ff.
87. Article 50 (Johnson 254f; cf. also Lê Code 41; Deloustal, 41).
88. See chapter 9, 219f.
89. On 'protection' see chapter 6, 143.
90. Ming 1.47 (op.cit., 372); Ch'ing article 43, Philastre I, 276; Staunton, 43. See also a sub-statute translated by Bodde and Morris, op.cit., 176 (though cf. the translation of Philastre I, 277 and especially Chen, On Analogy in Ch'ing Law, 223), and a further sub-statute translated by Philastre I, 260.
91. Philastre I, 276 with a different translation of the reasons (parce que, dans les deux cas, il s'agit de la perte d'un objet qui intéresse la sûreté d'un territoire).
92. Some are translated in Boulais, 1724-1738, and all by Philastre II, 751ff.
93. Bodde and Morris, op.cit., 176f suggest that many such decisions stopped at the level of the Board of Punishments and were not in fact submitted to the throne as required by the code.
94. There has been some difference of opinion over the role of analogy in Ch'ing law. See Bodde and Morris, op.cit., 176ff, 517ff, and Chen, On Analogy in Ch'ing Law.
95. On the liability of officials see chapter 6.
96. T'ang article 487 (translated Bünger, über die Verantwortlichkeit der Beamten nach klassischen Chinesischen Recht, 190); Ming 21.15 (MLCCFL, 1990); Ch'ing article 374, Philastre II, 669; Boulais, 1682f; Staunton, 447.
97. The rules are most clearly set out in Boulais, 1686-91.
98. For the precise way in which these punishments were calculated see the Ch'ing general commentary, Philastre II, 673, and cf. Ch'ü, op.cit., 283 n.116.
99. Article 40. See further chapter 6, at note 18.
100. Cf. however, the remarks of Ch'ü, op.cit., 282, n.113.
101. Philastre II, 672.
102. See generally Ch'ü, op.cit., 128f who also gives a survey of the administrative sanctions additionally applied in Ch'ing law to magistrates who gave wrong decisions.
103. See further chapter 6, 138ff.
104. MLCCFL, 1990. A translation of this can be found in Philastre II, 688.
105. Philastre II, 670.
106. Article 361, considered above.

5

The Punishments

This chapter will consider first the five traditional punishments established by the codes, certain supplementary punishments and the possibility of redemption. It will also examine certain special rules governing the imposition of punishment, and look at its distribution or incidence. This will involve a consideration of the 'privileged' groups who were entitled to redeem punishment and of the persons to whom punishments might be extended even though they had not themselves committed the offence in respect of which it was imposed. Finally something will be said of the possibility of escape or relief from punishment by amnesties.

Punishment proper for the Chinese was always strictly physical. Fines as such played a minimal role in the traditional system of punishment, although the payment of money or grain was the main means by which a physical punishment might be redeemed. From antiquity until the end of the imperial age the traditional legal punishments were classified as five, although their nature did not remain the same throughout this period. Until the Han they consisted of death and various mutilations such as amputation of the nose, hands or feet.[1] In 167 B.C. the emperor Wen abolished the mutilating punishments consisting of amputation, remarking that once a limb was cut off it could not grow again, and replaced them with beatings.[2] Later Han rulers and those of the succeeding dynasties experimented with punishments involving flogging or whipping with various instruments, forced labour or exile, until the Sui code settled the five punishments in the form which essentially they were to keep until the end of the Ch'ing. These were beating with the light stick, beating with the heavy stick, penal servitude, life exile and death.[3]

One may start with the form these punishments assumed in the T'ang code (which adopted them from the Sui) and consider the extent to which they were altered, refined or supplemented in the law of later dynasties. Beatings with the light stick were inflicted for trivial offences in order to shame the offender. The punishment was divided into five grades consisting of 10, 20, 30, 40 and 50 strokes of the bamboo, the code prescribing the exact number of strokes to be inflicted for a given offence.[4] Beatings with the heavy stick started at 60 blows and progressed upwards in step of ten to a maximum of 100. The dimensions of both sticks were prescribed by the law and likewise the parts of the body on which the blows could be inflicted. The light stick might be used only on buttocks and legs, whereas the heavy stick might be used also on the back (considered a more vulnerable part of the body), the blows to be distributed evenly over these areas.[5]

Penal servitude,[6] that is, forced labour in a fixed place, also had its five regular grades, namely, one year, one and a half years, two years, two and a half and three years.[7] Where a convict undergoing the punishment of penal servitude commits a further offence he may be sentenced to an additional year of labour, a total of four years being the maximum he would suffer.[8] The commentary to article 492 quotes a fragment from the statutes (*ling*) according to which those convicted in the capital area are to work in prison, and those in the provinces are to be sent to a suitable place to work for the government. Hence it seems that those sentenced to penal servitude were kept in prison and put to work, though especially in the provinces one cannot be sure of the extent to which the convicts were actually kept in prison. Special rules were introduced from time to time changing the nature of the work to be performed. Thus an edict of 745 provided that those sentenced to penal servitude might, according to the circumstances of the case, be assigned to military service.[9]

Life exile had only three regular grades: exile to a distance of 2000 *li* from one's place of origin, to 2500 *li* or to 3000 *li*,[10] each entailing in addition one year of penal servitude, and, in special circumstances, three or four years.[11] The punishment was originally introduced as a commutation of the death penalty for specific offences. Wives and concubines were required to accompany the exile, other relatives being permitted to join him if they wished.[12] There were two death penalties, strangulation and decapitation, the former, although the more painful, being regarded as the less severe, probably because of the belief that a person should have a whole body for his spirit to inhabit in the afterlife.[13]

Although the penal code of the Sung dynasty reproduced the T'ang articles of the 'five' punishments' the law with respect to their application was drastically changed. The two death penalties were left but exile, penal servitude and beating were all very significantly reduced. According to the Sung Legal Treatise the government paid attention to Confucian principles, especially those of humanity (*jen*) and mercy (*hu*), and the founder of the dynasty ordered a reduction of the punishments. 50 blows with the light stick was reduced to 10 or less, and 100 blows with the heavy stick was reduced to 20, in each case the blows to be applied on the buttocks; there were corresponding reductions for the other grades of beating. Irrespective of whether the rules stipulated a beating with the light or heavy stick, the same kind of stick of a defined length and thickness was to be used.[14] Penal servitude for 3 years was reduced to a beating of 20 blows on the back (more serious than a beating on the buttocks), with reductions in proportion for the other grades of penal servitude. Life exile coupled with penal servitude for 3 years was reduced to penal servitude for three years together with 20 blows on the back, the normal exile to 3000 *li* was reduced to penal servitude for one year and 20 blows on the back; and exile for lesser distances was correspondingly reduced.[15] Of course, bearing in mind the relative unimportance of the penal code in the legal practice of the Sung, one has to note that the actual punishment of an offence may have been more severe under the terms of a particular edict.

Yüan law did not adopt the reduced punishments of the Sung code but reverted more to the pattern of the T'ang, introducing some modifications. For beating a light and a heavy stick were used but the number of strokes differed from that prescribed by T'ang law. Punishment with the light stick was 7,17,27,37,47 or 57 blows and with the heavy stick 67,77,87,97 or 107 blows (in all cases on the buttocks), the dimensions of both sticks being defined by the law.[16] Five degrees of penal servitude were fixed, as in T'ang law, but to each was added a certain number of blows with the heavy stick, three years penal servitude, for example, entailing a beating of 107 blows. The Yüan punishment thus appears harsher than the T'ang. Convicts sentenced to forced labour were, according to the Yüan Legal Treatise, fettered while working during the day and kept in jail during the night. The nature of the work seems to have varied: if convicts have not been assigned to any particular labour they are to serve out their time in one of the Salt Offices.[17]

Exile was retained as a punishment but not operated in the same way as under the T'ang, the degrees of distance being dropped. Basically exiles from the south were sent to the north and those from the north to the south, the intention often being that they should serve as colonists in newly developed frontier areas and work as farmers under the supervision of authorities.[18] For grave crimes, such as repeated theft with violence, which yet did not attract the death penalty, offenders might be sent to serve with the army in distant regions.[19] There were two forms in which the punishment of death was applied, decapitation and slicing of the body, the latter reserved for the most serious offences.[20] The form of capital punishment is again more severe than under the T'ang.

Article 1 of the Ming code lists the 'five punishments' in a manner very similar to the T'ang code.[21] The most obvious difference is that both penal servitude and exile were supplemented with a beating with the heavy stick ranging from 60-100 blows for penal servitude, and being 100 blows for each of the degrees of exile.[22] The dimensions of the two sticks are given in one of the introductory tables to the codes;[23] they were to be used only on the buttocks.[24] From other sources one knows that those sentenced to penal servitude were normally required to work in the salt pits or mines and expected to produce a certain quantity of salt of iron per day, although they could be deployed for other kinds of work, such as the construction of official buildings, fortifications or roads.[25] In addition to the two death penalties of strangulation and decapitation of T'ang/ Sung law, the Ming retained from the Yüan period death by slicing for the worst offences. Although this form of death is not mentioned in the article, the introductory material in the code lists those offences punishable by slicing.[26]

With respect to life exile the true position was very different from that portrayed in the article. The Ming Legal Treatise states that the three ordinary punishments of exile were not in fact used, but were replaced by military service, either life-long or hereditary (passing to sons and grandsons) on the frontiers, the gravity of the offence determining the distance to which the conscript was sent and the nature of the region (whether it was malarial or not).[27] What appears to have happened is that at the beginning of the dynasty sentences of life exile in accordance with article 1 were imposed, each entailing forced labour for four years, but that gradually by special enactments more and more offences that were punished by ordinary exile under the code were given the punishment of military exile.[28] This may at first have been used primarily for military personnel who committed offences but came to be extended to many classes of the civilian population.[29] In Ming times it was regarded as a particularly severe punishment.

In taking as their model the Ming code the Ch'ing legislators naturally adopted the article specifying the 'five punishments'. Thus the article (*lü*) still largely followed the prescriptions of the T'ang code. Nevertheless important modifications were introduced by special enactment. The result was that in some respects the punishments were no longer applied as they had been either in T'ang or in Ming times.[30] Thus the practice with respect to beating was changed. A light and a heavy stick were still used, but each was considerably larger and heavier than its Ming counterpart. Hence the number of blows to be given was reduced. When the code prescribed 100 blows with the heavy stick only 40 were in fact to be given, when it prescribed 50 blows with the light stick only 20 were to be given, the strokes still being applied to the buttocks. Corresponding reductions were made in the other cases.[31] The rules for penal servitude were the same as under the Ming, with the difference that from 1725 offenders were put to work in the government post service in their own province and not sent to salt or iron mines in other provinces.[32] According to a table in Boulais each degree of the punishment was also supplemented by the wearing of the cangue (a wooden frame placed around the neck, and supported on the shoulders) for a certain number of days.[33] But it is not entirely clear that the wearing of the cangue was always imposed in sentences of penal servitude.[34]

The death penalties remained the same as under the Ming, but major changes were made in the exile system. First, the three standard punishments of life exile were revived. A complicated system existed for the determination of the place to which the exile was to be sent. The sentence also entailed the infliction of a beating of 100 blows with the heavy stick (in actuality 40), and, according to the table given in Boulais,[35] the wearing of the cangue for a specified period but not, it seems, compulsory labour. The Ch'ing code adopted from the Ming the provision requiring the exile's wife to accompany him, but in fact from the latter part of the 18th century this rule was no longer observed.[36] Military exile was retained by the Ch'ing as a punishment but lost its association with the army. Four degrees were established, that to 2000 *li*, that to 2500 *li*, that to 3000 *li* and that to more remote or malarial regions, each being supplemented with a beating of (nominally) 100 blows and the wearing of the cangue (for a period longer than that prescribed for ordinary exile). In fact only the last kind of military exile, that to very distant or malarial regions, was in effect more serious than ordinary exile since no military or other labour was required.[37] However the Ch'ing did introduce a particularly severe form of military exile which involved the offender being sent as a slave to the Mongolian garrisons outside China proper. This was the most severe Ch'ing punishment short of death.[38]

During all dynasties the physical punishments might under certain circumstances be the subject of redemption. The sentence was passed in the normal way but the offender was given the opportunity of paying a sum of money in lieu of receiving punishment. One may distinguish three categories of case in which redemption was allowed: (i) for certain specific offences such as accidental killing, (ii) to certain classes of 'privileged' person such as officials, the old, young or infirm and (iii) generally to anyone who could afford the payment. Categories (i) and (ii) were known to all the main dynastic penal codes from the time of the Han, but category (iii) appears to have been a creation of the Ming adopted, though modified, by the Ch'ing. Something will be said at this point about categories (i) and (iii), the treatment of category (ii) being reserved to a later stage of the chapter.

The only specific offence in the T'ang code for which redemption was allowed was accidental killing or injury where the appropriate amount of copper was paid to the family of the victim.[39] It was also allowed for the general class of 'doubtful' offences.[40] The Ming and Ch'ing codes retained the rule for accidental killing, abandoned it for 'doubtful' offences and added a further case. Where a person made a false accusation in principle he was to be subjected to at least the same punishment as that prescribed for the offence falsely imputed to another.[41] However where a person had committed some offence but was falsely accused of having committed a more serious one the codes under certain conditions introduced the possibility of redemption. Where the person falsely accused had in fact suffered the punishment for the offence (before the falsity of the accusation was discovered) the false accuser was to receive as punishment the difference between the punishment prescribed for the offence actually committed and that of the more serious offence for which sentence was passed. But should the person falsely accused not in fact have suffered the punishment, the false accuser was to be allowed to redeem the punishment appropriate to his case where it was a beating. Should it be more serious than a beating, penal servitude or above, he was to receive 100 blows with the heavy stick but might redeem the balance of the punishment. It does not appear that in this case the payment went to the person falsely accused.[42]

One can see there are acceptable reasons for the grant of redemption in the cases of accidental killing and false accusation. In the first there has been no fault, and in the second, although there is fault, the accused had committed some offence and at the same time had not actually suffered for the offence of which he was falsely accused.[43] When one comes to the wholesale extension of the availability of redemption in Ming and Ch'ing times the position is different. The reasons have nothing to do with the nature of the offence, the presence of absence of fault or the extent of the harm suffered by the victim. They are to do with the necessities of the state. The government required money, goods or labour and saw a means to obtain them by allowing offenders the possibility of redeeming their punishment by a particular payment or service. Indeed Ming practice on occasion went further and actually required offenders to redeem their punishments, whether they wished to or not.

During the Ming dynasty there was constant experimentation with the forms of redemption and a very considerable increase in its scope.[44] The reason for both developments, no doubt, lay in the necessities of the time. The Ming Legal Treatise itself points out that redemption payments were used to stockpile goods for use in emergencies and to help finance the cost of construction of imperial palaces and the running of government departments.[45] At different times and for different purposes the payment might be required in money (paper, copper or silver), in labour, in the delivery of rice, grain or materials, or in other services. Where a rule required payment in labour or provision of goods or services it or a later rule might also stipulate that the labour, goods or services should be converted into a money payment. All crimes other than the most serious might be redeemed, or indeed be required to be redeemed.

A good example is provided by the scheme established for the payment of rice as redemption in 1429. The emperor approved a proposal by senior officials to the effect that within Peking and the northern provinces 'officials, lesser functionaries, soldiers and civilians who rate the death penalty only as secondary criminals, and all lesser offenders (i.e. all offenders of any status except 'true' criminals rating the death penalty, whose guilt could not be subject to commutation) should pay in rice to the Peking granaries', the amount varying according to the punishment to be redeemed. A similar rule was established for offenders in Nanking and the southern regions, the principal difference being that the quantities of rice specified were much greater. However even at the time of this enactment it was clear that many people could not find the quantity of rice appropriate to redeem their sentence and were being kept in prison until they could. Hence a further proposal was accepted by the throne that those without the means to pay should be permitted to undergo the normal punishment provided by the law.[46]

The problem of those who could not pay led in fact by the end of the Ming to the establishment of a tripartite classification: those who had resources, those who had some resources and those who had none. The first group redeemed their offences - where permissible - through the payment of rice, and the second through the payment of money calculated according to the labour they should have performed by way of redemption. For the third group the normal punishment was imposed, if a beating, and, if not, labour in the army or courier service, such labour counting as redemption of the punishment prescribed.[47] These distinctions were adopted in the final version of the Ming code with slight modifications. The table specifying the scheme of redemption applicable under the *li* (sub-statutes) shows that those without resource are simply to be punished in accordance with the provisions of the code, those who have some resource are to pay silver equivalent to the value of the labour they should have contributed by way of redemption, and those with resource are to pay grain into the government storehouses.[48]

The Ch'ing dynasty operated two general schemes of redemption, one imported from the Ming and one introduced for the first time in 1743 and thereafter supplemented, both still appearing in the late 19th century editions of the code. Thus the code reproduces with some changes the Ming table which distinguishes between those with resource, with limited resource or without resource, showing the same payments under each head as the Ming.[49] The commentaries which follow the tables specify the offences which are not subject to redemption, in particular those not covered by the ordinary grants of amnesty.[50] Immediately after the conclusion of these commentaries there is inserted in the code a further table headed 'offences for which pardon is not granted by ordinary amnesties'. The table lists these offences and specifies that redemption is not allowed in their case. It then, with respect to all other offences, sets out in detail the price in silver to be paid for each grade of punishment from beheading down to beating with the light stick. It differs from the preceding table in two principal respects. The classification adopted is not that based on the possession or not of resources, but one based on status. Officials pay sums that increase proportionately to their rank and ordinary people pay at a lesser rate. The second difference is that the amounts to be paid are far higher. For example an ordinary person pays 480 ounces of silver as redemption for any sentence of penal servitude, whereas under the earlier table a person with resources pays 17.5 ounces. Furthermore the new scheme clearly contemplates the bestowal of a privilege, not a duty or a right. Anyone wishing to seek redemption under it must petition the emperor and show that his offence was characterised by extenuating circumstances warranting the extension of imperial clemency.[51]

Although even late editions of the code contain rules on both schemes of redemption, it is difficult to see how they could have applied contemporaneously. Both relate to the same kind of offence and yet differ markedly in the amounts to be paid and the personal criteria for payment. Sense can only be made of the position if we assume that in effect the later scheme replaced the earlier, although, as could happen, the latter still kept its formal place in the code. In a memorial from the Board of Punishments on the functioning of the system of punishments submitted to the throne in 1902, the only scheme of redemption referred to is that introduced in 1743. The point, in fact, is made that the amounts to be paid are so high that 'applications for redemption occurred only once in many years'.[52] This suggests that the 1743 scheme of redemption had become unworkable, and perhaps always had been.[53]

Three groups of rules relating to the determination of punishment are worthy of note because they can all be said to reflect, and arguably are to be explained at least in part by, the traditional Chinese concern for compassion. They appear in the T'ang code and from there passed substantially unchanged into the Ming and Ch'ing codes. The first group regulates the use of the degrees into which each of the five punishments is divided. A distinction is drawn between 'increasing' and 'decreasing' punishment. When a rule specifies that punishment is to be increased by a degree then the sentence is to the given punishment taken to the next degree higher. Thus if the rules show that the punishment for a particular offence is life exile to 2000 *li* with an increase of one degree, the appropriate sentence is life exile to 2500 *li*. The same calculation of degrees applies where the sentence is to be reduced, with the important difference that for this purpose the three distances of life exile and the two punishments of death respectively count as one degree. Thus if the punishment is beheading with a reduction of one degree, the sentence is to life exile to 3000 *li* not to strangulation, and if the punishment is to life exile to 3000 *li,* with a reduction of one degree, the sentence is to penal servitude for three years, not life exile to 2500 *li.*[54] Furthermore when a rule provides that the punishment is to increase proportionately to the value of goods stolen, for example by stating that there is to be a one degree increase for every X unit value of goods, the punishment must stop at life exile to 3000 *li,* unless the rule specifically authorises the infliction of the death penalty. Where a death penalty is authorised in these circumstances it is always strangulation and never beheading.[55]

This group of rules derives from the same wish to limit the number of offenders exposed to the most serious punishments, especially death, as the rules, already noted, on the review of executions for capital offences. Shen's 'upper commentary', included in the Ch'ing code, describes the rules in this group as exhibiting the utmost degree of humanity or benevolence (*jen*).[56]

The second group relates to a situation in which a person has already been convicted for one offence and, while serving his sentence, commits a further crime or crimes. The general rule was that he should undergo separately the punishment for each offence committed. Problems arose in the application of this rule when the initial sentence was to life exile or penal servitude. Should the convicted criminal subsequently, while serving his sentence, commit further offences punishable by beating, then he might readily receive the appropriate punishment, though the total number of blows inflicted with the light to heavy stick was not to exceed 200. But what was to be the position when a person serving a sentence of life exile committed a further offence entailing a sentence of life exile, or when a person serving a sentence of penal servitude committed a further offence entailing a punishment of penal servitude? The problem in the two cases was different.

The essence of the punishment of life exile was the removal of the offender to a considerable distance from his home; when this had been accomplished once, it was not practically possible to do it again. As the general commentary of the Ch'ing code states, the distance to which the exile would require to be sent if the second sentence of life exile were fully implemented 'would far exceed the boundaries of the empire'.[57] Hence the exile who committed a further exile offence remained in the same place but was given 100 blows and 3 years additional labour, the total number of years of labour to which he was subject not to exceed four.[58]

When a person sentenced to penal servitude committed a further offence entailing penal servitude there was nothing impracticable in simply adding on the requisite number of years to the existing sentence. However the codes provided that the total number of years of labour should not exceed four. Thus if he had originally been sentenced to penal servitude for three years and then committed an offence entailing a punishment of penal servitude for two years, only a year of labour was added to the original sentence. The general commentary[59] states that, were the normal rule followed and the sentences simply added, the number of years of labour would be excessive. The implication is that, on compassionate grounds, the maximum sentence involving forced labour to which an individual should be submitted is four years.[60]

Finally there are the rules which deal with the case where an offender is known to have committed several offences before any one of them has been brought to light and sentenced. Here the general rule was that the offender should only receive the sentence for the most serious of the offences which he had committed. Sentences for lesser offences or for offences of the same degree of gravity were not to be imposed. Should the offender have been sentenced for one offence and afterwards it became known that, prior to his conviction, he had committed other offences, then he might additionally be sentenced for any offence that was more serious than the one already sentenced, but the punishment assigned under the latter should be deducted from that assigned under the new sentence.[61] The commentaries do not give an explanation for this rule but arguably it stems, at least in part, from a reluctance to pile on an individual more punishment than he can reasonably bear; perhaps also some logical notion of the lesser being comprised within the greater influenced the legislators. The view may have been that an offender, on receiving the punishment of the most serious offence, could be deemed to have been punished also for the less serious.

Varying principles determine the distribution of punishment both with respect to classes of person and particular individuals. These principles may point to circumstances under which there should be an exemption from, or mitigation in, punishment, or to circumstances in which persons other than the one who committed the offence should also incur punishment for it. These principles have been enshrined in specific rules of the codes. The procedure followed here will be, first, an investigation of the rules and, second, an attempt to identify the underlying principles. There were several classes of person assigned by the codes a privileged position with respect to punishment, in particular officials, the aged, the young or the infirm and women. The law relating to officials will be left for consideration until a later chapter.

Already the T'ang code possesses a fully worked out and very carefully structured set of rules on the old, the young and the infirm.[62] Article 30[63] distinguishes between three groups of age and youth and two groups of infirmity, the extent of privilege or exemption from punishment varying according to the grade. The three 'age' grades are (i) those 70 and over or 15 and under, (ii) those 80 and over or 10 and under, (iii) those 90 and over or 7 and under. There are two grades of infirmity (i) the disabled (*fei-chi*), defined elsewhere in the code as those who had lost the use of one limb, or have a broken hip or backbone, or who are dumb or feebleminded or who are dwarfs, and (ii) the incapacitated (*tu-chi*) defined as those lacking the use of two limbs, blind in both eyes, inflicted with a loathsome disease (leprosy?), with tongue severed, with procreative organs destroyed, with ten fingers missing, or those who are insane.[64] These two grades are assimilated respectively to the first two 'age' grades.

The least degree of privilege is accorded those 70 and over, 15 and under, or those who are disabled (*fei-chi*). Persons within this category do not receive special treatment in the case of offences involving the death penalty. But in the case of those entailing a punishment of ordinary life exile or less, the punishment may be redeemed by payment of the appropriate quantity of copper.[65] The principal exception was that exile was still imposed when required under the rules of collective prosecution for rebellion or great sedition.[66] For those aged 80 and over, ten and under, or who counted as incapacitated (*tu-chi*), the degree of privilege was greater. Article 30 states that in cases where they commit rebellion or great sedition, or kill someone, or commit other offences entailing the death penalty[67] a petition is to be sent to the throne for decision. For other offences there is no liability, with the exception of theft or personal injury for which the payment of copper by way of redemption is required. If the offender is aged 90 or above or 7 and under, even for capital offences, punishment is not imposed. However young children aged 7 or under are still to be sent into slavery under the rules on collective prosecution where their father or paternal grandfather commits the offences of rebellion or great sedition. Should someone else have prevailed upon a person within this third category to commit an offence, the instigator is to be prosecuted himself.

By article 31[68] the benefits of article 30 are accorded to those who fall within the prescribed categories of age or infirmity at the time the offence is discovered, even though they did not qualify when it was committed. Further, if a person was 15 or under at the time he committed an offence, he is still entitled to the protection accorded youth, even though he should be older at the time of discovery. Finally article 474 provides that those within the first category or age and infirmity (70 and over, 15 and under, or disabled) should not, when involved in the investigation of an offence, be subjected to beating by way of torture. If accused, they should be convicted only on the evidence of three or more witnesses. Those in the second category (80 and over, ten and under, or incapacitated) might not be called as witnesses.[69]

Ming and Ch'ing law[70] are similar but there are some differences.[71]

Those aged 90 and over are not to be exempt from punishment where they have committed the offence of rebellion or great sedition. Curiously the Ming and Ch'ing commentaries give slightly discordant reasons for this rule (stricter than that of the T'ang code). According to the 'incorporated commentary' of the Ming code persons aged 90 and above can still be strong and robust or capable of instigating others, whereas those aged 7 and under possess neither quality.[72] The general commentary of the Ch'ing code points out that the former class of persons, although they lack the strength physically to engage in the affair, may possess the mental ability to organise the plot.[73] A difference may be signalled between the Ming and Ch'ing codes with respect to those aged 80 and over, 10 and under, or who are incapacitated. Whereas the Ming provision followed the T'ang, the Ch'ing specified that the privilege of memorialising the throne was not to be granted this category of person in cases of rebellion or great sedition.[74]

Furthermore there are differences with respect to what is understood by 'disabled' and 'incapacitated'. In T'ang law a person blind in one eye counted as 'infirm' (*ts'an-chi*) but not disabled (*fei-chi*),[75] whereas the 'incorporated commentary' of the Ming code[76] and the official commentary of the Ch'ing code (that in small characters)[77] give blindness in one eye as an example of *fei-chi*. In fact a sub-statute introduced in 1745 provided that a person blind in only one eye was not to be permitted redemption in the case of non-capital offences.[78] More important is the fact that both Ming and Ch'ing definitions of *fei-chi* and *tu-chi* were confined to physical defects and remove the T'ang examples respectively of 'feeblemindedness' (*ch'ih*) and 'insanity' (*tien k'uang*). The result is that in the later law mental defects in principle no longer counted as a ground of mitigation in, or exemption from, punishment.[79]

Whereas in Ming and early Ch'ing law no special provision for the insane appears to have been made, during the course of the 18th century a number of sub-statutes were added to the Ch'ing code. These were designed partly to impose on the family or the local authority the duty of supervising and confining the insane (the term now in use being *feng-ping*) to prevent their being a danger to the public, and partly to determine the legal consequences when an insane person killed either himself or another person. Should he kill one person he is thereafter to be kept chained in perpetuity and his relatives are to pay a set sum as funeral expenses to the victim's family. But should he kill two or more persons he is to be sentenced to strangulation or beheading (depending on the number or whether they are of the same family or not). Even so the circumstances will be re-examined at the autumn assizes with the possibility of a reprieve.[80]

Two more general differences between T'ang and Ming/Ch'ing law may also be noted. In the later period a special tariff governed redemption granted to the aged, young or infirm. They paid what in effect was a nominal sum, considerably less than a person would pay, for example, in the case of accidental homicide.[81] Whereas there is nothing in the T'ang code to suggest that, except in the case where a petition was to be submitted to the throne, persons falling within the various categories of the aged, young or infirm, acquired anything other than a right to redemption of, or exemption from, punishment, in Ch'ing law, at any rate, they appear merely to have been granted a privilege. Studies of the decided cases involving these categories of person have suggested that the Board of Punishments exercised a discretion as to the grant of redemption or exemption, despite the apparently mandatory terms of the code itself.[82]

The rationale for the special treatment of the old and the young is to be found in the Confucian conception of the old as deserving of respect and the young as deserving of compassion.[83] This is expressed in the main ritual classic, the Book of Rites (Li Chi), when it is said that 'a person of eighty or ninety is called a venerable greybeard. A person of seven is called a child deserving of pity. A child deserving of pity, or a venerable greybeard, even though they may have committed a crime, are not to be subjected to punishment'.[84] Another of the ritual classics, the Rites of Chou (Chou Li) declares that the very old, the very young and the mentally deficient are entitled to pardon for their offences.[85] Both these passages are cited in the T'ang shu-i commentary, the first in relation to the group comprising those aged 80 and over or 7 and under,[86] and the second in relation to the group comprising those aged 80 and over or 10 and under, or those who are incapacitated (tu-chi).[87] The T'ang shu-i commentary treats the general concept of 'pity' as the factor justifying lenient treatment of the three categories of the old and young and the two categories of the infirm (both mentally and physically).[88] Sometimes reference is made to the little intelligence or strength possessed by the old or young or to the fact that they, like the infirm, cannot endure physical punishment such as beatings or forced labour.[89] There is no systematic exposition of the reasons for extending compassion to the different categories, but generally it appears that physical or mental weakness was the main ground of pity cited.

The brief comments in the Yüan Legal Treatise suggest that the main consideration for the (considerably restricted) privilege granted the aged, young or infirm was the factual point that they were unable to endure beatings. No specific mention is made of pity.[90] The Ming commentaries show varying attempts to explain the rules, not always mutually consistent. Thus the official 'small' commentary explains the rule making liable only those who have instigated the very old (90 and over) or very young (7 and under) to commit crimes on the ground that persons so old or so young have little judgment (knowledge) or strength.[91] On the other hand the 'incorporated commentary', a propos of the rule that those aged 90 and over are still held liable for rebellion or great sedition, says that such persons may be robust and have the ability to instigate others.[92]

Two general statements from the Ming 'incorporated commentary' are worth noting. First it is said that one cannot not pity the old, be indulgent to the young and have compassion for those who are not whole.[93] Here a more differentiated approach seems to be taken. Indulgence for youth is not quite the same as pity for weakness. Further the reference to the 'infirm' is interesting. The ground for compassion is clearly physical imperfection - a body that is not whole - and not mental deficiency. The second cites the rules which permit the old to be dealt with according to their age at the time the crime was discovered and the young at the time of commission as the height of benevolence or humanity (*jen*).[94] One probably has in this fundamental Confucian concept the ultimate source of the whole complex of rules dealing with the aged, young or infirm.

From the 'upper commentary' of the Ch'ing code one has an explanation that follows more closely that of the Book of Rites on the position of the young and old. It is said that there is respect for the old, indulgence for the young and pity for those who are not whole.[95] Respect again is not quite the same as pity. More practical considerations are expressed in some of the Ch'ing cases. D. Bodde cites from one case the statement that clemency may be extended to the aged because, with the decline of their powers, they are not in a position to repeat their offence. The implication is that they no longer constitute a danger to the public and therefore need not be punished in the usual way.[96] Such judicial comment appears as a secondary justification. One has to take as the primary explanation of, and justification for, the leniency accorded the old, young and infirm the Confucian emphasis upon benevolence and humanity (*jen*). This focuses attention upon the particular condition of an individual who is to be subjected to punishment. Age, youth, illness or disablement are all human conditions which suggest the need for special treatment. Although one finds frequent reference to a factor they arguably have in common, their ability to arouse pity through the exhibition of physical or mental weakness, other notions such as respect for age and indulgence for the young also played a part in dictating a benevolent or humane solution to the issue of criminal liability.[97]

Another group to which special treatment was accorded was that of women. One should distinguish the case in which a woman herself had committed an offence from that in which she is liable to punishment on account of an offence committed by someone else. The latter will be considered below in the section on 'collective prosecution'. In T'ang law the leniency accorded a woman who had committed an offence was limited. For offences entailing as punishment death, penal servitude or beating there was no mitigation or exemption. Only where the appropriate punishment was exile did the law offer a concession on the ground that a woman should not be sent into exile alone. Hence in such a case the punishment was changed into a beating with the heavy stick ranging from 60-100 blows depending upon the distance to which the woman should have been exiled for her offence, together with labour for three years in her home locality. There was thus no redemption permitted, simply a change in punishment from exile to penal servitude with an additional beating.[98] An exception to the general rule is made by article 262 on the making or storing of *ku* poison.[99] A woman who commits this offence is to be strangled, and even should there be an amnesty, she is still to be exiled to 3000 *li*. The commentary to article 28 says that 'making and keeping *ku* poison falls within what is intolerable and women who do so are expelled to the frontiers of the empire in order to cut off the root of this evil'.[100]

In Ming and Ch'ing law, in keeping with the general availability of redemption, women were placed in a more favourable position. Both codes contained an article providing *inter alia* that when a woman committed an offence punishable by penal servitude or exile she was to receive a beating of 100 blows with the heavy stick and be permitted to redeem the balance of the punishment, the tariff being the same as that prescribed for the old, young or infirm. The article also specifies that for the infliction of the beating the woman may wear an outer garment unless she has committed the offence of illicit sexual intercourse. In that case, since she has already forfeited her modesty, she may wear only an under garment.[101] The provisions of the article were supplemented by a sub-statute, contained in both codes, which established certain exceptions to, and enlargements of, the primary rule. Women were still to receive the ordinary punishment prescribed for their offence where it consisted of illicit intercourse, theft or lack of filial piety or where they altogether lacked resources. However, subject to these qualifications, two further benefits were accorded them: (i) commutation of the death penalty for 'miscellaneous offences' (the less serious ones normally comprised within the terms of an ordinary amnesty) into a beating of 100 blows plus redemption, and (ii) the conversion even of the beating into a redemption payment established according to a special tariff.[102]

Although, so far as I have been able to see, none of the codes explicitly introduces the concept of *jen* into the discussion of the special treatment accorded women, the explanation probably lies in the general notion of benevolence or humanity. The particular aspect of benevolence upon which emphasis is laid differs in the codes. For the T'ang code the primary consideration was that women could not be allowed to go into exile on their own, except when it was absolutely necessary to remove the source of an evil as in the case of *ku* poison. But the T'ang legislators saw no objection to their undertaking labour, perhaps because the labour prescribed was that suitable for women.[103] However the Ming and Ch'ing commentaries emphasise rather that hard labour is not something a woman can endure, and hence she should not be subjected to punishments which involve it.[104] Here the labour under contemplation seems to be something like working in the salt or iron mines or in the government courier services.

One further example of leniency in punishment, resting upon a somewhat different principle, may be given. Where the offender is the sole support of aged or infirm parents or paternal grandparents he might be accorded favourable treatment. The reason in this case lay not in the individual circumstances of the offender himself but in those of his closest senior relatives. T'ang law differentiates the treatment of the offender according to the nature of the punishment he has merited. If the offence is capital, provided that it is not one of the ten abominations, and the offender's paternal grandparents or parents are aged 80 or over or are incapacitated (*tu-chi*) and require to be supported and there is no other year of mourning (or closer) adult relative in the family, then a petition may be sent to the throne. Should the offender be granted permission to remain at home and look after a parent or grandparent in need of support, then on the death of the relative supported or the attaining of the age of 21 by a year of mourning or closer relative, a further petition is to be sent to the throne requesting a decision on the fate of the offender. No doubt where he had faithfully performed his filial duty, imperial clemency would be extended to him.[105]

Where the offence entailed a punishment of life exile, provided it was not excluded from the scope of ordinary amnesties, the offender was allowed as of right - without the necessity for a petition to the throne - to remain at home until either the relative supported died or a year of mourning relative attained the age of 21. On either of these events occurring the offender was, within a year, to be sent into exile to serve his sentence. Even where the offender has already gone into exile, the article appears to contemplate that he will be recalled should parents or paternal grandparents by reason of age or infirmity require his support.[106]

Where the offence entailed a punishment of penal servitude and there were no other adults in the household, the punishment was commuted into a beating of 120 blows with the heavy stick for the first year of penal servitude and 20 blows for every half year thereafter making a possible maximum of 200 blows. No such commutation will be made if the offence has been robbery or wounding unless there are old or infirm parents or paternal grandparents requiring support. This provision contemplates a different situation from the others. It is based not upon the presence of parents or grandparents who require to be supported but upon the offender being the only adult in the family, and therefore, perhaps, the main source of its livelihood. Hence if the offence is merely one punishable by penal servitude he is allowed to receive a beating instead. But this benefit is not available under any circumstances for more serious offences punishable by death or exile and, in the case of robbery or wounding, is extended only under the circumstances defined by the article. One notes also that 'adult' refers to any person over 21 in the household, not just to year of mourning or closer relatives. Oddly, unmarried women whatever their age do not count as adults, but a wife does.[107]

In Ming and Ch'ing law the treatment of the offender was even more generous, although it dealt basically only with the situation in which old or infirm relatives required support and not with that in which the offender was the only adult in the household. In the first place the circumstances of 'age' or 'infirmity' were extended, the Ming article still treating 'aged' as 80 and above but including physical 'disablement' (*fei-chi*) under 'infirmity', and the Ch'ing reducing 'aged' to 70 and over. In the second place, whereas the rule applicable to capital offences remained broadly the same as the T'ang, a new rule was adopted for exile or penal servitude offences. In these cases the offender was simply to receive a beating of 100 blows with the heavy stick and be allowed to redeem the balance of the punishment (according to the nominal tariff provided for the old, young and infirm). Under both rules, that is those applying to capital and non-capital offences, the condition for the availability of the benefit was that there should be within the family no second adult, defined now as someone 16 or over (presumably again a male or wife), upon whom the grandparent or parent could rely for support.[108]

These were the main rules contained in the articles of the code. In addition during the Ch'ing period a large number of supplementary rules were issued from time to time. These in part extended the benefit of the rules even further and in part, perhaps because of the fear of abuse, imposed a number of restrictions. Thus an offender who was the only son of a woman who had been widowed for 20 or more years was also to be allowed to remain at home to look after her, even though she was aged less than 70,[109] and offenders were also allowed the benefit of the rules on remaining at home where their paternal grandparents and parents were all dead and they were the only person qualified to undertake the ancestral sacrifices.[110] Other rules introduced a number of additional burdens, such as the requirement that offenders be sentenced to wear the cangue for specified periods of time, or defined circumstances under which the benefit of remaining at home was not to be available, as where the offender had killed someone who was the only support of his parents, unless the latter had been unfilial.[111]

The reasons for the T'ang rules appear to have varied. In the case of paternal grandparents or parents who were aged or infirm, the reason for allowing the offender to remain at home and support them clearly lay in the duty of filial piety. So imperative was this duty that the *shu-i* commentary makes no explicit reference to the fact that it overrode the normal application of the criminal law. For the case of the family in which the offender was the only adult, the reason for extending leniency was again pity, derived from the fundamental concept of humanity (*jen*). The commentary at one point says that the commutation of the offender's sentence of penal servitude is 'due to pity that the criminal's household may have their food supply cut off, and the further fear that there may be difficulties and poverty within the household'.[112] The Ming and Ch'ing commentaries invoke both the concept of pity and the importance of filial piety, though the notion that the circumstances of the case are deserving of pity is given the greater emphasis.[113]

Collective Prosecution

Punishment might extend not just to the person guilty of an offence but to varying numbers of his relatives who had not themselves been involved. Such a degree of punishment, in its most severe form sometimes termed 'the extermination of the family', was reserved for the most serious offences, especially those directed against the state or the ruling house. It is known to have been a feature of Ch'in law and, despite some hesitation under the Han,[114] was applied by all dynasties thereafter. Only at the end of the Ch'ing did those in favour of reforming the law, imbued with Western ideas, argue that a true application of the principle of benevolence required punishment to be restricted to the person who had actually committed the crime and not be extended to innocent relatives.[115]

T'ang law knew a very carefully worked out and graduated system of 'collective prosecution' in which both the precise degree of relationship taken into account and the extent of punishment varied according to the gravity of the initial offence.[116] The most serious offences, attracting the greatest range of liability, were plotting rebellion, defined as plotting 'to endanger the Altars of Soil and Grain', that is, the state itself,[117] and committing great sedition, defined as attempting 'to destroy the ancestral temples, tombs or palaces of the reigning house'.[118] In both these cases large numbers of relatives were punished. The father and sons aged 16 and above of the principal offenders were to be strangled; their sons aged 15 and below, mother, daughters (neither married nor engaged),[119] wives and concubines (whether their own or their sons), paternal grandfather (including great and great-great grandfather), grandsons by sons (including great and great-great grandsons) brothers and sisters were all forfeit to the state as slaves. Their paternal uncles and nephews by brothers were to be exiled to 3000 *li*.[120]

The selection of relatives reflects the patrilineal structure of Chinese society. Those to be punished are relatives on the father's side, the only exceptions being the mother herself, the wife and concubines. The range of female relatives brought within the scope of punishment is considerably smaller than the male. Neither the paternal grandmother nor the father's sisters or nieces by sons are included. Under the general law the wives and concubines of those sentenced to exile were to accompany them, although, on grounds of pity, not being involved in any way in the offence, they are exempt from forced labour or beating.[121]

Age, infirmity and sex were grounds of mitigation or exemption. Sons aged 15 and under escape with their lives, as emerges clearly from the terms of article 248. Less clear is the position of men aged 80 and over or younger men who are incapacitated (*tu-chi*). After the section prescribing the punishments of death and enslavement but before that prescribing the punishment of exile, the article states that men falling within these categories are to be exempt from punishment. This makes it clear that they are to be exempt from death or enslavement, but one may infer from the position of the clause that they are still to suffer the punishment of exile. The same part of the article also declares women aged 60 and over or younger women who are disabled (*fei-chi*) to be exempt from punishment. In this case it is made clear that exemption is to be from exile as well as enslavement, since a note inserted in the text of the article specifies that the same is to apply for the other offences in which women (it does not mention men) are involved in collective prosecution. Under these offences the only punishment imposed on women who are made jointly liable is exile and hence one may conclude that the article was intended to exempt women falling within the categories described from exile as well as enslavement.

If the plot to rebel was unsuccessful in the sense that the plotters were unable to induce the masses to follow them, they themselves are beheaded but the extent of 'collective prosecution' is less. The only relatives affected are the father, mother, sons and daughters (neither married nor engaged), wife and concubines (of the offender), all of whom are to be sent into life exile to 3000 *li*.[122] The circumstances under which the aged, young, infirm or women might be entitled to mitigation are not entirely clear. One is entitled to infer from the first part of article 248 that the mother if 60 or over or disabled would not be sent into exile, but article 30 and its commentary introduce a complication. The article provides that where life exile is imposed on account of collective prosecution for rebellion or sedition those aged 70 or over, 15 or under or who are disabled are not allowed to redeem the punishment by payment of copper.[123] However the *shu-i* commentary explains that the law is not the same for women as for men. It quotes the exception already made by article 248 in favour of women aged 60 and above or who are disabled and further adds, with reference to the case where the plot to rebel has been unsuccessful, that wives, concubines or daughters aged 60 or above or 15 or less may redeem their sentence of exile by payment of the appropriate amount of copper.[124] The difficulty is that article 248 appears to accord complete exemption to women aged 60 and above or to those who are disabled; it says nothing about redemption. One has to conclude either that article 248 was an incomplete statement of the law and that 'exemption' meant 'redeem by payment of copper', or that the commentary to article 30 was incorrect in including women of this category within the group from whom redemption was required. On the latter view the result would be that girls aged 15 and under would be allowed to redeem their punishment, but women aged 60 or over or disabled would have complete exemption.[125] Even for girls aged 15 and under redemption would be possible only where the plot to rebel had proved unsuccessful in the technical sense defined, not where it had actually mobilised support.

For another group of offences, regarded as somewhat less serious, it is enacted that the wife and sons of the offender are to be exiled to 2000 *li*. These are plotting treason (defined as betraying the country, as by going over to the enemy), where acts in furtherance of the treason have already been committed,[126] divulging to the enemy information about impending military attacks,[127] and killing three persons in one family or dismembering a person.[128] The commentary to article 251 (on plotting treason) states an important rule which is applicable to all three offences. If the offender only has a wife and/or a son aged 15 or under, the punishment may be redeemed by payment of the appropriate amount of copper. Since the law provides that women cannot be sent into exile alone they are to remain at home, receive a beating with the heavy stick and do forced labour. But should a son be aged 16 or more the sentence of exile will be implemented for the mother as well as the son,[129] though she will be exempt from forced labour at the place of exile.[130]

An offence which presents some special features is that of making or keeping *ku* poison (made from noxious insects and able to kill persons or drive them mad).[131] The principal offenders are to be strangled. Members of the same household, who are unaware of the circumstances, are to be exiled to 3000 *li*. Should there be an amnesty the principal offenders escape death but are still to be exiled (with the other members of the household) to 3000 *li*. However those who are aged 80 or over or 10 or under, or who are incapacitated (*tu-chi*) and have no family members to accompany them into exile are to be exempt.[132] The commentary explains that the whole household is to be kept together, and so if there are members capable of being exiled then all are to go irrespective of age or infirmity. Elsewhere in the code it is explained that in view of the intolerable nature of the offence the normal rule prohibiting the sending of women into exile alone is not to apply.[133] Not just the women who make or keep *ku* poison but also all those who live in their household are to be sent into exile (despite any amnesty).[134]

The rather complex position in T'ang law of the aged, young, infirm or women involved in collective prosecution may be summarised as follows. For men aged 80 and over or younger men who are incapacitated (*tu-chi*) there was exemption from death or enslavement, though it appears that they were still to be sent into exile. One exception is stipulated in the context of the offence of making or storing *ku* poison. They are not to be sent into exile unless there is an adult and fit family member to accompany them. Since the *shu-i* commentary to article 262 states that the reason for the exemption is that persons so old or infirm could not survive on their own, it may be that the same rule was applied to other cases of collective prosecution. Boys aged 15 and under were exempted from death but not enslavement. They were also to be sent into exile except in the following two cases: (i) where the boy was aged 10 or under and there was no adult to accompany him (stated in the context of the *ku* poison offence but possibly of more general application), and (ii) where, in the case of offences less serious than plotting rebellion or great sedition (treason, divulging information to the enemy, or killing three persons in one family) the only relatives of the offender to be exiled were his wife and/or sons aged 15 or less (the punishment here being redeemable).

Women aged 60 and over or younger women who are disabled (*fei-chi*) were exempt from enslavement and exile (the death penalty not being imposed on women who were collectively prosecuted). Probably, although the matter is not certain, they were not required to redeem a sentence of exile. There are two exceptions. A sentence of exile imposed in connection with collective prosecution for making or storing *ku* poison is to be implemented except where the woman is aged 80 and over or is incapacitated and there are no adult persons to accompany her. The other exception, applicable to the three less serious offences described above, is where a wife is left with no son aged 16 or over. Should she be under 60, the sentence of exile may be redeemed. Girls aged 15 and under are enabled to redeem a sentence of exile by payment of copper and those aged ten and under were not sent into exile unless there was an accompanying adult (generalising from the rule stated in the context of *ku* poison). One qualification is necessary. It is not entirely clear that girls aged 15 or under were able to redeem a sentence of exile in case of plotting rebellion or great sedition.

In some respects the Ming/Ch'ing law of collective prosecution was more severe than the T'ang.[135] In the first place rebellion and great sedition are treated in exactly the same way.[136] The full punishment is imposed for the mere plot whether or not anything has been done to carry it out and irrespective of the degree of success in mobilising others. The principal offenders are to be put to death by slicing; their paternal grandfather (up to great-great), father, sons, grandsons by sons (down to great-great), brothers and persons (male), living in the same household, whether or not their surname is different, paternal uncles and sons of brothers, provided they are aged 16 or over but irrespective of infirmity, are to be beheaded; males (within this class) aged 15 or under, their mother, daughters, wives and concubines, sisters, wives and concubines of their sons are to be given as slaves to deserving officials. Excepted from collective prosecution are daughters already promised in marriage, sons or grandsons who have been adopted by other families and betrothed girls who have not yet been sent to the family.[137]

Not only is the range of persons to be put to death much wider than in T'ang law but it includes non-patrilineal male relatives such as maternal or affinal relatives who happen to be living in the same household. A basic distinction is drawn between males (who are to be executed unless aged 15 or under) and females (who are to be enslaved). In fact a sub-statute of the Ch'ing code ameliorated the position of males involved in collective prosecution and established a punishment other than death. The sons and grandsons of the principal offenders, where it was clear that they had no knowledge of the facts, were to be castrated and given as slaves to the officials and soldiers of the newly acquired territories; other males jointly liable, without being castrated, were subjected to the same slavery.[138]

For the case of plotting treason where acts in furtherance of the plot had already been carried out, the principal offenders were to be beheaded, their wives, concubines, sons and daughters given as slaves to deserving officials, their parents, paternal grandfather, grandsons (by sons) and brothers were to be exiled to 2000 li. A sub-statute changed the punishment of exile and increased its severity. Those whom the law required to be exiled were now to be sent to the newly acquired territories to cultivate the land on behalf of the state.[139] Possibly it was an element of public need, rather than a mere wish to make the punishment more severe, that dictated this change.

For the other offences, with the exception of divulging military secrets to the enemy where the Ming/Ch'ing law does not impose collective prosecution,[140] the position was similar to the T'ang. Thus where three people in one family have been killed the offender's wife and sons are to be exiled to 2000 li,[141] and where ku poison has been made or kept the wife and sons of the principal offender(s) and the other members of the household who do not know the circumstances are to be exiled to 2000 *li*.[142] Ch'ing sub-statutes made some additional adjustments. Thus an enactment of 1779, finally revised in 1830, introduced a special rule determining the fate of the sons of a person who had killed three members of one family. Those who are aged 16 or more are to be exiled to the furthest frontiers at 4000 *li*, those aged 15 or under are to be sent with the wife and daughters to a near frontier.[143]

Ming and Ch'ing law make fewer concessions to the aged, young, infirm or women with respect to offences which entail collective prosecution than does the T'ang. Thus in the case of rebellion and great sedition the sentences of death and enslavement are carried out strictly in accordance with the law. There are no exemptions for men aged 80 and above or younger men who are incapacitated or for women aged 60 and above or younger women who are disabled. Although women were normally allowed to redeem sentences of exile, this privilege was not available in the case of offences entailing collective prosecution, even where they were aged 60 and above. The reason for the greater severity of the later law, as indicated in the commentaries noted below, appears primarily to have been the fact that close relatives (aged 16 and above) of the offender were deemed to know the circumstances of the offence. They must at least have had suspicions which they should have disclosed to the authorities. Hence, according to the thinking of the commentaries, the imposition of the punishments of death, enslavement or exile, irrespective of age or sex, is justified.

When one comes to consider generally the reasons for the punishment of persons other than the actual offenders, which are stated or implied in the codes, one can detect three lines of approach.[144] There is first the notion that some crimes are so wicked that they demonstrate the depravity not just of those who have actually committed them but also of the family to which they belong. Next there is the notion that the relatives and others who are collectively prosecuted have somehow been at fault because, although they did not participate in the offence or even know about it, they should have been aware of what was happening and acted to prevent it. Finally there is the notion of deterrence; potential offenders would be more effectively deterred if they knew that a consequence of their act would be the involvement of their relatives in harsh punishment. Some illustrations of these views follow; it is difficult to detect a consistent approach.

The T'ang *shu-i* commentary says 'Plotting rebellion and great sedition are criminal to the utmost degree of censure and extinction. Such crimes defile the whole family and the eradication of evil must reach to the roots'.[145] There is an implication here that the family to which the offender belongs is or has become evil and should therefore be exterminated. A similar thought seems to underly the commentary's explanation of the rule that women involved in the making or keeping of *ku* poison or those forming part of their household must be exiled; the whole household is defiled by the act.[146] At the same time there is a clear sentiment expressed elsewhere in the commentary that persons will take every care to prevent members of their family from committing the offences of plotting rebellion or great sedition since they know that the whole family will be involved in punishment.[147]

Ch'ing commentators seem to have favoured an arguably more rational, or at least just, approach and sought to locate the reason for collective prosecution in the personal fault of the relatives or members of the household made liable. The general commentary to article 223 on plotting rebellion or great sedition points out that males aged 16 or over already possess knowledge and discernment. Even though they have not participated in the plot they are still partisans or adherents of the rebellion and so deserve to be punished. The idea here, expressed more clearly in a later part of the commentary, is that the relatives and members of the same household must have some knowledge of the plotting even though they do not know the details and have not joined in the plot. They are virtually in the same position as those who actually know of, but fail to disclose, the plot. But males aged 15 or under and females lack discernment and therefore are not punished capitally. The same commentary also makes the point that the fundamental idea of the rules is to fill people with fear so that they will watch and stop rebellious plots coming to fruition. Here what is expressed is the idea of deterrence.[148] Similar points of view are expressed in Shen's 'upper commentary' on article 257 dealing with the dismemberment of a body for magical purposes. Those who live with a person given to malevolent practices cannot fail to be aware of this. The object of the law is to repress sorcery and ensure that those living with a person given to such practices will denounce him. Intermingled again are the thoughts of personal fault on the part of members of the household and the deterrent and preventive effect of the rule.[149]

Amnesties

Imperial acts of grace by which exemption from, or reduction of, punishment might be granted to various classes of offender were an integral part of the legal system. The codes did not prescribe that there should be amnesties, these being a matter of imperial discretion, but they did carefully regulate the way in which they should be interpreted, and provided clear criteria defining which offences should and which should not fall within the conventional amnesties. Generally the T'ang and Sung rulers appear to have made greater use of the grants of amnesty than the Ming and Ch'ing. The assize system of the latter dynasties already introduced a considerable measure of leniency into the application of the punishments, the process of review in capital cases frequently leading to a reduction in the normal sentence prescribed by the code. Hence the scope for mitigation of punishment by amnesty was perhaps less in the later dynasties than the earlier.[150]

The T'ang, Sung, Ming and Ch'ing codes all make a distinction of critical importance between offences which fall within the scope of an ordinary amnesty and those which do not, although the offences listed under the latter head were more numerous in Ming/Ch'ing than in T'ang law[151] Article 488 of the T'ang code provides *inter alia* that in the case of offences excluded from the scope of an ordinary amnesty either the regular punishment prescribed by the code or at least a reduced one, is to be imposed, even though an amnesty should have been granted. The *shu-i* commentary gives a number of examples. In the case of 'contumacy', the fourth of the ten abominations, namely, beating or plotting to kill paternal grandparents or parents, or killing paternal uncles or their wives, elder brothers or sisters, maternal grandparents, husband or husband's paternal grandparents or parents,[152] the punishment of death (prescribed by the code) is still to be imposed. In the case of rebellion or sedition, the killing of older paternal first cousins or relatives of a higher generation for whom mourning is worn for five months, or preparing or keeping *ku* poison, the sentence of exile is still to be imposed (reduced from death). In the case of the ten abominations, deliberate killing (*ku sha*), collective prosecution for rebellion of sedition, the offender, if an official, is still to be disenrolled.[153] In the case of an official committing the offences of illicit sexual intercourse, theft, kidnapping, receiving property and subverting the law, even though there is an amnesty, he is still to be dismissed from his office.

Article 489 adds a clarification. It provides that where one knows there is to be an amnesty and deliberately commits an offence, or commits 'contumacy', or a personal retainer or slave beats, plots to kill or forcibly has sexual intercourse with his owner, there is to be no forgiveness at all by an amnesty. In other cases, namely where one kills a relative of a higher generation for whom mourning is worn for five months, or an older paternal first cousin, or plots rebellion or commits great sedition, then although there is an amnesty, the offender is still to be exiled to 2000 *li*. The commentary points out that in the latter class of case the effect of an amnesty is to exempt the offender from the death penalty, but the punishment of exile is to be imposed in its place.[154]

These two articles in effect establish certain presumptions which apply to the interpretation of an amnesty, in the absence of any explicit and contrary indication of the imperial will. Only in one case does it appear that an amnesty was to have no effect at all. This is with respect to offences falling under the head of 'contumacy' for which, despite an amnesty - unless otherwise indicated - the death sentence is still to be imposed. But in other cases however serious, some reduction in punishment will be allowed. Thus those who plot rebellion or commit great sedition or prepare *ku* poison all escape death, though they are still sentenced to exile to 2000 *li*. For some very serious offences such as deliberate killing (of an unrelated person) there was to be complete exemption unless the offender was an official. In that event he was still to be disenrolled. The only offence which remained truly unforgivable was that involving attacks upon the closest paternal, maternal or affinal relatives ('contumacy'); the family was given in this context greater consideration even than the state or the emperor.

One has to remember that the reductions in punishment authorised by articles 488 and 489 applied only where the amnesty governed the offence in question. If, for example, it excluded the ten abominations then no reduction at all was permissible for the specific offences so classified. On the other hand if it included the ten abominations the principles described above applied. For 'contumacy' there was no forgiveness and for some other offences, although the death penalty was remitted, there was still to be exile to 2000 *li*.

Ming/Ch'ing law was simpler, although more rigorous, than T'ang. Essentially a wide range of offences was excluded altogether from the benefits of an ordinary amnesty. Among these offences were the ten abominations, theft, killing, arson, corruption, fraud, illicit sexual intercourse, instigating others to kill, and helping those who had committed crimes to evade the authorities. However special amnesties might extend complete exemption or, perhaps more likely, grant a reduction in punishment to persons who had committed one of the offences normally regarded as unforgivable. In such a case the amnesty must specify exactly the nature of the offence and the degree of reduction in punishment accorded.[155]

The commentaries show that the underlying rationale was the wish to penalise most heavily those offences which had been intentionally committed. These should not be forgiven, whereas for inadvertent acts such as accidental killing or the accidental lighting of a fire (with resultant damage) the circumstances warranted pity, and forgiveness was appropriate.[156] One has enshrined here the very same thought which had led king Wu more than 2000 years prior to the Ming to declare that killing should be the punishment even for small offences deliberately committed, but not for offences committed accidentally even though they were great.[157]

Notes

1. Cf. Hulsewé, Remnants of Han Law, 102; MacCormack , Lü hsing: Problems of Legal Interpretation.
2. Former Han Legal Treatise (Hulsewé op.cit., 334f). Later amputations were revived and again discontinued. See Johnson, 94 (*shu-i* commentary to article 11).
3. See Balazs, Traité juridique du 'Souei-Chou', 74.
4. Article 1 and commentary (Johnson, 55); Bünger, Quellen zur Rechtsgeschichte zur T'ang Zeit, 143.
5. Article 482 and commentary. See also Bünger, op.cit., 93 (where the Old T'ang Legal Treatise summarises the rules), 138, 219 (for edicts restricting beating on the back).
6. See generally Johnson, 58; Bünger, op.cit., 143; Ou, La peine d'après le code des T'ang, 29f.
7. Article 3 (Johnson, 58f).
8. Article 29 (Johnson, 166f).
9. Bünger, op.cit., 215, and cf. an edict reproduced in the New T'ang Legal Treatise (Bünger, 164) stating that a like opportunity was allowed to those sentenced to be beaten with the heavy stick. The same edict refers to convicts doing their work while fettered in the cold and heat.
10. Article 4 (Johnson, 59).
11. See articles 24, 29 (Johnson, 147, 166).
12. Article 24. See Bünger, op.cit., 143f; Ou, op.cit., 33f.
13. Article 5 (Johnston, 59f). Another reason suggested is that filial piety required a person to keep whole the body he had received from his parents (Johnson, 59 n.74). Cf. also the remarks of Granet, Religion of the Chinese People, 88f.
14. Seidel, Studien zur Rechtsgeschichte der Sung-Zeit, 47f, 81.
15. So the Chinese text of the Sung Legal Treatise (p.4967 of the Peking edition published by Chunghua Publishing House), and the table inserted in the Sung code in the article on punishments between 'exile' and 'death'. Seidel appears to have misunderstood the position (cf. his translation at 80f and introduction at 47).
16. So the Yüan Legal Treatise (Ratchnevsky, Code des Yüan I, 5, 343f) and

cf. Ch'en, Chinese Legal Tradition under the Mongols, 49ff.

17. Ratchnevsky, op.cit., I, 6, 340 and cf. II, 147. Ch'en, op.cit., 48 observes that persons sentenced to penal servitude were normally put to work in the mines and salt wells.

18. Ratchnevsky II, 8, 340; Ch'en 47f.

19. Ratchnevsky II, 63 and n.2; Ch'en, 48.

20. Ratchnevsky I, 9, and Ch'en, 42f.

21. See also the account in the Ming Legal Treatise (Munzel, Strafrecht im alten China, 38f).

22. MLCCFL, 179f and see also the table of the five punishments at 71.

23. Op.cit., 22.

24. Munzel, op.cit., 39.

25. See Munzel, 83, and 38, 86 (special sentences of penal servitude for 4 or 5 years).

26. MLCCFL, 97.

27. Munzel, 39, 71f, 74.

28. The Ming Legal Treatise gives the number of offences so punished in the latter part of the 16th century as 213 (Munzel, 72).

29. For details see Munzel, 127f (notes 481 and 491) and cf. Bodde and Morris, Law in Imperial China, 88.

30. Generally see Bodde and Morris, 76ff.

31. See Boulais, p2f; Philastre I, 114f; Bodde and Morris, 77, 80f.

32. Boulais, 195; Bodde and Morris, 81.

33. Boulais, p.3.

34. Cf. Bodde and Morris, 95f.

35. Boulais, p.4.

36. Bodde and Morris, 83ff.

37. For a late Ch'ing appraisal of the problems posed by both ordinary and military exile see Meijer, Introduction of Modern Criminal Law in China, 137ff.

38. Boulais, p.4f; Philastre I, 281f; Staunton, 44f; Bodde and Morris, 87ff where an account can be found of other supplementary punishments such as tattooing.

39. Article 339. Johnson, citing the Japanese scholar Niida Noboru, also instances the case of false accusation (55, n.45), but the code itself in the articles on false accusation (342-4) simply provides that the false accuser is to bear the same punishment as that of the offence falsely charged, or the difference between that punishment and the one really merited by the accused.

40. See chapter 4, 89f.

41. See chapter 7, 167f, 172f.

42. Ming 22.5 (MLCCFL, 1666); Ch'ing article 305, Philastre II, 407f; Boulais, 1478; Staunton, 366f.

43. Cf. the reasoning of the general commentary of the Ch'ing code, Philastre II, 412.

44. Generally see Munzel, op.cit., 58ff, 114ff.

45. Munzel, 58.

46. Hucker, Censorial System of Ming China, 143ff.

47. So Munzel, 122.
48. MLCCFL, 59.
49. Philastre I, inserted between pp.34-5.
50. Philastre I, 35f. See further the section on 'amnesties' below.
51. Philastre I, 41f (wrongly stating 400 ounces); Boulais, p.15f.
52. Meijer, Introduction of Modern Criminal Law in China, 147.
53. Although Staunton reproduces the tables of the two general schemes (lxxii, lxxiii), assuming that the earlier relates to redemption necessarily to be paid, the latter to those offences not necessarily redeemable, Boulais (p.15f) gives only the table for the later scheme.
54. T'ang article 56 (Johnson 268); Ming 1.38 (MLCCFL, 351); Ch'ing article 35, Philastre I, 259; Staunton, 38.
55. See previous note.
56. TCLLHCPL, 740. Cf. Boulais, 111.
57. Philastre I, 177.
58. Thus, if his original sentence of exile had entailed 4 years of labour and he committed a further exile offence the only additional punishment he received was the infliction of 100 blows.
59. Philastre I, 177.
60. T'ang article 29 (Johnson, 166); Ming 1.20 (MLCCFL, 280); Ch'ing article 20, Philastre I, 176 (criticising the rules at 182); Boulais, 145; Staunton, 23.
61. T'ang article 45 (Johnson, 235); Ming 1.7 (MLCCFL, 215); Ch'ing article 25, Philastre I, 215 (criticising the rule at 218); Boulais, 152; Staunton, 29.
62. For the Han position see Hulsewé, Remnants of Han Law, 298ff, and the same author's Han China - a Proto 'Welfare State'?, 266f.
63. Johnson, 169; Bünger, Punishment of Lunatics and Negligents according to Classical Chinese Law, 3.
64. Articles 303, 305, 474, and cf. Bünger, op.cit., 4, and especially, Bodde, Age, Youth and Infirmity in the Law of Ch'ing China, 150, 167, n.30.
65. Article 1 which lists the five punishments also specifies the amount of copper needed to redeem each grade of each punishment (Johnson, 55ff). In T'ang law there were no differential tariffs for redemption, and so the old or young paid according to the same scale as those, for example, who had accidentally killed.
66. See further the section on 'collective prosecution' below.
67. This interprets the Chinese text differently from Johnson and Bünger who take the phrase 'entailing the death penalty' as qualifying the other offences, rather than as establishing a separate category. I here follow the explanation given in the 'incorporated commentary' of the Ming code (MLCCFL, 287).
68. Johnson, 176.
69. Cf. Lê Code, 665.
70. For Yüan law see Ratchnevsky, Code des Yüan I, 21f, IV, 21, 288ff; Ch'en, op.cit., 52.
71. Ming 1.21 (MLCCFL, 286), 28.10 (op.cit., 1972); Ch'ing articles 21, 22, 369, Philastre I, 185, 191, II, 656; Boulais, 131ff, 716; Staunton, 23f,

441, Bodde op.cit., 159ff.

72. MLCCFL, 290.
73. Philastre, 186.
74. Philastre I, 185. For special rules introduced under the Ch'ing on killing by young children see Philastre I, 188; Boulais 134; Bodde, op.cit., 162, and for a Ch'ing rule allowing the privilege of redemption only for a first offence see Philastre I, 188f; Boulais, 135; Bodde, op.cit., 162.
75. The statute is translated by Twitchett, Financial Administration under the T'ang Dynasty 212, n.21.
76. Cf. Ratchnevsky, Code des Yüan I, 22 n.5.
77. Philastre I, 185.
78. Philastre I, 188; Boulais, 133; Bodde, op.cit., 161 (and cf. his remarks at 151).
79. Cf. Bodde, op.cit., 151 as against Bünger, Punishment of Lunatics and Negligents, 7f.
80. See in particular Philastre II, 226f; Boulais, 1287-1290, and cf. the remarks of Alabaster, Notes and Commentaries on Chinese Criminal Law, 92ff; Bünger, op.cit., 8; Bodde, op.cit., 151f.
81. See, for example, the table in Boulais, p. 10, and cf. that inserted in Philastre I between p.34-5.
82. Bodde and Morris, Law in Imperial China, 170f, 173.
83. Generally see Johnson, 30; Bunger, op.cit., 6; Bodde, op.cit., 139f.
84. Bodde, op.cit., 140, and cf. Legge, Li Chi I, 66.
85. Biot, Tcheou-li II, 356.
86. Johnson, 178.
87. Johnson, 171 and cf. 169.
88. Johnson, 169, 173.
89. Johnson, 171, 175f, 177.
90. Ratchnevsky, Code des Yüan I, 21.
91. MLCCFL, 287.
92. Op.cit., 290.
93. Op.cit., 289.
94. Op.cit., 295.
95. Philastre I, 187.
96. Op.cit., 139.
97. See also the section on 'collective prosecution' below.
98. Article 28 (Johnson, 162f).
99. Cf. Lê Code, 424, Deloustal, 423 and below at note 131.
100. Johnson, 163.
101. Ming 1.19 MLCCFL, 270; Ch'ing article 19, Philastre I, 172; Boulais, 127; Staunton, 22.
102. MLCCFL, 279; Ch'ing, Philastre I, 114 decree VIII, the Ch'ing version differing from the Ming in that it leaves out any reference to the resources possessed by the woman, perhaps taking this point for granted. For the tariffs see the table in Philastre I, between pp.34-5 and cf. his remarks at 175.
103. Johnson, 58, n.66.
104. MLCCFL, 272-3; Ch'ing, Philastre I, 172-3.

105. Article 26 (Johnson 152f).
106. Johnson, 155 (26.2d).
107. Article 27 (Johnson, 156f).
108. Ming 1.18 (op.cit., 267); Ch'ing article 17, Philastre I, 162; Boulais, 96; Staunton, 20.
109. Boulais, 97.
110. This extension was introduced in 1769 (Boulais, 98).
111. See generally Boulais, 99ff.
112. Johnson, 157.
113. MLCCFL, 267, 268; Ch'ing, Philastre I, 163. See also generally, Ch'ü, Law and Society in Traditional China, 76ff.
114. Cf. the Former Han Legal Treatise (Hulsewé, Remnants of Han law, 341f).
115. Meijer, Introduction of Modern Criminal Law in China, 167.
116. For a general discussion see Johnson, Group Criminal Liability in the T'ang Code.
117. Johnson, 63.
118. Johnson, 64.
119. See article 249.
120. Article 248 (cf. Lê Code, 411; Deloustal, 410).
121. Johnson, 170.
122. Article 248, second part.
123. Johnson, 170.
124. Johnson, 171.
125. See also article 18 (Johnson, 119f) which implies that men aged 80 and over or younger men who are incapacitated are altogether exempt from punishment under the rules of collective punishment, but the generality of the expression has to be read subject to the specific qualification inferable from article 248.
126. Article 251 (cf. Lê Code, 412; Deloustal, 411); but where 100 or more have been induced to participate or actual harm has been done the parents, wife and sons are to be exiled 3000 *li*.
127. Article 232 (cf. Lê Code, 255; Deloustal, 254).
128. Article 259 (cf. Lê Code, 420; Deloustal, 419).
129. In this case younger sons will also presumably accompany the mother.
130. The privilege accorded the wife under the rule does not appear to apply to the more serious case of treason described in note 126.
131. On *ku* poison see De Groot, The Religious System of China V, 826ff; Feng and Shyrock, The Black Magic in China known as *Ku*.
132. Article 268 (cf. Lê Code, 424; Deloustal, 423).
133. Johnson, 163.
134. Johnson, 171 and cf. article 24 at 150.
135. For material on Yüan law see Ratchnevsky, Code des Yüan IV, lff.
136. Generally see Ch'en, Disloyalty to the State in Late Imperial China.
137. Ming 18.1 (MLCCFL, 1299); Ch'ing article 223, Philastre II, 8; Boulais, 1024; Staunton, 269. Ch'ing commentators (Philastre II, 11) regarded the exceptions in favour of adopted children and so on as constituting the height of benevolence or humanity (*jen*).
138. Boulais, 1025, and cf. Philastre II, 13f. The sub-statute was introduced

in 1801 and subsequently revised a number of times.

139. Boulais, 1029 - also introduced in 1801 and subsequently revised.

140. Ming 3.7 (MLCCFL, 498); Ch'ing article 184, Philastre I, 708; Boulais, 904; Staunton, 213.

141. Ming 19.8 (op.cit., 148); Ch'ing article 256, Philastre II, 195; Boulais, 1249; Staunton, 308.

142. Ming 19.10 (op.cit., 1488); Ch'ing article 258, Philastre II, 203; Boulais, 1260-1; Staunton, 310. The previous article in both codes deals with the dismemberment of persons for magical purposes and has a like rule.

143. Boulais, 1253, and cf. Philastre II, 197 decree V. It also contained some other provisions.

144. See also Ch'en, op.cit., 168ff, and cf the observations of Leong and Tao, Village and Town Life in China, 12.

145. Johnson, 183.

146. See above at note 100.

147. Johnson, 170.

148. Philastre II, 9f.

149. Philastre II, 202 and cf. the observations of Staunton, 310n, on collective liability in the *ku* poison case.

150. See in general on amnesties McKnight, The Quality of Mercy, and cf. also Ch'ü, Law and Society in Traditional China, 215f. For the Han see Hulsewé, Remnants of Han Law, 225ff. From amnesties proper one should perhaps distinguish imperial measures which dispensed certain categories of offence from the punishments normally applicable to them. Thus in 782 an edict limited the imposition of the death penalty to the first four of the ten abominations (rebellion, great sedition, treason and contumacy; on them see chapter 8). See Bünger, Quellen zur Rechtsgeschichte der T'ang-Zeit, 166f, and cf. Wallacker, The Poet as Jurist, 526.

151. For the Sung see Eichhorn, Bemerkungen über einige nicht amnestiarbare Verbrechen im Sung-Rechtswesen.

152. Cf. Johnson, 66. For the ten abominations see chapter 8.

153. For disenrollment and dismissal from office see chapter 6.

154. McKnight, op.cit., 60f, does not seem to be correct in his remarks on the distinction drawn within the class of 'contumacy'.

155. Ming 1.16 (MLCCFL, 260); Ch'ing article 15, Philastre I, 156; Boulais, 89; Staunton, 18.

156. See the Ming 'incorporated commentary', op.cit., 762.

157. *K'ang kao* para. 8 (see chapter 1, note 2). Cf. also Biot, Tcheou-li II, 356 for the 'three cases of indulgence'.

6

The Legal Position of Officials

A considerable portion of all the penal codes is concerned with the legal position of officials, where this term is understood to cover not only those involved in the administration of the government at local or capital level, but also persons of high rank, military officials and imperial guardsmen. This study will be concerned only with the legal position of civil officials or other persons of high status, not with military personnel. Not only do the 'Specific Offences' sections of the codes contain numerous articles prescribing punishments for offences committed by officials, but the 'General Principles' sections establish some important rules governing their liability and in particular determining the extent to which they are entitled to preferential treatment. Broadly speaking offences committed by officials were divided into two principal categories 'private' or 'public'. 'Private offences' were those intentionally committed by officials, with a view to obtain some profit or gratify some passion. 'Public offences' were those committed inadvertently or carelessly in the course of administration such as the failure to meet a deadline or the giving of a mistaken decision.[1]

The distinction between 'private' and 'public' offences is central to an understanding of the way the rules determining the extent of an official's liability operated. Generally one can say that in the case of private offences the liability was greater and the availability of special concessions less than in the case of public offences. More particularly this difference can be seen in the level of punishment imposed for an offence, in the operation of the rules imposing collegiate responsibility, and in the extent to which an official, who has committed an offence, might claim privileged treatment. These points will be examined in turn. As a preliminary, however, a short description of the kinds of punishment or sanction to which officials were subject is appropriate.

Although the codes themselves do not distinguish between administrative and criminal punishments, all punishments which they prescribe being criminal, it is useful, for the purpose of exposition, to make this distinction. The reason is that officials are liable, on the one hand, to the ordinary 'five punishments' which may be incurred by any subject of the emperor, and, on the other, to special punishments which relate to the fact of office itself. The former may be designated 'criminal' and the latter as 'administrative' even though both are equally 'criminal' in being prescribed in the penal codes as punishments for offences. Two general points are worth making at the outset. First the Ming/Ch'ing law made greater use of administrative punishments than the T'ang/Sung. Second the availability of administrative punishment in itself already appears as part of the apparatus of privilege and concession afforded an official. An administrative punishment is often prescribed as a commutation of an ordinary criminal punishment, the latter constituting the standard legal response to the commission of an offence.

The only administrative punishments presented in the T'ang code are dismissal from office or disenrollment.[2] Dismissal might take two forms. For certain categories of offence the official was required to resign from both his active duty and honorary offices,[3] though he might keep titles of nobility. After three years he was permitted to resume office with a reduction of two degrees in rank. Among offences entailing this punishment were illicit sexual intercourse, robbery, kidnapping, taking bribes without suberting the law and making music or marrying while his paternal grandparents or parents were in prison on a capital charge.[4] For less serious offences the official was required to resign only from his active duty office and might resume this after one year with a one degree reduction in rank. Examples of offences entailing this kind of resignation are not caring for aged or infirm paternal grandparents or parents, or having a child during the period of mourning (27 months) for parents, or having illicit sexual intercourse with women of one of the 'mean' categories from within the area of his jurisdiction.[5] To Western eyes the admixture of offences entailing dismissal is curious, some being intrinsically reprehensible such as robbery or kidnapping, others being infringements of the code of family behaviour.

More serious was disenrollment. This punishment required the official to lose all his ranks and titles, whether active duty, honorary, titular or noble. Only after six years might a disenrolled official resume office and then with a considerable reduction in rank, the actual reduction varying according to the circumstances.[6] Among offences requiring disenrollment were illicit sexual intercourse, robbery, kidnapping, or taking bribes and subverting the law, all committed by supervisory or custodial officials within the area of their jurisdiction, or other crimes punishable by life exile.[7] It is apparent that the commission of certain crimes by an official within his area of jurisdiction was treated more seriously than the commission of the same crimes outside the area of jurisdiction. In the former case there is disenrollment, in the latter dismissal from active duty and honorary offices.

The Ming and Ch'ing codes also know dismissal and disenrollment as administrative punishments, although the way in which they are regulated differs from that found in the T'ang and Sung codes. Dismissal from office occurs in the context of punishment constituted by demotion. One has to distinguish the following possible punishments: degradation in rank by one or more degrees; retention of office at the same rank but assignment elsewhere; dismissal from existing office but reemployment; and dismissal from office altogether without re-employment.[8] These punishments may be combined; thus both degradation in rank and dismissal from existing office (with re-employment) may be imposed. For especially severe offences such as those involving corruption the official was disenrolled, a punishment entailing reduction to the position of a commoner with loss of all rank and titles. Neither code contains rules providing for the return to office after final dismissal or disenrollment, though it appears that this was often possible.[9]

Some administrative punishments found in the Ming and Ch'ing codes were not present in the T'ang and Sung codes. The Ming code makes considerable use of 'demerits', that is, a note placed on an official's record to the effect that he has committed an offence. A certain number of demerits would entail degrading. Another sanction, mentioned in the Ming code, but more frequently utilised in the Ch'ing, was loss of salary. Depending upon the seriousness of the offence the official forfeited his salary for one or more months. Loss of salary might be combined with other administrative punishments such as degrading.[10]

With regard to the incidence of punishment as it affected officials, one may make the following general points. For many private offences the punishment prescribed for the official would be the same as that for a commoner committing the same offence. In some cases, however, the commission of such an offence would entail a heavier punishment than that incurred by a commoner. Furthermore the seniority of the official might be a factor increasing the severity of the punishment. Three examples may be given, two from T'ang and one from Ch'ing law. The T'ang code by article 283 punished officials in charge of storehouses who stole from them or officials who stole within the area of their jurisdiction two degrees more severely than an ordinary person who stole goods of the same value.[11] The same code by article 146 imposed a punishment on supervisory officials where their relatives begged or borrowed money from persons within the area of their jurisdiction, even though they had no knowledge of the circumstances.[12] Under the Ch'ing code high officials such as censors, viceroys or governors who accepted presents or borrowed money from those subject to their jurisdiction were punished two degrees more severely than junior officials who committed the same offence.[13] What is apparent in these rules is a concern for what one may term the fiduciary aspect of an official's position; hence the greater severity with which offences involving the property or person of those entrusted to his care are treated.

Where the offence committed is a public one the punishment is generally lighter, reflecting the fact that it has been committed through inadvertence, not deliberately. The T'ang, Sung and even Ming codes still imposed in principle a criminal punishment such as beating with the light or heavy stick for these offences, but provided for their redemption. This is most clearly seen in the Ming code which, in the relevant article, specified that the punishment of a beating with the light stick was to be redeemed.[14] On the other hand the Ch'ing code, although taking as its starting point the criminal punishment, provided that an administrative punishment (loss of salary and degradation in rank) was to be substituted.[15] Generally the Ch'ing legislators in the context of public offences placed greater weight on administrative rather than criminal punishments.

More will be said below on the principles determining an official's liability to punishment and the nature of the punishment. For the moment one may consider the set of rules, found in all the traditional penal codes, which imposed, both for public and private offences, a collegiate liability on officials. Essentially the rules allocating liability flow from the way in which the administrative hierarchy was organised and the procedure for the making of decisions.[16] Each administrative unit was in theory composed of four layers of officials who generally may be dominated as the senior officer, the second officers, executive officers and clerical officers. An example may be taken from the commentary to article 40 of the T'ang code.[17] The Supreme Court of Justice in the capital had as senior officer, the president, as second officers the 2 vice-presidents and the revisory judges, as executive officers the 6 assistants, and as chief clerks 28 archivists and 56 secretaries.

Within each unit the decision making was complex. It started at the lowest level, proceeded upwards through successive layers until completed by the senior officer. The division of responsibility was roughly as follows. The clerical officers prepared the detailed documents setting out the facts of the case and the matters calling for decision. These went to the executive officers who might propose that a certain course be taken. Their proposal was considered by the second officer(s) who might reject, alter or affirm it. Their proposal in turn was submitted to the senior officer who took the final decision. Where the unit had a numerous staff (as the T'ang Supreme Court of Justice) not all officials would be involved in every decision. For the purpose of the allocation of responsibility it appears that only those officials who were jointly concerned, that is, had signed the relevant documents, were held liable should the decision turn out to be mistaken.

Administrative units themselves were not free-standing. They occupied a particular place in a hierarchy constituted by the office of the district magistrate at the bottom and the various organs of the central government at the top. Thus a proposed decision might need to proceed from an inferior unit to its superior in the hierarchy for reconsideration and equally, for the purpose of implementation, a decision might be sent down from a higher to a lower unit. Such other units likewise were involved in responsibility should they fail to detect a mistake made by the unit originally responsible for the decision. Even co-ordinate administrative units such as adjacent district or prefectural courts incurred liability should they have been in any way involved in a mistaken decision.

In setting out the rules apportioning liability for wrong decisions one may start with the T'ang code which provided the basis for the subsequent law of the whole imperial period.[18] The code utilises a distinction (that between principal and accessory) drawn from the law dealing with the joint commission of offences such as murder or robbery. Normally the principal is understood to be the person who forms the idea of committing the offence, who takes the lead in planning it, and the accessories are those who adopt his suggestion and help to implement it.[19] However in the context of the collegiate liability of officials a different sense is given to these terms. The principal is defined as the person from whom the mistake originated, whether or not he was aware he was doing something wrong, and the accessories are those who have joined in the mistaken decision, even though they do not know that a mistake has occurred.

The official within the unit who first commits the mistake, the principal, is punished according to the offence which he has committed. For example if he has recommended a wrong sentence in a criminal case he is punished according to the law on wrongful conviction or acquittal.[20] Under the ordinary law an accessory is punished one degree less than the principal. In determining who are the accessories and the order in which they are liable, the law moves up from the level within the unit at which the mistake originated to the top and then down from the originating level to the bottom. Suppose the mistake originated with an official of the executive class. Moving up, one comes to the second officer who constitutes the second degree accessory and is punished one degree less than the executive officer (the principal). Moving up further one comes to the senior officer who is punished, as third degree accessory, one degree less than the second officer. Finally one goes down below the executive officer and comes to the chief clerk who is punished, as fourth degree accessory, one degree less than the senior officer. Where the mistaken decision was sent for approval or examination to a superior or co-ordinate administrative unit and the mistake was not discovered, the officials of the latter unit are collectively punished one degree less than those of the originating unit. Where a mistaken decision is sent down to a lower unit, the members of which fail to discover the mistake, they are collectively punished two degrees less than the officials of the higher unit. In both cases the distinction between principal and accessory is applied.

The rules described above applied where the initial offence was a public one, that is, had been committed inadvertently through an oversight. However it might happen that an official deliberately, for some corrupt reason, gave a wrong decision or contributed wrong information to secure a wrong decision. The official who committed the private offence is naturally liable to the appropriate punishment. But the rules of collegiate responsibility still imposed liability on his colleagues who knew nothing of the offence, the perpetrator, perhaps, having done everything in his power to conceal it. The other officials were held to be liable as though they had made a mistaken decision. Suppose, for example, an executive officer deliberately proposed to his superiors a wrong judgment in a criminal case and this was accepted by the latter who failed to notice that there was anything wrong. The executive officer was punished according to the law on deliberately making a wrongful conviction or acquittal. The other officials associated with the decision at the various levels of the unit were punished as though they had by mistake given a wrongful conviction or acquittal. Since they were accessories an appropriate reduction in the degree of punishment was made. Thus the second officer, in the example, was to be sentenced to the punishment appropriate to the case of giving a mistaken judgment with a reduction of one degree as second accessory. The senior officer, as third accessory, receives a further degree of reduction and the chief clerk, as fourth accessory, also a reduction of one degree.

The range of liability imposed by these rules was potentially so wide that one must query, on practical grounds, the extent to which they were actually enforceable. However, apart from the practical consideration of enforceability, there were built into the system a number of rules providing for a mitigation of the general collegiate liability. Thus where the senior officer himself gave the correct formal decision, even though a mistake had been made at a junior level, there was no liability, because the decision emanating from the unit as a whole was correct. Further where the mistake originated at the level of the second officer or above, those below - the executive officers and chief clerks - were to be exempt from liability. This is an important rule because it safeguards junior officials from liability for the mistakes of their seniors. Where a private offence had been committed the actual offender would still be liable, but those who otherwise would be liable as accessories might be exempt under either of these rules.

Even where a mistake originated with the chief clerk and was subsequently adopted by all officials participating in the decision there might still be exemption from liability. Article 41[21] provides that where anyone of those involved 'becomes aware of and brings out the mistake'[22] all are to be free from liability provided that the mistaken decision has not yet been implemented. This is an important qualification reflecting a principle, elsewhere found in the code, that leniency may be extended where no harm has actually been done. Should the offence have been a private one, uncovered and disclosed by one of the officials associated with the decision, then it seems that all except the actual offender will escape liability.

For one class of public offence the code was less generous. This is 'delay' in the production or copying of official documents or imperial edicts. Where the time specified by the law for producing or copying a document had been exceeded, then should one of the officials - other than the chief clerk - disclose the error all will be exempt from liability except the chief clerk himself. Should it be the chief clerk who discloses the error he and the other officials involved in the matter will be entitled to a reduction in punishment of two degrees. The reason for this exception seems to be that the prime responsibility for the issue of the document within the prescribed time rested with the chief clerk. Because of concern for the general efficiency of the system - entirely dependent upon the production and circulation of documents - and perhaps because the very fact of delay itself created a harm, complete exemption could not be granted. In particular the official primarily responsible for the production or copying of the document (the chief clerk) was not to be excused except, to a limited extent, where he had himself disclosed and brought out the mistake.

These rules are on the whole reproduced in the Ming and Ch'ing codes but there is one important change reflecting what appears to have been a shift in responsibilities within administrative units. In the later dynasties it appears that the officials belonging to the lowest of the four levels - that entrusted with clerical functions - were held to be responsible not only for the actual drafting of documents but also for the accuracy of their content. For example clerks were expected to have the requisite knowledge to prevent errors of law or to uncover them once they had occurred. The general commentary of the Ch'ing code says that the clerk (*li ts'ao*) ought to have knowledge of the penal law, and ought to examine documents in detail to ensure that they are free from errors.[23] Hence in all cases of public offences the Ming and Ch'ing codes stipulate that the principal is to be the clerk involved in the preparation and checking of the document. The second degree accessory is to be his immediate superior, the staff supervisor, the third degree accessory is to be the second officer and the fourth degree accessory is to be the senior officer. Where the offence is a private one the perpetrator is to be punished accordingly and the four classes of official are to be punished as though a mistake had been made, again with the clerk as second accessory.[24]

Other less important changes have been made in the later law. Thus the Ming and Ch'ing codes slightly lessen the liability of inferior or superior units involved in the mistake. Where a superior unit does not notice a mistake in a document sent up from an inferior the collective punishment is to be two degrees less; where an inferior does not pick up a mistake in a document sent down from a superior its collective punishment is to be three degrees less.[25] Furthermore the rules on liability for 'delay' were applied a little differently in Ming/Ch'ing law and there also appear to have been differences between the laws of these dynasties. The 'incorporated commentary' of the Ming code states that where the clerk responsible for the 'delay' himself brought out the mistake he was entitled to a reduction in punishment by two degrees, and the staff supervisor (an official belonging to the third layer in the unit) was entitled to a reduction in punishment of three degrees.[26] The implication is that neither the second nor the senior officer was to be punished. The Ch'ing code makes it clear that in these circumstances only the clerk is to be punished, the officials belonging to the other layers of the unit escaping liability.[27] One also has in this relaxation of the T'ang rules a reflection of the fact that matters concerning the production and accuracy of documents were the responsibility primarily of officials at the clerical level, and should not involve their superiors in liability.

There is almost no discussion in the legal commentaries of the reasons for the rules imposing collegiate liability. The isolated comment one does find is directed at specific instances of liability. Thus the 'incorporated commentary' of the Ming code, in dealing with the position of units superior or inferior to the one from which the mistake originated, remarks that the superior unit is punished for its 'idleness and indifference' in not spotting the mistake, whereas the inferior unit is punished to a lesser degree out of pity for the fact that it is acting on orders received from a superior.[28] One might generalise from the remark on 'idleness and indifference' and argue that the whole complex of rules on liability for public offences (and collegiate liability for private offences) was derived from the wish, on the part of the legislators, to ensure the highest possible standards of administration. Each official should watch not just his own actions but those of his colleagues, in case he should be incriminated on account of another's mistake or, indeed, deliberate wrongdoing.

While some such view might have been held and even offered as a justification of the rules, it is not necessarily the factor that explains the origin of the system. A more basic reason can be found in the perception entertained by the Chinese of administrative duty. It was the duty of an official to carry out his functions in accordance with the law. Should he fail to do so, albeit inadvertently, he had thereby committed an offence. When one considers this point in the light of the administrative procedure under which officials from the four layers within the unit were jointly involved in the taking of a decision, one has the result that all have committed an offence in that they have been parties to a mistaken decision. From this perspective increased efficiency - if in fact achieved - might have been the consequence of the rules, but was not the motive force behind them.[29]

Although officials committed offences - whether private or public -

for which they incurred the punishment established by the code, they had access to a further complex of rules under which certain privileges were conferred. These privileges might relate to the procedure with which the offence was investigated, to the level of the punishment imposed, or to means by which the actual sentence might in some way be commuted. Furthermore such privileges might be available not just to officials or persons of high rank or standing but also to certain categories of their relatives. To modern Western eyes this apparatus of legal privilege is one of the most striking features of the traditional Chinese law. First the rules adopted by the various dynasties all showing an underlying consistency, though with variation in detail - will be discussed, and then something will be said on the reasons for official privilege.

Although the T'ang is the first of the known codes to have presented a fully worked out system of rules regulating the operation of official privilege, elements of the system are found much earlier.[30] The Chinese themselves believed that even the most ancient law knew at least some privilege for those of the highest rank and the greatest worth. The Rites of Chou (*Chou-Li*) which purports to describe the legal and administrative institutions of the Chou empire, includes the 'eight deliberations' in much the same form as they appear in the law of the imperial dynasties. Since the recent archaeological finds have shown that aristocratic rank entailed privilege even in the legalist state of Ch'in after the time of Lord Shang, it is likely that the laws of various states from early Chou times did, by and large, recognise some privilege in favour of those of high rank and standing. Certainly this was so in Han law, although the precise extent of privilege is not clear.[31] According to E Balazs all the penal codes from that of Wei (220-264 A.D.), one of the successor states to the Han, contained the 'eight deliberations'.[32] Not until the T'ang is there sufficient information for a full study of the law to be possible.

The T'ang code contains a number of articles dealing with the privileges accorded those of high rank, officials and their relatives. The rules are complex, making a number of careful distinctions, the general effect of which is that the higher the rank the greater the range of privilege, the smaller the category of excepted offences and the wider the range of relatives entitled to 'protection' (i.e. also placed in a privileged position vis-a-vis the law). Some of the rules made available a special procedure for the investigation and sentencing of offences; others simply permitted a sentence less than that which would normally have been imposed or provided for the total or partial commutation of the punishment. At the heart of the whole system were the 'eight deliberations', possibly representing its most ancient component.

Article 7[33] sets out the classes of person entitled to 'deliberation' and article 8[34] defines the content of the right. The eight classes are in sum relatives of the emperor, long standing personal retainers of the emperor, the morally worthy, those of great talent, those of great achievement, those of high rank, those who have shown exceptional diligence in the service of the state, and the members of former ruling houses. Of these the most important (for practical purposes) are the first and sixth; it is worth looking more closely at the way in which these two classes are defined.

'Imperial relatives' comprises all relatives of the emperor himself within the sixth degree of mourning or closer, all relatives of the emperor's paternal grandmother or mother within the fifth degree of mourning (i.e. those for whom mourning was worn for three months) or closer, and all relatives of the empress within the fourth degree of mourning (i.e. those for whom mourning was worn for five months) or closer. The commentary makes it clear that the relatives meant are predominantly (though not exclusively) patrilineal. If one takes the emperor himself as the focal point of the rules the following pattern emerges. His own relatives constitute the widest circle to whom privilege is extended; they go even beyond the fifth degree of mourning, the limit normally recognised by the code for the existence of rights and duties between relatives. Then come the relatives of the emperor's most important patrilineal female relative (his father's mother) and his most important matrilineal relative (his mother), but they comprise those one degree of mourning closer than his own relatives. Finally there are the emperor's affinal relatives - those acquired through his wife - but comprising only those two degrees of mourning closer than his own relatives.

The class composed of persons of high rank is again carefully defined and subdivided. The most important category is the official on active service, currently in the employment of the government. For such active duty officials there were nine ranks, the first being the highest and the ninth the lowest. Deliberation is allowed to those holding the first, second or third rank. A less important category is that of officials holding only titular rank, not actively employed in government service. Again there were nine ranks, only those holding the first or second being allowed deliberation. Finally there were officials holding honorary rank and various grades of nobles. Only honorary officials or nobles of the first rank were included within this class of privilege.

Article 8 confers two important rights upon those entitled to deliberation, one being procedural the other substantive. For offences entailing capital punishment no proceedings were to be instituted until the emperor had been memorialised for permission. Even after permission to try the case had been given, no sentence could be passed by the court. The record of the case, with a note of the relevant article of the code, was referred to the emperor and his decision awaited. Clearly such a procedure gave those who benefited from it a chance of avoiding the death penalty. A substantive right was conferred by the rule providing that in the case of offences punishable by life exile or less an automatic reduction of punishment by one degree was to be granted. Since, for the purpose of reduction, the three kinds of life exile counted as one, this right meant that any sentence of life exile, except for the cases listed in article 11[35], was reduced to a sentence of penal servitude. However neither of these rights was to be available where the offence fell within the category of the ten abominations.

A wider circle of officials and their relatives was accorded the right of petition. Article 9[36] establishes the following classes: relatives of the wife of the crown prince who are within the third degree of mourning or closer; relatives of all persons entitled to deliberation within the second degree of mourning or closer together with grandsons by sons; active duty or titular officials of the fourth or fifth rank and honorary officials or nobles of the second to fifth rank. To be noted again is the very careful grading of rank and degree of mourning and the way in which the degree and grade established in the article on petition interlock with those established in the article on deliberation.

Those entitled to petition were also given procedural and substantive rights. Although a capital offence could be investigated without prior permission of the emperor, the record of the case stating the circumstances, the fact that the law prescribed death, and the ground of petition was sent to the emperor who thereupon decided the sentence. Such a procedure, as with deliberation, provided an opportunity for the exercise of imperial clemency. For non-capital cases the sentence was automatically to be reduced by one degree, as for deliberation. But the range of offences excluded from the ambit of the privilege is wider than in the case of deliberation. Not only the ten abominations, but joint liability for rebellion or great sedition, homicide, and illicit sexual intercourse, robbery, kidnapping, acceptance of bribes and subverting of the law committed by officials within the area of their jurisdiction are also excepted.

The third right is purely a substantive one, that of reduction of punishment. This is available to yet a wider circle of officials. Article 10[37] provides that officials (active duty, titular or honorary) of the seventh or sixth ranks together with the paternal grandparents, parents, brothers, sisters, wives, sons and grandsons in the male line of all officials or nobles entitled to petition, are, for non-capital offences, to receive a reduction in punishment of one degree. The same exceptions apply as in the case of petition. Finally article 11[38] goes further and allows all those entitled to deliberation, petition or reduction of punishment, together with a further class composed of officials of the ninth or eighth grade and the paternal grandparents, parents, wives, sons or grandsons in the male line of officials entitled to reduction, for non-capital cases to redeem the punishment by payment of copper.

Examination of the structure of articles 9, 10, 11 reveals the following principle. In determining which relatives are to be entitled to 'protection', the legislators have generally enacted that where an official is entitled to a particular category of privilege his relatives (within defined limits) will be entitled to the category immediately below, and further have correlated the number of relatives with the rank of the official from whom they derive protection. The higher the rank the larger the number of relatives to whom the official's 'protection' extends.

A further important procedural right was conferred by article 474.[39] This accorded all those entitled to deliberation, petition or reduction of punishment (but not those entitled merely to redemption), just as the aged, young or infirm, immunity from the application of torture by beating in the trial of offences. Since no exceptions are stated one assumes that the right obtained even in the case of the ten abominations or the other offences excepted from the scope of deliberation, petition or reduction. However it is possible that since these privileges were not available to persons accused of an offence falling within the ten abominations or certain other offences, article 474 should be interpreted in the sense of 'with respect to offences for which there is deliberation, petition or reduction'. The matter is not entirely clear.

Article 11 and the succeeding articles introduce further points respecting official privilege. They define more exactly the circumstances under which an official may claim privilege, specify additional offences in respect of which privilege does not attach, introduce the notion of surrender of office as a means of commutation of sentence and regulate the relationship between surrender of office and redemption as mechanisms of commutation. These points will be taken in turn. Article

15[40] provides that former officials, where they have left office for an acceptable reason such as retirement or ill-health, are still to be entitled to the same privileges they had enjoyed as an official. By article 16[41] limited privilege also attaches with respect to offences committed before, but discovered only after, an individual became an official. In such cases for non-capital crimes redemption by payment of copper is to be allowed, and there is not to be loss of office. Even more generous is a further provision of article 16 allowing officials immunity from punishment where they have committed a public offence punishable by life exile or less and the offence is discovered only after they have left the particular office in which it was committed. According to the commentary, 'the principle involved is that completion of the assignment is considered to be leaving office so that public offences punished by life exile in accordance with this law are exempted from punishment'.[42]

Offences additional to those already listed in the articles on deliberation and petition (8, 9) are withdrawn from the sphere of privilege by articles 11 and 15. Article 11 states that the sentence of life exile in certain cases is to be carried out, the official committing the offence being disenrolled and sent into life exile. These are those regarded as more serious than the ordinary life exile offences. Examples are the accidental killing of a paternal grandparent or parent, or concealing the fact of a parent's death and not mourning.[43] The same article also states that neither reduction of punishment or redemption by payment of copper is to be allowed for certain offences entailing penal servitude. Examples are accidentally killing or wounding a relative of a higher generation or of the same generation but older, for whom mourning is worn for one year or more, robbery committed by men or illicit sexual intercourse committed by women.[44]

Article 15 restricts the category of offences for which relatives of an official can claim 'protection'. Thus there is no privilege where one commits an offence against a relative of a higher generation or of the same generation but older on whose protection one generally relies for privilege; or, interestingly, where one is entitled to 'protection' through a collateral relative and commits an offence against that relative's paternal grandparents or parents; or where one beats or accuses to the court a relative of a higher generation or of the same generation but older for whom mourning is worn for nine months, or a relative of a higher generation for whom mourning is worn for five months.[45] The importance attached to seniority in relationship emerges very clearly from these rules, most strikingly in that which withdraws privilege in the case of the paternal grandparents or parents of a collateral relative but appears to allow it in the case of the relative himself.

Article 17[46] introduces a very important principle of T'ang law, namely the use of office to replace punishment. Whether an official commits a public or a private offence, provided the punishment is life exile or less, it is open to him to surrender one or more of the offices which he holds and thereby cancel or reduce the punishment. The tariff adopted by the article relates the particular rank of the office to the punishment of penal servitude and distinguishes between private and public offences. In the former case one office of fifth rank or above is equivalent to two years of penal servitude, and one office of the ninth to sixth rank to one year of penal servitude. In the latter case the equivalent terms of penal servitude are respectively three years and two years. For the purpose of the calculation the three kinds of life exile are all treated as four years penal servitude. The article prescribes the order in which offices (where more than one is held) are to be surrendered, first the active duty office, then any honorary office, and finally if there still remains uncancelled punishment any further offices held.[47] This avoids the possibility that an official might still retain his highest rank by surrendering lesser ranks.

Surrender of office was used to cancel punishments of penal servitude or life exile as converted into penal servitude. This left unaffected sentences of beating with the light or heavy stick. Even in the case of a sentence of penal servitude it might be the case either that all offices held were insufficient to replace the full sentence or that a single office held was more than sufficient to replace the punishment. It was in these situations that the privilege of redemption by payment of copper was relevant. Where the sentence was purely a beating, or where surrender of all offices still left a portion of the sentence of penal servitude uncancelled, or where the office to be surrendered exceeded the amount of the sentence, the official was permitted to redeem his punishment by payment of copper, and thereby, in the first and third of these cases, retain his office.[48]

As stated so far the rules are straightforward. But there are difficulties in understanding the precise operation of the rules on surrender of office and redemption, especially in the content of offences punished by disenrollment or dismissal. For example it is not, at first sight, clear whether office can be used for a double purpose: that is, can it both be surrendered to cancel a punishment of penal servitude and in addition be the object of resignation or disenrollment?

A consideration of articles 11 and 22 allows one to establish a number of points. It is clear from the terms of article 11 both that the five kinds of life exile there denominated cannot be cancelled through surrender of office or redeemed, and further that an official who commits an offence entailing such punishment is to be disenrolled and sent into exile. Article 11 also lists other offences entailing punishments of exile or penal servitude coupled with disenrollment or dismissal from office where cancellation of punishment through surrender of office (though not necessarily redemption) appears to be excluded. Examples are the deliberate beating (producing disablement) of a relative of a higher generation or of the same generation but older for whom mourning is worn for five months, and theft of goods of sufficient value to yield a punishment of penal servitude. The former offence entails disenrollment with no possibility of surrender of office or redemption. The latter entails dismissal from office but noble rank may be retained and, it seems, the punishment of penal servitude redeemed by payment of copper. The article further specifies offences where not only surrender of office operates to cancel punishment but there is also a limited facility of redemption. Suppose an official accidentally (*kuo shih*) kills or wounds a relative of a higher generation or of the same generation but older for whom he wears mourning for one year or longer where the particular offence entails a punishment of penal servitude. In these circumstances neither disenrollment nor dismissal is required, but he may surrender his offices, retain noble rank and redeem any uncancelled portion of the punishment.[49]

The possibility of redemption requires some additional comment since the article states that for the various offences which it lists there is to be neither reduction in punishment nor redemption. However in a later section of the article an important qualification is introduced. Where the offence entails disenrollment both official and noble rank are to be removed and there is no possibility of redemption. Should the offence entail merely dismissal or permit surrender of office to cancel punishment, noble rank may be retained and redemption allowed.[50] What appears odd, in light of the previous statement in the article precluding redemption, is the fact that redemption now appears to be possible. Is the meaning that copper is paid to permit redemption of the noble rank, leaving the offender to serve the balance of the punishment (if any), or is it that the offender, after surrender of his offices or dismissal from them, may still keep his noble rank and in addition redeem the punishment or any uncancelled portion of it? The normal usage of the phrase 'receive redemption' would suggest the latter interpretation, and this, in fact, is confirmed by the last part of article 22 which explicitly states that redemption is not to be allowed where noble rank is revoked.[51] It follows that the general rule enunciated in article 11 according to which, for the offences specified, there is to be no redemption must be understood as having a very limited scope, or as applying primarily to cases where the offender is not an official.

Article 22 establishes the general rules that are to apply to offences punished by disenrollment or dismissal, excluding those especially considered and enumerated in article 11. It provides that where an official commits an offence entailing disenrollment or dismissal and the punishment prescribed is 'heavy', then both surrender of office and redemption may be used to cancel, reduce or commute the punishment. For example where an official commits an offence for which a punishment of life exile *and* disenrollment is prescribed (there being in this case no reduction by one degree), then, provided it is not one of the offences listed in article 11, he may use such offices as he has to cancel the punishment of exile (equivalent to four years penal servitude) and with respect to any uncancelled portion he may redeem by payment of copper.[52] Thus for such cases of disenrollment or dismissal as are not subject to the special rules of article 11, the offices from which the offender is removed may also serve to cancel or reduce punishment.

Under the Sung the formal rules remained the same and were reproduced in the text of the penal code. However in 1202 some important modifications were introduced in a collection of rules described by Brian McKnight as 'the late Song code'.[53] In the first place the different kinds of privilege were distributed more widely among the whole official class. Thus those entitled to deliberation now included officials of the fifth rank, those entitled to petition officials of the sixth rank and those entitled to a reduction of sentence officials of the eighth rank (held by a very large number of officials). Further the protection accorded the wives of relatives of officials was also extended: the wives of the sons or grandsons (in the male line) of officials of the eighth rank or above were to have the same privileges as their husbands. Finally titles of nobility were to be disregarded in the determination of privilege; only offices involving actual service to the state counted.[54]

Under the Yüan there seems to have been a considerable reduction in the privileges accorded officials. The eight classes of persons entitled to deliberation remained, but the content of the privilege may not have been the same as in T'ang/Sung law. In particular it may not have involved an automatic reduction of one degree in the punishment for non-capital offences.[55] Otherwise the main rule on privilege seems to have been that stated in the Yüan Legal Treatise as follows: 'Every official charged with the government of the people who has committed a light fault of a public nature is permitted to redeem his punishment by a fine'.[56] The implication is that for serious public and all private offences the official was to be punished in accordance with the ordinary law.[57]

The Ming inherited from earlier dynasties the system of official privilege but introduced many changes. The most important were the abolition of the rules granting an automatic reduction of punishment by one degree for non-capital offences and permitting the cancellation of punishment through surrender of office, a remodelling and extension of the scope of redemption and a greater use of administrative punishment (salary fines, demotion or transfer). The eight classes of those entitled to deliberation were retained, with some change in their order, but the first class, that of imperial relatives, had added to it the relatives of the wife of the crown prince of the third degree of mourning or closer. In T'ang law these persons had been entitled only to the privilege of petition. Furthermore the scope of deliberation was extended from capital offences only to all offences other than those falling within the category of the ten abominations. Three memorials were now required, the first requesting imperial permission to take cognisance of the offence, the second to proceed to 'deliberation', that is, undertake the investigation, and the third requesting the imperial determination of the sentence.[58] Thus generally one can say that the privilege of deliberation was considerably strengthened by Ming law.

Petition was also retained but its manner of working altered. Where officials of the fifth or fourth rank committed an offence (whether capital or not) there was to be a petition to the emperor for authority to investigate the offence. In the case of officials of the sixth or lower rank regional inspectors or other appropriate officials might conduct the investigation on their own authority. But in both cases a memorial had to be sent to the throne stating the proposed sentence and requesting the imperial decision. A special rule applied in case of prefectural, sub-prefectural or district officials. Here their immediate superiors were not allowed themselves on their own authority to investigate an alleged offence, but must memorialise the throne for permission. If granted, a second memorial in due course was sent stating the proposed sentence, but this was not to be implemented until an official appointed by the emperor had confirmed its correctness. However in the case of light offences, those punished by a beating with the light stick, a salary fine, receipt of redemption (*shou shu*) or a note placed on the official's record, these special procedures were not to apply.[59] One assumes also, although this is not said explicitly, that the ten abominations were to be excluded from the sphere of privilege.[60]

These rights have all been procedural. In addition a number of substantive rights were available to officials in the form of special punishments. Where the offence was a public one, punishable by a beating with the light stick, then all officials were allowed to redeem the punishment by the form of redemption known as 'receive redemption' (*shou shu*), and no note of the offence was placed on the official's record. Where the public offence entailed a beating with the heavy stick or more serious punishment, a note was to be placed on the official's record, ultimately, at intervals of nine years, to be taken into account in a review of his rank. There is nothing in the article to suggest that receipt of redemption (*shou shu*) was permitted.[61] However the 'incorporated commentary' says that under sub-statutes (*li*) all specific offences, whether public or private, are subject to 'payment of redemption' (*na shu*).[62] There are two kinds of redemption involved here. The first known as *shou shu* was regulated by the articles of the code and allowed in various cases, such as where offences had been committed by the old, young or infirm, or, as here, where a light public offence had been committed by an official. A special tariff applied to this kind of redemption. The second known as *na shu* was available to anyone, whether or not an official, and permitted redemption according to another tariff which itself varied according to whether the offender was wealthy or merely had some resources.[63]

For private offences more serious administrative punishments were prescribed. If the offence entailed a beating of 40 blows with the light stick, a note was to be placed on the record but the official was retained in office. If the punishment was 50 blows the same applied with the difference that the official was transferred to other employment. If the punishment was from 60-90 blows with the heavy stick the official was degraded one or more ranks in proportion to the number of blows and also transferred. For private offences entailing a beating of 100 blows the official was to be dismissed from office altogether.[64] Nothing is said as to the position where more serious offences are committed or as to the possibility of redemption. On these points one assumes that, for private offences punishable by penal servitude or above, the ordinary law was applied and that for all private offences the possibility of redemption by the *na shu* method remained (except where specifically made unredeemable).

Rules for relatives also differ from the T'ang. The paternal grandparents, parents, wife, son or grandson in the male line of those entitled to deliberation are themselves to be entitled to the same procedural privileges.[65] Other close relatives of persons falling within two only of the eight classes of deliberation were given protection. The maternal grandparents, father's brothers and their wives, father's sisters, brothers, sons-in-law and sons of brothers of imperial relatives (whether by blood or marriage) or of meritorious officials, where they committed an offence, might be tried without prior imperial permission, but no sentence could be carried out until the emperor had been memorialised for his decision. The same privilege was accorded to the parents, the wife or the heir (son or grandson) of officials of the 5th or 4th rank. However a number of offences was withdrawn from the scope of protection accorded relatives, namely the ten abominations, collective prosecution for rebellion or great sedition, theft, illicit sexual intercourse, homicide, and receipt of property with subversion of the law.[66]

One or two further differences from T'ang law may be noted. The Ming article on offences committed prior to the taking of office but discovered while the offender is in office is similar to, but not identical with, the corresponding T'ang article. Where it is a question of a public offence committed prior to the taking of office receipt of redemption (*shou shu*) is to be allowed.[67] Where an official occupying a subordinate position commits an offence discovered only after promotion, or where any official commits such an offence while in employment, discovered only after departure from office, the consequence depends upon the gravity of the offence. Where the prescribed punishment was a beating with the light stick, there was to be no liability; where it was a beating with the heavy stick or above, a note of the offence was to be placed on the record.[68] Should dismissal from office be involved there is no further punishment. Further, should the offence involve the concealment of money or grain or the loss of government property, there must be reimbursement. In the case of private offences judgment is to be in accordance with the ordinary law.[69] Finally the Ming article on exemption from torture restricts this privilege to those falling within the eight classes entitled to deliberation.[70]

It appears that prior to the revision of the code in 1725-7 Ch'ing law was broadly the same as that of the Ming.[71] However at that time certain changes were made bearing on the punishments to be incurred by officials who committed public or private offences. Whereas under the Ming and early Ch'ing there had been some scope for the investigation (as distinct from the sentencing) of offences committed by officials without reference to the emperor, this was now reduced. Article 6[72] requires permission to be obtained from the emperor before any offence, whether public or private, committed by an official can be investigated; the only exception, added by the official 'small' commentary, is that where the matter is unimportant.[73] Once permission to investigate had been obtained, a further memorial stating the result had to be submitted. No sentence could be implemented until an affirmative response had been received.[74]

By article 7[75] officials who committed an offence punished by a beating with the light stick were to forfeit a portion of their salary, the amount depending upon the number of blows prescribed for the offence. If the punishment prescribed was that of a beating with the heavy stick, for 60 blows there was again forfeiture of salary but for 70 blows upwards there was a successively severe degrading in rank, though the official was to keep his employment. At 100 blows he was to be both degraded and transferred. Article 8[76] established the same kind of punishments for private offences punishable by a beating with the light or heavy stick, but the degree of punishment was more severe. For example should the offence entail a beating of 100 blows the official was to be degraded and dismissed from office.

Article 12[77] also modified the Ming rules on the position of officials who have committed offences prior to the employment. Where a public offence was discovered after the official had obtained office, then irrespective of whether the punishment was a beating, penal servitude or exile, redemption was to be allowed. The term used for redemption here is *na shu*, expressing the position obtaining under the general law by which most offences might be redeemed according to a certain tariff by those with at least some resource.[78] Where an official in employment commits a public offence, punishable by a beating of 90 blows or less, which is discovered after he has been promoted or has left office, he is to be punished by forfeiture of salary or degradation in rank according to the scale prescribe by article 7. At 100 blows or above he is to be sentenced in accordance with the code. Otherwise the article reproduces the Ming rules.

Certain other points, suggested by Thomas Metzger's full discussion, may be made with respect to Ch'ing law and practice. Throughout the period there appears to have been a reluctance to allow officials to benefit from the full extent of the privileges accorded by the code, and a desire to see that bad officials were in fact appropriately punished. Two facts suggest that there is some substance in this hypothesis. The Yung-cheng emperor, responsible for the 1725-7 revision of the code, only permitted the retention of the right to deliberation with considerable hesitation. He affirmed that prior to his reign the articles of the code conferring it had never in fact been used by the dynasty, and indeed did not accord with the ideal of equality before the law.[79] Further, cases decided by the Board of Punishments involving serious offences by officials show that frequently no exemption from, or reduction or commutation of, the punishment prescribed by the code was allowed.[80]

On the other hand in the case of public offences greater leniency was allowed. The punishments prescribed by the code and applied through the Board of Punishments were in practice displaced by the system of administrative sanctions falling within the jurisdiction of the Board of Civil Office. Thus where a magistrate in a case decided around 1826 had given a mistaken judicial sentence entailing under the code a punishment of two years penal servitude and 80 blows with the heavy stick, the Board of Punishments refused to impose the punishment and handed the case to the Board of Civil Office for the imposition of administrative punishment. The normal practice appears to have been for all cases of public offence - unless they were particularly grave - to have been handled by the Board of Civil Office.[81] It was also possible for public offences to be 'cancelled' by an appropriate number of notes of merit entered on an official's record, a kind of commutation that was abolished for private offences in 1768.[82].

Imperial policy on the question of what privileges of redemption should be allowed officials fluctuated during the Ch'ing. The matter is complex, but generally one can say that the early Ch'ing took a more generous approach than the late Ch'ing.[83] The first edition of the Ch'ing code incorporated a sub-statute from the Ming code.[84] This not only made available to officials the possibility of redemption for all offences short of serious capital ones, but actually required them to redeem their sentences of beating, penal servitude, exile or death (imposed for less serious capital offences). However the position reflected in this sub-statute was changed during the course of the 18th century and especially in the 19th century. The late 19th century edition of the Ch'ing code contains sub-statutes dating from 1801 which severely limit the scope of redemption. One authorises the payment of redemption (*na shu*) for trivial offences punished with a beating of the light or heavy stick, although where the official is dismissed from office, neither the beating nor the redemption payment is to be imposed. Where the offence entails penal servitude, exile or death the punishment is to be implemented.[85] Another reaffirms these rules but adds that in cases of offences entailing penal servitude or exile the offender may request the throne for permission to redeem the sentence.[86] However it is stated that such redemption would never be permitted in cases where the offender had corruptly made a profit.

When one seeks to uncover the reasons for the procedural and substantive rights accorded officials, one is to some extent entering the realm of speculation. The orthodox Confucian position appears to be simple. The *li*, the moral code, enjoined that physical punishments should not be inflicted on those holding high office.[87] Of course this precept was not always honoured in practice, but it probably had, at least at times, some influence in moderating both the harshness of the punishments inflicted upon officials and the degree of public humiliation to which they were exposed.[88] But what were the reasons for the adoption of such a standpoint? The clearest expression I have seen is contained in a memorial submitted by the great Han scholar Chia I in 176 B.C.[89] Pointing to the proximity of high officials to the throne, Chia I argued that ill-treatment inflicted upon them not only manifested disrespect to the emperor but might also be damaging to the standing of the throne. He also advanced the moral consideration that true gentlemen (of whom ministers of the emperor were examples) should govern their conduct by a sense of shame, not out of regard for possible punishment, and the pragmatic consideration that people respond better to good treatment than to bad.[90]

One or two of these points are echoed in the commentaries of the Ch'ing code which occasionally refer to the respect with which people of high standing should be treated, the leniency which the moral code (*li*) required to be shown, and even to the concept of pity.[91] At the same time not all Confucian rulers shared this viewpoint. As has already been noted the Yung-cheng emperor regarded the retention of the eight deliberations as contrary to an ideal of fair and equal treatment. Not only did he think that officials should not be privileged, but that, being models for others, any misconduct on their part was especially reprehensible. Ch'ing practice, at least in the later period, also tended to be sparing in its accord of privileged treatment. Thus, at a very general level, one may say that the reasons stated by Chia I were given less credence in Ch'ing times; the attention accorded them probably varied throughout the history of the great imperial dynasties.

Some modern scholars have explicitly or implicitly discounted the relevance of the Confucian dictum excluding high officials from harsh punishment. H.G. Creel, in stressing the cruel treatment even of high officials in the pre-imperial period, remarks 'The controversial passage in the Book of Rites was thus no doubt written by some official as an expression of hope'.[92] He also suggests that since the holding of high office in Han times entailed considerable risk to the holder, there was a strong element of self interest in the support by officials of a doctrine advocating privileged treatment.[93] Brian McKnight in his study of official privilege under the Sung[94] stresses the relationship between political power and privilege in T'ang and Sung times. The implication of his analysis is that the class wielding political power under the emperor simply did what it could to secure privileged treatment for itself.[95]

To the above suggestions one may add a reflection on the sense of shame by which, according to Chia I, the true gentleman should regulate his conduct. Should the true gentleman not behave in accordance with the standards of proper conduct, the shame he experiences is in itself a punishment. Where an official misconducts himself to such an extent that he is dismissed or demoted the shame and humiliation, apart from other adverse consequences (social and financial), already constitute a severe punishment. In many cases - not perhaps all - it might legitimately be regarded as unjust to inflict additional punishment upon the official in the form of one or more of the five standard punishments. Some such thought may underly the T'ang rules on cancellation of punishment by surrender of office and the Ch'ing preference for purely administrative sanctions (dismissal, demotion and salary fines) in the case of less serious offences.

Notes

1. A note in the T'ang code defines 'public offences' as those 'connected with public matters which do not involve secret crookedness', and the *shu-i* commentary defines 'private offences' as those 'committed in a private capacity which have no connection with public affairs. Even though connected with public affairs, if the motive is prejudiced or partial, it is considered to be a private offence' (Johnson, 113). The general commentary of the Ch'ing code says 'une faute publique est une faute commise sans intention et sans aucun mobile privé' (Philastre I, 226), and further says 'L'erreur en affaires publiques ne peut pas, par la nature même, provenir d'une idée d'intérêt privé et elle ne dépasse pas les limites d'une faute d'attention' (op.cit., 230). On the other hand a private offence occurs where 'un seul ait agi dans un but privé, soit à cause d'un relation de parenté soit à cause d'un sentiment d'inimitié soit par corruption, soit pour écouter des suggestions' (op.cit., 226).
2. See below for the different notion of 'surrender' of office.
3. See Johnson, 25.
4. Article 19 (Johnson, 27ff, and cf. also article 21.2 at 136).

5. Article 20 (Johnson, 129f, and cf. also article 21.3a at 136f).

6. Article 21 (Johnson, 133f).

7. Article 18 (Johnson, 119f).

8. Slightly simplified. Cf. Metzger, Internal Organization of Ch'ing Bureaucracy, 300.

9. See generally Metzger, op.cit., 314ff.

10. See generally Ming 1.7, 8, 14 (MLCCFL, 215, 218, 256); Ch'ing article 7 (Philastre I, 138; Boulais, 70; Staunton, 10), 8 (Philastre I, 139; Boulais 71; Staunton, 11), 13 (Philastre I, 149; Boulais, 78; Staunton, 16). See also Metzger, op.cit., 273 n.84.

11. Cf. Lê Code, 437; Deloustal 436. The matter was handled differently in Ming (18.11, MLCCFL, 1330) and Ch'ing law (article 233, Philastre II, 36; Boulais, 1051; Staunton, 277).

12. In Ming/Ch'ing law he was not punished in such a case. Cf. Philastre II, 464; Boulais, 1545; Staunton, 388.

13. Boulais, 1546; Staunton 388.

14. Ming 1.7 (above note 10). See also below at notes 61, 62.

15. Ch'ing article 7 (above note 10), and cf. the remarks of Metzger, op.cit., 274f.

16. See generally Bünger, Über die Verantwortlichkeit der Beamten nach klassischen chinesischem Recht, and MacCormack, Liability of Officials under the T'ang code.

17. Johnson, 216; MacCormack, op.cit., 150.

18. See especially article 40 (Johnson, 216), and the literature cited note 16.

19. See article 42 (Johnson, 255).

20. See chapter 4, 91f.

21. Johnson, 222.

22. The *shu-i* (Johnson, 222) distinguishes this from 'confessing' but the Ch'ing commentaries equate the position of the official bringing out the mistake to that of a relative who confesses on behalf of another (Philastre I, 231).

23. Philastre I, 226, II, 672.

24. Ming 1.26 (MLCCFL, 323); Ch'ing article 27, Philastre I, 225; Staunton, 30.

25. Cited previous note.

26. MLCCFL, 329.

27. Article 28, Philastre I, 230; Staunton, 31.

28. Op.cit., 376.

29. For further discussion see MacCormack, op.cit., 160f.

30. See generally Ch'ü, Law and Society in Traditional China, 170ff.

31. Cf. Hulsewé, Remnants of Han Law, 285ff, arguing that only a very few imperial relatives actually benefited, and Balazs, Traité juridique du 'souei-chou', 145 n.185, suggesting a rather wider range.

32. id.

33. Johnson, 83.

34. Johnson, 88.

35. See below.

36. Johnson, 89f.

37. Johnson, 92f.
38. Johnson, 93ff.
39. Cf. Lê Code 665; Deloustal, 664.
40. Johnson, 104f.
41. Johnson, 108.
42. Johnson, 111.
43. Johnson, 94f.
44. Johnson, 97f.
45. Johnson, 106ff.
46. Johnson, 112ff.
47. This refers to offices previously held at an earlier stage of the official's career (article 17.5, Johnson, 118).
48. Article 22 (Johnson, 141ff and cf. article 21, 139f).
49. Johnson, 97f.
50. Johnson, 98f.
51. Johnson, 143.
52. id.
53. Song Legal Privileges, 96 and n.4.
54. See generally McKnight, op.cit.
55. Cf. Ratchnevsky, Code des Yüan I, 17f.
56. Ratchnevsky, op.cit., 20.
57. Cf. also the remarks of McKnight, op.cit., 103; Ch'en, Chinese Legal Tradition under the Mongols, 57f.
58. Ming 1.3, 4 (MLCCFL, 187f).
59. Ming 1.5 (op.cit., 199).
60. This again is more generous than under the T'ang where a larger number of offences was excluded (see above).
61. Ming 1.7 (cited note 10).
62. Op.cit., 217.
63. See chapter 5, 107f.
64. Ming 1.8 (cited note 10).
65. In T'ang law they would have been entitled only to petition.
66. Ming 1.9 (MLCCFL, 224).
67. 'Public offence' means one committed inadvertently in the course of exercising official functions; the T'ang article simply spoke of offences punished by life exile or less.
68. Although nothing is said about redemption, this would be available under the *na shu* tariff.
69. Ming 1.13 (op.cit., 252).
70. Ming 28.10 (op.cit., 1972).
71. Generally for the Ch'ing see Metzger, Internal Organization of Ch'ing Bureaucracy, chapter IV.
72. Philastre I, 135; Boulais, 63; Staunton, 9.
73. Philastre I, 137 comments on this: '...il ne s'agit que des fautes graves, c'est-à-dire de toutes celles qui sont prévues dans le code et entraînent une peine; les fautes légères dont il est question sont les petites irrégularités, négligences, ou erreurs qui peuvent être commises dans le service, et pour lesquelles les fonctionnaires supérieurs peuvent demander

directement des explications aux délinquants ou leur adresser leurs observations; ces dernières fautes sont punies administrativement d'après les règlements des ministères. Voila dù moins comment ce passage est généralement interprété en Cochin-chine, et l'explication paraît rationelle'. Cf. the Ming rule above.

74. Cf. the remarks of Metzger, op.cit., 298f.
75. Philastre I, 138; Boulais, 70; Staunton, 10.
76. Philastre I, 139; Boulais, 71; Staunton, 11.
77. Philastre I, 148; Boulais, 77; Staunton, 15.
78. Cf. generally Philastre I, 112 ('verser le rachat'), 118.
79. See McKnight, Song Legal Privileges, 103; Metzger, op.cit., 85f.
80. Bodde and Morris, Law in Imperial China, 169; Metzger, op.cit., 306.
81. Metzger, 311f.
82. See Boulais, 69; Metzger, 303, 313.
83. See especially Metzger, 304ff.
84. MLCCFL, 182; Metzger, 304. For details on the highly complicated Ming position see Munzel, Strafrecht im altem China, 58f, 116f.
85. Boulais, 37; Philastre I, 112 decree I.
86. Metzger, 306, notes that the relatively light tariff provided by the *na shu* scale for those with resources was no longer available, and Boulais, p.25, n.5, observes that where extenuating circumstances were present the emperor might consent to accept a 'gift to the treasury' (according to a very high tariff) in lieu of punishment.
87. See chapter 2, 31f.
88. One knows of course that there were still many cases of severe and humiliating punishments imposed on officials, especially for offences against the emperor.
89. Hulsewé, Remnants of Han Law, 287f.
90. This was very much a Confucian, not a legalist perception.
91. Philastre I, 120f, 131, II, 656.
92. Legal Institutions and Procedures during the Chou Dynasty, 39.
93. Op.cit., 52, n.65.
94. Song Legal Privileges.
95. Cf. also the remarks of Hulsewé op.cit., 294.

7

Confession, Mutual Concealment and Accusation

Complex rules on these matters are found in all the main dynastic codes. They provide (i) that a person who confesses that he has committed an offence, before that offence has come to light, is to be pardoned, (ii) that persons who 'conceal' offences committed by their relatives or help them to escape the consequences of their illegal acts are to be exempt from punishment, and (iii) that persons who accuse their relatives of having committed offences, whether the accusation is true or false, themselves commit an offence. The details of these rules, including the qualifications to which they are subject, will be set out below.

The three sets of rules are found in different articles of the codes, and also in different sections, confession and mutual concealment being treated in the General Principles and accusations in the Specific Offences part. Despite this spatial separation the rules interlock in the sense that the operation of any one set cannot be understood without reference to the other two sets. One reason for the interest of the rules is the light they throw upon legislative technique. Three core notions, confession, concealment and accusation, form the subtratum of a highly complex and wide ranging network of legal consequences. The rules are a good example of the technique of 'economy of means' used by the legislators.

Another, perhaps more compelling, reason for interest is the insight provided by the rules into the moral and social values which the codes were intended to implement. The two main moral values which the rules enshrine are those of personal recognition of fault together with repentance, and the obligation of help and mutual support imposed by relationships of kinship and marriage. The main social value, which indeed qualifies the effect given by the law to the moral values, is the preservation of the state and the emperor from harm. The latter was given priority by the codes in that the protection (immunity from prosecution) afforded individuals through the rules on confession and concealment was not extended to cases in which the offence threatened the emperor or the state. More is said on these points below.

The rules appear fully fledged in the T'ang code but hints and precedents can be found in earlier dynasties. For the Spring and Autumn period one has evidence supplied by the anecdote of the father who stole a sheep.[1] From this it appears that at least some states knew a rule under which a son who accused his father of theft himself committed a crime punished by death. In this case the value of filial piety was preferred to that of loyalty to the ruler. The existence of such a rule implies the existence of a further rule, namely that the son should 'conceal' and not divulge the offence of his father. What is not clear is the extent to which the actual penal rules of any given state incorporated either or both of these rules. Certainly the Confucian and probably also the pre-Confucian ethic emphasised the duty of the son to protect his father and shield him from the consequences of his wrong doing.[2] A passage in the *K'ang kao* has sometimes been cited as the ultimate source, or perhaps inspiration, of the legal rules on confession,[3] but it is by no means clear that it deals with confession at all.[4] Nevertheless one can accept that acknowledgement of guilt and genuine repentance may in practice, from a very early period, have led to exemption from, or mitigation of, punishment.

Rules relating to confession, concealment and accusation of relatives were all known to the codes of the Han dynasty although there is difficulty in determining the date at which they were introduced and their exact content. From an account in the *Shih chih*[5] and the *Han shu*[6] it appears that in 122 B.C. the code contained a clause pardoning those who voluntarily acknowledged their crimes. Although the account in question states that a prince who confessed to planning with others a revolt was exempted from punishment under this clause, one cannot be sure of its exact content.[7] On the other hand there do not apppear at this time to have been firm rules on concealment or the accusation of relatives. The precise position is difficult to determine. The account already mentioned records that a prince was executed in 122 B.C. for informing against his father.[8] Yet in the record of the debates of the literati held in 81 B.C. there is a passage which suggests that at that date the law contained a rule punishing as accomplices those who took the lead in hiding a criminal. From the context one gathers that a father or son might be liable under this law for concealing each other's crimes even though it was recognised as a moral principle that each should 'screen' the other.[9]

The historical development of the rules on concealment and accusation is uncertain. Still it remains likely that for more than a century the Han dynasty produced no clear rules on the entitlement of relatives to concealment. This is shown by the fact that an important innovation was made in 66 B.C. by edict of the emperor Hsüan.[10] This law provided that sons, grandsons or wives who took the lead in hiding their parents, grandparents or husbands committed no offence. In capital cases should a grandparent, parent or husband hide a grandson, son or husband, the matter was to be referred to the throne for special consideration. The benefit of this edict applied only to the classes of relatives mentioned. An incident is reported by the *Han shu* for 55 B.C. A marquis was disposed from his fief for concealing his brother-in-law whom he knew had committed an offence.[11]

For the unsettled period from the end of the Han until the beginning of the Sui and T'ang dynasties one has some fragments of evidence. The most interesting is from the Eastern Tsin dynasty (317-419 A.D.). This is a memorial to the throne in 317 A.D. which condemns the practices of punishing the son on behalf of the father, or torturing parents to ascertain the whereabouts of the son, or beheading the senior member where a family has absconded, or punishing grandparents or parents on account of offences committed by absconding grandsons or sons. The argument is made that if the principles of mutual concealment are destroyed, the proper relationship between a ruler and his subjects is also destroyed.[12] Some of the offences for which parents or grandparents were punished on behalf of their sons or grandsons or vice-versa may have been rebellion or treason to which the protection of the rules of concealment was not extended. Yet the language of the memorial is sufficiently broad for it to be probable that other offences also were meant. Hence one can see that mutual concealment, although no doubt always a subject of moral injunction, did not invariably form a part of the law of the dynasties that intervened between the Han and the T'ang. It has been argued that the T'ang rules on confession can be identified in the law current at the beginning of the Western Tsin dynasty (265 A.D.)[13] In fact while again one can detect evidence of the moral value ascribed to confession and to the fact that it might entail forgiveness or a mitigation of punishment, it is by no means certain that the penal code of the Western Tsin contained rules similar to those of the T'ang.

Although the exact course of the development of the legal rules on confession, mutual concealment and accusation of relatives prior to the T'ang cannot be reconstructed, one can say that rules on these matters appeared in at least some of the codes of the preceding dynasties. But no fully worked out set of interlocking rules is evidenced prior to the Sui/T'ang code. The investigation will therefore start with the rules in the T'ang code and from there proceed to consider the changes effected by the codes of the later dynasties. The general rule on confession is stated in article 37.[14] Where a person who has committed an offence confesses before it has come to light, in principle - subject to various qualifications - he is to receive pardon for his offence. The commentary by way of explanation states 'To have faults and not to correct them, this is indeed a fault'.[15] What is meant is that genuine repentance and recognition of error coupled with a desire to reform are the important matters; should they be manifest there is no need for legal punishment.

A sub-section of article 37 deals with the case where one person confesses on behalf of another and links confession with the rules on mutual concealment and accusation.[16] The exact interpretation of the clause presents difficulty.[17] On the interpretation adopted here the article first puts a general case in which someone is sent to confess on behalf of another and then introduces two specific cases in which, although the person to obtain the benefit does not send the person making the confession, the relationship between the two is such (in virtue of the law of mutual concealment) that where one confesses for the other or both accuse each other, the law can attribute the same result to the confession or accusation. One may then distinguish the following three cases (i) A sends B to confess on his behalf, (ii) a person confesses on behalf of a relative whose offence he is entitled conceal, and (iii) relatives who are entitled to conceal each other's offences proffer mutual accusations. In each case the position is to be treated as though the offender had himself confessed.

The commentary to the article adds one or two further details, though again there have been differences of opinion over its interpretation. It illustrates the statement on the sending of someone to confess with the following example. Suppose A commits an offence and sends B on his behalf to confess, then, irrespective of whether B is a close or distant relative,[18] this is the same as A himself confessing. The statement concerning those entitled to mutual concealment is explained by reference to the article permitting mutual concealment to those who live together or relatives standing in a mourning relationship of nine months or closer.[19] There then follows an illustration of a different relationship of concealment, namely that between personal retainers or slaves and their master. A confession of the former on the part of the latter is treated as though the master had himself confessed.[20] The statement in the article concerning mutual accusations is explained as referring to situations still based on mutual concealment. What appears to be meant is that the mutual accusations in question are brought only by those relatives who stand in a relationship of mutual concealment.[21]

Finally the commentary introduces a special rule for relatives standing in a five or three months relationship of mourning. This rule again is taken from the article on mutual concealment which provides that where such relatives conceal each other's offences they are punished three degrees less than would be a person who concealed the offence of an unrelated person. Where a relative of this kind confesses on behalf of another the latter is also entitled to a reduction in punishment of three degrees.

There is one particularly important factor which limits the degree of exemption to be obtained through confession. This is what may be called the principle of the restoration of the *status quo*. Where goods have been taken they are still to be restored, and where physical injury has been inflicted the offender, despite confession, is still to be sentenced.

To understand the rules providing for confession on behalf of a relative one has to look at those on mutual concealment set out in article 46 which allows the following classes of person to conceal each other's offences.[22]

(i) those who live together, whether or not there is a relationship of mourning between them,

(ii) close patrilineal relatives, that is, those standing in a relationship of 9 months mourning or closer, even though they live apart,

(iii) one category of matrilineal relatives, namely, maternal grandparents and grandchildren

(iv) certain categories of affinal relatives, namely wives of grandsons and grandparents, husband's brothers and sisters-in-law, and brother's wives and brothers-in-law,[23]

(v) slaves on behalf of masters but not vice versa.

Relatives who stand in a five or three month relationship of mourning to those whose offences they conceal are not exempt from punishment but are entitled to a reduction of punishment by three degrees below that appropriate for a person who conceals the offence of an unrelated person. Someone who informs a relative that he is being sought by the authorities or actively assists him to escape their pursuit is also declared to be exempt from liability. An important exception to the protection given by the rules of mutual concealment is constituted by the offences of plotting rebellion, plotting great sedition and plotting treason.[24]

Thus the general position is that where a relative entitled to conceal does so he is exempt from punishment. The normal rule for unrelated persons was that to hide a criminal knowing of his offence or help him to escape justice entailed punishment one degree less than the punishment prescribed for the offence committed by the person helped (article 468).[25] However the relative whose offence was concealed was not treated as though he had confessed. Should he be subsequently caught he would be sentenced in accordance with the code.

'Mutual concealment' should be analysed in terms both of rights and duties and of privileges. A relative of the prescribed category has not merely a privilege that his offence be concealed in the sense of not being disclosed but a right. Conversely the relative aware of the offence is under a duty not to divulge it. However the active taking of steps to conceal an offence or give shelter to a fugitive is not a right that can be demanded, merely a privilege. The law does not compel a relative actively to give assistance to an offender, but nor does it punish him should he choose to do so. The duty to conceal an offence is made legally enforceable through the law relating to accusations.

Although the details of the law are complicated the general position with respect to accusations may be represented as follows. Subjects of the emperor were under a duty to report to the authorities those whom they knew to be engaged in rebellion, great sedition or treason. Failure to report entailed a heavy punishment, in some cases capital.[26] With respect to other offences there was no duty to inform, although persons might be encouraged to give information through the offer of rewards. However anonymous accusations were prohibited; if sent in they were to be disregarded and the accuser, if discovered, was liable to a heavy punishment.[27] When a person knowingly made a false accusation he was in principle to suffer the same punishment as that prescribed for the offence of which accusation was made,[28] though true accusations might be made with impunity.

These general rules were modified in their application to accusations made by one relative against another. In considering these rules one needs to distinguish the position where the accusation was true from that where it was known to be false. First may be taken the case in which the accusation is true.[29] Contrary to the position that obtained where the parties were unrelated, the making of a true accusation against a relative in itself normally constituted an offence. The seriousness of the offence and hence the severity of the punishment varied according to the exact relationship of the parties and in particular according to whether the accuser was a 'senior' or a 'junior' relative of the person accused. By 'senior' is meant a relative of a higher generation or of the same generation but older, and by 'junior' a relative of a lower generation or of the same generation but younger. Thus a son or grandson who accused a parent or paternal grandparent of an offence, even though the accusation was true, himself committed an offence entailing capital punishment. On the other hand a paternal grandparent or parent who accused a grandson or son of an offence which the latter had committed was not liable. In their case one can say that there was no legally enforceable duty to conceal the offence.

Where a 'junior' relative accused a 'senior' to whom he stood in a one year mourning relationship the punishment was a minimum of two years penal servitude. When the accuser was the 'senior' relative the punishment was only a beating of 60 blows with the heavy stick. These are just examples; there are rules covering every degree of relationship. The relative accused is to be treated as though he had himself confessed; the rule on confession is applied to his offence and he may consequently (depending on the nature of the offence) escape all liability.

There is one important class of exceptions to the rule prohibiting accusations between relatives. In the case of the most serious offences against the state or emperor the prohibition does not apply and indeed a person commits an offence if he fails to accuse a relative who has committed any of these offences, namely, plotting rebellion, great sedition, plotting great sedition, treason or plotting treason. Of these five, three attracted 'collective' or 'joint' liability, that is, entailed the liability of innocent relatives together with the actual offender. These were plotting rebellion, great sedition and treason. Accusation of a relative of such offences, if true, entailed his conviction in accordance with the code, but those relatives who would normally be liable with him are treated as though they had themselves confessed and so escape liability.

One other exception to the rule prohibiting accusations should also be noted. Relatives entitled to conceal each other's offences may lawfully accuse each other of physical injury or wrongful taking of property. In such a case the accuser is not punished; nor is the accused treated as though he had himself confessed. Nor are accusations of this kind within that section of the code which applies the rule on confession to relatives (entitled to mutual concealment) who accuse each other of offences.

Where the accusation is false the ordinary rules are modified. 'False' refers to an accusation known to be false and made out of enmity.[30] The general rule is that the person making the false accusation is to receive the punishment prescribed for the offence which he alleges has been committed.³¹ This is subject to qualification where the parties are related, the punishment being heavier for false accusations of 'senior' than of 'junior' relatives. Thus any accusation (not falling within the limited class of exceptions) of a paternal grandparent or parent (whether true or false) entails the punishment of strangulation. When a 'senior' relative for whom mourning is worn for one year is falsely accused, the minimum sentence is two years penal servitude (that prescribed for a true accusation). But where the accusation is 'serious' the punishment is increased by three degrees. This is explained by the commentary to article 346 as meaning that where an increase of three degrees would raise the punishment of the offence falsely accused above two years penal servitude, the increase is to be applied. For example where the offence attracts a punishment of 1 1/2 years penal servitude an increase of three degrees raises it to 3 years penal servitude; this is then to be the punishment imposed on the relative making the false accusation. A similar principle is applied in the case of false accusations directed against other 'senior' relatives for whom mourning is worn for nine, five or three months, but in these cases the applicable increase is only one degree.

Article 347 applies a similar principle to false accusations of 'junior' relatives. First one may note that paternal grandparents or parents who bring false accusations against their grandsons (whether in the male line or not) or sons are not punished. False accusations against a 'junior' for whom mourning is worn for one year attract a minimum punishment. of 60 blows with the heavy stick (that prescribed for true accusations). Where the punishment of the offence falsely accused is heavier than this, a reduction in punishment of two degrees is made (provided it would not reduce the punishment below 60 blows). Thus if the offence falsely accused attracts a punishment of 90 blows with the heavy stick, the punishment actually imposed on the 'senior' relative who makes the false accusation is 70 blows. For 'junior' relatives for whom mourning is worn for 9 months the applicable reduction is one degree, but for other 'juniors' (for whom five or three months mourning is worn) the punishment is the same as that which would be imposed for the false accusation of an unrelated person.

Two particular problems in the interpretation of the T'ang rules may be instanced. The first, concerning the position of relatives standing in a mourning relationship of 5-3 months, is an example of illogicality. Here there is no proper relationship of mutual concealment, although a relative of this kind who conceals an offence is entitled to a reduction of punishment by three degrees, and a similar reduction is accorded the relative who committed an offence where confession is made on his behalf. However according to the *shu-i* commentary a relative of this kind who is *accused* is not treated as though he had himself confessed (article 346). It thus seems that he is to be sentenced for the offence without any reduction in punishment. This creates an anomaly since under the rules on accusations the person who accuses a relative for whom he wears mourning for five or three months himself commits an offence entailing punishment. Logically one would have expected the relative accused to be in the same position as though confession had been made on his behalf, that is, that he would have been entitled to a reduction in punishment by three degrees. The fact that he was not shows that there was an important difference between an *accusation* of a person and a *confession* made on his behalf, though it is not easy to know how the one was distinguished from the other.

The second problem is one of interpretation. A note inserted in the article on confession states (a propos of a special case) the general rule that where a year of mourning relative is accused of one of the offences against the state, ranging from plotting treason up to plotting rebellion, he is to be treated as though he had confessed. This seems to conflict with the law as stated in the context of mutual concealment, namely that that benefit does not obtain in the case of these offences against the state. There are two ways in which the note may be understood.

From the statement of the position where a son or grandson accuses a parent or paternal grandparent of plotting rebellion etc. one knows that those jointly liable are to be treated as though they had themselves confessed. Hence the note on year of mourning relatives may simply mean that in the cases of plotting rebellion, actual sedition, or treason those who would be collectively prosecuted - other than the offender himself - would escape liability, but the offender would still be sentenced in accordance with the code. On this interpretation the inclusion of plotting great sedition or plotting treason in the list of offences specified in the note would be redundant, since in these cases no joint liability or collective prosecution obtained.

For the second interpretation two assumptions have to be made: (i) that a relative might be entitled to the benefit of the rules on confession even though the offence of which he was accused was not within the ambit of mutual concealment, and (ii) that anyone who confessed at least to plotting great sedition or plotting treason,[32] where nothing had been done in furtherance of the plot, was entitled to exemption. On the basis of these assumptions the note may be explained as meaning that year of mourning relatives can be treated as though they had themselves confessed, in the sense that they are exempt from liability in cases of plotting great sedition or plotting treason. Some support for this interpretation may be gathered from a further section of the article on confession which specifies for the case of treason, where matters had progressed beyond the mere plot, a reduction in punishment of two degrees for one who confessed. If one follows this interpretation for year of mourning relatives one would have to conclude that the same applied where a son or grandson accused a parent or paternal grandparent, namely that the latter would be treated as though they had themselves confessed and so be exempt from liability in cases of plotting great sedition or plotting treason, and furthermore be entitled to a reduction in punishment by two degrees in the case of treason where something had been done in furtherance of the plot.

One proviso (giving a further complication) still needs to be added. The rule laid down for 3-5 month mourning relatives (already considered) may suggest that the reduction of two degrees for the case of treason was allowed only in the case of one who confessed, not in the case where a person was accused, even by a relative entitled to conceal (in the normal case) his offences.

The Ming and Ch'ing codes preserve the essential structure and content of the T'ang rules but there are some changes on points of detail. The principal difficulty in comparing the early and the later codes is in knowing whether a rule clearly stated in the Ming and Ch'ing code, but not obviously present in the T'ang, is merely a clarification or restatement of what was already understood to be the law in T'ang times, or whether it in fact represents a change in the law.

With respect to confession[33] the Ming and Ch'ing rules are virtually the same as the T'ang, although rather more clearly stated. In particular it is clear that the rules allow the benefit of confession in the following circumstances:

(i) where someone sends another person - whether a relative or not - to confess on his behalf;

(ii) where a relative entitled to conceal that offence confesses on the offender's behalf even without his authorisation;

(iii) where relatives entitled to mutual concealment accuse each other of offences (provided they do not fall within the class of exceptions, such as theft or physical injury).

The position of relatives for whom mourning is worn for three or five months is the same as under the T'ang code, but a new rule is introduced with respect to relatives with whom there is no mourning relationship. They are entitled to a reduction in punishment of one degree in the case of confession on their behalf.

The rules governing the various offences against the state are made clearer than in T'ang law. This is one of the areas where it is difficult to be sure whether one has a clarification of an earlier position or an innovation. At any rate for Ming/Ch'ing law it is clear that where nothing has been done in furtherance of a plot to rebel, to commit sedition or treason, the offenders on whose behalf confession is made are treated as though they had themselves confessed and escape punishment. Where the plot had actually been carried out, although those jointly liable were exempt in the event of confession, the actual offenders on whose behalf confession had been made were still to be punished in accordance with the law; with the proviso that in the case of treason, where something had already been done (although the act of treason had not been completed), a reduction of punishment by two degrees was allowed.

The law on mutual concealment differs in two respects from the T'ang.[35] The range of relatives between whom mutual concealment is allowed is extended to include a wife's parents and a son-in-law. This extension is sharply criticised by the late Ch'ing legal scholar Hsueh Yun-sheng as disturbing proper relationships by including 'remote' relatives within the class of 'near' relatives.[36] Second, relatives who had no mourning relationship were entitled to a reduction in punishment of one degree where they concealed each other's offences.

The general rules on accusation were the same as for the T'ang, but there were some differences, especially in relation to false accusations. First one may note the more important differences in the Ming and Ch'ing law on accusations against relatives which were true.[37] The punishments are generally lighter in Ming/Ch'ing law than in T'ang law. Thus under the later codes a son or grandson who accused parents or paternal grandparents incurred a punishment of three years penal servitude and a beating of 100 blows with the heavy stick, not death as under the T'ang code.

Where 'senior' relatives accused 'juniors' of offences they had in fact committed, the latter were still treated as though they had themselves confessed and so might acquire exemption, but the former did not, in making the accusation, commit a punishable offence. In this respect 'seniority' in the relationship was given greater weight than under T'ang law . If one regards the 'senior' as still under a moral duty to conceal the 'junior's' offence, one has to conclude that the duty was no longer legally enforceable. Where an accusation is made by a relative for whom mourning is worn for 3-5 months the offender is no longer (as under the T'ang code) punished in accordance with the code, but is entitled to a reduction of three degrees in punishment, just as though there has been a confession on his behalf. Logically this is a more satisfactory result.

The Ch'ing code extends the range of offences of which accusation between relatives might lawfully be made. In addition to accusations of physical injury and depredation of property inflicted by a relative on the accuser the code permits an accusation to be made of illicit sexual intercourse, illegally passing through a boundary gate, wounding another person, and damaging another's irreplaceable property.[38] These last offences represent an important extension because they are not confined to injuries inflicted by one relative on another.

It is with respect to false accusations that the Ming and Ch'ing codes show the most marked difference from the T'ang, in that the calculation of the punishment proceeds on a different basis.[39] The Ming/Ch'ing law graduates the severity of the punishment according to the nature of the punishment prescribed for the offence of which a false accusation is made. Where the original punishment is a beating of 10 to 50 blows with the light stick the punishment for the false accusation is this punishment with an increase of two degrees. Where the original punishment is more serious, that is, consists of life exile, penal servitude or a beating with the heavy stick, the punishment for the false accusation is the original punishment with an increase of three degrees, provided that it should not exceed a beating of 100 blows with the heavy stick and exile to 3000 *li*. Should the accusation be of a capital offence and the person accused actually have been put to death, the accuser is himself to suffer capital punishment. In addition half his property is to be given to the family of the person falsely accused. Should the falsity of the accusation be revealed before the death penalty has been carried out the accuser is to be exiled to 3000 *li* and do penal servitude for 3 years.[40]

These are the rules which apply where there is no relationship of mourning between the accuser and the accused. If there is such a relationship the punishments are calculated through the application of principles similar to those of the T'ang code.[41] For example false accusation of a paternal grandparent or parent by a grandson or son, entails the death penalty (strangulation). Where a 'senior' relative standing in a relationship of mourning of three months to one year is accused, one first takes the punishment that would be applied if the accusation were true. If the punishment for the offence of which false accusation is made is less than that which would be entailed if the accusation were true it is the latter punishment that is applied. But if it is more serious than this, one takes the former punishment (that prescribed for the offence of which false accusation is made) and increases it by three degrees.

In the case of false accusations of 'junior' relatives a sliding scale is adopted. There is no liability where paternal grandparents, parents or maternal grandparents falsely accuse a son or grandson. For a false accusation of a year of mourning 'junior' the punishment is three degrees less than than prescribed for the offence of which false accusation is made; in the case of a nine month relationship the decrease is two degrees, and for five or three months one degree.[42]

One is now in a position to attempt an assessment of the complex rules, whose content has been broadly described. The core element connecting the three sets of rules and explaining their content is the fact of blood relationship and the moral obligations held to flow from it. This is particularly evident in the rules on mutual concealment and accusation. The moral principle that close relatives should help each other becomes, in the context of the concealment of offences, the legal rule that one relative should help another escape the normal consequences of his offence. The principle and the rule are an implementation of the Confucian teaching on the value of reform and education through moral guidance. Where a relative commits an offence he should be reprimanded and made to see the error of his ways, but he should not be delivered into the hands of the authorities. Shen's 'upper commentary' explicitly cites the natural affection of relatives for each other as the underlying principle.[43]

The rules punishing a relative who accuses another make enforceable the duty of concealment, although, as has been seen, there is no strict correlation between concealment and prohibition of accusation. Sometimes, as in the later law where a 'senior' accuses a 'junior' relative, there is no offence constituted by the accusation, even though the 'senior' would have been entitled to conceal the 'junior's' offence.

These rules appear to have been a means, adopted under Confucian influence, by which more legalist and authoritarian policies were softened. A despotism attempting to control a large country through a tiny bureaucracy has to rely upon informers for the detection and punishment of criminal offences. Since informers are likely to come from the same family as the offender the rules on mutual concealment and accusation must have operated effectively to deny the state the opportunity of detecting and punishing many offences. The state, of course, may have been the more willing to accept this position, since it relied upon the clans to ensure good behaviour on the part of their members and to punish such less serious offences as did occur.[44] In the really important cases where the safety of the emperor or state was threatened, there was no benefit of concealment and a relative who knew of the offence was under a duty to inform. What is interesting is that the Ch'ing law saw a considerable increase in the number of offences withdrawn from the protection of mutual concealment. In particular a relative might lawfully accuse another of illicit sexual intercourse, of unlawfully passing through boundary gates, of wounding another or damaging another's irreplaceable property. However it does not necessarily follow that a person who knew a relative had committed one of these offences was liable to punishment if he failed to inform; merely that he committed no offence if he did inform.

The rules on confession originally developed independently of those on mutual concealment and indeed exhibit a distinct value, that of repentance and individual regeneration through acknowledgment of fault. The essential linking of the confession and mutual concealment rules appears again to have been due to the obligations which the Confucians derived from the fact of blood relationship. An individual should voluntarily confess his faults, but should he not do so then a close relative should help him by confessing on his behalf and so, as it were, performing his moral duty for him.

There may sometimes have been a difficulty in deciding whether information that another had committed a crime counted as a confession on that person's behalf or as an accusation. The point is important since a relative who levied an accusation against another himself committed an offence, but he did not do so where he merely confessed on the latter's behalf. How was *accusation* distinguished from *confession*? If it was enough to use the language of confession, then what in reality was an accusation (made out of enmity) could readily be presented in the form of a confession, with the result that the accuser would escape liability.

By the Ch'ing dynasty, if not before, the impact of the benefit of concealment and the prohibition of accusation was considerably lessened through the exceptions which came to be allowed. Some of these exceptions as where one relative took another's property or inflicted physical injury on him - can still be explained in terms of Confucian orthodoxy. According to the 'incorporated commentary' of the Ming code,[45] accusation in these cases is justified because the hatred and division which the offences reveal show that the offender has rebelled against the relationship and, in effect, does not acknowledge it. But with respect to the other offences listed in the Ch'ing code, the motivation of the legislator may have been more one of concern for the victim of the offence. Some encouragement was provided for the laying of information as to offences committed by a relative against the person or property of a non-relative. Perhaps also there is reflected greater reluctance to rely upon clan discipline.

Notes

1. For versions of this see Analect 13.18 (Soothill, Analects of Confucius, 136); Liao, Han Fei Tzu II, 285; Wilhelm, Frühling und Herbst des Lü Bu We, 138.

2. Cf. Mencius's account of the legendary emperor Shun and his father (Lau, Mencius, 190).

3. See Kennedy, Die Rolle des Geständnisses im chinesischen Gesetz, 13f.

4. Para 8 (see chapter 1 note 2). See also Karlgren's gloss 1637 (Glosses on the Book of Documents, 288).

5. The *Shih chi* is the great history compiled by the Han scholar Ssu-ma Ch'ien around the beginning of the first century B.C. See Watson, Records of the Grand Historian of China II, 391.

6. The *Han-shu* is the official history of the Former Han Dynasty written by Pan Ku towards the end of the first century A.D. See volume 9, 2196 of the edition published in Peking by the Chung-hua publishing company. This section of the history has not, so far as I know, been translated into a Western language.

7. In later dynasties planning rebellion was in principle excluded from the benefit of the confession rules.

8. It is not clear exactly what the nature of the accusation was. Cf. Watson, op.cit., 390, 392. The case may simply have been one in which the conduct of the prince was held to constitute lack of filial piety, although he had not accused his father of any specific offence.

9. The passage is translated by Dubs, History of the Former Han Dynasty II, 224, note 10.1.

10. Dubs, op.cit., 224.

11. See *Han shu* 2, 474 (edition cited note 6). I am grateful to Professor Hulsewé for his help with the interpretation of the Chinese text.

12. See Ch'ü, Law and Society in Traditional China, 71.

13. Kennedy, Rolle des Geständnisses, 15.

14. Johnson, 201.

15. id.

16. This is translated by Johnson as follows: '37.3a - Cases where a representative is sent to confess and the person who makes the confession is one who is allowed mutual concealment by the law, or where a person who is allowed mutual concealment makes an accusation to the court are each decided according to the law on the criminal himself confessing' (202). As will be apparent I have not followed his interpretation.

17. See Kennedy, Rolle des Geständnisses, 68 n.58.
18. Johnson, 202, translates 'need not be a relative'. I have here followed Kennedy's translation (op.cit., 21). In fact the position may have been that although a relative would normally be sent as substitute the authorities would not hold the nature of the relationship between offender and the messenger to be relevant.
19. Article 46. See below.
20. Hence the relationship of concealment operated only in favour of the master.
21. This interpretation accords with the punctuation of the edition of the code published in Peking in 1983.
22. Johnson, 246.
23. Johnson (wrongly) translates 'husband's brothers and their wives'.
24. The fact that only plots are mentioned and not, for example, actual sedition or treason, is to be explained by the fact that it is only where nothing has been done in furtherance of the plot that the offence, properly speaking, can be concealed.
25. Cf. Lê Code, 654; Deloustal, 653.
26. Article 340 (cf. Lê Code, 500; Deloustal, 499).
27. Article 351.
28. Article 342. See note 31 below.
29. The relevant articles are 345, 346 and 347. Cf. also Lê Code 504; Deloustal, 503. Article 345 deals with any accusation against paternal grandparents and parents, article 346 with accusations by senior against junior relatives, and article 347 with accusations by junior against senior relatives, both (346 and 347) distinguishing between the case where the accusation is true and that where it is false.
30. Cf. article 341 and commentary where the distinction is made between the case where the accusation is known to be false and that where it is false but believed, through a failure to make a proper examination of the situation, to be true.
31. Article 342 (cf. Lê Code 502; Deloustal, 501).
32. Plotting rebellion may not have been treated in the same way.
33. For a general discussion of confession in Ch'ing law see van der Valk, Voluntary Surrender in Chinese Law.
34. Ming 1.23 (MLCCFL, 305); Ch'ing article 24, Philastre I, 205; Boulais, 115f; Staunton, 27.
35. Ming 1.30 (op.cit., 336); Ch'ing article 31, Philastre I, 247; Boulais, 173ff; Staunton 34.
36. In his commentary on the mutual concealment article in his parallel text edition of the T'ang and Ming codes (T'ang Ming Lü Ho Pien).
37. Accusations by relatives are dealt with in a single article - Ming 22.6 (op.cit., 1709); Ch'ing article 306, Philastre II, 429; Boulais, 1495f; Staunton, 371.
38. Illicit sexual intercourse and illegally passing through a boundary gate appear in the T'ang article on confession as offences for which confession does not entail exemption (Johnson, 209). One may have here not so much a change in the law as a making explicit of what had been implied

in the earlier code.

39. Ming 22.5 (op.cit., 1666); Ch'ing article 305, Philastre II, 406; Boulais, 1474f; Staunton, 364. On the special provisions for redemption see chapter 5, 105f.
40. Further financial consequences are established by the article.
41. The rules are contained in the article cited note 37 above.
42. These rules specifying the way the punishment is to be increased or decreased as the case might be are similar to, though not identical with, the T'ang rules.
43. Philastre II, 435.
44. For clan control see chapter 3, 63f.
45. MLCCFL, 339f.

8

The Ten Abominations and Offences Against the Person

The Ten Abominations

In the previous chapters on several occasions mention has been made of the 'ten abominations'. It is convenient at the start of the discussion of the main specific offences regulated by the codes, to give a brief account of them. The phrase 'ten abominations' expresses a classification, known from pre-T'ang times,[1] in which a large number of specific offences are grouped. The content of the classification is almost, although not entirely, identical in all the major codes.[2] These offences range from the most serious that can be committed by a subject, namely, plotting rebellion, to what appear to be the comparatively trivial acts of making music during the period of mourning for one's husband or beating an older relative of the same generation for whom mourning is worn for five months. Likewise some offences within the classification are capital, others are not. The terms used to describe collectively each of the abominations range from the highly specific to the highly general. Thus the first three cover respectively the single offences of plotting rebellion, plotting great sedition and treason, whereas under the seventh abomination in the T'ang code, entitled 'lack of filial piety' (pu-hsiao), are grouped at least nine offences.

Several distinct criteria seem to have been adopted in the compilation of the classification. First was the protection of the state (including its rites) and the emperor, second the desire to outlaw particular kinds of magical activity, and third, the preservation of the most fundamental family or social values.[3] Included under the first criterion are the treasonable offences already mentioned. In addition one has a variety of offences directed against the person or dignity of the emperor. The sixth abomination entitled 'great irreverence' (ta pu-ching) comprises certain ritual offences, namely, stealing objects used in the great state sacrifices or by the emperor, stealing or forging the imperial seals, and certain offences evidencing disrespect for the person of the emperor (making a mistake preparing the imperial medicine or food or in the construction of imperial boats).[4] The T'ang code contains some offences of disrespect not found in the Ming or Ch'ing list of abominations, namely, criticising or complaining of the emperor, driving away messengers carrying imperial decrees or generally exhibiting improper behaviour towards the emperor.[5]

Offences regarded as being cruel and irrational to an exceptional degree are subsumed under the head of the fifth abomination entitled 'depravity' (*pu-tao*). These are the killing of three persons in one family (not guilty of a capital offence) or the killing and dismemberment of a person,[6] and certain dangerous magical practices, namely the making or keeping of *ku* poison, various forms of sorcery and, in the Ming/Ch'ing law, dismemberment of a person specifically for magical purposes.

By far the majority of offences falling under the 'ten abominations' can be regarded as implementing different values associated with the family or other relationships approximated to it. These offences are further dominated by the notion of hierarchy; generally they are committed by 'junior' against 'senior' relatives, especially parents and paternal grandparents. For convenience of exposition they may be sub-divided into two groups: those evidencing direct attacks upon the person or reputation of a relative, and those exhibiting more generally a failure to show proper respect. Under the head of the fifth abomination, 'contumacy' (*o-ni*) are grouped the most serious offences against the person of 'senior' relatives: beating or plotting to kill one's paternal grandparents or parents, or killing one's paternal uncles or their wives, father's sisters, elder brothers or sisters, maternal grandparents, husband or husband's paternal grandparents or parents. This list reflects the degree of importance attached in Confucian thinking to different classes of relatives. The killing of a paternal uncle is placed upon the same level as merely plotting to kill parent or paternal grandparent; maternal grandparents are placed upon a lower level than paternal; elder but not younger brothers or sisters are included; and there is no mention of the wife or her parents and paternal grandparents.

A miscellaneous collection of offences against the person or reputation of a broader number of relatives is included under the eighth abomination, 'discord' (*pu-nu*): plotting to kill or selling relatives for whom mourning is worn for three months or more (junior relatives would be included here), or beating or reporting to the authorities one's husband or relatives of a higher generation or of the same generation but older for whom mourning is worn for nine months or more, or relatives of a higher generation for whom mourning is worn for five months. Reflected here is one of the most important Confucian obligations obtaining within the family, the duty to conceal offences committed by relatives and refrain from reporting them to the authorities (discussed in chapter 7). Generally to be noted is the very careful way in which the clauses on 'contumacy' and 'discord' are drafted. There is a fine differentiation both between the gravity of the offence and the degree of relationship, the principle applied being the more senior the relative and the longer the period of mourning, the wider the range of acts constituting the most serious offences.

Other offences against the reputation of 'seniors' are classified under the seventh abomination, 'lack of filial piety' (*pu-hsiao*), namely, cursing or reporting to the authorities one's parents, paternal grandparents or husband's parents.[7] Here, as with other offences listed under this head, the underlying rationale is the failure to show proper respect. This may be manifested in different ways viz: failing to look after one's paternal grandparents or parents, forming a separate household or holding separate property during their lifetime (without their consent), marrying, making music or leaving off mourning attire during the period of mourning for one's parents, concealing the death of one's paternal grandparents or parents or falsely to state that they have died.[8] The general commentary of the Ch'ing code states that the instances listed of lack of filial piety are only some of those actually made the subject of criminal liability.[9] One may compare the analogous offence committed by a wife (the junior relative) against the husband classified under the ninth abomination 'unrighteousness' (*pu-yi*), namely her concealing the death of her husband or remarrying, making music or leaving off mourning attire during the period of mourning for him.

One respect of family life not dependent upon the relationship between 'senior' and 'junior' reflected in the ten abominations is sexual conduct. The tenth, entitled 'incest' (*nei-luan*), comprises sexual intercourse with any relative for whom mourning is worn for five months or more, as well as with the concubines of the paternal grandfather or father (notions of hierarchy and respect again entering). Such conduct is designated as the degradation of man to the level of the animal, and a violation of the most fundamental moral principles. Finally the ninth abomination 'unrighteousness' evidences the treatment of certain non-family relationships as requiring the kind of behaviour expected from a 'junior' to a 'senior' family member. Under it is subsumed the killing of one's official superior (of a certain rank), magistrate, prefect or teacher.[10]

The ten abominations have primarily a symbolic significance. They enshrine the values deemed to be the most important in traditional China and at the same time express the horror with which their rejection was regarded. While some of the acts mentioned, such as those threatening the safety of the state or its ruler, would no doubt be included in any country's list of the most serious offences, the majority stem from the characteristic Confucian value system of the traditional Chinese. In legal terms the fact that an offence is classified as an 'abomination' is relatively insignificant. No additional punishment is thereby incurred. The main consequences were the exclusion of these offences from the various procedural or substantive privileges accorded officials and those of high standing, and the fact that normally they were also excluded from the scope of amnesties.

Killing

The fundamental categories operated by the traditional law are already fully apparent in the T'ang code. Indeed the principal articles reappear almost unaltered in the later codes.[11] Hence I propose first to discuss the T'ang law and then consider the most important changes affected by the Ming and Ch'ing law.[12] With respect to killing the T'ang code distinguished five basic categories. These are *mou-sha* (plotting to kill), *ku sha* (deliberate killing), *tou sha* (killing in the course of a fight or brawl), *hsi sha* (killing in the course of a game) and *kuo-shih sha* (accidental killing). The code does not present and dissect these categories in the manner of a modern textbook of criminal law. When introducing or using them it places most emphasis on the physical circumstances from which the killing results and on the status of the victim or the killer. The former emphasis is most evident in two of the categories, killing in a fight or a game, but is also reflected in the treatment of deliberate and accidental killing. The emphasis on status is seen in the fact that the rules are concerned more with the relationship of victim and offender than with any other aspect of the act. The punishments vary according to the precise degree of relationship by blood or marriage between victim and offender, or to their exact official rank.[13]

Mou sha (plotting to kill) is of significance as a separate category in cases where no killing has actually resulted.[14] For example to plot to kill one's parents or paternal grandparents and certain other 'senior' relatives was an offence punishable by beheading even though the victim suffered no actual harm. Where the relationship was less close or a 'senior' plotted against a 'junior' the punishment was less.[15] Plotting to kill an unrelated person who held no special official rank was punished by three years penal servitude.[16] 'Plotting' is defined by article 55 as involving 'two or more persons' but 'if the circumstances of the plot are clear and evident then one person may be considered to be the same as two persons'. The commentary gives an instructive example:

> 'If someone enters another person's house carrying a knife or a club, and investigation proves them to be enemies who each desires to kill the other, then even though there be only one person, this situation is considered the same as a plot.[17]

The definition of 'plot' as including the case in which one person intends to kill where that intention has become manifest by some physical act is important because it shows that attempted killings may often have been punishable as instances of *mou sha*.

Ku sha (deliberate killing), although one of the central categories, is not properly defined; nor is it even given a specific article to itself. The principal article introducing *ku sha* is that which primarily is concerned with *tou sha* (killing in a fight). Hence these two categories are best considered together. Article 306 states: 'if a person is killed in the course of a fight, the punishment is strangulation; if he is killed in a fight by means of sharp-bladed weapons or if the killing is deliberate (*ku*), the punishment is beheading'.[18] The commentary supplies the reasoning for the distinctions made in the article. In the case of an ordinary fight there is no intention to kill and hence the lesser punishment of strangulation is justified. Although the commentary does not articulate it, the principle involved is that of requital; the taking of a life must be requited with a life. If sharp-bladed weapons are used then there is evidenced an intention to destroy. The implication is that the killing in this case falls under the head of *ku sha*. Or, the commentary continues, if the killing is not an account of a fight or quarrel and lacks any particular affair, it is called *ku sha*.

The phrase 'lacks any particular affair' is not without difficulty. Does it mean the same as 'not on account of a fight or quarrel'? If not, what is the kind of 'affair' meant? These questions were discussed in the celebrated opinion of the poet and jurist Po Chü-i to which some reference has already been made.[19] Prior to the year 822, in which his opinion was delivered, the view taken by the Supreme Court of Justice had been that 'affair' must be given a meaning different from that of 'quarrel' or 'fight'. Thus if the accused could show that an 'incident' had preceded and provoked the act of killing, he was sentenced under *tou sha* (strangulation) and not under *ku sha* (beheading). The case in which Po was asked for his opinion concerned a husband who, in a fit of anger, had beaten his wife so savagely that she had died from her injuries. The highest judicial bodies held this to be a case of *tou sha* (killing in a fight) on the ground that the killing had resulted from an 'affair', namely the circumstances responsible for the husband's anger. Po rejected this conclusion on two grounds. First, the context showed, in his view, that 'affair' should be understood in the same way as 'fight' or 'quarrel' and therefore its mention was strictly redundant. Second, unless this construction was placed upon the phrase, the absurdity would be produced that no-one could ever be convicted of *ku sha* since on every occasion an 'affair' could be alleged to have preceded the act of killing. Po's opinion was approved by imperial edict and thereafter held to constitute the law.

Two aspects of the T'ang code's treatment of *ku sha* should be noted. The first is the context in which this category is introduced. What is of importance is not an abstract, general definition of *ku sha* but the concrete situation from which the killing results. Hence the emphasis is on one of the most common situations which leads to someone's death (a fight), and the category of *ku sha* itself is treated as killing not resulting from a fight where the circumstances permit the inference of an intention to kill. The second point is a related one. The case in which sharp-bladed weapons are used also discloses an emphasis on the particular circumstances of the killing. But here the specific reason for singling out the type of weapon used in the fight is the nature of the intention held to be revealed. The intent is not presented abstractly as an ingredient of the offence, but is inferred from one aspect of the total factual situation. Both these features, the emphasis on the situation from which the killing results and the reliance upon a specific state of affairs as evidence of intent, can be seen as characteristic of a not yet fully developed legal art.

Hsi sha (killing in a game or sport) is given a separate article,[20] but its treatment suggests that, like *ku sha* itself, it was considered primarily in relation to *tou sha* conceived as the main or standard category. The article and the note distinguish two types of game or sport. If the game is merely a competition of strength based on mutual agreement and one of the participants is killed by another, the latter receives a punishment two degrees less than that applicable for killing in a fight. But if sharp-bladed weapons are used or dangerous feats are attempted, for example, those involving high places or water the punishment is only one degree less.

The important point about the punishment - in both cases - is that the effect of the decrease by one or two degrees was to substitute respectively exile or penal servitude for death.

The commentary emphasises the importance of mutual accord. If the participants 'glare at each other in anger' and there is an obvious case of hatred, the death cannot be treated as having occurred in the course of a game; depending upon the circumstances the case will be one of *tou* or *ku sha*. The commentary also gives a reason for the higher punishment where the game or larking about occurs in dangerous circumstances involving knives or high places and so on. If the intrinsic situation is dangerous, special care and caution are necessary. To indulge in games is not to exercise such care and hence, if death results, a punishment higher than that imposed in the ordinary case of a game is justified. B Wallacker, emphasising more the element of acceptance of risk, observes:

> Apparently the principle is this: Where there was inherent risk in the activity, then the victim's responsibility for his own death rises measurably above that in which the horseplay is on the face of it innocuous... The point is that the risk of the situation is so great as to make the concept of consent inoperative. The players are not permitted, by law, to consent to horseplay in circumstances which are in themselves so risky as to make the activity of horseplay therein tantamount to asking to be injured or killed. Therefore the law will not grant the surviving wrongdoer clemency of two degrees but only of one degree.[21]

The code generally employs the phrase *kuo-shih sha* to describe non-intentional killing other than that occurring in the course of a game or a fight. The central article states that in cases where someone is killed or injured *kuo-shih* (accidentally) the manner in which the death occurred is to be followed and the judgment is to be by means of copper.[22] The meaning is that the nature of the facts justifies financial redemption of the capital punishment normally applied in cases of killing. The commentary to article 483 states that the copper (the amount of which was specified by article 5)[23] was to be paid to the family of the victim. From a modern perspective one may say that the criminal law provides a civil remedy. The state extracts compensation (a fixed amount) from the offender and pays it to the family of the victim. From the perspective of the T'ang legislators and officials the position probably was that the government, by an act of benevolence, allowed a fine due to it to be paid to the family of the victim.

A note to the article explains *kuo-shih* by means of a phrase which became a classic definition adopted throughout the legal history of imperial China. Literally this states: 'what ear and eye do not reach, what thought and care do not contemplate'. The following examples are given in the note and the commentary: throwing a brick or tile and not hearing the sound of anyone or seeing anyone appear (illustrating the phrase 'what ear and eye do not reach'), throwing a tile or rock in a lonely place where there should not be people and accidentally killing someone, lifting with others a heavy object where their collective strength is insufficient, or climbing with others a high and dangerous place, and in either case one's foot slips with the result that one of the others is killed, or in the course of hunting wild beasts accidentally killing someone, or, while engaged with others in arresting robbers, by mistake killing a bystander (illustrating the phrase 'what thought and care do not contemplate').

There has been some difference of opinion over the interpretation of the phrase 'what ear and eye do not reach, what thought and care do not contemplate'. One view treats it as a statement of liability on account of negligence.[24] This is probably wrong. Literally regarded the phrase seems to express something like 'what could not in the circumstances have been seen or heard, or what could not have been contemplated by the exercise of thought and care'. Some of the examples, however, might strike a modern reader as rather awkward illustrations of the phrase interpreted in this sense. Where people lift a beam too heavy for their collective strength, climb high places, or traverse dangerous passages, it might be thought that they ought to have contemplated the possibility of accidents and hence have exercised special care or not have undertaken the venture at all. But it is probable that the T'ang legislators attributed the death in these situations to external circumstances which in their view could not have been avoided through the exercise of care and thought at the time.[25] Hence one has what may be termed a situation of strict liability in the sense that the fact of someone being killed imposes a liability on the person from whose act the death had resulted. On the other hand the fact that there was deemed to be no carelessness or other personal fault determines the nature of the punishment as payment of copper.[26]

The code uses the five basic categories of killing to cover not only standard instances but also a wide variety of circumstances which do not readily fit into any one category. Its technique is to provide that if circumstances x, y, z result in someone's death the killing is to be treated as *ku sha*, *tou sha* and so on, as the case might be. Further refinement is possible through the use of the notion of degree. Thus a killing which occurs in particular circumstances may be treated not just as killing in a fight but as such killing with a reduction in punishment by two degrees.[27] By this method weight can be given to factors considered by the legislator to be important, such as the status or relationship of offender and victim, and the level of blame involved. Generally nothing explicit is said on the latter question but one has the impression that where there has been intent to do a wrongful act or where the legislator deems the act to have been particularly foolish or hazardous an appropriate adjustment is made in the way the killing resulting from the act is categorised or in the degree of punishment assigned to it. Some examples of the code's technique follow.

Where arrows or other missiles are fired in the direction of the imperial palace and someone is killed, this is treated as *ku sha*.[28] Deliberately to terrorise someone in a dangerous place with the result that he dies,[29] or deliberately to mix medicine not in accord with the original prescription with the result that someone dies is *ku sha*.[30] Likewise if one deliberately breaks open a dike because one has a grudge against a person or simply because one fears that the water will harm oneself and as a result someone is killed, there is *ku sha*.[31] On the other hand, if one deliberately creates a disturbance in the market and as a result someone is killed, this is still treated as *ku sha* but with a decrease in punishment of one degree.[32] If several persons plot to kill A but by mistake at night kill B instead of A, it is *ku sha*.[33] The main point about these various cases is that the killing is treated as *ku sha* even though the offender had not intended specifically to kill the victim. In the estimation of the legislator the act leading to the death is still sufficiently blameworthy to attract the punishment for *ku sha*.[34]

The category of killing in a fight is also applied to varied situations where there is a killing but not necessarily a fight. Thus if anyone is killed through an object being pushed into his nose or ear or other bodily opening, or through the removal of his clothing or food, the case is treated as *tou sha*.[35] Sometimes what determines the treatment of killing as *tou sha* is the quality of the offender's initial intention. Thus if a person engaged in robbery accidentally (*kuo-shih*) kills someone, the killing is held to fall under *tou* and not *kuo-shih sha*.[36] The commentary explains that the reason for applying the law of *tou sha* is the original intention to rob. Likewise if there is an original intention to fight but one of the contestants by mistake kills a bystander, the killing falls under the head of *tou* and not *kuo-shih sha* because again, according to the commentary, the offender's original intention was to cause harm. However the punishment is one degree less than that prescribed for *tou sha*, that is, exile rather than strangulation.[37]

Several other situations are dealt with by a combination of the category of killing in a fight and a variation in the degree of punishment. If one is driving a cart or riding a horse in the city without reason and thereby kills someone, the punishment is two degrees less than that for killing in a fight, namely, penal servitude.[38] The same punishment is imposed where an official neglects to repair dikes or repairs them at the wrong season and as a result someone is killed,[39] or where someone is killed in a collision of boats caused by the offender's faulty navigation.[40] In determining the punishment in these cases it is likely that the legislators considered the extent to which the offender was at fault. They may have taken into account both the absence of an initial wrongful intention, and the fact that death resulted from failure to observe the proper conduct demanded by the circumstances.

If one compares the situations held to fall under the category of *kuo-shih sha* with those held to fall under the category of killing in a fight (*tou sha*), one can conclude only that the legislators were guided in their classification by some assessment of the element of fault. A decision must have been taken that the degree of fault was not sufficient to justify the imposition of the category of *tou sha* and hence that of *kuo-shih sha* was to be followed. An ox which has once gored or injured someone should be marked or fettered in a certain way, and a dog which had become rabid should be killed. If these prescriptions were not followed and someone was killed by the ox or dog, the killing was treated as *kuo-shih*.[41] Likewise if the owner failed to fulfil his statutory obligation to burn poisonous meat with the result that someone ate it and died, he was liable on the ground of *kuo-shih sha* (unless the eater stole the meat in which case the owner's liability was simply that constituted by his failure to burn it).[42]

With these examples may be contrasted a case in which a killing has occurred *wu* (without intention) and yet the law of *kuo-shih sha* is not applied. Where construction or demolition work is in progress and due care is not taken with the result that someone is killed, a punishment of penal servitude for 1 1/2 years is imposed on the workman or supervisor responsible.[43] Both the article and the commentary emphasise the fact that the killing, although not intended, results from a failure to exercise proper care. It is probable that the evident fault displayed in the circumstances of the killing led to the imposition of penal servitude rather than to the application of the *kuo-shih sha* law.[44]

The few examples given are sufficient to bring out a great technical merit of the T'ang code, the organisation of material according to a precise and highly developed system of classification. The circumstances under which a person kills or brings about the death of another are of an infinite variety. The objective of the legislators is not only to co-ordinate the variety of circumstance in such a way as to permit a manageable legal regulation, but to devise a set of rules under which the judge is able to find the predetermined punishment for any particular state of affairs. This objective is achieved by the combination of two processes. First, there is the division of killing or acts which produce death into a number of basic categories. The main criteria for the selection of these categories appears to be the frequency with which death results from a particular activity, and the presence or absence of an intention to kill. Application of the first criterion yields the categories of *tou* and *hsi sha*, and application of the second those of *ku* and *kuo-shih sha*. The second process is the establishment of the punishment for the standard or normal case of killing within each category, and the use of the notion of degree in marking differences from the standard case. A very large number of situations can be accommodated in the code by allocation to a basic category, and determination of the degree of punishment appropriate within that category, to the particular case.[45]

Although not articulated as such an important factor controlling the final classification of a particular case appears to have been the element of culpability. Account was taken of the degree of fault exhibited by a person who caused another's death, especially of whether he had intended to do an unlawful act from which a death resulted (even though he had not intended the death itself) or whether, in the situation in which he found himself, he had simply failed to behave in the proper way. Cases of the second kind attracted a lower punishment than those of the first. One cannot go further than to suggest that such matters of fault were material in the framing of the rules, not establish precisely for each rule how far any particular kind of fault was built into its composition.

The five basic categories of T'ang/Sung law also formed the substratum of the Ming/Ch'ing law.[46] Before examining the form which they take in the later law, one may note that the Ming and Ch'ing codes introduced a few special rules not known in the T'ang code. The most important of these concerned the liability of those who drove another to commit suicide. A person who exerted pressure upon another with respect to some affair such as a marriage, sale of property or a loan, and as a result drove the latter to suicide is to be punished with a beating of 100 blows with the heavy stick. A much more serious punishment was imposed where the one exerting the pressure was a 'junior' relative. To drive to suicide in this way a 'senior' relative for whom mourning was worn for one year entailed the punishment of strangulation, with proportionate reductions in punishment where the mourning relationship was less close. Specially severe rules were introduced by sub-statutes for the case where sons or grandsons by their obstinate and perverse behaviour drove their paternal grandparents or parents to suicide; the punishment was to be beheading. It is even provided that where a son was poor, unable to earn a living and support his parents with the result that they killed themselves, he is to be given 100 blows with the heavy stick and exiled to 3000 *li*.[47]

In the Ming and Ch'ing law the category of *mou sha* is more sharply differentiated and more clearly distinguished from *ku sha* than in T'ang law. In the T'ang code the category appears to have found its main utility in connection with attempts. This is not so in the Ming and Ch'ing codes where it primarily covers a plot followed by actual killing. One can see the difference in perspective reflected in the formulation adopted respectively by the T'ang/Sung and Ming/Ch'ing codes. Whereas the T'ang code (article 256) takes the plot itself as the central offence and specifies what additional punishment is to be imposed where injury or death in fact results from it, the Ming and Ch'ing codes make central the fact of killing itself. The article provides that in the case of a plot to kill the one who forms the idea is to be beheaded, those (accessories) who contribute their active support (*chia kung*) are to be strangled, whereas those who join in the plot but do not contribute active support are to receive 100 blows with the heavy stick and be exiled to 3000 *li*.[48] The article - and this is the significant point - then stipulates that liability to these punishments arises only where the killing has been completed. If the victim is injured, but does not die the punishments are less; if he is not even injured they are still further reduced.[49]

An important consequence of the different conceptions of *mou sha* in the T'ang and Ming/Ch'ing codes is that more attention had to be paid in the later codes to the nature of the intention by which *mou* was to be distinguished from *ku sha*. For the T'ang legislators and commentators this was not a problem since *mou sha*, if successful, became *ku sha*. In Ming and Ch'ing law the same result did not follow and it therefore became necessary to specify exactly how the intention constituting *mou sha* differed from that constituting *ku sha*. The difference was located in the time at which the intention to kill was formed. If it was formed only at the time of the actual killing the offence was *ku sha*, but if it was formed in advance of the act the offence was *mou sha*. The 'incorporated commentary' of the Ming code has the following definition of *mou sha*: 'whenever one harbours a grievance, devises means and decides upon a plan to kill a person and executes the plan he is guilty of planned homicide'.[50]

Ku and *tou sha* appear in the same article in the Ming and Ch'ing codes but the logical separation between them is more clearly made than in the T'ang. Thus the Ming/Ch'ing article contains three separate sections, the first establishing the punishment of strangulation for killing in a fight (*tou sha*), the second the punishment of beheading for deliberate killing (*ku sha*), and the third specifying the punishments to be applied where there has been a plot to join together and beat a person with the result that he died.[51] Nevertheless the two categories remain closely associated in the thought of the legislators. The fact that they appear in the same article is not due just to an unreflecting, albeit somewhat modified, adoption of the arrangement of the corresponding T'ang article. Both *ku* and *tou sha* enshrine an 'evil intention' with respect to the victim, in the one case to kill him, in the other to inflict harm, which distinguishes them from killing in a game (*hsi sha*) or accidental killing (*kuo-shih sha*). Furthermore as is evident from discussions in the legal commentaries, in practice many cases of *ku sha* did result from fights. Where a fight ended with the death of one of the participants the main problem for the law was to determine whether the offence should be treated as *ku* or *tou sha*. The fact that *mou sha* in the Ming and Ch'ing codes covered all cases of premeditated killing also contributed to the association of *ku sha* with fights, since the impulse to kill arising more or less instantaneously with the act of killing was again likely to appear in the context of a fight. Hence although a clear distinction between *ku* and *tou sha* is made in the article, in practice it was often difficult to decide which was the appropriate offence.

There is a clear formulation of the conceptual distinction between *ku* and *tou sha* in the commentaries. At its most concise this is found in the introductory words of the official, 'small' commentary to the Ch'ing article: 'when a person at a given moment (*lin-shih*) feels the desire to kill and the others (who participate in the affray) are not aware of it, his offence is called *ku sha*'.[52] A similar approach is found in the 'incorporated commentary' of the Ming code,[53] and is also expressed in Shen's 'upper commentary'.[54] It is clear that both the legislators and the commentators are trying to find a test which will enable *ku* to be distinguished from *tou sha* in the context of an affray. Where a person has been killed in a fight or brawl there were several possible legal outcomes. If only one other was involved he might be liable for *ku* or *tou sha*, depending upon whether or not he had the intention to kill at the moment of striking the fatal blow. If several persons were involved the choice was between holding all liable under the section of the article on 'plotting together and collectively beating' or one liable on the ground of *ku sha* and the others on the former ground or all liable for *ku sha*. Relevant here is whether the intention to kill was held only by one, or known to and shared by the others (in which event all would be liable for *ku sha*).

Difficult questions of proof arose. How was the existence of the intention necessary for *ku sha* to be determined? The most obvious method was to look at the circumstances of the killing and see if an intention to kill could reasonably be inferred, and this is in fact the method adopted by the commentaries. In particular they single out as relevant two circumstances: the presence or absence of a state of enmity between the parties, and the extent to which in a fight one participant had resorted to unnecessary force. Some instructive remarks are found in a commentary entitled *tu lü p'ei hsi*.[55] Here it is said that *ku sha* refers to a case where one has an enemy and kills him, not to a case where one knows one has an enemy and kills him. What this means is that in the case of knowledge the intention to kill is likely to have been formed prior to the actual encounter with the enemy. So, according to this commentary, where one is daily preoccupied with the enmity of another, then happens to see that person and kills him at that moment (*lin-shih*) this is *mou* and not *ku sha*. On the other hand if one comes across a former enemy (without previously being conscious of and brooding on the enmity) and beats him so that he dies, this is *ku sha*, the necessary intent being inferable from the previous state of enmity.

Having dealt with the case of enmity the same commentary turns to the case of two persons (not former enemies) who engage in a fight. If one yields but the other persists in striking until he has deprived him of life, how, says the commentator, can this not be *ku sha*? In such a case there is formed at that time (*lin-shih*) an intention to kill even though there was no such intention prior to the fight. Whenever one participant was unable to put up further resistance but implored mercy or fell wounded to the ground, the same analysis can be made. A similar situation may arise in a case where several persons have plotted to beat another. Originally they intended merely to beat, but if, inflamed by the victim's opposition or insults, they cry "kill! kill!" and the victim died from their blows the offence is that of *ku sha*.

While the category of *kuo-shih sha* in Ming/Ch'ing law remains essentially the same as the T'ang, that of killing in a game (*hsi sha*) is not.[56] Two important changes are found in the Ming and Ch'ing articles.[57] First, killing in a game is now treated, from the point of view of liability, in the same way as killing in a fight. The punishment is to be strangulation, not penal servitude as in T'ang law. Second, the T'ang distinction between ordinary games or sports and larking about in a dangerous place or with dangerous implements is no longer observed. All killings resulting from games, sports or horseplay are treated as being equally grave.

The Ch'ing code itself makes clear that what is meant by a 'game' in the context of *hsi sha* is an activity of an intrinsically dangerous nature. The official commentary inserted in the article states that 'the affair must be one capable of causing death' and cites by way of example contests with fists or sticks. Shen's 'upper commentary' emphasises the point that the participants know that what they are doing is potentially harmful and so deliberately assume the risk of injury or death. Where death results from some ordinary amusement which the participants could not have foreseen would lead to harm the case cannot be treated as *hsi sha*. For example if two persons are eating plums in an orchard and one in play throws the stones at the other who in trying to dodge knocks his head against a rock and dies, this is a case of *kuo-shih sha* and not *hsi sha*.[58]

With respect to accidental killing (*kuo-shih sha*) one may merely note the Ming/Ch'ing provision that the redemption payment was to be applied to the funeral expenses of the victim. The specification in this case of the destination of the redemption payment derives from a more far reaching change in the law, stemming from Mongolian practice and passing into Ming/Ch'ing law from the Yüan. This is the general requirement that in cases of homicide the offender (or his family) should make a contribution to the funeral expenses of the victim.[59]

Ch'ing jurists and perhaps also Ming recognised a sixth category of killing, *wu sha* (killing by mistake).[60] The T'ang code had known some of the rules which later appear as part of the complex associated with *wu sha*,[61] but had not identified *wu sha* explicitly as a separate category of killing. Even in Ming and Ch'ing law, although *wu sha* is separately mentioned in the same article that deals with *hsi sha* and *kuo-shih sha*,[62] in essence it is no more than a variant of *mou, ku, tou* or *hsi sha*. Thus the Ming and Ch'ing article itself simply states that where one of the participants in a fight by mistake (*wu*) kills a bystander or third party the case is to be treated as *tou sha* and the punishment of strangulation after the assizes imposed. Should a person plan to kill (*mou sha*) or be engaged in deliberately killing (*ku sha*) another and by mistake (*wu*) kill a third party the case is to be treated as *ku sha* and the punishment of beheading after the assizes imposed. The case of *hsi sha* is regulated by a sub-statute introduced in 1735 which provided that where someone was killed by mistake (*wu*) on account of a game (*hsi*) the case was to be treated as *hsi sha* and the punishment of strangulation after the assizes imposed.[63]

Generally the law of homicide, especially in Ch'ing times, was developed through the enactment of a large number of sub-statutes which introduced rules for various concrete situations. One of these may be instanced here because it provides a vivid illustration of what appears to have been a fundamental principle of the criminal law, that for the life of the person who has been killed another life must be taken in requital. Normally the life to be taken in requital was that of the person who had brought about the death. But under certain circumstances the life of another person involved in the offence was permitted to substitute for that of the person who had killed and the latter escaped with a punishment of exile.

A sub-statute, emanating from the end of the Ming dynasty, provided, in the version contained in 19th century editions of the Ch'ing code:

> Whenever in the case of a joint affray an offender is tried for injury which he has inflicted and for which he should be sentenced to strangulation, it happens that the person who had originally conceived the plan for the affray or one among the other persons who had joined in the affray and inflicted mortally serious injury has committed suicide for fear of punishment in that particular case, before having been led before the magistrate or when either of them after having been led before the magistrate has died of illness in jail, or when he was being transported to the court of his trial died as a consequence thereof on the way, it shall be permitted to consider such person to have paid with his life for the homicide and to reduce by one degree the punishment of the (principal) offender who deserves to be strangled, and to sentence him to permanent banishment.[64]

One notes, of course, that it is not just any life that is deemed sufficient compensation. It must be the life either of the person who had instigated the fight or of one of those who had inflicted a serious wound, although not that which actually produced death. Furthermore the circumstances under which the death of such a person counts as requital are very narrowly defined by the sub-statute: suicide prior to the official investigation, or death from illness while the offender is in jail awaiting trial or on the way to be tried.[65]

Personal Injury

The rules on personal injury in all the main codes (T'ang, Sung, Ming and Ch'ing)[66] show certain characteristic features. First I propose to examine the rules applicable to injuries inflicted by one person upon another and then, by way of addendum, to look briefly at the rules determining liability for injuries inflicted on people by animals. One may summarise the principal characteristics of the first group of rules as follows. Liability is made to depend upon a variety of factors: the type of implement with which the injury is caused, the nature and extent of the injury, the social, official or family relationship between the offender and the victim, and finally the consequences of the injury as manifested within a particular period of time. The third of these features may be quickly dismissed, not because it is unimportant but because it has been adequately examined in Tung-tsu Chü's book on *Law and Society in Traditional China*. The essential point is that the punishment was more severe where a person of low status beat or wounded a person of high status, as where a 'junior' family member or subordinate official or 'mean' person wounded respectively a 'senior' family member, a higher ranking official or a free person. Many rules in the code are devoted to working out the implications of such relationships of status.[67] To illustrate the other features I take as my main model the T'ang code and indicate to what extent the Ming and Ch'ing law introduced changes. In fact in all codes the rules are very similar.

With respect to the type of implement, a tripartite distinction is made between hands or feet, 'other objects' and military weapons. Article 302 provides that merely beating a person with hands or feet entails a punishment of 40 blows with the light stick (Ming/Ch'ing 30 blows); actually inflicting a wound - defined as 'where blood is visible' (Ming/Ch'ing as a bruise) - by such means or simply beating (without wounding) with 'another object' entails a beating of 60 blows with the heavy stick (Ming/Ch'ing 40 blows with the light stick), 'another object' being anything apart from hands or feet or military weapons but including the latter where the blade is not used.[68] Article 304 deals with military weapons (bows and arrows, knives, spears, javelins, lances and so on) and provides a punishment of 100 blows with the heavy stick merely for attempting to injure a person with such a weapon, even though the attacker in fact misses his victim. Thus provision is not found in the Ming/Ch'ing law. If a wound is actually inflicted the punishment is penal servitude for two years (same in Ming/Ch'ing law with the addition of a beating of 80 blows with the heavy stick).[69]

With respect to the nature of the injury, many different situations are put. Only some examples are given here. Thus article 303 provides that where a tooth is broken, the ear or nose damaged, one eye damaged though still capable of sight, a finger, toe or bone broken, or a wound inflicted with fire or hot water, the punishment is penal servitude for one year (Ming/Ch'ing 100 blows with the heavy stick). It further provides that where two or more teeth, fingers or toes are broken, or the head is deprived of all hair, the punishment is penal servitude for one and a half years (Ming/Ch'ing one year penal servitude and 60 blows with the heavy stick).[70] Article 305 provides *inter alia* that for breaking or destroying a limb or blinding in one eye the punishment is penal servitude for 3 years (Ming/Ch'ing the same with the addition of 100 blows with the heavy stick), and for cutting out the tongue or inflicting two or more injuries of the kind mentioned in the article, the punishment is exile to 3000 *li* (Ming/Ch'ing the same with the addition of 100 blows).[71] The Ming and Ch'ing articles add two matters not found in the T'ang code. For defiling a person's face with foul substances such as dung a punishment of 80 blows with the heavy stick is imposed, and 100 if the substance is introduced into the victim's mouth or nose. In the case of serious injuries amounting to incapacity (*tu-chi*) the offender is to surrender half his property to the victim for his maintenance.

Once a person had been wounded, the liability of the offender could not be fully determined until the consequences of the wound had become clear. While the mere fact of wounding itself imposed liability, according to the detailed prescriptions of the codes, that liability could be increased where the victim subsequently died. The problem was: under what circumstances could the initial wound itself be treated as the cause of death? The T'ang code established the broad rule that should the victim die within a specified number of days, and no other cause had intervened, the offender was to be liable for killing under whichever category was appropriate. The periods of time established by article 307 are: beating or wounding with hands or feet, 10 days (Ming/Ch'ing 20 days); 'other articles', 20 days; knives, fire or hot water, 30 days; maiming or dislocating a limb or breaking a bone, 50 days. Except where indicated the Ming and Ch'ing rules were the same.[72] A special rule was also applied to cases of maiming or the breaking or dislocation of bones. If the injury was cured within the prescribed period the punishment was reduced by two degrees.[73] An important gloss is found in the Ming and Ch'ing, though not the Tang codes. The offender is to be ordered to undertake the cure of the wound and thus help to prevent possible consequences that would be more adverse to himself.

In the context of the rules on personal injuries occurs a rare and interesting reference to, and recognition of, a limited right of self-help. Article 310 after stating that where two people beat and fight each is to be liable in respect of the injuries inflicted on the other, adds 'where someone strikes a blow afterwards (i.e. in response to an attack) and is in the right, the punishment is to be reduced two degrees, but this is not to apply where the person struck dies'.[74] As the *shu-i* commentary makes plain there are two conditions that must be satisfied before the person striking the blow is entitled to the reduction in punishment. First, he must be in the right, in the sense that he is perfectly innocent and has not committed any offence against the other party, and, second, he must strike the blow only to defend himself in response to a blow already inflicted on him. An even more serious limitation upon the extent of the right is that it does not apply where death results from the blow struck in self defence. One probably has here an application of the principle already noted that when a life has been taken, the life of the person responsible is forfeit by way of requital.

In all the codes the rules on liability for personal injury are expressed in terms of 'beating and fighting'. This is natural in that fights are not only themselves frequent but are generally productive of an injury of some kind. However this treatment does raise the question: what is the liability for injuries inflicted in circumstances other than a fight? This question is easily answered for T'ang law since each of the main articles on killing also includes wounding. Thus where a wound is deliberately (*ku*) inflicted (that is, does not arise accidentally or naturally in the course of a fight or game) the punishment is to be one degree higher than that for wounding in a fight (article 306). Wounding in the course of a game entails a punishment one or two degrees less - depending on the circumstances - than that for wounding in a fight (article 338), and for accidental wounding redemption by payment of copper may be made (article 339).

The position in Ming and Ch'ing law is somewhat less clear. Wounds are specifically mentioned in the articles on *hsi* and *kuo-shih sha*, the punishment in the former case being the same as for wounding in a fight and in the latter being redeemed through the appropriate payment. However the article on *ku sha* says nothing about wounds deliberately inflicted. One has to infer that the distinction between such wounds and those inflicted in the course of a fight, known to T'ang law, was suppressed and that the former were subject to the same punishment as the latter. If this were the position one can see the benefit obtained, an avoidance of the many practical problems that would arise in determining whether an injury should be treated as deliberately inflicted or merely as incurred in the course of a fight. Yet where death resulted from the injury the practical problem of deciding whether the killing should be treated as *ku* or *tou sha* remained; in this context it would be necessary to determine whether the initial wounding had been deliberate.

From the perspective of comparative legal history the rules on personal injury present a phenomenon of considerable interest. It is generally thought that rudimentary or archaic legal systems are characterised by the cataloguing of numerous different and specific injuries to each of which is assigned an economic value. Loss of a toe is held to be worth one piece of silver and so on. The tariff for injuries in such archaic legal systems is further influenced by the respective statuses of offender and victim. If a person of low rank causes a person of high rank to lose a toe the amount to be paid is now two pieces of silver and so on. Rules of this kind characterised, for example, Roman law at the period of the Twelve Tables, and the Anglo-Saxon and other early Germanic codes. The Chinese rules assign physical punishments, not a monetary value to personal injuries. But in so far as they provide a lengthy catalogue of specific injuries each entailing its appropriate legal consequence, and provide for the variation of such consequences according to relationships of status, they fit the archaic model. The point, however, is that these rules not only made their first appearance (collectively considered) in a sophisticated and technically advanced code, but survived for many centuries into the modern period and finally disappeared only with the end of imperial China in the twentieth century.

Killing or Injury by Animals

The rules are substantially the same in all three codes. They are concerned partly with the regulation of precautionary measures to be taken in the case of animals known to be dangerous, and partly with the determination of liablity where death or injury to a person results from the neglect of these precautions, or through the owner's deliberate act. Article 207 of the T'ang code provides that where a domestic animal is known to be given to goring, kicking or biting it is to be appropriately marked or fettered. The *shu-i* commentary states that the horns of an animal given to goring are to be removed, and likewise the ears of an animal given to biting. A dog known to be rabid must be killed. Failure to comply with these requirements in itself entails a punishment of 40 blows with the light stick.[75]

If the precautions required by the article are neglected and as a result an animal kills or injures a person the law of accidental (*kuo-shih*) killing or injury is to be applied. Consequently the offender may discharge his liability by payment of the appropriate amount of copper to the victim or his family. However if the owner, knowing of the animal's disposition to kick, gore or bite, deliberately releases it with the result that it kills or injures a person, the law of killing or injuring in a fight is to be followed with a reduction in punishment of one degree. The effect is to impose a punishment of life exile to a distance of 3000 *li* (supplemented in Ming and Ch'ing law with a beating of 100 blows with the heavy stick). There is no requirement that the owner should actually intend that the animal should kill or injure, or even attack another person. He may, for example, have released it merely in order to terrify.

It thus appears that where an animal injures or kills a person, and the owner has neither omitted to take the precautions required by the code nor has deliberately released the animal, there is no liability. Even in the case of a goring ox or rabid dog (for example) there would be no liability where the owner had not known of the animal's propensity or condition. In certain other cases, too, the codes provide that there is to be no liability. The T'ang article states that when a person has been hired for a fee to treat a sick animal but does not know how to control it and is killed or injured, there is no liability. The reason for this exception may be that the person who receives payment thereby accepts the risk of injury, and perhaps also that he has held himself out as having the ability to control the animal and so is precluded from complaint if he fails to exhibit the requisite skill. Likewise, for obvious reasons, there is held to be no liability where a person deliberately provokes or teases another's animal and in consequence is killed or injured. The same rules are found in the Ming and Ch'ing articles.

Insulting Words

Generally associated with beating, although punished less severely, is the offence of uttering insulting words, comprising, it seems, not just actual insults or cursing but even immoderate language used in scolding or reproof. In T'ang law the offence is strictly circumscribed and seems to be derived from the obligation to show respect imposed on a junior vis-a-vis a senior relative or upon a subordinate vis-a-vis a superior officer or representative of the emperor. The only circumstances under which insulting words imposed liability appear to be the following: (i) concubine (though not wife) cursing or scolding husband, 80 blows with the heavy stick;[76] (ii) junior relatives cursing or scolding elder brothers or sisters, 100 blows with the heavy stick, or father's brothers or their wives, father's sisters or maternal grandparents, penal servitude for one year;[77] (iii) grandchildren or children cursing or scolding parents or paternal grandparents, death by strangulation,[78] (iv) wife or concubine cursing or scolding husband's paternal grandparents or parents, penal servitude for three years;[79] (v) wife or concubine who has remarried cursing or scolding her deceased husband's paternal grandparents or parents, penal servitude for 2 years;[80] (vi) wife or concubine cursing or scolding senior relatives of the husband for whom she wears mourning for three months or more, the punishment depending upon the degree of mourning, being one degree less than that imposed on the husband for cursing or scolding the same category or relatives;[81] (vii) slaves or personal retainers cursing or scolding their masters, exile (converted into a beating of 200 blows with the heavy stick), or their master's year of mourning relatives or maternal grandparents, penal servitude for 2 years (converted into 160 blows with the heavy stick),[82] or their former masters, penal servitude for 2 years (also converted into a beating);[83] (viii) cursing or scolding messengers bearing imperial decrees or one's military commander, district magistrate or prefect, or subordinates cursing or scolding their superiors of the 5th rank or above, penal servitude for 1 1/2 years, or subordinates cursing or scolding officers in charge of the 6th rank or below, 90 blows with the heavy stick.[84]

The T'ang articles contain notes specifying further the conditions under which liability attaches. For situation (iv) it is specified that the person insulted must personally bring the accusation. Although this requirement is not explicitly stated in the rules determining liability for insults between other family members, it is possible that, as in the later law, it also applied to these cases. For situation (viii) it is specified that the imperial messenger or official in question must personally hear the insulting words. One should not necessarily infer that for the other situations personal hearing was not necessary. Perhaps the point is that although the official or superior need not bring the accusation personally, he must at least have heard the insult; otherwise one might have a plethora of actions of the kind in which A asserted B had insulted C who in fact had been unaware of the insult. Only in the later legal commentaries does one find reasons given for the rules requiring personal prosecution and personal hearing.

Whereas in T'ang law there is nothing to suggest that an action for insult lay except in the few cases specified by the code, the position in Ming and Ch'ing law was not the same. In the first place a much broader conception of 'insult' was taken; it was no longer restricted to cases evidencing a failure to respect on the part of junior to senior relatives or subordinates to superiors. The codes provide that where one person abuses, reviles or curses another a punishment of 10 blows with the light stick is to be imposed, and, should there be a bout of mutual abuse, both parties are to be similarly punished irrespective of who was the first to begin.[85] It follows that if there was an action in the case of unrelated persons, there must always be one in any case of a junior abusing or cursing a senior. Hence the commentaries of the codes specify that where a given case is not expressly established the rules on beating are to be consulted and an appropriate reduction in punishment made.[86] However, as in T'ang law, it remained true that the relationship between two individuals might preclude an action for insult. Thus it was not possible for junior relatives or subordinates to bring accusations of abuse against senior relatives or superiors. To have allowed such action would have been fundamentally contrary to the duty of respect imposed by the relationship.

One case caused difficulty in the later law. Although the wife vis-a-vis the husband counts as a junior relative there is no text which specifies that she is liable for cursing or abusing him. Only in the official commentary of the Ch'ing code is there a reference to the position of the wife vis-a-vis the husband. It is said that the law does not make the wife liable for cursing or insulting the husband because within the inner apartments both hold the same rank and there ought to be indulgence. However the commentary adds that should the wife in fact curse or insult the husband and should he bring an accusation, then she should be punished under the 'catch-all' article on 'doing what ought not to be done' where the matter is light, the punishment being a beating of 40 blows with the light stick.[87]

The special rules regarding personal hearing or personal making of the accusation remain broadly the same as in T'ang law, but the treatment of these matters is fuller in the Ming and Ch'ing codes. It is made clear that in all cases of abusive language arising within the family or among relatives the person abused must personally make the accusation. Furthermore the commentaries provide some explanation of both qualifications. Officials must personally hear the insult because, given the difficulties of proof, there is otherwise too much scope for misunderstandings and slanders.[88] The Ming 'incorporated commentary' advances a similar reason for the rule that relatives must personally make the accusation.[89] However the Ch'ing official commentary contrasts relationships based on mutual dependence (as between subordinates and superiors) and those based on natural affection (as between relatives), and points out that in the latter case a relative may choose, out of affection, to conceal an insult; hence it should not be open to a third person to make the accusation.[90] One general point should be added. It is likely that cases of cursing and scolding, where they occurred among relatives were dealt with by family or clan disciplinary procedures rather than referred to the state authorities for the infliction of the statutory punishment.

Sexual Offences

Under the head of 'illicit sexual intercourse' the codes treat three basic situations: adultery, incest and sexual relationships between single, unrelated persons.[91] Distinctions are drawn according to whether force is used or, where there is consent, according to the circumstances under which the act takes place. The later law also introduced a liability for indecent suggestions which prompted the recipient or a close relative to commit suicide.[92] At no time could traditional Chinese society, at least in official terms, be described as permissive. It has been argued that Ch'ing attitudes, under the influence of the then current doctrines of neo-Confucianism, dictated an even harsher line on sexual matters than that taken by earlier dynasties.[93]

In its general article on the subject of illicit sexual intercourse the T'ang code provides that where both parties have consented, and the woman has no husband, each is to be sentenced to penal servitude for 1½ years, to be increased for the woman to 2 years where she has a husband. Should force be used the man's punishment is to be increased by one degree (penal servitude for 2 years) and the woman is not to be liable.[94] Heavier punishments are imposed where the parties are related. Some examples, not an exhaustive list, follow. Sexual intercourse with a relative for whom mourning was worn for three months or more or the wife of such a relative is punished by penal servitude for 3 years and exile to 2000 *li* if force is used.[95] If sexual intercourse takes place between great nephew and great paternal aunt, or between brother and brother's wife the punishment is exile to 2500 *li* and if force is used death by strangulation;[96] if between nephew and wife of paternal uncle or brother and sister, the punishment is death by strangulation whether or not force is used.[97]

Sexual intercourse between persons of different social classes or occupying certain social positions also attracted heavier punishments. Where a male slave has sexual intercourse with a free woman the punishment for both is penal servitude for 2¹/₂ years; if force is used the man is to be strangled.[98] Nothing is said of female slaves having sexual intercourse with free men.[99] When a supervisory or custodial official has sexual intercourse with a woman under his jurisdiction his punishment is to be increased by one degree.[100]

Ming and Ch'ing law presents a more nuanced picture which appears to owe much to rules introduced under the Mongols.[101] In its general article on illicit sexual intercourse it adopts and supplements the T'ang distinctions, reducing the punishment for cases of consent but very considerably increasing them where force has been used.[102] Ordinary illicit sexual intercourse by consent where the parties are single and unrelated is punished by a beating of 80 blows; if the woman is married her punishment is increased to 90 blows. But the law now introduces a refinement. Even though the woman has consented, should she have been lead astray and seduced, evidenced by her agreeing to go with her lover to another place to consummate the act, the punishment for both is heavier (100 blows) and remains the same whether or not the woman is married.

Use of force is given more attention than in the earlier law. A distinction is drawn between the completion of an act of rape and a forcible attempt.[103] In the former case the punishment is death by strangulation (much more severe than in T'ang law), and in the latter it is reduced by only one degree to exile to 3000 *li* and a beating of 100 blows with the heavy stick. One sees from the observations in the Ch'ing general commentary how sternly the law regarded the use of force in this as in other contexts.[104] It thus became very important to determine whether illicit sexual intercourse should be treated as 'forcible' or not. In this respect the Ch'ing code in its official commentary introduced a particularly stringent requirement. It emphasises that the use of force must be such as to preclude any possibility of resistance on the part of the woman, that there must be evidence supplied either by witnesses or the state of the woman's clothing and body, and, most important, the woman must resist for the duration of the act. Should she be subjected to force, initially resist, but then acquiesce the act itself cannot be treated as forcible. Furthermore the character of the woman is itself relevant to the classification of the act. Should someone after witnessing a woman engage in illicit sexual intercourse himself use force in raping or attempting to rape her he can be convicted only under the rule on seducing a woman.[105]

Other important rules contained in the article, not all of which are found in the T'ang code, are: (i) sexual intercourse committed with a girl aged 12 or under is to be deemed forcible even though the girl should have consented; (ii) should a child be born of the act the responsibility for upkeep rests with the man;[106] (iii) where the woman is married, in addition to being punished, she may at the option of her husband be retained by him or sold or married to another, though not to the adulterer; (iv) both a go-between and those who make their home available for the act are also to receive punishment reduced by one degree from that of the guilty parties;[107] (v) where someone knows of, but arranges to conceal, the act he is to be punished 2 degrees less than the guilty parties; (vi) in view of the difficulties of proof and the danger of false accusations it is enacted that no liability for illicit sexual intercourse can arise unless the parties are caught in the place where the act is committed; (viii) should a woman become pregnant and it is not known who the father is she alone is to be punished.

Incest is taken further than in T'ang law. Where persons belonging to the same clan or their wives have sexual intercourse, even though there is no relationship of mourning between them, the punishment is 100 blows with the heavy stick. As in T'ang law sexual intercourse with relatives of three months mourning or closer or their wives is punished by penal servitude for three years (with the Ming/Ch'ing supplement of 100 blows with the heavy stick), though where force is used the punishment is again much heavier (death by beheading). If a great nephew and great paternal aunt or brother and brother's wife commit the offence the punishment is death by strangulation (heavier than in T'ang law) and by beheading if force is used. Beheading is the punishment for sexual intercourse with a concubine of the father, wife of paternal uncle, sister or wife of son or grandson. These examples show that generally the Ming and Ch'ing law punished sexual intercourse between relatives more severely than in T'ang law.[108]

The position of slaves is regulated more fully than in T'ang law. Where a slave has sexual intercourse with the wife or daughter of the head of the family, both man and woman are to be beheaded.[109] Generally where a slave has sexual intercourse with the wife or daughter of a free man the punishment is that which would have been imposed where both were free with an increase of one degree. On the other hand where a free person has sexual intercourse with another's slave woman, the punishment is one degree less than that imposed in the ordinary case. Where both parties are slaves the case is to be treated in the same way as if both were free.[110] The rules as to officials having sexual intercourse with a woman under their jurisdiction, or as to sexual intercourse during a period of mourning for parents or husband, or where one or both parties were Buddhist or Taoist priests or nuns are the same as the T'ang.[111]

The extent to which these detailed rules on sexual morality were actually enforced must remain a matter of some doubt. The authorities would certainly take cognizance of a sexual offence where someone had died as a consequence of violence used in the commission of the act or been killed by an irate husband and the like. Otherwise they would be required to act if the matter was brought to their attention as a prosecution instituted by the appropriate person. Still one suspects that the intervention of the state was comparatively rare and that sexual morality was largely left to the discipline of the family and the clan.

Notes

1. Some of the terms used to designate the individual 'abominations' are known in Han law (Hulsewé, Remnants of Han Law, 156ff). During the subsequent period the list of the ten abominations was itself gradually put together. See Balazs, Traité juridique du 'Souei-Chou', 142, n.184; Rosner, Die "Zehn schimpflichen Delikte" im chinesichen Recht der Yüan-Zeit 54f; Johnson, 62 (*shu-i* commentary).

2. For T'ang/Sung law see T'ang article 6 (Johnson, 61ff); for Yüan law, Ratchnevsky, Code des Yüan I, 13ff and cf. IV, lff, and generally see Rosner, op.cit.; for Ming law, article 1.2 (MLCCFL, 186); and for Ch'ing law, article 2, Philastre I, 122; Boulais, 45; Staunton, 3f.

3. See Rosner, op.cit., 105. Balazs holds the governing principle to be 'désobéissance à l'autorité supérieure: Etat, dynastie, fonctionnaires-chefs, potestas du père et des aînés' (op.cit., 144).

4. The general commentary of the Ch'ing code (Philastre I, 123) draws specific attention to the lack of respect in these circumstances.

5. Johnson, 73.

6. All the standard translations of the Ch'ing code fail to distinguish properly between dismemberment (motivated by enmity) and dismemberment for magical purposes or to distinguish either from the preparation of *ku* poison or the practice of sorcery (Philastre I, 122; Boulais, 45; Staunton, 3).

7. Husband's parents are omitted from the T'ang code.

8. Since an official whose parents had died was required to resign from office for the duration of the period of mourning, he might wish to avoid the consequence by concealing their death, or indeed to have an excuse for resignation by falsely asserting the death of one of them.

9. Philastre I, 123.

10. The Ming/Ch'ing definition of 'official superior' is not quite the same as the T'ang. Cf. Johnson, 80 with Philastre I, 123f.

11. Although the categories are operated by Yüan law, the form of the rules

seems to have been rather different from that found in other dynasties. Cf. Ratchnevsky, Code des Yüan IV, 255ff.

12. I am drawing to some extent upon two previous writings: The T'ang Code: Early Chinese Law, and the T'ang and Ming Law of Homicide.

13. On the way in which family relationships affected punishment see especially Ch'ü, Law and Society in Traditional China, 41ff.

14. The commentary to article 18 (Johnson, 119) states 'Plotting to kill if the victim has already been killed is considered the same as deliberate killing (*ku sha*)'.

15. Article 253. Cf. Lê Code, 415; Deloustal, 414.

16. Article 256. Cf. Lê Code, 416; Deloustal, 415.

17. Johnson, 268.

18. Cf. Lê Code, 467; Deloustal, 466; Meijer, The Concept of *Ku-sha* in the Ch'ing Code, 87ff.

19. See chapter 3 at note 32.

20. Article 338. Cf. Lê Code, 498; Deloustal, 497, and generally Wallacker's comprehensive study, The Chinese Offence of Homicide through Horseplay, discussing the T'ang law at 272ff.

21. Op.cit., 274f.

22. Article 339. Cf. Lê Code, 499; Deloustal, 498; MacCormack, Mental States as Criteria of Liability in the T'ang Code, 69f (on which I have drawn for what follows).

23. Johnson, 60.

24. See especially Bünger, The Punishment of Lunatics and Negligents According to Classical Chinese Law, 13f.

25. The situation, as has been seen, was different where those engaging in a dangerous activity also larked or fooled around with the result that someone was killed.

26. On *kuo-shih* see Meijer, Review of Nakamura Shigeo, Studies in Ch'ing Law, 230f.

27. One of the basic categories itself *(hsi sha)* already provides an example of this.

28. Article 73. Cf. Lê Code, 64; Deloustal, 64.

29. Article 261. Cf. Lê Code, 422; Deloustal, 421.

30. Article 395.

31. Article 425.

32. Article 423. Cf. Lê Code, 557; Deloustal, 556.

33. Article 336. The case is considered in the final question and answer of the commentary; the reason for the decision is stated to be that, since there was an original intention to kill one person (A), although another (B) is killed by mistake, the killing falls under *ku sha*.

34. Of the Ch'ing law Meijer, Concept of *Ku-sha* in the Ch'ing Code, 100, observes: 'The justification of sentencing someone as if he had committed *ku-sha* lies in the fact that the offender had performed his action under circumstances when he could certainly expect fatal results for others and his taking that risk meant that he did not care, a circumstance which was comparable to his battering an adversary so much that he did not care whether the victim died or not, which comes very near to the intention

of killing'.

35. Article 261. Cf. Lê Code, 422; Deloustal, 421.
36. Article 289.
37. Article 336. Cf. Lê Code, 497; Deloustal, 496.
38. Article 392.
39. Article 424.
40. Article 427.
41. Article 206. The implication is that in the normal case the owner was not liable where his animal (acting of its own accord) killed or injured someone. See further the section below on 'killing or injury by animals'.
42. Article 263.
43. Article 244. Cf. Lê Code, 568; Deloustal, 567.
44. In Ming and Ch'ing law this case was reclassified and subsumed under the category of *kuo-shih sha* with the consequence that the punishment was changed from penal servitude to payment of redemption (Ming 29.2 (MLCCFL, 2045); Ch'ing article 390, Philastre II, 733; Boulais, 1709; Staunton, 484).
45. Not all cases of killing were subsumed under one of the basic categories. In some instances special rules were deployed such as that punishing the killing of three persons in one family (article 259) or that dealing with a death resulting from construction or demolition work (article 244).
46. Cf. the remarks above on the ordering of the material in the Ming/Ch'ing code (chapter 1 at note 71).
47. Ming 19.18 (MLCCFL, 1529, and for the sub-statutes, 1533); Ch'ing article 268, Philastre II, 247; Boulais, 1322-5; Staunton, 321, and for the sub-statutes see Philastre II, 253 decree IX, 443 decree I; Boulais, 1329, 1504. For a detailed discussion of the law see Meijer, Criminal Responsibility for the Suicide of Parents in Ch'ing Law.
48. The T'ang article (256) contained similar rules for accessories.
49. Ming 19.1 (op.cit., 1461); Ch'ing article 251, Philastre II, 164; Boulais, 1121f; Staunton, 303.
50. MLCCFL, 1462, translated by Meijer, Concept of *Ku-sha* in the Ch'ing Code, 94.
51. Ming 19.9 (op.cit., 1496); Ch'ing article 259, Philastre II, 209; Boulais, 1268f; Staunton, 311.
52. Translated by Meijer, op.cit., 92.
53. Op.cit., 1497.
54. Philastre II, 217.
55. This can be found among the commentaries to Ming 19.9 in Hsüeh Yunsheng's parallel edition of the T'ang and Ming codes (T'ang Ming Lü Ho Pien).
56. See Wallacker, Chinese Offence of Homicide through Horseplay, 278ff.
57. Ming 19.11 (op.cit., 1505); Ch'ing article 261, Philastre II, 222; Boulais, 1283; Staunton, 313.
58. Philastre II, 229f.
59. See especially Ratchnevsky, Code des Yüan IV, 255f, and cf. Ch'en, Legal Tradition under the Mongols, 52; MacCormack, T'ang and Ming Law of Homicide, 70f.

60. See the 'upper commentary', Philastre II, 164.

61. For an example see note 33 above.

62. For the reference see note 57 above.

63. Philastre II, 225 Decree IV.

64. Translated by Meijer, Aspect of Retribution in Traditional Chinese Law, 204f. Cf. also Boulais, 1275; Philastre II, 215 decree IX.

65. Generally see Meijer, op.cit., 199ff.

66. Further rules appear in the Yüan legal compilation. See Ratchnevsky, op.cit., IV, 235ff.

67. For details see Ch'ü, op.cit., 41ff, 183f, 186f.

68. Cf. Lê Code, 465; Deloustal, 464.

69. Cf. Deloustal, 465, 466. For the Ming rules see article 20.1 (MLCCFL, 1541), and for the Ch'ing article 271, Philastre II, 266; Boulais, 1344ff; Staunton, 324.

70. Cf. Lê Code, 466; Deloustal, 465, and for the Ming and Ch'ing rules the articles cited in the previous note.

71. See previous note.

72. Cf. Lê Code 468; Deloustal, 467; Ming 20.2 (op.cit., 1551); Ch'ing article 272, Philastre II, 275; Boulais, 1357f; Staunton, 327.

73. T'ang article 305; Ming and Ch'ing articles cited in the previous note.

74. Cf. Lê Code 471; Deloustal, 470 and the slightly expanded rules in the Ming and Ch'ing articles cited above.

75. Cf. Lê Code, 582; Deloustal, 581; Ming 18.7 (op.cit., 1235); Ch'ing article 208, Philastre I, 268; Boulais, 997; Staunton, 248. See generally MacCormack, Liability for Animals in Traditional Chinese Law, where a translation of the relevant T'ang articles can be found.

76. Article 326. Cf. Lê Code, 481 (where the T'ang article is misinterpreted, as it is by Ch'u, Law and Society in Traditional China, 126); Deloustal, 480 (more accurate account of the T'ang rules). In Ming and Ch'ing law the position is the same: Ming 21.7 (op.cit., 1647); Ch'ing article 299, Philastre II, 385; Boulais, 1454; Staunton, 357.

77. Article 328. Cf. Lê Code, 477; Deloustal, 476. The Ming and Ch'ing rules are the same, though the relevant articles add the case of elder brothers and sisters born of different parents in respect of whom the mourning period and hence the punishment varied: Ming 21.5 (op.cit., 1643); Ch'ing article 297, Philastre II, 382; Boulais, 1452; Staunton, 356.

78. Article 329. Cf. Lê Code, 475; Deloustal, 474. The Ming and Ch'ing rules are the same: Ming 21.6 (op.cit., 1645); Ch'ing article 298, Philastre II, 383; Boulais, 1453; Staunton, 357.

79. Article 330. Cf. Lê Code, 476; Deloustal, 475. In Ming and Ch'ing law the punishment was death by strangulation (articles cited in previous note).

80. Article 331. Cf. Lê Code 476; Deloustal, 475. The Ming and Ch'ing punishment was death by strangulation: Ming 21.8 (op.cit., 1648); Ch'ing article 300, Philastre II, 386; Boulais, 1455; Staunton, 358.

81. Article 334. Cf. Lê Code, 483; Deloustal, 482. The Ming and Ch'ing law simply provides that the wife or concubine is to receive the same punishment as the husband should he commit the offence (articles cited

note 76).

82. Article 323. Cf. LêCode, 480; Deloustal, 479. For the former case the Ming and Ch'ing law prescribed the penalty of death by strangulation, and for the latter penal servitude for two years together with a beating of 80 blows with the heavy stick. It also added some further cases: Ming 21.4 (op.cit., 1642); Ch'ing article 295, Philastre II, 379; Staunton, 355.

83. Article 337. Cf. Lê Code, 486; Deloustal, 485. Ming and Ch'ing law (article cited in note 80 - Boulais, 1456) provided the punishment was merely to be that for insulting an ordinary (unrelated) person, that is, a beating of 10 blows with the light stick.

84. Article 312. Cf. Le Code, 487; Deloustal, 486. The Ming and Ch'ing law had more distinct categories within the class of officials and generally imposed somewhat lesser punishments: Ming 21.2, 3 (op.cit., 1637, 1641); Ch'ing articles 294, 295, Philastre II, 377, 379; Boulais, 1450; Staunton, 354, 355.

85. Ming 21.1 (op.cit., 1637); Ch'ing article 293, Philastre II, 377; Boulais, 1449; Staunton, 354.

86. Ming 'incorporated commentary', op.cit., 1645; Ch'ing 'upper commentary', Philastre II, 379 with his own remarks, and the official, small commentary inserted at the end of article 297 (op.cit., 382).

87. Article 299, Philastre II, 385; Boulais, 1656; Staunton, 419.

88. Ming 'incorporated commentary', op.cit., 1640; Ch'ing general commentary, Philastre II, 378, and the official, small commentary inserted in article 296, op.cit., 381.

89. Op.cit., 1643.

90. Article 296, op.cit., 381.

91. Generally see Ch'ü, Law and Society in Traditional China, 64f, 187f. For homosexual offences introduced into the law in Ch'ing times by substatutes see Boulais, 1588; Ng, Ideology and Sexuality: Rape Law in Qing China, 67f; and especially Meijer, Homosexual Offences in Ch'ing Law.

92. Cf. Meijer, Price of a P'ai-Pou, 290f, 293f.

93. Cf. the remarks of Ng, op.cit., 57.

94. Article 410. Cf. Lê Code, 401; Deloustal, 400, and for the immunity from punishment of women against whom force is used, article 415.

95. Article 411.

96. Article 412. Cf. Lê Code, 406; Deloustal, 405.

97. Article 413. Cf. Lê Code, 406; Deloustal, 405.

98. Article 414. Cf. Lê Code, 407; Deloustal, 406.

99. Cf. the remarks of Ch'ü, op.cit., 187.

100. Article 416. This article also imposed an increase of punishment by two degrees on persons engaging in sexual intercourse while in mourning for parents or husband, and on Buddhist or Taoist priests or nuns who had sexual intercourse.

101. See especially Ratchnevsky, Code des Yüan IV, 47f.

102. Ming 25.1 (op.cit., 1833); Ch'ing article 332, Philastre II, 524; Boulais, 1581f; Staunton, 404.

103. This distinction between 'completed' and 'attempted' act is not applied to situations in which there is consent.

104. Philastre II, 525 and cf. chapter 9 on forcible theft.
105. Philastre II, 524, and see especially Ng, Ideology and Sexuality.
106. Detailed rules on these matters are contained in a T'ang Household Statute inserted in the Sung code after the group of articles on illicit sexual intercourse in the book on Miscellaneous Offences.
107. The T'ang code (article 415) knew the case of the go-between.
108. Ming 21.56 (op.cit., 1843): Ch'ing article 334, Philastre II, 534; Boulais, 1599f; Staunton, 406f.
109. Ming 21.8 (op.cit., 1848); Ch'ing article 336; Philastre II, 539; Boulais, 1608; Staunton 407.
110. Ming 21.11 (op.cit., 1854); Ch'ing article 339, Philastre II, 545; Boulais, 1628; Staunton, 409.
111. Ming 21.9.10 (op.cit., 1850, 1852); Ch'ing articles 337, 8, Philastre II, 542, 544; Boulais, 1617, 1624; Staunton, 408, 9.

9

Theft and Damage to Property

Tsang

A basic concept running through the rules on theft and damage to property which requires preliminary explanation is that of *tsang*. Although strictly speaking the term is untranslateable by a single expression, the meaning having to be gathered from the varying contexts in which it occurs, the best approximate English rendering so far suggested is 'illicit goods'.[1] In this broad sense *tsang* designates either property which the law treats as having been unlawfully acquired and with respect to which it establishes a punishment, or property which has been lost, destroyed or damaged as a consequence of someone's act and with respect to which again the law establishes a punishment.

All the codes distinguish between six kinds of *tsang* or rather between six offences involving *tsang*.[2] However the nature of the six differs in the earlier (T'ang/Sung) and later (Ming/Ch'ing) codes. The T'ang classification (adopted by the Sung) was: forcible theft, secret theft, the acceptance of bribes by officials with a consequent subversion of the law, the acceptance of bribes by officials without subverting the law, acceptance of property by supervisory or custodial officials within the area of their jurisdiction, and the imposition of liability on account of *tsang* (*tso tsang*) in cases not falling under one of the other heads.[3] In Ming and Ch'ing law there is greater emphasis upon the notion of theft itself. Thus the six offences now become: theft by supervisory or custodial officials of public property entrusted to their care, theft by ordinary persons of public property, the acceptance of property by officials who subvert the law, secret theft, the acceptance of property by officials without subverting the law, and the general liability on account of *tsang* (*tso tsang*).[4] The omission of forcible theft from the Ming/Ch'ing classification of *tsang* offences is explained by the fact that the punishment in all cases where goods were forcibly taken was decapitation, irrespective of their value.

For each of these six offences (whether in Tang/Sung or Ming/Ch'ing law) the punishment is determined by reference to *tsang*. This means that its severity is proportional to the value of the illicit goods involved in the particular offence: if goods worth X have been stolen, then the punishment is to be Y. However the scale or tariff adopted varied according to the specific offence. In those deemed most serious such as forcible theft or the acceptance of bribes and the subversion of the law, illicit goods of a given value attracted a much higher punishment than those of the same value involved in one of the miscellaneous *tso tsang* offences. Some examples from both the earlier and the later periods follow.

In T'ang law the forcible theft of goods worth a piece of silk one *ch'ih* (approximately one foot) in length is punished by penal servitude for three years, and of goods worth 10 *p'i*[5] or more by strangulation.[6] In the case of secret theft the punishment for taking goods worth one *ch'ih* of silk is 60 blows with the heavy stick, and that for taking goods worth 50 *p'i* or more is exile with added labour.[7] Where a supervisory or custodial official accepts a bribe and subverts the law the scale ranges from 1 *ch'ih*, 100 blows with the heavy stick, to 15 *p'i*, strangulation; if the law is not subverted 1 *ch'ih* entails 90 blows with the heavy stick and 30 *p'i* exile with added labour.[8] A supervisory official who accepts goods worth 1 *ch'ih* within his area of jurisdiction is punished by 40 blows with the light stick, the maximum punishment for accepting goods worth 50 *p'i* or more being exile to 2000 *li* (article 140). For the miscellaneous class of *tsang* offences (*tso tsang*) the punishment starts with 20 blows with the light stick for 1 *ch'ih* and progresses to a maximum of 3 years penal servitude (article 389).

In Ming and Ch'ing law the same principles applied although the scales were different. Goods are assessed in terms of ounces of silver (or in Ming law the equivalent in strings of cash).[9] Most serious was the theft of goods entrusted to their care by supervisory or custodial officials. Theft of goods worth one ounce of silver or less was punished with a beating of 80 blows with the heavy stick and of those worth 40 ounces nominally with decapitation (commuted in Ch'ing law to the exceptional punishment of penal servitude for 5 years). Next in order of seriousness were theft of public property by ordinary people and acceptance of bribes by officials with subversion of the law. In both cases punishment started at a beating of 70 blows with the heavy stick in respect of goods worth

1 ounce of silver or less and ended with strangulation at 80 ounces.[10] Next came secret theft and acceptance of property by officials without subversion of the law. In these cases punishment started with a beating of 60 blows with the heavy stick in respect of goods worth 1 ounce of silver or less, and ended with strangulation at 120 ounces or more.[11] Finally, rated least serious, were the miscellaneous *tsang* offences where the range of punishment (starting at 20 blows with the light stick at 1 ounce or less and ending at penal servitude for three years and 100 blows with the heavy stick at 500 ounces) was approximately the same as under the T'ang.

Theft

From the detailed provisions found in the codes one can establish certain general points concerning the treatment of theft both in T'ang/Sung and Ming/Ch'ing law.[12]   Several factors might determine the way the punishment was assessed in a particular case of theft. First, the law singled out certain species of property, possessing little intrinsic value, the unauthorised appropriation of which was regarded as a serious offence. In such cases, for example, the taking of objects used by the emperor or official documents or seals, a fixed punishment was imposed.   For property not excepted in this way the severity of the punishment depended upon the value of the goods taken (*tsang*).   Sometimes these two methods of assessment were combined, as where a minimum punishment was stipulated and a proviso added to the effect that should the property taken have a high value the punishment was to be assessed according to the *tsang*. Second, a distinction was drawn between forcible and secret theft, the punishments being considerably heavier for the former. Third, the status or legal position of the offender or victim was important. In particular officials who stole property in respect to which they occupied a position of trust were punished more heavily than ordinary persons who stole property of the same value. Significant also was the fact of family relationship. Persons who stole from others towards whom they stood in a relationship of mourning were punished less severely than unrelated persons, and, indeed, the longer the period of mourning, the less severe the punishment. Fourth, statements which establish the conditions for the accomplishment of an act of theft were concerned exclusively with physical requirements and in particular the degree of asportation necessary to constitute a completed act of theft. Nothing is said of the mental requirements, it obviously being assumed by the legislators that the intention to take was clearly manifested in the physical act and required no independent mention. Finally the law imposed an obligation on the thief to make restitution - in some case onerous - as well as liability to punishment.

Objects for the theft of which fixed punishments were imposed were those of particular importance to the emperor or the state, although their monetary value might be slight. The Ming/Ch'ing punishments tended to be considerably more severe than the T'ang. Thus T'ang law punished theft (whether forcible or secret) of articles personally used by the emperor (such as clothing or chariots) or used in the imperial sacrifices to the spirits with exile to 2500 *li*.[13] In Ming and Ch'ing law the punishment was decapitation.[14] T'ang law (article 273) punished theft of imperial decrees with penal servitude for two years (Ming/Ch'ing decapitation), of other official documents with a beating of 100 blows with the heavy stick (Ming/Ch'ing the same plus branding, but strangulation if they concerned military operations).[15] By article 271 the theft of imperial seals was punished with strangulation,[16] and by article 272 that of other official seals with penal servitude for 2 years (Ming/Ch'ing punishment for both being decapitation).[17] The theft of plants or trees from an imperial mansoleum was punished in T'ang law (article 278) by penal servitude for 2 1/2 years (Ming/Ch'ing, 100 blows with the heavy stick and 3 years penal servitude), and that of trees from other grave sites by a beating of 100 blows with the heavy stick (Ming/Ch'ing 80 blows with the heavy stick).[18]

The theft of horses or cattle presented one or two special features deriving from the particular value which attached to them. This is evident most clearly in the rule common to all codes imposing a punishment even on a person who killed his own animal. Article 203 of the T'ang code imposed a punishment of 1 1/2 years on anyone who deliberately killed a horse or beast falling within the class of cattle, reduced to 1 year for a person who killed his own animal.[19] In Ming and Ch'ing law the punishment was only a beating of 100 blows with the heavy stick for killing one's own animal but penal servitude for 1 1/2 years and a beating of 70 blows with the heavy stick for killing anyone else's.[20] According to the T'ang *shu-i* commentary the reason lies in the necessity of cattle for the conduct of agriculture and of horses for military transport. The general commentary of the Ch'ing code adds a reason that appears to be drawn from Confucian morality: since such animals employ their strength in the service of man, to kill them is an act of ingratitude.[21]

T'ang law links what are inherently the separate offences of killing and theft and provides that for stealing horses or cattle (whether owned by the government or private persons) and killing them the punishment is to be penal servitude for 2 1/2 years. Nothing is said of the theft of these animals alone.[22] Presumably in this case the assumption is that their services for agriculture and transport are not lost and therefore the theft can be dealt with according to the normal rules. The corresponding articles in the Ming and Ch'ing codes retain the connection between theft and killing but impose a heavier minimum punishment, penal servitude for 3 years and 100 blows with the heavy stick. They explicitly distinguish the case where the animals are merely stolen, without being killed, and provide that the normal rule is to be applied under which the punishment depends upon the value of the stolen property.[23]

For all cases in which a fixed punishment was prescribed and there was no calculation of the *tsang*, the T'ang code established a general rule. When in fact the calculation of the value of the property stolen would have yielded under the normal tariff applied in theft (either forcible or secret) a punishment as high as, or higher than, that prescribed in the fixed minimum, than the case was to be treated as theft with an increase in punishment of one degree (article 280). For example, according to the commentary, where another person's horse or beast of the class of cattle worth 20 *p'i* is stolen and killed, the punishment under the ordinary rules would be penal servitude for 2 1/2 years. This is the same as the minimum punishment provided by article 279. Hence an increase of one degree is applied and the thief sentenced to penal servitude for 3 years. No such general rule was contained in the Ming and Ch'ing codes. The reason probably was that in many of the cases for which a fixed punishment was prescribed, it was so heavy, especially where property owned, used or emanating from the emperor was taken, that there was no point in having a supplementary rule permitting the punishment to be calculated according to the value of the *tsang*. Where this was to be permitted the particular article establishing the fixed punishment also provided for punishment in accordance with the value of the *tsang*. For example the article on theft and killing of animals contained such a provision (similar to the T'ang) after the establishment of the fixed punishments.

Where no fixed punishment was prescribed the punishment in all cases of theft was determined by reference to the value of the goods taken but the tariff depended upon the kind of theft. If there was an element of 'force' the punishment proportionately was much higher than in the case where the theft was 'secret'. The T'ang code defines forcible theft as that in which physical force or intimidation is used and states that it makes no difference whether the force is used prior to or after the actual taking of the goods. Equally the drugging or stupifying of a person with wine and a subsequent removal of his property are acts amounting to forcible theft (article 281). Secret theft is defined as that which is done in secret with a disguise of one's appearance as through the wearing of a mask (article 282). In both forcible and secret theft there is punishment for what one might term unsuccessful (rather than attempted) theft, that is, where an act of theft has been completed but the thief has not succeeded in getting away with property. Where 'force' has been used the punishment is penal servitude for two years; otherwise it is a beating of 50 blows with the light stick. Where property has been obtained, that is, where the thief has succeeded in getting away with the stolen goods, more severe punishments are imposed in accordance with the value of the *tsang*. If weapons are carried the punishments are again increased. Even should no property be obtained, the punishment is exile to 3000 *li*; for obtaining goods worth 5 *p'i* the thief is to be strangled (article 281).

Two special rules are worth noting. These specify how the value of the *tsang* is to be calculated, and therefore have a bearing upon the eventual punishment imposed. In cases of repeated (two or more) thefts the value of all the stolen goods is to be totalled and then halved, the figure so reached determining the punishment. The commentary to article 45 gives as an example a person who commits several acts of secret theft at different places, obtaining in all goods worth 82 *p'i*. Half this figure (41 *p'i*) is taken as the determinant of the sentence which is life exile to 3000 *li*.[24] Sometimes the law is more severe as where supervisory officials commit repeated thefts within the area of their jurisdiction; the illicit goods are totalled and not halved for the determination of the punishment.[25] Where two or more persons take part in a theft, the rule is that each is liable with respect to the total value of the goods taken (or the half in the event of repeated thefts) even though he may personally have received only a proportion of this. Thus if ten people steal goods worth ten *p'i* and each takes one *p'i* for his share, he is still liable with respect to the full amount of ten (article 297).

Forcible and secret theft can be regarded as basic categories utilised by the code in the sense that they are focal points around which a number of other offences is clustered. As in other areas of the law the code adopts a technique of assimilation and resolves an issue of punishment by stating that certain conduct is to be treated as the same as (*i . . . lun*) or as comparable to (*chun . . . lun*) forcible or secret theft. *I . . . lun* and *chun . . . lun* are both technical expressions which have a different significance. Where an offence is to be treated in the same way as theft, all the rules applicable to theft apply also to that offence. Where it is merely to be treated as comparable to theft, not all the penal consequences of theft are applied. For example the rule requiring restitution of double the *tsang*[26] was applied to offences to be treated in the same way as theft, not to those to be treated merely as comparable. Some examples follow.

The kidnapping of a slave is treated in the same way as forcible theft, the punishment being determined according to the value of the slave (*tsang*) on the scale laid down for that offence, with a maximum sentence of exile to 3000 *li*.[27] Where someone deliberately sets fire to another's house and takes property both the property taken and that lost through the fire constitute the *tsang* and are to be treated as having been forcibly stolen (article 284). If someone for a reason unconnected with theft assaults another, then afterwards sees property and seizes it, the case is treated as one of forcible theft. But since there was originally no intention to steal, where the value of the *tsang* taken warranted the death penalty, the offender was to be sentenced merely to exile with added labour (article 286).[28]

Many offences are subsumed under the head of secret theft. Those to be treated in the same way include cases in which market officials have established unfair practices in the markets and thereby made a personal profit (article 419), or in which persons have made a profit by exchanging personal for government property or vice versa,[29] or by using privately made, unfair weights and measures for the giving out or taking in of official goods.[30] Similarly one who has profited from another's labour by appropriating some material product on which the latter has expended effort (for example mown and stored grass) is treated as a thief (article 291). Also included are certain cases in which officials 'borrow' government property, viz, the borrowing of interest yielding or fruit producing property belonging to the government by supervisory or custodial officials where there is no written record of the transaction,[31] and the private employment by officials of corvee labour which should have been applied to public works.[32]

If one takes the essence of theft to be the removal of another's property without his permission one can see why a number of offences are classified not as theft itself but as comparable to theft. The main criterion for membership of this class appears to be the negative one of a clear failure to satisfy the conditions for theft. First, there are some offences in which property is obtained by threats or deceit. These resemble theft but perhaps were not classified as being theft because to all appearances the property was obtained with the consent of the owner. Using blackmail or threats to obtain property is treated as comparable to theft but the punishment is increased by one degree.[33] Obtaining property by deceit or through the falsification of private or governmental documents is also treated as comparable to theft but here there is no increase in punishment.[34] Second, there are offences treated as comparable to theft which involve merely the destruction or loss of, or damage to, property with no necessary element of deceit or personal profit.[35] Possibly the connecting link lies in the fact that the owner has been deprived of property or caused economic loss. Finally there are several miscellaneous offences treated as comparable to theft such as accepting a slave knowing him to have been kidnapped where there is a decrease in punishment by one degree (article 296), or the winning or losing of property by gambling where those who lose are punished as accessories, that is, by one degree less than those who win.[36]

Ming and Ch'ing law show some differences from the T'ang and Sung with respect to the categories of theft, the particular rules for the calculation of the *tsang*, and the nature of the punishment.[37] The basic distinction remains that between forcible and secret theft but two further special kinds of theft not found in T'ang/Sung law are now present. First the later law treated more seriously the theft of property from government storehouses or granaries by private individuals and established a tariff for the calculation of *tsang* more severe than that applied to the normal case of secret theft.[38] According to Shen's 'upper commentary' the explanation lies in the greater importance attached to goods belonging to the state.[39]

Second, there was a specific offence of robbing a person in broad daylight for which a minimum punishment of penal servitude for 3 years and a beating of 100 blows with the heavy stick was imposed. Should the value of the goods taken, on the scale applied to secret theft, yield the same or a higher punishment, then this was to be applied with an increase of two degrees. To be treated in the same way was the pillage of a ship that had capsized or been wrecked or of an individual's property in the event of an accidental fire on his premises.[40] The commentators have some difficulty in distinguishing theft in broad daylight from forcible theft. Both appeared to be brazen acts involving the use of some force. According to the official commentary prefixing the Ch'ing article the distinction lay in the number of persons and the nature of their weapons. If they were numerous and bore murderous weapons the offence was forcible theft; if they were few and did not bear such weapons it was robbery in broad daylight.   However Shen's 'upper commentary', probably rightly, located the distinction not so much in the number of persons involved as in the degree of violence exhibited, that is, according to whether murderous weapons were carried or not.   A Ch'ing sub-statute in fact extended the provisions of this law to cover robbery committed by bands of marauders on the roads, even though it took place in the obscurity of night.[41]

The distinction between forcible theft and robbery in broad daylight was of crucial importance because of the severity with which Ming and Ch'ing law treated the former. In an effort to stamp out violent acts the most stringent punishments were imposed where the act qualified as 'forcible theft'. Where acts of force, with a view to taking property, had been completed such as the assembling of armed persons, the proceeding to a person's house irrespective of whether they were seen or not, and the breaking of doors and windows, then even though no property was actually taken, perhaps because of successful resistance, a punishment of exile to 3000 *li* together with a beating of 100 blows with the heavy stick was imposed. Should any property in fact be taken then, irrespective of its value, all, without distinction between principals and accessories, are to be punished with decapitation. Both the Ming and the Ch'ing commentaries emphasise that the essence of the offence is the employment of force not the actual taking of property.[42]

Secret theft, defined by the commentaries as that accomplished by stealth so that the owner is unaware that it is taking place, is treated in the same way as in T'ang/Sung law, although the punishment now entails the branding of the criminal with words indicating his offence.[43] As in T'ang law both theft by threats or blackmail and theft by deceit are to be treated as comparable to secret theft, the former entailing an increase of punishment by one degree.[44] Further, generalising from the T'ang position, the codes introduced a special rule for the taking of unharvested crops, vegetables, fruit or unguarded implements or articles (that is, not in a house or under special watch), or of objects from the mountains or uninhabited places on which someone has expended labour, such as trees cut down for firewood. Since these items of property have either not been appropriated by their owners through being taken into their homes or placed under guard, or are intrinsically open to anyone, the law is slightly less strict and treats the act as comparable to theft; the tariff for that offence is to be applied in the calculation of the punishment but the offender is to be exempt from branding.[45]

With respect to the calculation of the *tsang* for the purpose of determining the appropriate punishment the T'ang rules were maintained only in part. Where several persons took part in a theft each, as in T'ang law, was held liable on account of the total value of the goods taken, irrespective of the amount which he individually had received. However where a person or persons had committed several distinct acts of theft either against the same owner or against different owners the T'ang rule which prescribed accumulation of the *tsang* and then the halving of the total, to reach the amount fixing punishment, was abandoned. Instead Ming and Ch'ing law adopted a rule under which the goods taken on each occasion were separately valued and the thief was liable to punishment only in respect of whichever figure should prove to be the highest.[46] This not only prevented what the commentators regarded as excessive severity (should he have been made liable for the total) but also accorded with the general principle governing cases of multiple offences.[47]

In Ming and Ch'ing law where property had been obtained by an actual act of theft, as distinct from an act treated as comparable to theft, the thief in addition to receiving the appropriate punishment was also to be branded on the right arm with letters stating 'secret theft'. Should a thief once branded commit a second act of theft he is to be branded with the same letters on the left arm. Should he subsequently commit yet a third theft he is to be strangled.[48] The Ch'ing general commentary makes two important points.[49] It is only acts of theft which themselves entail branding that count for the purpose of the rule that the third theft is to be punished with strangulation. Further the purpose of the branding is to deter the culprit from future offences and encourage him to reform. Should he still commit theft even after the second he is to be deemed incorrigibly evil and deserving of death.

Officials occupying what may be termed a fiduciary position with respect to persons or property were punished more severely than ordinary persons if they committed theft. In T'ang law supervisory or custodial officials who stole goods entrusted to their care (that is, from storehouses of which they had charge) or from persons within their area of jurisdiction were punished two degrees more than an ordinary person who stole property of an equivalent value.[50] In Ming and Ch'ing law the emphasis is more clearly placed on the protection of public goods kept in public storehouses. For their theft two special tariffs were introduced, one, particularly severe, applying to the theft of such goods by officials placed in charge of them,[51] and the other, less severe though still more stringent than that used for secret theft, applying to their theft by ordinary persons.[52] It thus appears that the Ming and Ch'ing law, with respect to theft, placed less weight on the relationship of an official to the people of the district over which he presided than did the T'ang and Sung.

There is nothing particularly striking to Western eyes in the imposition of severe penalties on officials who breach fiduciary obligations. What is striking is the complex of rules found in all codes drastically reducing the punishment where theft occurs between relatives. The two principles governing this matter were that theft might occur only between relatives who were not living together and that the closer the relationship between the thief and the victim the lighter the punishment. Thus the T'ang code provided that where a person stole from a relative for whom he wore mourning for three or five months (irrespective of who was 'senior' and who 'junior') the punishment was one degree less than for theft between unrelated persons; if the mourning was for nine months the punishment was two degrees less, and if for one year three degrees less.[53] The Ming/Ch'ing law was even more lenient. Theft from a year of mourning relative was punished five degrees less than that from an unrelated person, from a nine month mourning relative, four degrees less, from a five months mourning relative, three degrees less, from a three months mourning relative, two degrees less, and from a relative for whom no mourning was worn (a case not contemplated by the T'ang code), one degree less. Further the thief in each case was exempt from branding.[54]

These rules apply essentially to the case of secret theft only. For forcible theft account is taken of the distinction between 'senior' and 'junior' relatives. The T'ang code provided that where a relative of a lower generation or of the same generation but younger committed forcible theft the reductions in punishment normally applied to theft between relatives were not to be available and the matter was to be governed by the law on forcible theft between unrelated persons (article 285). Since no special rule is laid down for the case where a relative of a higher generation or of the same generation but older committed forcible theft, it is to be inferred that the reductions in punishment were here applicable. The same rules with respect to forcible theft are found in the Ming and Ch'ing codes.[55]

A significant feature of the rules on theft between relatives is that they do not apply where there is wrongful appropriation of goods by relatives who live together. The reason is that the 'junior' as well as the 'senior' members of the household have an interest in the family property which in due course will devolve to them. However the management of the property was in the hands of the family head (normally the most senior male) and it was not open to juniors to act on their own authority, without the permission of the head, and appropriate to themselves or dispose of family property. If they did they committed a particular offence, not theft, but one designated the improper and unauthorised use of family property. The punishment depended upon the value of the family property so appropriated, but in all codes might not exceed 100 blows with the heavy stick.[56] Where relatives did not live in the same household the law recognised that the offence of theft could be committed. But the reduced punishments imposed, and the fact that, except in the case of forcible theft, no distinction is made between 'senior' and 'junior' are probably also to be explained as a consequence of the notion that relatives had some kind of interest in property held by any of them.[57]

Only at the end of their respective sections on theft, after an enumeration of all the special cases, do the codes establish the criteria for the determination of the question, has an act of theft taken place? These criteria are concerned with the question of possession, the assumption apparently being that there can be no theft unless the offender has taken possession of the goods. What amounts to the taking of possession varies according to the nature of the object. The relevant articles, virtually identical in all the codes, are exceptional in that they are concerned purely with a definitional point and do not themselves establish either an offence or a punishment. It is perhaps for this reason that they are to be found after the articles specifically providing the punishments for theft.

Article 300 of the T'ang code provides that whether the theft is public (that is, forcible) or secret there must be a 'taking' of the property,[58] evidenced primarily by removal from its location, though not necessarily from the premises themselves. It was the requisite degree of removal that varied according to the nature of the object. Thus for utensils or ordinary objects, for example money or silks, it was necessary to move them from their original place. For objects like gold, jade or precious stones it was enough if they were concealed in the hand, although not yet actually taken away. If an object was too heavy to be removed by human strength alone and had to be conveyed by horse or mule, theft was not completed until it had been placed on the beast for transport, even though it had been removed from its original place. Special rules applied to animals or birds. In the case of animals kept in enclosures or fettered it was necessary to move them from their usual place; as to wild birds (like falcons) and beasts it was necessary to exert special control over them. Where one ox or horse was taken and others of the same species followed the latter were not to be included in the estimate of the property stolen (the *tsang*) unless they were offspring following their mother.[59] The distinctions made in the Ming and Ch'ing articles are the same, although it is stipulated that objects such as silk and money should be moved 'far' from the place of theft.[60]

It is a remarkable fact that the Ch'ing code utilises the same criteria and the same distinctions and even the same examples as the T'ang code so many centuries earlier. Throughout its history the traditional law can be seen to have focused sharply upon the physical aspect of theft. For an act of theft to be completed there must essentially be asportation, signifying the taking of possession by the offender. There might still, according to the codes, be liability in theft, even though the act had not been followed by the actual obtaining of the property in the sense that the thief made good his escape with it. However great care must be taken in establishing the circumstances. The general commentary of the Ch'ing code states that there must be certain and precise indications of the act of theft or the testimony of reliable eye witnesses.[61] Again the emphasis is on the physical circumstances of the act.

It is perhaps also remarkable that nothing is said in the text of the articles or commentaries as to any possible mental requirement (*mens rea*). No doubt what Roman law calls the *animus furandi,* the intention to steal, was deemed to be sufficiently manifest in the physical act, so much so that there was thought to be no need even to refer to it. Yet one wonders whether the very conservatism of the legal tradition perhaps had a stifling effect in preventing a fresh analysis or a fresh contribution. The T'ang code itself was an admirable legal creation, and the rules it established were frequently and rightly accepted by the later codes. Yet even where arguably there was room for further development or refinement the sanctity attached to the T'ang rules may have restricted or prevented this.

A thief was not only liable to punishment but was also under an obligation to make restitution, that is, to restore to the victim the stolen goods or their value (the *tsang*). The content of this obligation is more onerous in T'ang law than in Ming or Ch'ing. The *shu-i* (T'ang) commentary explains that, because a thief has been covetous of another's property, the matter is more serious than in other offences involving illicit goods and he should be required to restore double their value. This rule applied to all cases which were to be treated as theft, though not to those which were to be treated as comparable to theft.[62] Later law did not accept this reasoning. Both the Ming and Ch'ing codes merely require restoration of the goods stolen or their value.[63]

There is an important exception to the rule requiring restitution of the *tsang*. Article 33 of the T'ang code provides that in cases where the punishment is death or exile and the *tsang*, for example the goods stolen, have already been spent or dissipated, there need be no restitution. The commentary, as in many other contexts, invokes the concept of pity as the reason for leniency.[64] The Ming and Ch'ing position was less lenient. In principle the offender's family was only exempt from the obligation to restore where he had himself died and the *tsang* had been spent or dissipated.[65] This general rule may have been applied under the Ming to the case of theft. During the Ch'ing, however, practice seems to have changed. Shen's 'upper commentary' states that in cases of forcible or secret theft, even where the offender has been executed or had died of illness, restitution to the victim is to be made out of his property.[66] The implication is that it made no difference whether the goods originally stolen were still in the possession of the thief or his family or not. Furthermore a sub-statute, apparently introduced in 1801, though stating a rule applied earlier, requires compensation to be paid to victims from the property of the thieves, and adds that where the latter have been captured and the stolen property found to be irrecoverable the local magistrate is himself to provide compensation up to a certain amount.[67]

Damage to Property

The treatment of destruction or loss of property or damage to it in the codes is markedly similar to that of theft. A double regime of punishment and compensation is established. There is concentration on particular types of property, the rule applicable to each kind being set out in separate articles, although a certain level of generality is reached. The social or public value (not the economic) of the property destroyed lost or damaged primarily determines the severity of the punishment. In cases where this value is high the legislators prescribe that the offence is to be treated as theft or as comparable to theft. In other cases the normal rule is that there is to be liability on account of *tsang*. Thus the first task in determining the punishment for a particular act of destruction, loss or damage is to identify the applicable tariff, for example that for theft or liability on account of *tsang*. Once the tariff has been identified the economic value of the property becomes relevant, the scale of punishment being in accordance with the value of the *tsang*. Again, as in the case of theft, for particular kinds of property a fixed punishment is prescribed. Generally it does not appear that the codes drew a sharp distinction between the offences of theft and damage to property. The rules vary to some extent according to whether the property is government or private, the loss, damage or destruction has occurred deliberately or not, and whether the property has been physically damaged or just lost. First will be examined the rules on damage done by persons and then those on damage done by animals.

The T'ang code equates theft and destruction of the principal Taoist and Buddhist statues. For either act a punishment of 3 years penal servitude is imposed.[68] A fixed punishment of penal servitude for 1 year is also imposed for the destruction of the stone tablets or stone animals erected at the tombs of officials.[69] To be treated as theft is the deliberate throwing away or destruction of objects used in the great imperial sacrifices (article 435). More frequently used is the technique of treating the damage as comparable to theft. Thus the deliberate killing of horses, cattle or other domestic animals,[70] the loss and damage of property through flooding caused by the wanton and deliberate breaking through a dyke where a minimum punishment of 3 years penal servitude was imposed,[71] the deliberate throwing away or destruction of government or private utensils or goods or the destruction of trees or crops,[72] the deliberate throwing away of official seals, keys of public buildings, imperial decrees and official documents (articles 437,8), the throwing away, destruction or removal of government food or drink (article 441), are all to be treated as comparable to theft and the punishment, other than a fixed minimum, calculated according to the tariff for secret theft. The references to destruction in the above cases must be taken as implying an intention to destroy.

For other cases the legislators deem it sufficient to impose liability on account of *tsang*, where the punishment is calculated according to a lighter tariff than that applied to theft. Treated in this way are the loss or damage of property caused through flooding where a dyke is broken with the object of stealing water for personal use, a minimum punishment of a 100 blows with the heavy stick being imposed (article 425), the damage suffered by goods or articles in public granaries and storehouses where they have not been arranged according to the proper rules, or not aired and dried at the proper time,[73] loss of property caused through a disturbance deliberately created in a market or crowded place,[74] loss or damage caused through flooding when a dyke has not been kept in proper repair, the official responsible being liable on account of *tsang* with a reduction in punishment of five degrees,[75] the loss or destruction of official or private property through the failure to keep a boat seaworthy or to navigate it properly, again with a decrease in punishment of five degrees (article 427), damage to property resulting from the accidental lighting of a fire, with a decrease in punishment of 3 degrees (article 430), provided the fire was not within a government building or storehouse; if so there is no decrease and a minimum punishment of penal servitude for 2 years is imposed (article 431),[76] the damage or destruction of minor Buddhist or Taoist statues on which labour has been expended,[77] and wrongfully eating, throwing away or destroying fruit in government or private orchards (article 441).

In most of these cases the reason for treating the loss, damage or destruction as imposing merely liability on account of *tsang* and not as comparable to theft is the fact that the offender had not intended to harm the property in question.[78] In other cases also punishment was excluded or reduced where there was no intention to destroy or harm. For the accidental (non-deliberate) killing or wounding of a domestic animal, or the accidental destruction, or loss of damage of privately owned goods, trees or crops, there was no liability to punishment; if the goods, trees or crops are owned by the government there is still liability but with a decrease of 3 degrees (article 203, 442).[79] When objects used in the great imperial sacrifices, official seals, keys of public buildings, imperial decrees or official documents are accidentally lost or destroyed, the offence is still treated as comparable to theft but there is a decrease in punishment of 2 degrees (articles 435, 437, 438). Furthermore where there was liability for the accidental loss of government property (of various kinds) and the object was found and restored within thirty days by the person who had lost it there was to be exemption from punishment; if the property, whether government or private, had been deliberately abandoned but found and restored within the same period, there was to be a decrease in punishment of 1 degree.[80]

What is surprising in view of the treatment of theft is that the T'ang code does not appear to have provided what was to be the case where a person lost, damaged or destroyed property belonging to a relative. The only article mentioning relatives deals with the killing of domestic animals. If someone kills horses or cattle belonging to a relative for whom mourning is worn for three months or more, the punishment is to be the same as that applied where the owner himself kills the animal; for other domestic animals there is to be liability on account of *tsang* with a maximum punishment of 100 blows with the heavy stick.[81] Where other property was lost, damaged or destroyed it seems that the case was treated as though the parties were unrelated.

In addition to punishment an obligation to make restitution was often imposed. However in a number of cases an exception was made and the obligation excluded. Thus where the nature of the object was such that no restitution or payment of compensation was possible only a punishment was imposed. This rule is laid down in article 445, the note and commentary giving as examples tallies, emblems of command, seals, gate keys, contracts, official documents and imperial decrees. In other cases one infers that no obligation to make restitution was imposed because the relevant article makes no mention of it. Thus nothing is said of restitution in the article on damage to goods resulting from the unseaworthiness of a vessel, faulty navigation or the deliberate creation of a disturbance in the market. The reason may have been the remoteness of the connection between the offending act and the damage.

Sometimes the code states that the value of the *tsang* is to be paid to the owner only where the loss, destruction or damage has arisen from a deliberate act. Article 434 provides that in all cases of damage or destruction caused by fire or water there is to be payment of compensation only where the offender's act responsible for the damage had been deliberate.[82] Thus there is no obligation to pay the value of the property lost by the owner in cases where flooding has occurred through the failure to keep a dyke in repair, or a fire lit for a proper purpose has accidentally spread. However should a person have deliberately broken open a dyke, whether the intention was to appropriate water for his own use, simply to cause damage, or directed at some other improper object, he must pay compensation to the owners of property lost, destroyed or damaged in consequence of the resulting flood. With respect to public property kept in government storehouses there was also an obligation to pay compensation only in the event of deliberate loss or destruction (article 445). For the eating, throwing away or destruction of fruit from government or private orchards there was an obligation to pay the value of the *tsang* to the owner, but not, it seems, where there had been non-deliberate destruction (article 441).

In other cases there was an obligation to pay compensation whether or not the damage had been deliberately caused. Article 203 stipulates that where a domestic animal has been killed or injured the amount by which it is now worth less is to be paid to the owner as compensation; this is also to apply where the animal belongs to a relative (article 205). Where the stone tablets or animals adorning the tombs of officials, or a person's house, tower or walls have been damaged or destroyed, whether accidentally or deliberately, the offender is to repair or restore (article 443). Perhaps the same applied where Buddhist or Taoist statues have been destroyed or damaged, although no express distinction between 'deliberate' and 'accidental' is drawn in the language of the text (article 276). Article 445 stipulates that in the case of government or private utensils and goods, whether they have been deliberately or accidentally lost or destroyed, compensation is to be paid to the owner. The article (442) imposing punishment in this class of case mentions also trees and crops. The fact that they are omitted in article 445 suggests that there may have been no obligation to pay compensation for such property. If so it is difficult to see what could have been the reason for the distinction between 'utensils and goods' and 'trees and crops'. On the other hand it is possible that the phrase 'utensils and goods' used in article 445 may have been deemed to include the 'crops and trees' specifically enumerated in article 442.

No reason is stated in the *shu-i* commentary for the exclusion of the objection to make restitution in a number of cases where destruction, loss or damage has resulted from a non-deliberate act. One might conjecture either that the relationship between act and damage in these cases was deemed to be too remote or that the absence of an intention to cause harm or perform an unlawful act induced leniency on the part of the law. These two possible reasons are not related since comparative legal history shows that where there is *dolus,* an evil or unlawful intention, the causal connection between act and damage and the question of remoteness may be disregarded. Why, then, should the distinction between deliberate and non-deliberate acts have been disregarded in some cases and the obligation to make restitution imposed whether or not there was present an intention to cause harm or commit an illegal act? From the cases put in the rules one may perhaps infer that the law treated the classes of properly specified, namely animals, stone tablets, houses etc, government or private utensils and goods as of sufficient importance to warrant the imposition of an obligation to make restitution in all cases of loss, destruction or damage. The matter is something of a puzzle since where goods stored in government warehouses were detroyed or damaged though carelessness on the part of the officials in charge there was no obligation to make restitution, although one would have thought such property was valued by the government.

The principles and rules of the Ming and Ch'ing law were similar, although a number of the detailed prescriptions found in the T'ang and Sung codes do not reappear in the later codes. Thus the Ming and Ch'ing codes do not contain specific provisions on the theft or destruction of Taoist or Buddhist statues,[83] damage to property caused through the deliberate creation of a disturbance in the market or through unseaworthy vessels or faulty navigation. On the other hand there are articles dealing with the killing or injury of animals,[84] flooding and damage to property caused by the breaking open of dykes,[85] or the failure to keep them in proper repair,[86] damage to goods in public storehouses through the failure to arrange them properly or keep them dried and aired,[87] damage by fire,[88] the throwing away or destruction of a person's utensils or goods, the felling and destruction of trees and crops, or the destruction or damage of grave tablets and stone animals or houses and walls,[89] the eating, throwing away or destruction of fruit from government or private orchards[90] and the throwing away or destruction of imperial edicts, official seals and documents and the like.[91]

The rules in all these cases remain broadly the same as the T'ang, although there may be some variation in the level of punishment imposed. However the Ming and Ch'ing legislators appear to have taken a stricter approach to the question of compensation than the T'ang. There is no general article requiring compensation, and the specific authorisation stated in particular articles suggests that the circumstances under which an obligation to pay compensation arose were fewer in Ming/Ch'ing law than in T'ang/Sung. Thus the Ming and Ch'ing articles on the killing or injury of animals (whether deliberate or not), on deliberately burning houses or property, on throwing away or destroying someone's utensils or goods, felling and destroying trees or crops, destroying or damaging grave tablets or stone animals, or destroying or damaging houses or walls (whether deliberate or not) specifically require the payment of compensation or the repair of the damaged object. But the articles on the breaking open of dykes say nothing of compensation to be paid to the owners of goods lost through the resultant flooding. Nor is anything said about compensation in the article on eating, throwing away or destroying fruit in government or private orchards. On the other hand where goods in government storehouses are damaged through a failure to place them properly or to keep them aired or dried, there is an obligation on the official responsible to pay compensation to the government, not a rule that obtained in T'ang law.[92]

With respect to damage to property done by animals the codes - all containing the same rules - distinguish between two basic situations: that where the damage is to inanimate property and that where an animal kills or injures another animal. Where inanimate property is eaten or damaged, the codes consider the position according to whether the owner of the property kills the offending animal at the time it is committing the damage or not. If he does he is still liable to a punishment for the killing but with a reduction of 3 degrees. In addition he is to pay as compensation to the animal's owner the amount by which it is now worth less (the decreased value). On the other hand the latter is also to pay to the owner of the property compensation for the damage done by the animal. Should the animal not be killed or injured its owner remains under an obligation to pay compensation for the damage done and in addition is liable to punishment either where he has deliberately let it loose or where he has been careless in keeping it under control, the severity of the punishment depending upon the value of the property damaged.[93]

On the subject of animals killing or injuring each other the T'ang code contains a more embracing group of rules than the Ming or Ch'ing codes. Article 206 distinguishes between dogs and other animals. Where a dog acting of its own acccord kills or injures someone's domestic animal the owner of the dog is to pay as compensation the 'decreased value'. Where another animal (for example, a horse or ox) acting of its own accord has killed or injured someone else's animal only half the 'decreased value' is to be paid. In neither case is punishment incurred. One may infer from the *shu-i* commmentary that the reason for the higher degree of compensation imposed in the case of dogs is that these animals were a particularly frequent source of trouble. The commentary says that since it is in the nature of dogs to bite they must be controlled by their owners. Since it does not give a reason for the limit of half the 'decreased value' in the case of other animals, one may infer that a particularly strict onus (requiring explicit justification) was placed upon owners with respect to their dogs.

The code further provides that where an owner deliberately releases his dog or other animal and it kills or injures someone else's animal the case is to be treated as though the owner of the offending animal had deliberately killed or injured the other animal. Here the legal result is the imposition of punishment together with the obligation to pay the 'decreased value'. The standard situation contemplated by this provision appears to be that in which the owner goads his animal to attack another's animal. But it is probable that liability was imposed under this head where an owner released his animal under circumstances where he could be deemed to know that it might attack another's animal, even though he had not intended that it should attack. Where separate owners set their respective animmals to fight each other and one is killed or injured, a fixed punishment of a beating of 80 blows with the heavy stick is imposed on each owner. In addition compensation is to be paid for the 'decreased value' of the animal killed or injured.

Of these rules the only one explicitly preserved in the Ming and Ch'ing codes concerns the case in which dogs have been deliberately released with the result that they have killed or injured another's animal. The matter is not treated as seriously as in the T'ang code since only a beating of 40 blows with the light stick is imposed, together with an obligation to pay as compensation the 'decreased value'.[94] One may conjecture that the reason for this solitary survival lies in practical considerations. It was only the case of owners setting their dogs onto another's animal or the like that caused much trouble in practice.

Notes

1. See Johnson, 297. Seidel, Die Sanktion der ungerechtfertigten Bereicherung im chinesischen Recht der T'ang Zeit, 140 suggests 'unrechtes Gut', and cf. the remarks in Lê Code II, 27 (at p.51). See for further discussion MacCormack, The Concept of *tsang* in the T'ang Code, upon which I have drawn for what follows.

2. The concept is also important in Yüan law. See Ratchnevsky Code des Yüan, 172 under *tsang*, translated here as 'produit d'une action illicite'.

3. Cf. Johnson, 184.

4. For the Ming see the table in MLCCFL, 49 and for the Ch'ing see Boulais, p.7f; Philastre I, 26f; Staunton, lxxi.

5. One *p'i* is a piece of silk 1.8 *ch'ih* by 40 *ch'ih* (Johnson, xiii). See generally article 34 (Johnson, 189).

6. Article 281. Cf. Lê Code, 426; Deloustal, 425.

7. Article 282. Cf. Lê Code, 429; Deloustal, 428.

8. Article 138. Cf. Lê Code, 138; Deloustal, 138.

9. See generally the tables cited note 4, that in Philastre being the most reliable.

10. Ch'ing law distinguished between the case where an official drew a salary from the state and that where he did not, allowing slightly more favourable treatment in the latter case.

11. In Ming law the maximum punishment was exile to 3000 *li* and a beating of 100 blows with the heavy stick.

12. For Yüan law, where the basic principles appear to have been much the same as those of the other dynasties, see Ratchnevsky, op.cit., lV, 103ff. On the little known pre-T'ang law see Hulsewé, The Wide Scope of Tao 'Theft' in Ch'in-Han law.

13. Article 270. Cf. Lê Code, 431; Deloustal, 430.

14. Ming 18.4.7 (MLCCFL, 1312, 1318); Ch'ing articles 226, 229, Philastre II, 22-27; Boulais, 1039, 1043; Staunton, 274, 5.

15. Ming 18.5 (op.cit., 1315); Ch'ing article 227, Philastre II, 24; Boulais, 1040-1; Staunton, 274.

16. Cf. Lê Code, 430; Deloustal, 429.

17. Ming 18.6 (op.cit., 1317); Ch'ing article 228, Philastre II, 25; Boulais, 1042; Staunton, 275.

18. Ming 18.10 (op.cit., 1326); Ch'ing article 232, Philastre II, 32; Boulais,

1047; Staunton, 277, both referring only to 'trees'.

19. Cf. Lê Code, 580; Deloustal, 579.

20. Ming 16.7 (op.cit., 1225); Ch'ing article 207, Philastre I, 762; Boulais, 988; Staunton, 245.

21. Boulais, p.450 n.l; Philastre I, 764.

22. Article 279. Cf. Lê Code, 444; Deloustal, 443.

23. Other animals were also included in the Ming/Ch'ing articles with lesser punishments. See Ming 18.17 (op.cit., 1372); Ch'ing article 239, Philastre II. 84; Boulais 1135; Staunton, 285.

24. Johnson, 240; see also the commentary to article 282.

25. Johnson, 241.

26. See below at note 62.

27. Article 293. Cf. Lê Code, 453; Deloustal, 452.

28. If the goods are merely stealthily taken, the case is treated as secret theft.

29. Article 290. Cf. Lê Code, 449; Deloustal, 448.

30. Article 420. Cf. Lê Code, 190; Deloustal, 190.

31. Article 212. Cf. Lê Code, 558; Deloustal, 557. I have followed Deloustal's account. Lê Code has 'borrow at interest' instead of 'interest bearing property'. Where there was a written acknowledgement of the loan the case was treated as comparable to theft.

32. Article 247. Cf. Lê Code, 571; Deloustal, 570.

33. Article 285. Cf. Lê Code, 436; Deloustal, 435. Apparently the difference between this case and that of forcible theft proper was that for the latter there must be a physical, overpowering element in the intimidation exercised.

34. Article 373. Cf. Lê Code, 551; Deloustal, 550.

35. See below under 'damage to property'.

36. Article 402. Cf. Lê Code, 188; Deloustal, 188. Further examples of offences assimilated to theft will be found in MacCormack, The Concept of *tsang* in the T'ang Code, 28ff.

37. Only the most important differences are here signalled.

38. Ming 18.12 (op.cit., 1338); Ch'ing article 234, Philastre II, 43; Boulais, 1054; Staunton, 249.

39. Philastre II, 45.

40. Ming 18.15 (op.cit., 1358); Ch'ing article 234, Philastre II, 43; Boulais, 1054; Staunton, 249.

39. Philastre II, 45.

40. Ming 18.15 (op.cit., 1358); Ch'ing article 237, Philastre II, 68; Boulais, 1092f; Staunton, 283.

41. See Philastre II, 68, 71, 73f and his own discussion at 74f.

42. Ming 18.13 (op.cit., 1342); Ch'ing article 235, Philastre II, 47; Boulais, 1061f; Staunton, 280.

43. Ming 18.16 (op.cit., 1365); Ch'ing article 237, Philastre II, 76; Boulais, 1117f; Staunton, 284.

44. Ming 18.20, 21 (op.cit., 1390, 1393); Ch'ing articles 242, 3. Philastre II, 103, 108; Boulais, 1166f, 1171; Staunton, 288f, 289f.

45. Ming 181.18 (op.cit., 1378); Ch'ing article 240, Philastre II, 89; Boulais, 1143; Staunton, 286.

46. See the article on secret theft cited above.

47. Cf. Philastre II, 78 and see chapter 5, 110.

48. See the article on secret theft cited above. This rule was varied and to some extent mitigated by sub-statutes which made the ultimate punishment of strangulation depend upon the value of the property taken at the third offence. See Boulais 1122, 4, 5. The T'ang code was less severe. It provided that where an individual has successively committed three acts of theft each punishable by penal servitude he is to be sentenced to exile to 2000 li, and if each is punished by life exile he is to be strangled (article 299).

49. Philastre II, 78.

50. Article 283. Cf. Lê Code, 437; Deloustal, 436.

51. Ming 18.11 (op.cit., 1330); Ch'ing article 233, Philastre II, 36; Boulais, 1051; Staunton, 287.

55. See previous note.

56. T'ang article 162 (cf. Lê Code, 292; Deloustal, 291); Ming 4.14 (op.cit., 588); Ch'ing article 83, Philastre I, 391; Boulais, 414; Staunton, 92, and see the explanation given by the 'upper commentary' (Philastre I, 392).

57. See the discussion in Ch'ü, Law and Society in Traditional China, 67f.

58. For a discussion of the concept of 'taking' in the Ch'ing law of theft see Jones, Theft in the Qing Code.

59. Cf. MacCormack, The T'ang Code: Early Chinese Law, 139.

60. Ming 18.27 (op.cit., 1455); Ch'ing article 249, Philastre II, 154f; Staunton, 300f, and cf. Philastre's remarks on the difficulty posed by the interpretation of 'far from the place of theft' (156f).

61. Philastre II, 156.

62. See articles 33 (Johnson, 186) and 53 (Johnson, 262).

63. Ming 1.23 (op.cit., 295)' Ch'ing article 23, Philastre I, 194; Boulais, 62; Staunton, 26.

64. Johnson, 186.

65. See note 63.

66. Philastre I, 198.

67. Boulais, 167.

68. Article 276. Cf. Lê Code, 433; Deloustal, 432.

69. Article 443. Cf. Lê Code, 599; Deloustal, 598.

70. Article 203. See above at note 19.

71. Article 425. See Twitchett, The Fragment of the T'ang Ordinances of the Department of waterways, 69.

72. Article 442. Cf. Lê Code, 601; Deloustal, 600.

73. Article 214. Cf. Lê Code, 559; Deloustal, 558.

74. Article 423. See Twitchett, The T'ang Market System, 247.

75. Article 424. See Twitchett, Fragment of the T'ang Ordinances, 68.

76. For the provisions on fire cf. Lê Code, 617; Deloustal, 616. In the case of arson a special and severe tariff governing the punishment applies (article 432).

77. Commentary to article 276 (on which see note 68 above).

78. Only in the cases of the minor Buddhist and Taoist statues and private or government fruit does an intention to destroy constitute a component

of the offence. The reason for lessening liability, despite the presence of such an intention, was probably the nature of the property harmed (held not to be of sufficient importance to warrant an increased liability).

79. See notes 19, 72 above.

80. Article 466. Cf. Lê Code, 565; Deloustal, 564.

81. Article 205. Cf. Lê Code, 584; Deloustal, 583.

82. See note 76.

83. This may reflect the stronger position of Confucian orthodoxy in the later period.

84. Ming 16.7 (op.cit., 1225); Ch'ing article 207, Philastre I, 702, Boulais, 998f; Staunton, 245f. For killing one's own horse or beast the punishment was a beating of 100 blows with the heavy stick, and for killing someone else's, a minimum punishment of one and a half years penal servitude together with a beating of 70 blows with the heavy stick was imposed. For other animals the punishments were less.

85. Ming 30.1 (op.cit., 2059); Ch'ing article 295, Philastre II, 742; Boulais, 1715f; Staunton, 471. The articles distinguish two cases (i) the 'secret' breaking open of the banks of a dyke where the punishment is 100 blows with the heavy stick if it is government property and 80 blows if it was constructed by a private individual; should the water escape and do damage there is liability on account of *tsang* where, on the appropriate tariff, the punishment would be heavier than the minimum prescribed, and (ii) the 'deliberate' breaking open where the punishment is much heavier (three years penal servitude and 100 blows with the heavy stick, reduced by two degrees if the dyke is privately owned); should water escape and do damage the matter is treated as comparable to secret theft and punishment imposed according to the appropriate tariff, if heavier than the prescribed minimum. The difference between 'secret' and 'deliberate' breaking open was a matter of controversy among the Ming and Ch'ing jurists. The Ming 'incorporated commentary' (op.cit., 2060) defines 'secret' as the stealing of water for personal profit, and 'deliberate' as the breaking open of the dyke with the intention of harming another. This follows the T'ang approach. Shen's 'upper commentary', on the other hand, holds 'secret' to be that which is done stealthily and clandestinely and 'deliberate' to be that which is done publicly and flagrantly (Philastre II, 744).

86. Ming 30.2 (op.cit., 2062); Ch'ing article 396, Philastre II, 744; Boulais, 1718; Staunton, 472. Where damage was caused through the flooding the only punishment imposed on the official responsible is a beating of 60 blows with the heavy stick.

87. Ming 7.20 (op.cit., 803); Ch'ing article 127, Philastre I, 584; Boulais 695; Staunton, 141. Liability on account of *tsang* (according to the appropriate scale) is imposed on the official in charge.

88. Ming 26.7, 8 (op.cit., 1877, 1881); Ch'ing articles 347, 8, Philastre II, 559, 563; Boulais, 1649f; Staunton, 415f. The punishments vary according to whether the fire is started deliberately or not and according to the type of property burnt.

89. Ming 5.9 (op.cit., 628); Ch'ing article 91, Philastre I, 477; Boulais, 514f;

Staunton, 104. In the case of utensils, goods, trees and crops the offence is treated as comparable to secret theft, with exemption from branding and an increase of two degrees if the property is owned by the government. Should the loss or damage be non-deliberate there is no liability to punishment in the case of private property, and for official property there is a reduction in punishment of three degrees. In the case of grave tablets and stone animals a beating of 100 blows with the heavy stick is imposed; in the case of houses, walls and the like there is liability (according to the appropriate tariff) on account of *tsang* with an increase of two degrees for damage to official buildings.

90. Ming 5.10 (op.cit., 633); Ch'ing article 92, Philastre I, 482; Boulais, 516; Staunton, 105. Liability on account of *tsang* is imposed for eating, throwing away or destroying fruit on another's land , with an increase of two degrees for unauthorised removal, or eating government owned fruit or officially prepared food and drink.

91. Ming 3.3 (op.cit., 476); Ch'ing article 61, Philastre I, 323; Boulais, 276f; Staunton, 65. For edicts or seals the punishment is decapitation, for ordinary official documents merely a beating of 100 blows with the heavy stick, in each case reduced by three degrees where the destruction was not deliberate. For the loss of edicts etc. lesser punishments are imposed.

92. Since nothing is said in the Ming and Ch'ing codes on the position were a person destroys property belonging to a relative - except in the case of animals - one assumes the normal rules applied.

93. T'ang articles 204, 209 (cf. Lê Code, 581; Deloustal, 580); Ming 16.7 and Ch;ing article 207 (cited note 84). Cf. generally MacCormack, Liability for Animals in Traditional Chinese Law.

94. Ming 16.8 (op.cit., 1236); Ch'ing article 208, Philastre I, 768; Boulais, 998; Staunton, 248.

10

Contract

Introduction[1]

A contract, interpreted in the light of developed Western legal systems (whether derived from Roman law or the English common law) is an agreement between two or more parties which the law makes enforceable, provided certain conditions are met. Sometimes the mere agreement is made enforceable, as in the case of the Roman consensual contracts, sometimes the law requires an element apart from agreement such as consideration (the English common law), delivery of an object (the Roman real contracts) or an oral or written formality (the Roman verbal and literal contracts). In all cases, however, the law has evolved a separate branch concerned with actionable agreements, whatever the precise conditions for actionability, and has provided a systematic exposition of the formation of contract, the rights and duties of the parties and remedies for breach.

Traditional Chinese law, even by the end of its history, never attained this result. At least such a conclusion holds if one thinks of the official law contained in the penal codes and the decisions of the Supreme Court of Justice or Board of Punishment. The reason is that the codes themselves dealt with contract only in a scattered and fragmentary fashion, intervening primarily to protect the fiscal interests of the state or the interests of the family, to prevent grievances that might lead to public disorder or particularly gross or prevalent abuses, and to ensure impartial administration by officials. Hence no legislative rules governing the formation of contracts, the rights and duties of the parties, and remedies for breach were ever comprehensively established. Nor did the legislature even provide a framework within which the courts might develop such rules.

On the other hand, it seems that by the 19th century, if not earlier, commercial practice had established a set of rules which governed contracts for the sale of goods. These rules were often not formally stated in the contract by the parties but were well understood by them and the transaction was assumed to be conducted and regulated on their basis. Their operation depended primarily upon the good sense and readiness to co-operate of the parties. Such contracts appear seldom to have been considered by the magistrates and, even should they come before the court, no attempt was made by the judge to apply or develop the law, except where a provision of the code itself was relevant.[2] For the early part of the 20th century there is also evidence of what one may term developed customary law in relation to other contracts, such as hire.[3]

This chapter will confine itself to the law relating to contract as stated in the penal codes from the T'ang to the Ch'ing.[4] Even within this sphere one aspect will have to be left aside since it contributes nothing to an understanding of the rules of contract themselves. A number of rules in the codes impose punishments on officials who enter into certain contracts with persons subject to their jurisdiction or deal in certain ways with government property. These rules are concerned primarily not to define the legal conditions under which contracts might validly be made, but to ensure that the official administers the territory entrusted to him impartially and without corruption.[5] Apart from contracts made by officials, the penal codes deal with contracts, or rather particular aspects of contracts, of the following kind: the sale or pledging of property, with a particular emphasis upon land and houses; the sale and purchase of goods in the markets; contracts which establish debts; and contracts under which property is entrusted to or 'deposited' with another. No attempt is made by the codes to provide a comprehensive set of rules for any of these contracts. In particular there is hardly anything in the way of a definition of contract or of particular contracts given, and no specification as such of the requirements necessary for the conclusion of a valid contract. Rather, isolated rules are established which apply to one or other of the designated contracts. These rules are all 'criminal' in the sense that they impose punishments for non-compliance.

Sale or Pledge

Legislative rules on these contracts are found in the article and commentary of the T'ang code, in statutes and edicts (from the late T'ang) inserted in the Sung code and in the articles and sub-statutes of the Ming and Ch'ing codes. The reasons for the interference of the legislature varied. On the one hand it was concerned with the economic stability of the family. By and large property acquired by individual members of a family was held to be for the use and support of all its members under the direction of the head.[6] Although the latter might authorise the alienation of property the state introduced some safeguards designed to ensure that the family was not too easily deprived of its assets. Hence some rules established by the codes or other forms of legislation reflect this general policy that property should, if possible, be kept within the family.

On the other hand, the state was also intent upon the protection of interests of its own, especially in regard to land. These derived either from the emperor's ultimate ownership of land (leading to restrictions on alienation) or from the financial benefits accruing to the state through the payment of taxes and labour services (leading to the regulation of contracts by which land was transferred). While all dynasties adopted a similar fiscal policy with respect to land and therefore operated roughly similar rules on the registration of contracts providing for the transfer of land, there was a major difference between the T'ang and the later dynasties on the question of alienability. Basically until the middle T'ang, marked by the outbreak of the rebellion of An Lu-shan, only certain categories of land might validly be alienated. After this time, in practice land became freely alienable, subject to certain conditions, but the statutory law for a very long period, did not reflect this change. Thus not only were the provisions of the T'ang code itself never revised but the Sung code also adopted them although they were never applied during that dynasty.

I propose to discuss first the question of alienability of land, then the rules on registration of contracts dealing with land, and finally the rules designed to keep property within the family. The general principle accepted by the T'ang code was that all land belonged to the emperor who might allocate it to individuals. There were two important categories of allocated land. First, what is called 'personal share' land was allocated to an individual for cultivation on condition that it reverted to the state when the occupier attained the age of 60. Second, what is called 'land in perpetuity' was allocated to an individual on the understanding that it would be inherited by his heirs.[7] Both categories appear in principle to have been inalienable. The code by article 163 provided that those who sold 'personal share' land are to receive a beating the severity of which depends upon the amount sold. The land is to revert to the original owner and the price is forfeit to the state.

Although the text of the article speaks only of 'personal share' land it is possible that the same rule applied where 'land held in perpetuity' was illegitimately sold. That this was the position is suggested by the *shu-i* commentary to the article. This enumerates the cases in which it was permitted to sell either 'personal share' land or 'land held in perpetuity':

> In cases where one is entitled to sell: that is, in the case of land in perpetuity, where the family is poor and it is sold to defray funeral expenses, or in the case of personal share land, where it is sold to provide the cost of a homestead, or a mill or store, or something of like sort, or where one was moving from a restricted to a broad locality,[8] one is allowed to sell it according to the statutes. Those who wish to sell donated land also do not come within the scope of the prohibition. The lands in perpetuity of officials of the fifth rank and above, and of honorific officials, are also allowed to be sold.[9]

It is clear that even from its inception there had been problems with the enforcing of this system. After An Lu-shan's rebellion it seems that it largely became inoperative. By the end of the T'ang and the beginning of the Sung, despite the continued enactment of the codified provisions, the distinction between 'personal share' land and 'land held in perpetuity' had become obsolete as had the general prohibition on alienation. Article 163 of the T'ang code does not reappear in the Ming and Ch'ing codes.

Where land was alienable – under certain restricted circumstances in the early T'ang, freely in later periods – the state required that it be informed of the contracts by which the disposition was made, that (at least in the later law) the contract itself be registered, and that the name of the purchaser or creditor acquiring the land be registered as the lawful occupier. Implicit in the rules is the requirement that the contract be in writing.[10] The principal reason for the interest taken by the state was the fact that the liability for taxes and labour services was assessed on the basis of land held by households. Hence where transfers of land were contemplated it was essential that the transferee be registered as the person responsible for the payment of taxes.

With respect to alienation of land, and the requirement of registration, one has to distinguish three kinds of contract.[11] There is first the outright, unconditional sale (*mai*). This appears to have been relatively rare. More common was a conditional sale (*tien mai*) reserving to the seller a power of redemption. Should the seller subsequently not wish to redeem, the parties might agree, on payment of a further sum, to convert the conditional into an absolute sale. Finally there was the simple pledge of land under which possession was acquired by the creditor but the expectation was that the debtor would redeem within a fairly short period (*tien* or *chih chu*). The difference between the conditional sale and the pure pledge of land seems to have been that in the case of the latter the period within which the power of redemption was exercisable might not exceed ten years.[12]

Some examples of the statutory rules follow; they do not claim to constitute an exhaustive account of what is a highly complex topic. A T'ang land statute (*ling*) enacted in 737 provided:

> In all cases of the sale and purchase of lands, a report should be sent to the official under whose jurisdiction the case comes. At the end of the year then lands will be placed under the new holder in the registers. If a sale or purchase is made improperly without a report being rendered, the price will be confiscated and not recoverable, and the lands will revert to the original owner.[13]

The requirement of registration under this statute may have been understood as applying also to cases in which land was pledged and passed into the possession of the creditor.[14]

Yüan law also contained far reaching rules on the registration of contracts. Generally it was provided that contracts for the absolute or conditional sale of land or houses required the permission of the local magistrate; both parties were to attend his office and ensure that the title to the property and thus the responsibility for taxes were registered in the name of the purchaser.[15] Further a decree of 1285 apparently required anyone selling or pledging land, houses, slaves or cattle to register the contract with the appropriate office for the payment of the duty levied on the transaction.[16] This is the first text which I have seen that specifies the payment of a duty on the contract.

The Ming and Ch'ing codes contain an article dealing with the registration of contracts of *tien mai* for land or houses. The expression *tien mai* causes difficulty. Sometimes it is taken just as referring to 'pledge' in the sense of 'conditional sale' [17] and sometimes as referring to both absolute and conditional sale.[18] The problem can perhaps be resolved on the basis that even if *tien mai* is taken to express only the conditional sale, one is entitled to assume that *a fortiori* the rules settled for this case would have applied also to absolute sale. The formulation probably reflects the fact that sales of land and houses were normally or often in the conditional form. These articles provide *inter alia* that a registration fee should be paid on the contract, and further that the property should be registered in the name of the buyer or creditor. Failure to comply with the first requirement entails a beating of 50 blows with the light stick and the forfeiture to the state of half the amount received for the land or house. Failure to comply with the second requirement entails a beating, the severity of which depends upon the acreage involved, with a maximum of 100 blows with the heavy stick and the forfeiture of land only (not a house) to the government.[19]

The wording of the article – referring to 'who takes by way of conditional sale' – suggests that the obligations and consequent punishments are imposed primarily upon the buyer/creditor and not upon the seller/debtor. The latter would be affected by the provision for forfeiture of the land only in the unlikely event of the price not having been paid to him. Should in fact this have been the position, it is possible that the contract would not be deemed to be operative at all. A Ch'ing sub-statute of 1759 draws a distinction between absolute and conditional sales of land or houses and the simple pledge of such property. A registration fee was payable only for sale (whether absolute or not) and not for the mere pledge.[20]

The legislative rules which appear to have been designed to keep property within the family or to deal with problems arising from the family's customary rights in land even after alienation, concentrate on three issues: the attempted disposal of property by junior members of the family, the sale of land by the family head, and the circumstances under which pledged land might be redeemed. A principle firmly applied in all dynasties was that the control and disposition of all property acquired by family members (with some unimportant exceptions) vested in the senior male member of the family or any other senior appointed specifically to be head of the household.[21] Several rules are concerned to protect this power of disposition vested in seniors.

Article 162 of the T'ang code imposed a punishment on junior members of a household who, without the consent of the senior male, on their own authority disposed of family property. The punishment ranged from a beating of 10 blows with the light stick to a maximum of 100 blows with the heavy stick, the number depending upon the value of the property wrongfully taken and used.[22] This general provision is supplemented by a Miscellaneous Statute of 737[23] which specifies the circumstances under which junior members might act in the absence of the family head. It provided that where the head of the family was available (defined as being within a distance of 300 *li*) junior members were not on their own authority to pledge (*chih chu*) slaves, domestic animals, land, houses or other property, or to sell land or houses.

Although the text of the statute refers specifically only to the sale of land and houses, the rule is probably to be understood as applying also to the other kinds of property mentioned. Where the head was not available the juniors might request the appropriate magistrate for permission to proceed with a pledge or sale. With some modification the same rule was applied under the Sung.[24]

The Ming and Ch'ing statutory law appears to have been stricter. Both codes contained an article, similar to the T'ang, punishing junior members of the family living in the same household who wrongfully, that is, on their own authority without the consent of the family head, used or disposed of family property. The punishment ranges from 20 blows with the light stick to 100 blows with the heavy stick, the number again depending upon the value of the property.[25] However I have not discovered in the codes any rules comparable to those established by the T'ang statute. Hence it does not appear that any provision was made for the alienation of property by junior members in the absence of the family head.

The rule which most clearly evidences the notion of the family interest in property (as well as of interests possessed by persons outside the family) is that which requires the head of the family, when he wishes to make a conditional or absolute sale of land or even to pledge it without surrendering possession, first to make the offer to senior agnatic relatives not of the same household, and then, if they refuse, to the neighbours (who are thus deemed to have a secondary interest in possible changes in the title to land). In this form the rule is found in one of the memorials included in the Sung code.[26] According to Gernet it represents a codification of earlier practice.[27] It reappears in the Yüan legislative corpus with some important additions. After the contract for the conditional or absolute sale of land has received official sanction, the seller should consult successively relatives of the same branch, not living in the household, neighbours, and anyone to whom the land has already been pledged. In effect he is required to offer the land to them and they have a certain period of time within which to accept or reject the offer. Punishments are imposed for failure to comply with the time limits or for the use of obstructionist tactics.[28]

Although these rules do not, so far as I can see, reappear in the articles or sub-statutes of the Ming and Ch'ing codes,[29] modern commentators assert that what is termed 'the right of prior option or preemption' in favour of relatives and the other classes of person mentioned continued to be part of the law.[30] Ch'ing contracts of sale often, though not always, contained a clause stating that the land had first been offered to other

members of the family who had declined to purchase.[31] What is not
entirely clear is the effect on the validity of the disposition of a failure
to give the required options. One would expect that, at the instance of
any class which should have been consulted but was not, the transaction
would be set aside, but one cannot be sure of the extent to which any
such rule would have been enforced in practice.[32]

Where land or houses had been transferred to another there were
several problems with which the law from time to time had to deal. These
centred primarily upon the question of redemption. In particular it was
sometimes uncertain on the wording of a document whether the
transaction contemplated the grant of a right to redeem or not, and,
further, where the existence of such a right was clear, the unlimited
period of time within which custom permitted its exercise created
difficulties for the person in possession.[32] Generally, as can be seen from
the following examples, the legislation attempted to strike a reasonable
balance between the interests of the person who had originally ceded the
property or his heirs and the interests of the person in possession.

One of the provisions contained in the T'ang Miscellaneous Statute
of 737 dealt with the problem that arose where property (of any kind)
was pledged as security for a loan and the debtor found himself unable
to keep up the interest payments. The general rule established is that the
creditor is not allowed on his own authority (without the consent of the
owner) to sell the property pledged. Should the unpaid interest come to
exceed the amount of the capital and the debtor still could not repay the
debt the creditor might approach the relevant public authority for
permission to sell. Where this was granted any surplus obtained on the
sale was to be returned to the debtor.[34]

A Sung decree of 963 provided that where land or houses had been
pledged, then not only the original possessor but his heirs were to have
the right to redeem at any time on payment of the original debt, provided
the written agreement recording the transaction could be produced.
However, if the original agreement could not be produced, or if, when
produced, it did not clearly state whether the property was subject to
redemption or not, the right to redeem might be exercised only within
a period of thirty years from the date of the original transaction. After
that time the possessor was to be at liberty to dispose of the land as he
wished.[35]

The Ming and Ch'ing article on the *tien mai* of land and houses, already
cited, imposed a beating on pledge-creditors who improperly sought to
prevent redemption where the pledge-debtor at the time fixed for

redemption proferred repayment. Ch'ing sub-statutes further established a number of important rules with respect to redemption. These may be summarised as follows: (i) a person alienating land must state clearly in the contract whether the transfer of property was absolute or conditional, that is, subject to redemption, (ii) where the transaction is not stated to be 'absolute', redemption is possible even though no clause specifically authorises it, (iii) where the property is redeemable but the owner (debtor) is unable to repay the debt at the time fixed for redemption, he may ask the creditor to pay a further sum to count as a price for the land and convert the transaction into an 'absolute' sale; should the creditor in possession not wish to do this, he is to have the right himself to sell the property to a third person and retain from the proceeds the amount of the debt, (iv) where deeds are produced for a time before the above rules were in force (1753)[35] and it is not clear from their tenor whether the property is to be redeemable or not, a period of 30 years from their date is to be allowed for redemption. After that time the property belongs unconditionally to the creditor/purchaser.[37]

Sale of Goods in the Markets

The state in all the dynasties under consideration exercised supervision over the markets in the large towns and enacted rules regulating the sale of goods in them. These were designed in particular to protect buyers from unfair practices. The T'ang code contains a more elaborate set of rules than that found in the Ming or Ch'ing codes.[38] Apart from prohibiting the use of incorrect and unauthorised weights and measures and requiring the officials in charge of the markets to fix just prices and prevent unfair trading practices,[39] the code contained important rules on the quality of the goods sold and on the procedure for the sale of slaves and animals. Article 418 imposes punishments on the seller of 'utensils and such things as hempen or silk cloth which are fragile, not made of the appropriate materials, are short in length or narrow in width'.[40] The minimum punishment is a beating of 60 blows with the heavy stick. Where the seller had made a profit which, according to the scale applied to secret theft, would yield a higher punishment, the latter was to be imposed. It makes no difference whether the seller is himself the manufacturer or a merchant dealing in articles made by someone else. The officials in charge of the markets incur the same punishment if they know the circumstances, but obtain a reduction of two degrees if they are ignorant of them.

The *shu-i* commentary provides that such objects as are fragile or not made of proper material are to be confiscated by the government, but cloth which is too short or too narrow is to be returned to the supplier. Presumably this difference in the fate of the defective commodity reflects the fact that the use of improper materials was considered more serious than the supply of cloth of the right quality but lacking the correct measurements. Nothing is said of the position of the buyer. One infers that he was entitled to recover the price.

For the sale of slaves or animals in the market special formalities have to be observed. Article 422 provides:

> In all cases of the purchase of male or female slaves, horses, cattle, camels, mules and donkeys, if within three days of the payment of the price a market certificate (*shih-ch'üan*) is not drawn up, the purchaser will be liable to a beating of thirty strokes, and the vendor to one degree less.
>
> If within three days of the drawing up of the certificate it should prove that there was some long standing weakness or sickness, it is permissible to cancel the sale. But if anyone should attempt to cancel a sale without there being any such sickness, so as to cheat the other party, the sale shall be held to be legal, and the offender will be liable to a beating of forty strokes.
>
> If after the sale is completed the market office (*shih-ssu*) does not issue the certificate at the correct time, the officers responsible will be liable to a beating of thirty strokes for a delay of one day, the punishment to be increased by one degree:for each further delay, the maximum penalty being a flogging of 100 blows.[41]

The commentary makes it clear that the power of rescission exists where the buyer first discovers the existence of the 'long standing weakness or sickness' after the certificate of purchase (the written contract) has been drawn up. It does not seem to have been relevant whether the seller had knowledge of the disease or not; at least no inquiry was conducted into this question. An enigmatic phrase at the end of the commentary appears to mean that the code does not affect contracts established outside the markets. Such contracts may establish any length of time the parties wish for the exercise of a power of rescission by the buyer.[42]

Perhaps the legislation dealing with transactions in the market was primarily designed, as Gernet has suggested,[43] to ensure the orderly conduct of proceedings in them, especially in the vast markets of the capital cities. If the rules contained in the code were observed the chances of public outcry and disturbance over unfair dealings were certainly much reduced. At the same time the rules on the qualities of the goods sold and the presence of disease in slaves or animals do show a particular concern with the position of the buyer. It is not difficult to detect in them a desire to protect the buyer against particular (and no doubt common) kinds of sharp practice on the part of the seller.

The Ming and Ch'ing codes preserve only part of the T'ang legislation. Particular kinds of unfair market practices, especially those concerned with the manipulation of prices as where sellers or buyers attempted to establish monopolies and 'made what is cheap dear, or what is dear cheap', were punished with a beating of 80 blows with the heavy stick. Where any profit so made would entail, on the appropriate scale, a heavier punishment, the offence was to be treated as comparable to secret theft and punished accordingly.[44] As in the T'ang code there are also rules punishing the use of unfair or unauthorised weights and measures,[45] as well as the manufacture and sale of articles which are not firm and strong, or silk and cotton which are defective, or short in length or narrow in width, in all cases not conforming to the normal standards of manufacture, size and quality. Whereas the Ming code for the case of the sale of defective goods imposes a beating of 50 blows with the light stick on the seller and provides that the goods are to be forfeit to the government, the Ch'ing code merely imposes the beating.[46] Although nothing is said in the article as to whether the criminal liability for defective goods applies to all contracts or only to those made in the markets there is an implication in Shen's 'upper commentary' (stating that the article applies to goods sold in markets and bazaars not to official goods) that the latter was the position.[47] The extent to which this legislation was actually applied in Ch'ing times is doubtful. It seems that the regulation of weights and measures, of prices, and even of the quality of the goods sold in the market was largely in the hands of the guilds; disputes rarely gave rise to the application of the criminal law.[48]

Debt

Two articles of the T'ang code deal with the general problem of debt. Article 398 provides that in all cases of debt (*fu chai*) where the written contract (*chi*) is disregarded and what is owed is not paid by the due time a punishment is to be imposed upon the debtor.[49] Its severity depends both upon the value of what is owed and the length of time for which there has been default. It starts with a beating of 20 blows with the light stick (where there has been default in the payment of property worth 1 *p'i* or more for a period of 20 days) to penal servitude for 1 year (where there has been default in the payment of property worth 100 *p'i* or more for 100 days). Repayment of the debt is also to be ordered. From the *shu-i* commentary it appears that the court might, in a suitable case, grant an extension of time to the debtor.

The article has a wide scope. It covers the case of any contract (loan, hire, sale or pledge) under which money or other property is owed. It is not restricted to specific cases of borrowing. However its provisions only seem to apply where there is a written contract specifying what is owed and the period of time within which it must be paid. Purely verbal arrangements would not attract the punishments prescribed by the article. Significantly nothing is said explicitly of a right of the creditor to be repaid. Nor is any remedy specifically to compel repayment given to him. The court itself is to order repayment, but it is not clear how such an order was to be put into effect. Perhaps failure by the debtor to honour it exposed him to further beatings under the article on 'what ought not to be done'.

Article 399 by implication permits the creditor a limited privilege of self-help. It provides that where a creditor does not inform the appropriate public authority of the debt due to him but instead seizes from the debtor property in excess of the debt he is liable on account of *tsang* to the extent of the excess.[50] There are two points to note here. First, the primary obligation of the creditor, where the debtor was in default, was to notify the court. Presumably the magistrate then summoned the debtor in order to determine what punishment was due as well as to see if any further delay should be accorded. But it does not seem that the court would directly help the creditor by official distraint on the debtor's goods.

Second, if the creditor, instead of notifying the court, helps himself to the debtor's property – as in practice was probably the most common step taken by those seeking repayment of debts – and takes no more than the value of the debt, he commits no offence. Presumably in this case the debt is deemed to be discharged and the debtor himself is exempt from punishment (even though in default at the time of the seizure of his property by the creditor). If the creditor takes too much the same consequences follow, with the addition that he himself commits an offence for which the court will impose a punishment. Possibly the court would also order the return of the excess to the debtor.

Indirectly, therefore, the code supplies a creditor with an effective remedy for the recovery of a debt, effective, that is, provided the creditor possesses the physical strength or can muster enough help to overcome any resistance offered by the debtor. Although he cannot make use of court personnel to obtain property from a debtor, he can exert considerable pressure in order to obtain repayment. In sum, should the debtor have property he is likely to repay rather than face the infliction of the punishment prescribed by the code for default. Alternatively, should the debtor refuse to repay, the creditor, if careful not to take too much, may resort to self-help. Even if the debtor personally has no property relatives may contribute to save him from a court appearance. The court will not take cognizance of the debt unless it receives an application from the creditor. He is in a position to use the threat of applying to the court as a bargaining counter with the debtor.

The Miscellaneous Statute of 737, already cited, contains further important rules, both as to the limits within which the parties were free to contract, and the possible remedies of the creditor.[51] Where movable property is lent (*ch'u chü*) the jurisdiction of the court is to be excluded provided the written agreement and its execution comply with certain conditions. These conditions are:

(i) the interest stipulated in the contract should not exceed 6 per cent per month and the total interest recoverable should not exceed the amount of the capital;[52]

(ii) the creditor should not in satisfaction of the debt seize from the debtor property not authorised by the contract, and the debt which the creditor seeks to enforce (by the seizure of the property) should be that from which in fact the overdue interest arises, and

(iii) if the debtor has insufficient movable property he himself or male members of his family are to enter the service of the creditor and work for him.

The last condition is of particular interest since it bears on the general problem of enslavement on account of debt. Article 400 of the code deals with the situation in which a free person gives himself or a young relative into slavery as security for a debt. Where a person gives himself into slavery under these circumstances he is to be punished three degrees less than the punishment he would have incurred if he had sold himself into slavery to another.[53] Where he gives a junior relative into slavery as security for a debt, he is to be punished three degrees less than the punishment he would have incurred if he had sold such a relative as a slave.[54] If the creditor knows the true status of the person given as pledge he is also held to have committed the same offence but obtains a further reduction in punishment of one degree. In this case, but not that in which the creditor is ignorant of the true position, the value of the labour obtained from the person pledged as a slave is to be calculated and set off against the debt.

Against this background the Miscellaneous Statute of 737 sets out the conditions under which a debtor or male members of his family may lawfully enter the creditor's service and by their labour work off the debt.[55] This provision may have been introduced in an attempt to regulate a widespread practice by which debtors and their relatives became personal slaves of their creditors. If so, it does not seem to have worked. T'ang lay sources evidence the continuing practice of debt slavery. The essays of the great T'ang statesman and writer Han Yü (768-824) contain passages on the plight of debtors and the means by which they may be relieved. In a memorial to the emperor on the subject he explains that in his term as prefect of Yüanchow (a relatively small district) he had discovered 731 free men and women who had been given as pledges to their creditors in contravention of the law. Their condition was indistinguishable from that of slave; they were beaten and made to work by their creditors until they died. Han Yü states that in accordance with the law – perhaps he was referring to article 400 of the code – he had the value of the labour provided by the debtors assessed and freed them.[56]

A similar account is given in the inscription composed by Han Yü for the tomb of a fellow official, Liu Tzu-hou who was prefect of Linchow in the early part of the ninth century. A local custom was the taking of men and women as security for debt. If the debt was not redeemed in time and the interest came to equal the capital, the surety was forfeit and became a slave of the creditor. Liu, when prefect, sought to rectify the situation by allowing the very poor to discharge their debt by means of their labour. Their creditors were to keep a written record of their services and release them as soon as the value of the labour equalled the amount of the debt. This rule, Han Yü states, was afterwards applied in other prefectures with the result that nearly 1000 sureties were released in the course of one year.[57] Despite the efforts of Han Yü, Liu Tzu-hou, and no doubt other worthy officials, it is likely that the laws prohibiting enslavement for debt were not fully observed.

A rule similar to that governing the period within which redemption is available is established by a decree of 824 generally for claims arising from debt (*fu chai*). The decree recited the problem arising from unclear, written contracts (*chi*) and provided that where a claim arising from a debt more than 30 years old is made the court is not to entertain it where none of the original guarantors (*pao*) can be produced and there is no clear written record of the transaction.[58] Two important consequences flow from this decree. If the period between the making of the claim and the constitution of the debt is less than 30 years, the court will have jurisdiction even though the guarantors are not available and no clear written evidence can be produced. On the other hand if the period is over 30 years the court will not have jurisdiction unless either the guarantors are available or a clear record of the transaction can be produced. Hence the 30 year period does not extinguish the claim (as would have been the case under rules of negative prescription in Western legal systems); it merely places an obstacle in the way of a claimant.

The Ming and Ch'ing codes contain regulations on the following matters: the use of free persons as payment for debts; the permissible rates of interest that might be charged; and the position where there is default in repayment of a debt. Although the rules show a general correspondence with those of the T'ang and Sung period there are some important differences. One of the dispositions contained in the most comprehensive Ming and Ch'ing article on debt imposes a severe punishment upon a person who takes a debtor's wife, concubine or child as compensation for debt.[59] In the absence of force the punishment is to be a beating of 100 blows with the heavy stick; if force has been used the punishment is to be increased by two degrees to penal servitude for one and a half years and 70 blows with the heavy stick. In both cases those taken in compensation are to be restored to their relatives and no further action on the part of the creditor to recover the debt is to be allowed.

To be noted is the fact that only the creditor is made criminally liable by this article. No punishment is imposed on the debtor even where he has voluntarily surrendered his wife, concubine or child as compensation. The reason is made clear in the general commentary of the Ch'ing code. What is postulated is a case where a wealthy and powerful creditor induces a poor debtor to surrender his wife, concubine or child. Although the debtor consents, he does so only in virtue of the pressure placed upon him. Hence, although the commentary does not make the point specifically, it is just that punishment should reach the creditor and not the debtor.[60]

With the article just described one has to compare another article of the Ming and Ch'ing codes which deals specifically with the liability of a person who pledges or hires his wife or daughter to another. This article imposes a beating of 80 blows with the heavy stick on someone who, in exchange for property, gives as a pledge (*tien*) or hires out (*ku*) his wife or concubine to another person so that she becomes his wife or concubine; a punishment of a beating of 60 blows with the heavy stick is imposed for the pledging or hiring out of a daughter as wife or concubine to another. If the person receiving the wife or daughter in pledge or hire knows her true status he is to receive the same punishment, and, further, any property he has given is to be forfeit to the government. If he does not know he is not liable to punishment and may recover the property. In all cases the wife or concubine given in pledge or hire is to return to her own family (both marriages being dissolved) and the daughter is to return to her parents (the marriage being dissolved.)[61]

The circumstances contemplated by this article are those in which a person obtains money, either pledging his wife, concubine or daughter in effect as security for the return of the loan upon terms that during the period of the loan she is to be the wife or concubine of the creditor, or hiring them out in return for a fee upon terms that they become for a period of time the wife or concubine of the hirer.[62] What the law is especially concerned to prohibit and to punish is the giving or taking of a wife or concubine under these conditions. What is not prohibited by this or any other law is, as Shen's 'upper commentary' explains, the pledging or hiring out of wives and daughters upon terms that the creditor acquires a right to their services but neither marries them nor acquires sexual rights. Such a practice is said to be very common among poor people.[63]

The amount of interest which a creditor might charge is subject to two restrictions. The monthly rate must not exceed 3 per cent, and the total amount of interest recoverable under the debt must not exceed the amount of the capital sum borrowed. Creditors who infringe these rules are to receive a beating, the number of strokes depending upon the amount of unlawful profit made, with a minimum of 40 blows with the light stick and a maximum of 100 blows with the heavy stick. Any interest obtained in excess of the permitted amount is to be returned to the borrower.[64] In practice it does not seem that the legal limitation on interest was observed.[65]

The same article establishes rules for the case in which the debtor is unable to repay his debt.[66] As in the T'ang code, a punishment is imposed, graduated according to the amount owed and the period of delay. The maximum punishment that can be imposed is a beating of 60 blows with the heavy stick. In all cases the capital and interest are still to be paid to the creditor. However the limited right of self-help available to the creditor under the T'ang code is now removed altogether. The Ming and Ch'ing articles provide that where powerful persons forcibly take their debtors' animals and goods, instead of prosecuting their claims before the courts, a minimum punishment of a beating of 80 blows with the heavy stick is to be imposed. Should the property so taken, according to the scale applied where one is made liable on account of *tsang*, yield a higher punishment, this is to be imposed subject to a maximum of three years penal servitude and 100 blows with the heavy stick.[67] It is thus clear that in all cases where the creditor resorts to self-help against the wishes of the debtor – he is to be punished. Shen's 'upper commentary' points out that the intention of the code is to punish the resort to violence itself.[68] However the official commentary modifies the position where the creditor takes no more than is due to him. In this case he may redeem the beating and keep the property.[69] Only where he takes property in excess of the debt does the debtor have the right to recover the excess.

Another important addition to the T'ang rules is found in a sub-statute contained in both the Ming and Ch'ing codes. It provides a mechanism by which pressure can be exerted on a defaulting debtor, with concealed resources, to pay what he owes. The mechanism is available not just against defaulting debtors but in any case where property may lawfully be claimed from another under the head of restitution of *tsang*. In its Ming version the sub-statute provides that where the value of the property to be restored to a private individual is 30 ounces of silver or more, and the offender, after he has been kept in prison for a year or more, is found not to have the means to pay, a full report of the circumstances is to be sent to the emperor for his decision. Where the amount to be recovered is less than 30 ounces of silver and the same circumstances obtain, then the restitution of the property is no longer to be enforced, and the offender merely submits to the punishment appropriate to his offence.[70]

This sub-statute was adopted by the Ch'ing code but revised in 1835, and its provisions somewhat modified. The periods of imprisonment were reduced to six months, where property valued at 30 ounces of silver or more was due, and to three months where the value was less. If, after the lapse of these periods, it was clear that the offender was insolvent, a petition was to be sent to the emperor giving him the choice of exercising clemency or passing a sentence of exile, having taken into account all the circumstances of the case.[71] It appears that the essence of this mechanism was first to subject the offender to a period of imprisonment in order to coerce him to restore the property due, and second, where it became clear that it was not possible for him to make restitution, to expose him to the possibility of an additional, severe punishment at the direction of the emperor.

Deposit of Property

The codes are concerned with the unauthorised disposition of property which has been entrusted by one person to another. Probably the matter merited legislative attention because it was deemed to be akin to theft. The word used to express the transaction (*chi*) appears to have the primary sense of 'deposit' or 'give in trust' and hence to designate a situation in which one person has left property with another for safe-keeping. However it is likely that no sharp distinction was drawn between deposit for safe-keeping and a gratuitous loan under which the recipient was permitted to put the property to its normal use. It is less certain that the rules applied when property had been received as security for a debt or had been taken on hire in return for a fee. However one cannot exclude altogether the possibility that these situations were also included under the head of *chi*.[72]

Article 397 of the T'ang code provides that a person who receives on deposit (*chi*) another's property is liable on account of *tsang* (with a decrease in punishment of one degree) where he, without authorisation, applies the property to his own use or otherwise disposes of it.[73] This means that the punishment is assessed according to the scale established for *tsang* offences and then decreased by one degree. The *shu-i* commentary states that the maximum punishment is to be penal servitude for 2 1/2 years. Should the recipient falsely state that an animal entrusted to him had died or that an object has been lost he is liable under the offence of obtaining property by fraud and deceit (with a decrease in punishment of one degree).[74] The reason for the difference is not explained. The commentaries of the Ming and Ch'ing codes say that in the case of unauthorised disposal there is still an intention on the part of the recipient to restore the value of what he put to his own use; hence he is to be liable only on account of *tsang*. But in the case of deceit he has in fact the intention of committing theft and therefore should be appropriately punished.[75]

A question and answer in the *shu-i* commentary raise the point: what is the position where an animal has died or an object genuinely been lost? Is the depositee in this case liable for the value, although he committed no offence? The answer distinguishes between the two cases. For the latter it cites as the appropriate analogy the article in the code on the loss of property owned by the government or a private person under which the person who loses it is bound to make restitution of the value unless the loss has been occasioned by forcible theft (article 445). Hence in the present case the depositee is required to make restitution of the value of the lost article unless it has been taken from him by force. For the former the relevant analogy is supplied by a statute dealing with the herding or stabling of animals. If the death was 'reasonable' no compensation need be paid. If it is not 'reasonable' the 'decreased value' of the animal is to be paid. 'Decreased value' is elsewhere defined to mean the difference between the value of the animal when alive and its value when dead.[76] 'Reasonable' is not explained but presumably refers to the exercise of proper care in looking after the animal.

This discussion is of interest because it suggests that the standard of liability applied to the transaction was partly 'strict' and partly based on fault. Where inanimate property was not returned it seems that the recipient was liable unless he could show that the goods had been taken from him by force or perhaps had been lost through some other irrepressible act such as fire or flood. Where an animal died liability, sensibly, was not strict but depended upon fault. If reasonable care had been taken of the animal and still it had died there was no fault and hence no liability.

The articles of the Ming and Ch'ing codes follow closely that of the T'ang but elaborate somewhat on the position where property has been lost or animals have died. The text of the articles excludes liability where objects have been lost through fire, water or theft (without specifying forcible theft alone) or where an animal has died of illness, provided there is clear proof of these eventualities.[77] The general commentary of the Ch'ing code uses language which suggests that the standard of liability applied to the transactions subsumed under the head of 'deposit' was one based on fault. It concludes with the observation that the eventualities described could not be expected and are not the fault (*kuo*) of the recipient.[78]

Sub-statutes in both codes deal with the question of deposit of goods with relatives and here there is a difference between the approach taken by the two dynasties. The Ming sub-statute provides that the case of deposit with relatives is to be decided in the same way as that of deposit with an unrelated person; it is not necessary, it declares, to decrease the punishments in accordance with the degrees of mourning.[79] However in 1725 under the Ch'ing this sub-statute was revised and account taken of mourning relationships.

Where property has been deposited with relatives for whom mourning is worn for nine months or more, or with maternal grandparents or relatives entitled to mutual concealment,[80] there is to be no punishment in the event of its wrongful disposal.[81] Where the relatives entrusted with the property are those for whom mourning is worn for five months, the punishment is to be reduced by three degrees, for relatives of three months mourning by two degrees, and for relatives for whom no mourning is worn, by one degree. In all cases the value of the property is to be restored.[82]

Further Ch'ing sub-statutes, dating in their final form from 1845, supply very detailed rules on the apportioning of loss where goods placed as security with pawn shops, or left to be dyed or cleaned have been lost through theft or fire.[83] It is possible that these sub-statutes varied the rules established by the article of the code. On this interpretation the article itself must be deemed to apply not just to goods left with persons on deposit or loan but also to those left with pawnshops as security for debt or with persons engaged in the business of dying or cleaning. A preferable interpretation, perhaps, is that the sub-statutes were dealing with situations not within the original scope of the article at all. On this construction the article would not have dealt with goods left with others under contracts of pledge or hire of services, but only with cases of deposit for safekeeping or gratuitous loan. Although it is only in the sub-statutes that there is any direct reference to the recovery of the property deposited or the payment of compensation for loss, the articles of the codes which are concerned with the imposition of punishments presuppose the right of the victim of the offence to recover the *tsang*. For this purpose the mechanism described in the section on 'debt' was available.

Notes

1. I here draw upon what I have said in The Law of Contract in China under the T'ang and Sung Dynasties.
2. See especially Brockman, Commercial Contract Law in Late Nineteenth Century Taiwan.
3. See, for example, Oyamatsu, Laws and Customs in the Island of Formosa, 32, 39f, 114ff, also the literature cited chapter 3 note 83.
4. For the Han see Hulsewé, 'Contracts' of the Han Period.
5. For the T'ang code see MacCormack, op.cit., 22ff.
6. For discussion of the notion of 'family property' see Hu, The Common Descent Group in China and its Functions, 15f; Schurmann, Traditional Property Concepts in China, 510ff; Shiga, Family Property and the Law of Inheritance in Traditional China; and see further below in chapter 11 under 'inheritance'.
7. For the terminology and details see Twitchett, Financial Administration under the T'ang Dynasty, 1ff, esp. 4-5.
8. A 'restricted locality' was one in which there was insufficient land for the subsistence of the population, a 'broad locality' one in which there was an abundance of land available for cultivation.
9. Twitchett, op.cit., 136, also giving a translation of the article.
10. Sometimes there is an explicit rule to this effect. Thus under the Sung the seller or debtor must sign the contract in the presence of the purchaser

or creditor. See MacCormack, op.cit., 40.

11. This is somewhat over-simplified. For a full description of late Ch'ing practice see Hoang, Notions techniques sur la propriété en Chine, 7ff. See also generally Palmer, The Surface-Subsoil Form of Divided Ownership in Late Imperial China.

12. See the Ch'ing 'upper commentary', quoted by Philastre I, 463; Hoang, op.cit., 8. Cf. Jamieson, Chinese Family and Commercial Law, 89, n.1. According to McAleavy the ten year rule was introduced around the middle of the 18th century (Dien in China and Vietnam, 410). Before the introduction of the rule it is difficult to see that there is any distinction between the conditional sale and the pledging of land (involving surrender of possession). Indeed even afterwards there is some doubt on the matter. McAleavy in the article just cited and Oyamatsu, op.cit., 38ff, 142ff (both based firmly on late Ch'ing customary law as found in Taiwan) distinguish merely between 'sale' and 'pledge' (*tien*) and do not introduce a third transaction, that of the conditional sale.

13. Twitchett, op.cit., 129, and cf. von Senger, Chinesische Bodeninstitutionen im Taiho-Verwaltungskodex, 78.

14. Another enactment of the same year (a 'Miscellaneous Statute'), on one construction, explicitly in its second part applies the requirement of approval by the public authorities to both pledge (*chih chu*) and sale (*mai*). However it is not clear whether the statute is referring only to the case where junior members of the household request permission from the authorities to dispose of property in the absence of the head, nor whether the reference is just to land and houses or also to other species of property listed in the first part (slaves, cattle and other property). Cf. the different versions given by Gernet, La vente en Chine d'après les contrats de Touen-Houang, 302-3 (Lorsque...les maisons), and 303 (last para.); Lin, Vergeiselung und dingliche Sicherungsrechte im chinesichen traditionellen Privatrecht, 142; Shiga, op.cit., 128f. Cf. also MacCormack, op.cit., 37f. See also below at notes 22, 23.

15. Ratchnevsky, Code des Yüan II, 100f.

16. Ratchnevsky, op.cit., 100, n.3.

17. So Philastre I, 459; Staunton, 101.

18. Boulais, 476; Jamieson, op.cit., 85 (translating 'all mortgages and sales of land or buildings...'). Cf. also the observations of Hoang, op.cit., 12.

19. Ming 5.6 (MLCCFL, 616); Ch'ing article 89, Boulais, 476; Staunton, 101; Jamieson, op.cit., 85 (omitted in Philastre I, 457).

20. Boulais, 482; Jamieson, op.cit., 89. See also above at note 12. It appears that in practice these rules on registration were often evaded. Cf. Jamieson, op.cit., 86; Wang, Land Taxation in Imperial China, 29f; Oyamatsu, op.cit., 45, 148. See also Ch'ü, Local Government in China under the Ch'ing, chapter viii; Zelin, The Magistrate's Tael, 250f; and for a Ch'ing magistrate's own accounts of his duties, Huang, Complete Book concerning Happiness and Benevolence, 233f.

21. On the head of the family see McAleavy, Certain Aspects of Chinese Customary Law in the Light of Japanese Scholarship, 538ff.

22. Cf. Lê Code, 292; Deloustal, 291.

23. See the literature cited at note 14.
24. See Gernet, op.cit., 303.
25. Ming 4.14 (op.cit., 588); Ch'ing article 83, Philastre I, 391; Boulais, 414 (and cf. his observations at 412); Staunton, 92.
26. Cf. Lin, Vergeiselung und dingliche Sicherungsrechte, 154; Burns, Private Law in Traditional China, 305; MacCormack, op.cit., 42f. For the history of the rule during the Sung see Burns, op.cit., 305ff.
27. Op.cit., 331.
28. Ratchnevsky, Code des Yüan II, 103f.
29. However a Ch'ing sub-statute states *inter alia* that where a buyer under a contract for the unconditional sale of land subsequently asserts that he need pay less than originally agreed because the seller had not first offered the land to the former owners or his kinsmen or neighbours he is to be liable under the article on doing what ought not to be done where the matter is serious (Boulais, 479 bis; Jamieson, op.cit., 87, and cf. his remarks at 89, n.l).
30. Cf. Jamieson, op.cit., 87, n.l; Haas, Gewohnheitsrechtliche Verträgstypen in China, 48; Freedman, Lineage Organization in Southeastern China, 105; Schurmann, Traditional Property Concepts in China, 514; Kroker, The Concept of Property in Chinese Customary Law, 137f; Brockman, Commercial Contract Law in Late Nineteenth Century Taiwan, 108.
31. Cf. Jamieson, op.cit., 88, n.l, 97; von Senger, Kaufverträge im traditionellen China, 172f, 179f, 183. Examples from the Yüan period can be found in Lin, op.cit., 175ff. The contracts given by Hoang, op.cit., 100ff do not contain this clause though some of them contain the assertion that the sellers are not in dispute with their relatives over the property.
32. It appears that from the beginning of the 20th century, if not earlier, the clause on prior offer to relatives, even where inserted in a contract, was treated as a fiction. Cf. Oyamatsu, op.cit., 37; Jamieson, op.cit., 101; Haas, op.cit.,48, 50 Nr 40.
33. Another aspect of pledge regulated by the codes was the fraudulent repledging of property. Both Sung legislation which may already be drawing upon late T'ang enactments (Lin, op.cit., 156; MacCormack, op.cit., 43f) and Ming and Ch'ing articles (cited note 19) hold that an owner who fraudulently repledges property already pledged to another is to be treated as comparable to a secret thief with respect to the profit he has made, and that the fraudulent transaction is to be undone. Cf. the remarks of McAleavy, Dien in China and Vietnam, 408f.
34. Lin, op.cit., 117.
35. Lin, op.cit., 152, MacCormack, op.cit., 41f.
36. In fact the 30 year rule was probably applied in the case of unclear contracts drafted even after this date. Cf. Hoang, op.cit., 7; Jamieson, op.cit., 100.
37. Boulais, 479 bis, 480; Philastre I, 469; Hoang, op.cit., 8f. For a history of the Ch'ing legislation, held by McAleavy to be motivated by the desire to improve the position of the recipient of the property, see his article cited note 12, 410f. He suggests that in practice this legislation may not have been observed, and that, for example, the customary rule under

which the person granting property as *tien* had in perpetuity to right to redeem continued to be followed. However Oyamatsu, in his account of Taiwan customs, says that the statutory rule under which the pledgor lost his right of redemption after 30 years prevailed in Formosa (op.cit., 145).

38. See generally MacCormack, op.cit., 33ff.

39. The relevant articles and statutes are translated in Twitchett, The T'ang Market System, 243ff.

40. Twitchett, op.cit., 244.

41. Twitchett, op.cit., 246.

42. Gernet, op.cit., 306f. An interesting parallel to the T'ang legislation is furnished by the edict of the aediles on the sale of slaves and cattle in the Roman market, though under Roman law the period within which the buyer might exercise a power of rescission was considerably longer.

43. Op.cit., 307.

44. Ming 10.3 (op.cit., 898); Ch'ing article 137, Philastre I, 613; Staunton, 164f.

45. Ming 10.4 (op.cit., 907); Ch'ing article 138, Philastre I, 617; Boulais, 756; Staunton 165.

46. Ming 10.5 (op.cit., 912); Ch'ing, Staunton, 167 (not in Boulais or Philastre).

47. TCLLHCPL, 2225.

48. See chapter 3, 64f. and cf. also Jamieson, op.cit., 113ff. There are also some interesting observations on commercial practices in Doolittle, Social Life of the Chinese II, 151ff.

49. Cf. Lê Code 588; Deloustal, 587.

50. Cf. Lê Code 591; Deloustal, 590.

51. See MacCormack, op.cit., 46ff; Gernet, op.cit., 299f, 334 and n.2.

52. The actual interest stipulated as lawful varied from time to time. See Yang, Money and Credit in China, 95f.

53. Article 295 determines this to be exile to 2000 *li*; three degrees less is penal servitude for two years.

54. Article 294 provides that the punishment for kidnapping and selling a junior relative is the same as that for killing such a relative in a fight with a reduction of one degree if the junior has consented to the sale. For example, if an elder brother, with his younger brother's consent, sells the latter into slavery, the punishment is penal servitude for 2 and a half years. A decrease of 3 degrees is penal servitude for one year.

55. Article 34 (Johnson, 190) provides that one day's labour is the equivalent of goods worth 3 *ch'ih* (feet) of silk.

56. See Liu, Chinese Classical Prose. The Eight Masters of the T'ang-Sung Period, 52f; Lin, Vergeiselung und dingliche Sicherungsrechte, 85.

57. Liu, op.cit., 92ff; Lin, op.cit., 86.

58. Gernet, op.cit., 344.

59. Ming 9.1 (op.cit., 876); Ch'ing article 134, Philastre I, 602; Boulais, 733; Staunton, 160.

60. Philastre I, 604. See also the extracts from Shen's 'upper commentary' at 605.

61. Ming 6.2 (op.cit., 650); Ch'ing article 95, Philastre I, 501; Boulais, 556;

Staunton, 110. Doolittle, Social Life of the Chinese II, 209f, records a common practice in which husbands sold their wives to be the wives of other men.

62. See the explanation in the Ch'ing general commentary of the difference between pledge and hire (Philastre I, 501).

63. Philastre I, 501, and cf. Boulais, 555.

64. Ming 9.1 (op.cit., 875); Ch'ing article 134, Philastre I, 601; Boulais, 730; Staunton, 158.

65. Yang, op.cit., 98ff, especially 100 para. 10.30; Boulais, 729.

66. Boulais, 731-3; Jamieson, op.cit., 109.

67. This maximum is stated only in the Ch'ing code.

68. Philastre I, 605.

69. The sense of this is best given in Boulais's version (732).

70. MLCCFL, 303 (translated in Philastre I, 198 decree I).

71. Boulais, 165.

72. Cf. the remarks of Philastre I, 609.

73. Cf. Lê Code, 579; Deloustal, 578.

74. Article 373 provides that the obtaining of property by fraud and deceit is to be treated as comparable to theft.

75. Cf. Philastre I, 608.

76. See chapter 9 at note 93.

77. Ming 9.2 (op.cit., 885); Ch'ing article 135, Philastre I, 607; Boulais 740; Staunton, 161. See also Jamieson, op.cit., 110f. The maximum punishment for liability on account of *tsang* is 2 and a half years penal servitude together with a beating of 90 blows with the heavy stick, and for fraud and deceit, three years penal servitude together with a beating of 100 blows.

78. Cf. Philastre I, 608 who here (wrongly I think) translates the word *kuo* ('error' or 'fault') by 'volonté'.

79. MLCCFL, 887.

80. See on this chapter 8.

81. No mention is made in the sub-statute of a fraudulent or deceitful appropriation of the property.

82. Boulais, 741.

83. See Philastre I, 609f; Boulais, 496-7, 742-5; Jamieson, op.cit., 110f; Brockman, op.cit., 86 (and cf. his observations at 87-8). For the rules on pledge in the period Yüan-Ch'ing see also Lin, op.cit., 119ff, esp. 122f, 133f.

11

Family Law: Succession, Adoption and Marriage

Introduction

Since the family and its proper ordering were at the heart of the Confucian system the codes are all concerned to see that the most fundamental requirements for the successful transmission of the family line through the generations are observed. These requirements are the conclusion of marriage according to the correct forms and the production of an heir who will continue the line and ensure the well-being of the ancestors through the maintenance of the sacrifices to them. They are intimately related in that it is normally from the marriage - and certainly this is the most strongly held expectation - that the heir is born. But it might happen that the wife produces no son. In such an event the heir must be found either in the son of a concubine or through recourse to adoption. Consequently the law governing the adoption of an heir is an integral part of the law on succession which in turn is designed to ensure maintenance of the proper links between the dead and the living.

Succession is thus not primarily concerned with the transmission of property but with the maintenance of continuity in the sacrifices to, and worship of, the ancestors. Nevertheless the codes do deal to a limited extent with succession to property, probably because of the perception that those with the duty of maintaining the ancestral sacrifices should share equally in the property. The codes speak only of transmission of property, not of liabilities; in fact those too automatically passed to the family head. A general point to be made is the extent to which the codified rules are merely reflections of the prescriptions found in the ritual classics. They make enforceable by means of penal sanctions the essential Confucian moral rules designed to ensure the successful continuation of the family.

A word of caution with respect to the codified provisions is necessary. Family law is an area in which custom is particularly important.[1] The statutory rules themselves, as already stressed, are largely a re-enactment of the moral rules accepted by Confucian literati as establishing the proper prescriptions for the conduct of family affairs. However such prescriptions were in reality accepted and applied only by the ruling and official class, not by the common people. The usages followed by the latter in the conduct of their family affairs may well have differed from those of the former.[2] A related point is that among all classes some of the legislative rules, such as those determining the conditions under which a divorce should occur, were not observed in practice. Local customs, varying in different parts of China, may also have led to the modification or even disregard of statutory rules.[3] For the practices followed or encouraged by particular clans with respect to such matters as the behaviour of wives and widows, the adoption of children and the exact distribution of property on the death of the family head the appropriate clan rules should be consulted.[4]

Succession and Adoption

In order to understand the provisions found in the codes one has to make a distinction between the following three sets of rules: (i) those designed to ensure the transmission of titles, ranks and dignities, (ii) those designed to ensure the continuation of the sacrifices to the ancestors, and (iii) those regulating the transmission of property. The relationship between these sets of rules is not entirely clear and has given rise to some difference of opinion. Nor can one be sure that the position during the T'ang (for example) was the same as that during the Ming and Ch'ing. The problem can be put in this way. The first two sets of rules, as they appear in the codes, prescribe the selection of an individual as the successor to the father. Such a successor inherited, on the one hand, any hereditary rank or dignity and, on the other, had the responsibility for the conduct of the sacrifices to the ancestors. Where there were sons born to the wife it was the eldest son who was selected as successor for these purposes. However with respect to the third set, on the transmission of property, no distinction was drawn between the ages of the sons; nor was it relevant whether they were born from the wife, a concubine or even (in the later law) a slave. All were entitled to an equal share of the property.

How is the rule on equal shares to be related to those which singled out the eldest son of the wife as successor? The answer probably lies in the fact that, with respect to the sons, no sharp distinction should be drawn between the entitlement to conduct the sacrifice to the parents and ancestors and the entitlement to share in the property. As has been observed by one of the leading Japanese scholars on Chinese family law, Shuzo Shiga: 'a man lives in those who sacrifice to him. The joint and simultaneous succession to sacrifices and property is indissoluble. This is the basic guideline of China's inheritance law'.[5] Any son may appropriately conduct the sacrifices to the ancestors and hence each is entitled to an equal share of the property with the others. Consequently it becomes important to single out the eldest son or any other individual as successor only in two situations: where it is a question of succession to rank or title, and where there are no sons who constitute the natural successors. In the latter event a successor to the sacrifices must be found in adoption. How important this was can be seen from the practice of the posthumous appointment of a legal successor to a person who has died without male issue or without himself securing the adoption of a suitable relative.[6]

The T'ang code contains rules on the apportionment of a legal successor, the position of children given in adoption and the partition of family property.[7] Article 158 imposes a punishment of penal servitude for one year on a person who selects his legal successor (*ti*) 'not in accordance with law (*fa*)'. The article assumes that the situation is one in which the wife is aged 50 and has not yet produced a son. Should there be a son or sons by the wife it is the eldest such son who automatically becomes successor. However where this is not the situation the article permits the appointment of the eldest of those sons born to concubines, and establishes the same punishment should a son other than the eldest be appointed. No doubt most eventualities would be covered by these provisions, at least for those among the better off who could afford concubines; normally there would be a son born either from the wife or a concubine.

In the *shu-i* commentary one finds quoted the relevant section of the Household statutes prescribing what is to be done where there is no son born to the wife, or where there is such a son but he has either predeceased the father or or by virtue of having committed crimes or incurred a disease (leprosy?) is not a worthy successor. The statute states that if the eldest son of the wife cannot be appointed successor (because he is dead or unworthy), his eldest son (that is, the eldest grandson in the principal line) is to be appointed. If there is no such person, the next eldest son of the wife should be appointed. If there is no such person, the eldest son born of a concubine is to be appointed. If there are also no sons of a concubine, the person to be appointed is a younger son of the wife of the (deceased) eldest son (that is, a younger brother of the eldest (deceased) grandson). If there is no such person, the eldest grandson of a concubine is to be established (that is, the eldest son of a son born to a concubine). Although the statute does not itself specify the appointment of the eldest son or grandson of a concubine, the fact that he - and not a younger son or grandson - should be appointed is inferable from the wording of the article itself.[8]

Neither the article nor the commentary specifies the precise purpose of the appointment of a legal successor. Certainly the appointment was not required for the purpose of inheriting the father's property. But it is not clear whether the purpose was to determine the succession to rank and title or to secure the continuance of the sacrifices, or both. In view of the fact that the necessity to secure the continuance of the sacrifices to the ancestors was paramount, it is difficult to escape the conclusion that the article was intended primarily to provide for this matter, though it would also have served to regulate succession of title. If this is the correct interpretation of the article, then it does not seem as though all the sons were equally entitled to conduct the sacrifices. This is particularly apparent in the situation where there are several sons but the eldest has predeceased his father, leaving a son. In this situation it is the grandson who is to be appointed the legal successor, not the eldest surviving uncle. Possibly the position was that although all the sons participated in the sacrifices the pre-eminent role was reserved for the eldest son, and after him, the eldest grandson in the same line. In other words although all the sons were entitled to conduct the sacrifices, and thus (according to Shiga) derived the right to share equally in the property, the main responsibility rested with the eldest male descendent in the principal line.

Nothing is said in article 158 about adoption. The only successors it contemplates are an individual's direct descendants, his sons and their sons. Being sons they automatically qualify as successors, even though one among them is alone the designated successor. However should there be no surviving sons or grandson it becomes necessary to appoint a successor from outside the ranks of direct descendants, though still from within the clan. The ritual rules prescribe who, under these circumstances, should be appointed successor. To effect the appointment the appropriate individual has to be brought into the family and adopted as a son. Once the adoption has taken place he has all the duties of the successor and is not normally allowed to break the bond and return to his old family.

Article 157 and its commentary specify the main rules governing adoption for the purpose of succession and establish punishments for their breach. Where parents lack a son they may adopt a male child from another branch of the clan, belonging to the appropriate junior generation. Once adopted the son may not of his own accord leave and return to his own family. Should he do so he incurs a punishment of penal servitude for two years. However he may choose to return should his adopting parents subsequently produce a son of their own, or should his own parents subsequently lose all their other sons. Should he displease his adopting parents they may send him back to his family (and presumably, although this is not said, adopt someone else).[9] Where an adopted son leaves in circumstances that entail a punishment of two years penal servitude, it thus appears to be open to his adopting parents to have him back or to return him to his own family.

Adoption of a child who belongs to another clan is punished by penal servitude for one year, the person giving in adoption receiving a beating of 50 blows with the light stick. To this rule there is one important exception. When a male child aged 3 years or less has been abandoned by his own family he may be adopted by another family and then takes the name of that family. Neither the article nor the commentary states explicitly that a child adopted in these circumstances might not, if there were no other children, constitute the legal successor. In the later law this was not possible. One might perhaps infer from the reason for the adoption given in the *shu-i* commentary - to save the life of the child, nothing being said of appointing a successor - that the position was the same in T'ang law. However it seems that in both T'ang and Sung practice such children, in the absence of legitimate issue, might be recognised as legal successors to prevent discontinuance of the family.[10] One has to accept that T'ang/Sung law may have been less strict in this matter than Ming/Ch'ing. Should the child merely have been lost, then if he is later recognised and claimed by his own family he should return upon repayment of the cost of his upkeep.[11]

Succession to family property is regulated by article 162,[12] the background to which is the fact that the sons and their families continue to live with the grandparents or parents until they have died, whereas the daughters have left their father's house on marriage and in effect passed permanently into their husband's family. It was a punishable offence for the sons to set up independent establishments or effect a separation of the property during the lifetime of their parents. Equally it was a punishable offence for grandparents or parents themselves to order their grandsons or sons to register a separate household.[13] However this prohibition did not apply to grandparents or parents ordering their grandsons or sons to hold property separately (article 155).[14]

Article 162 itself, after providing that junior members of the household are not allowed on their own authority to spend or appropriate family property, states that where the property ought to be divided then the division must be equal; where anyone who receives a share less than that to which he is entitled, the person who has unjustly benefited is liable on account of *tsang* with a decrease in punishment of 3 degrees. Nothing is said as to the identity of the persons entitled. However the *shu-i* commentary quotes a Household Statute which specifies that, where there should be a division of the land, houses and other property, these assets should be divided equally between elder and younger brothers. Where the wife of a brother has brought property with her as dowry, that is not included in the division but remains with the particular family (and ultimately passes equally to the sons within that family). Should a brother have died his sons take between them equally the share to which he would have been entitled had he lived.

No further information is provided by the text of the T'ang code itself. However fortunately a more complete version of the relevant Household Statute together with other material was inserted in the Sung code after the corresponding article prohibiting juniors from disposing of family property on their own authority.[15] The additional provisions of the statute, not given in the *shu-i* commentary, are (i) where all the brothers have died then their various sons share the property equally, (ii) where a son (or grandson) entitled to share has not yet married he is to be given betrothal property in addition to his share; (iii) women (unmarried) are to receive half the betrothal property accorded sons or grandsons, and (iv) where a wife has been widowed and lacks a son[16] she is to receive the share her husband would have received had he lived; if all her husband's brothers have died (at the time of division) she is to receive the share of one son. It does not appear from this that unmarried daughters or grandaughters are entitled to a share in the property - apart from the amount allocated them for betrothal[17]

A further T'ang statute,[18] included in the Sung code, deals with the situation where the household has been discontinued (*hu chüeh*), that is, where the father has died leaving no direct male descendants, and no legal successor has been adopted *inter vivos*, by testament or by posthumous appointment on the art of the clan elders. It provides that after sufficient property for the payment of the funeral expenses has been realised, the balance is to be given in the first instance to daughters (unmarried). If there are no daughters the property is to be divided equally among the closest agnatic, cognatic or affinal relatives. If there are no such relatives the state acquires.

Avery important provision is contained at the end of this statute, to the effect that the distribution of the property which it stipulates is not to take effect where the father in his lifetime has given a clear written direction as to the division of the property. This appears to concede a wide power of testamentary disposition to a father in circumstances where there are no natural or adopted sons or grandsons. However it is likely that the only persons who would qualify as objects of the power were relatives of the testator. It would not have been open to a father, for example, to pass over his daughters and leave his property to a friend. But he would have been able to choose which of his surviving daughters or other relatives should acquire the property and determine the proportion which each was to take.

A word may be added on the position of married daughters as determined by what appears to be a Sung enactment inserted immediately after the T'ang statute.[19] It states that where the household has been discontinued but there are married daughters (that is, none remain unmarried) the property, after payment of the funeral expenses, is to be divided into three parts. One part is to be divided between the married daughters and the other two are to go to the state. Where the latter include lands the closest agnatic male relatives are to be allowed to hold them as tenants from the state. Should a married daughter on being divorced or having lost her husband and having no son, return to her parents' home then, in default of male descendants, she shares in the property equally with unmarried daughters.[20]

Both the T'ang article and Household Statute which regulate the devolution of the property simply postulate a situation in which the division 'ought' to take place, without specifying further the circumstances which, as it were, activate the 'ought'. However it seems that what is contemplated is division of the family property on the death of the grandparents or parents after (although this is not specifically stated) completion of the prescribed period of mourning. Possibly it was only the death of the father or grandfather that was relevant to the question of partition of the property, that is, where the grandmother or mother survived there might still be a division, suitable arrangements being made for the support of the widow. Division was not compulsory on the death of the grandparents or parents. The brothers might choose to keep the property together and administer it jointly. But should any one brother request partition, then the division must be put into effect on the basis laid down in the statute. While the grandfather or father lived no junior member of the household could compel division or insist upon being given his share of the family property. Yet it was open to the grandfather or father, should he so wish, to proceed to a distribution of the property, between his grandsons or sons in his own life time. It seems that the division between the grandsons or sons should still comply with the rules of the statute, but the grandfather or father might retain for his own support any amount he thought fit.[21]

Ming and Ch'ing law make a clear distinction between the three sets of rules identified above.[22] One article establishes the succession to title and rank.[23] In the first place the title should descend to the eldest son of the wife, or if he is not alive, to the eldest grandson in the same line. Should there be a bar to succession, as where the son or grandson entitled to succeed has committed an offence precluding the holding of rank, the father's title and rank pass to the second son or his eldest son. Failing any male issue through the wife entitled to succeed, the eldest son or grandson of a concubine succeeds. Failing any such son or grandson the title and rank pass to that nephew who, according to the ritual rules, is the appropriate legal successor of the deceased, and failing a nephew, to a younger brother of the deceased.[24] By 'nephew' is here meant any junior collateral agnatic relative who would qualify under the ritual rules. An individual who disregarded these rules in the appointment of a person to succeed to his rank and title is to be punished with penal servitude for three years and a beating of 100 blows with the heavy stick.

The rules on the appointment of a legal successor responsible for the sacrifices follow the T'ang. In effect they are the same as those for the appointment of a successor to title and rank, except that a younger brother (not being of the right generation) may not be legal successor with respect to the sacrifices, though he may succeed to title.[25] The rule that a successor by adoption should be from the same clan is insisted upon more rigidly than in T'ang law. A child of three years or younger abandoned by its parents may be taken in adoption and given the same name as the adopting parents but cannot be appointed legal successor.[26] The punishments for disregard of the rules are somewhat less than under the T'ang (80 blows with the heavy stick where the rules on appointment are disregarded, and 60 blows where a person from a different clan is adopted as son). The improper appointment is to be set aside and a proper one made.[27]

Various sub-statutes added to the codes, especially the Ch'ing, provide more detail and make clearer the operation of the system. In particular it appears that an individual who lacked sons or grandsons competent to be legal successors had a wide degree of choice within the class of mourning relatives belonging to the appropriate junior generation. He might even, where there was no such relative, choose an appropriate person of the same surname even where no mourning relationship existed. Nor was he forced to appoint any particular individual within the clan. He might choose the person he deemed most wise or most talented, or the one for whom he felt most affection. Even where an appointment had been made, should enmity develop between the adopting father and the adopted son, on application to the authorities, the adoption might be set aside and a fresh successor appointed.[28] The most essential rules are that the person adopted as successor be from the same clan[29] and of the appropriate junior generation.

As to the transmission of property the Ming and Ch'ing rules are considerably stricter than the T'ang both with respect to the possible range of heirs and the freedom accorded an individual to determine the disposition of the family property. The only provision found in the articles of the code is the same as that in the T'ang: where there ought to be a division of the property among brothers it is to be carried out fairly so that each obtains an equal share.[30] However the Ch'ing sub-statutes, confirming rules already applied under the Ming, add a number of important details. These make clear,first, that where the property is to be divided among brothers, the sons of the wife, of concubines and of slave women are all to share equally. Even a son born in adultery is to obtain half the share of a legitimate son. Should he be the only son he is to obtain half the property, the other half going to the relative appointed as legal successor, and, in the absence of any other relative competent to succeed, the son born in adultery may himself be appointed legal successor, and take all the property. Should there be no sons, or male issue of sons, then the property is to be divided between unmarried daughters. Should there be no unmarried daughters (or granddaughters by deceased sons) it is to go to the state.[31] Other sub-statutes, again basically reiterating the Ming position, emphasise that adopted sons, even sons-in-law living with the family (an unusual but possible arrangement), are to share in the property with the legal successor; the latter is not to drive them away (something no doubt frequently attempted in practice).[32]

Under these rules not only are cognatic or affinal relatives but even agnatic relatives (other than direct descendants or the one appointed legal successor) excluded from succession to the property.[33] Nor are unmarried daughters entitled to share in the division of the property. Upon marriage they became the responsibility of their husband's family and might be entitled under certain circumstances to a share of that family's property. Another sub-statute, also repeating a Ming rule, provides that where a wife is left a widow without a son, on partition, she is to receive her husband's share of the property, though she may not take this with her should she remarry.[34]

Whereas the T'ang enactments permitted a father, where there was no direct male issue or adopted successor, to distribute his property by will (among his other relatives), it is less clear that this was the position in Ming and Ch'ing law. The generally stricter rules governing the devolution of the family property suggest that in fact in the later law the earlier (albeit still restricted) freedom of testamentary disposition was removed.[35] If this is correct it seems that all a person might validly achieve by a will was the disinheritance of a son for some grave reason such as unfilial or dissolute conduct, the appointment of a legal successor in a case where there was no direct male issue, and the making of minor bequests which did not seriously impair the rights of those designated by the law as heirs to the property.[36] This at any rate appears to have been the position under statutory law; custom may have determined otherwise.

Marriage[37]

In Confucian thought marriage was regarded as perhaps the most important of the five fundamental human relationships. It was compared to the interaction of Heavan and Earth from which all things spring. Both the Confucian ritual books and the law codes regulate the function of marriage and its consequences in great deal; more than in any other area of the law the codes simply repeat the prescriptions of the ritual books and attempt to secure compliance with them through the attachment of penal sanctions.[38]

The social - one may even say anthropological-background to marriage may be shortly described as follows. Since traditional Chinese society was dominantly patrilineal and patrilocal, a bride on marriage left her own family and went to live with the family of her husband.[39] He himself did not normally leave the parental household in the lifetime of his parents or grandparents.[40] Thus the grandparents, parents, sons with their wives and children, together with concubines and unmarried children formed a large family grouping that normally, though not necessarily, fragmented, on the death of the grandparents.

In her new home the bride's role was both that of a wife looking after her husband, of a mother raising her children, and of a daughter-in-law serving her husband's parents as well as his deceased ancestors through the part she played in the family cult. From the Confucian emphasis on the necessity to maintain a proper relationship between the wife and her husband's parents one forms the impression that this constituted her most important role. In effect the daughters-in-law replaced the daughters of the family lost to it on their marriage. A high status was accorded the wife in her husband's family, derived partly from her role in the sacrificial rites for the ancestors and partly from the fact that she was to be the mother of the legal successor. These features distinguish her sharply from, and placed her upon a more elevated plane than, any secondary wife or concubine whom her husband might also take.

Since marriage is one of the fundamental human relationships it was essential that it be accomplished in the proper way and that, once concluded, there should be no blurring of the respective roles of husband and wife. The marriage was arranged by the respective family elders, often through the medium of a go-between, and effected by an elaborate sequence of rites.[42] Once in her husband's house the bride should concern herself purely with domestic matters, with cooking, looking after the young children, serving her husband's parents and offering the sacrifices to the husband's ancestors. Above all she should not seek to direct the affairs of the household, a prohibition traditionally expressed in the graphic statement 'no hen should herald the dawn lest misfortune follow'.[43]

The two pre-eminent female virtues constantly stressed in the Confucian classic literature and such works as the Han compilation *Lieh Nü Chuan: Biographies of Eminent Women* are obedience and chastity. Applied to a wife this meant that she must be obedient and respectful, above all to her husband's parents whom she served. To displease them was to place a moral obligation upon the husband to divorce her, however much she may have pleased him. Chastity meant not so much that she must refrain from adultery - something taken for granted - as that she should 'follow one man' (her husband) for the whole of her life until she was buried in the same grave with him. In particular she was expected never to leave her husband, and, should he predecease her, not to marry again. One of the great Sung neo-Confucian scholars, Cheng I (eleventh century), went so far as to say that a virtuous widow should prefer death by starvation to remarriage.[44] Women who had distinguished themselves by their chastity, including widows who had refrained from remarriage for a long period of time, were given public marks of honour in the form of inscriptions and tablets commending their virtue.[45]

The Confucian moral code required the husband to treat his wife with respect and not to diminish her status as wife. But it was open to him to repudiate her, to send her back to her own home, if she failed in her duty to him or his parents. By Han times it was settled that she might be sent away for any of the following reasons: not serving her husband's parents, having no son, being licentious, being jealous, having a serious illness (?leprosy), talking too much, or committing theft. However even if one of these grounds was present she was still to be retained if there was no home to which she could return, or if she had already completed the three year period of mourning for her husband's parents (presumably even for one of them), or if her husband had been poor and lowly when she married him but subsequently became rich and honourable.[46]

Many, though not all, of these moral requirements and expectancies were made directly enforceable by the penal codes in the sense that punishments were established for their breach.[47] Generally to be borne in mind is the fact that the persons incurring the punishments were those responsible for the marriage, that is, the elders in the two families who had arranged it, not the boy and girl themselves. The legal rules will be considered under the following heads: betrothal and marriage, the position of the wife, and the ending of the marriage.

(i) Betrothal and Marriage

The T'ang code identifies three ways in which a betrothal may be made. In all cases the initiative must be taken by the parents of the bride and groom (or the grandparents or other senior relatives). The bride's father may formally promise her in writing to the groom's father. Such a formal written 'contract' is concluded through the intermediary of a go-between who ascertains and communicates to each party the necessary information leading to the promise to marry. Alternatively the two fathers may conclude a 'private' written agreement (without employing the services of a go-between) on the basis of particulars covering the age, health and status of the children to be married. The third mode - deemed equivalent to the making of a written promise - is constituted by the acceptance on the part of the bride's family of the appropriate betrothal presents; probably the services of a go-between were used.[48]

The nub of the provisions lies in the punishments imposed where one of these arrangements is made, that is, where a betrothal is validly contracted, and yet the marriage itself is not completed. The boy's family is treated much more leniently than the girl's. If the person in charge of the marriage on the girl's side repents and breaks the engagement, the punishment to which he becomes liable is 60 blows with the heavy stick. The marriage is still to take place. On the other hand if the boy's family repents the only legal consequence is that the betrothal property is not returned (there is no punishment and the marriage is not compelled). Where the girl's family not only breaks the engagement but promises her in marriage to another the punishment is more severe. The person in charge is to receive a beating of 100 blows with the heavy stick. If the second marriage was actually accomplished he is sentenced to penal servitude for 1 1/2 years. The girl is to be restored to the first fiancé; if he does not now wish to marry her, the betrothal property is to be returned to his family and the marriage to the second fiancé is to stand.[49]

Since the procedure for the betrothal meant that there was little opportunity for the boy and girl to be personally acquainted prior to the completion of the marriage, or even for those arranging the marriage to do more than inspect the bride or groom at the time of the betrothal, there was a certain danger of 'wrongful substitution'. A family might exhibit one child in perfect health at the interview with the other family but in fact conclude the marriage in the name of another child afflicted with a serious disease. Or the boy's family might say they were offering a son of the wife, but in fact supply an adopted son or the son of a concubine. Article 176 provided that where the girl's family made a 'wrongful substitution' the person in charge of the marriage is to receive a punishment of penal servitude for one year; if the boy's family made a 'wrongful substitution' the punishment is to be penal servitude for 1 1/2 years for the person responsible. Under a general rule stated in article 195 these punishments are very considerably reduced (by five degrees) when the wrongful marriage has not actually taken place. If possible the terms of the original agreement are to be fulfilled; but should the marriage with the person wrongfully substituted have been completed, although it is no longer possible to honour the original agreement, the parties are still to be separated.

The Ming and Ch'ing articles are formulated somewhat differently from the T'ang but proceed on the same basis, namely that a betrothal is concluded by a formal written promise, a private agreement or just the acceptance of betrothal property.[51] Shen's 'upper commentary' in the Ch'ing code explains the difference between the formal promise and the private agreement as lying in the presence or absence of a go-between.[52] However there are important differences between the T'ang and the

Ming/Ch'ing articles in the consequences entailed by failure to carry out the betrothal. In the first place the punishments are less severe. Where the girl's family repents the punishment for the person responsible is a beating of 50 blows with the light stick and the marriage is still to take place. If the girl is promised to another but the marriage is not yet completed the punishment is a beating of 70 blows with the heavy stick; if the marriage has been completed it is 80 blows. As in the T'ang code the girl is to be restored to the first fiancé. But his family is now placed in a more advantageous position should he not wish to have her back. Double the amount of the betrothal property is to be repaid and the girl is to go to the second fiancé.[53]

The punishment for wrongful substitution was also reduced: a beating of 80 blows with the heavy stick for the person in charge of the marriage where the girl's side is at fault, and 90 blows for the person in charge where the boy's side is at fault (again with a decrease of five degrees if the wrongful marriage has not been completed). In addition in the former case the betrothal property is to be restored, and in the latter it is to be kept by the girl's family. The Ch'ing general commentary adds an important gloss. Should the girl in the case of wrongful substitution where the marriage has taken place not wish to marry another, she is to be exempt from the rule requiring the parties to be separated.[54]

Furthermore an important change is made with respect to the boy's family. The person responsible for the boy's marriage is now subject to the same punishments as apply in the case where the girl's family repents, and the betrothal property is not restored. In the text of the Ch'ing article is inserted a fragment of the official, small commentary which states: 'still order the boy to marry the first fiancée and the second girl to whom he was betrothed is to be free to marry someone else'. As the general commentary emphasises, the second part of this fragment states only 'girl to whom he was betrothed' and not 'girl whom he married'. The effect of the wording is that the marriage to the second girl, if completed, cannot be undone, and it is now the first girl to whom the boy was originally betrothed who is to be free to marry someone else (and to keep the betrothal property given on the original engagement). The reason for the distinction drawn in this case between engagement and completed marriage is that in the latter event the second girl has 'lost her body' and, should the marriage be dissolved, has no-one to whom she can turn for a husband. Conversely in the case where the girl's family has married her to a second fiancé (where the marriage has been completed) this marriage may be undone provided the first fiancé is still prepared to accept her;

otherwise it also endures.[55] Althouqh the text of the Ming article does not contain this fraqment from the official commentary, the position was in fact the same in Ming law.[56]

Generally, therefore, one may conclude that in Ming and Ch'ing law there has been a considerable shift in the emphasis found in the T'ang code. The latter clearly placed greater value on the boy than the girl in that the punishments for withdrawal from the engagement were heavier on the girl's side than on the boy's, and further only the girl was compelled to honour the original engagement. In Ming and Ch'ing law both families were valued equally. The punishments for withdrawal from the engagement are the same, and the boy, just as the girl, can be compelled to honour the original engagement. The difference in the rules on the last point is due not to a superior value accorded the boy, but to a desire to protect the (second) girl who, once having lost her virginity, would find it difficult to obtain another husband should the marriage undone.

(ii) The Position of the Wife

First one may consider the rules concerned to ensure that in certain crucial ways the wife is treated properly by the husband. The codes imposed punishments on a husband who is guilty in his treatment of his wife of serious violation of the duty of respect imposed by the marital relationship. The explanatory commentaries in this context stress the fact that the husband and wife are paired together as equals.[57] There are no rules in the codes which specify as such the duties of the wife. This is perhaps due to the fact that the wife's duties are comprehensively listed in the rules defining the circumstances under which she may be repudiated.[58]

The T'ang code provides that the husband is to be sentenced to one year penal servitude if he takes a second wife (as distinct from a concubine) while he is still married to the first; furthermore the second marriage is to be undone.[59] The *shu-i* commentary compares the husband and wife to the sun and the moon. Both are indispensable parts of a whole and the wife, as the one in charge of the domestic arrangements, has an important role. The implication is that the relationship between husband and wife is unique; it cannot be diminished through the lessening of the position accorded the wife that would follow from the entrance into the household of a rival in the same position. The Ming and Ch'ing codes also prohibit the taking of a second wife, but the punishment is only a beating of 90 blows with the heavy stick; the second marriage is still to be undone.[60] The Ch'ing general commentary explains the offence as deriving from infringement of the correct behaviour demanded by the relationship (*i*) of husband and wife, namely, in establishing a second pair of mates where there should be only one pair.[61]

Common to the three codes are other provisions designed to prevent diminution of the wife's status.[62] The T'ang code imposes a punishment of 2 years penal servitude on a husband who relegates his wife to the status of a concubine or a man who takes a slave woman as wife.[63] The two faults appear to be different. In the one the husband is debasing the status of a woman who is already his wife, in the other he is raising to the status of a wife a woman who is a slave. Yet from the point of view of the code (reflecting here the accepted moral position) the misconduct of the husband in both cases is of the same kind. The *shu-i* commentary explains that husband and wife make a whole; they are a pair of (equally matched) mates. The wife is in a position of respect whereas concubines are acquired by purchase and slaves belong to an inferior class. To make the wife a concubine or to take a slave as wife is to lose 'the just way of husband and wife' and profane the laws of human relationships. A later part of the commentary to the same article points to the role of the wife in transmitting the family line and taking part in the sacrifices to the ancestors and asks 'how can a slave, even though manumitted, be worthy of receiving the important position of the mother of the heir?'[64] There is here an underlying notion of great moral iniquity attached to actions which depreciate the status of a wife as a person equal in standing to the husband.

The corresponding provision in the Ming and Ch'ing codes refers only to the reduction of the wife to the status of a concubine, imposing a beating of 100 blows with the heavy stick (lighter than that prescribed by the T'ang code) and requiring the wife to be restored to her proper status.[65] Attention is drawn in the Ch'ing general commentary to the fact that husband and wife are the one body. A concubine is of an inferior status; to make the wife a concubine is to confuse the 'noble' and the 'base'.[66]

One might infer from the dropping of the provision which prohibits the taking of a slave as wife that this prohibition no longer obtained in Ming and Ch'ing law. Such an inference receives confirmation from the article which regulates marriage between the 'free' and the 'mean'. All that this article prohibits is the giving of a free girl in marriage to a male slave. Nothing is said of the giving of a slave girl as wife to a free boy. A master who gives his slave in marriage to a free girl is to receive a beating of 80 blows with the heavy stick, and the person responsible for the girl's marriage, if he knows the circumstances, a beating of 70 blows with the heavy stick. The marriage is to be undone.[67] Consequently in Ming and Ch'ing law there seems in general to be no bar between the marriage of a free man and a female slave. An exception is constituted by a further article which specifically prohibits the marriage between an official and a girl belonging to the 'mean' class of singer or entertainer (deemed also to include prostitutes).[68] Did this article prohibit the marriage between an official and a slave woman? T'ung-tsu Ch'u holds that it did,[69] but the matter is not entirely clear.[70]

As has been seen the Confucian ethic did not regard the relationship of husband and wife as ceasing with the death of the husband. A virtuous wife was expected to 'follow one man' to the end of her life and keep her chastity by not remarrying. The codes do not go as far as prohibiting a widow from remarrying but they do impose some restriction on her freedom in this respect. First of all she was prohibited from remarrying during the period prescribed for the mourning of her husband (27 months). The T'ang code imposed the heavy punishment of three years penal servitude on a widow who remarried within the period of mourning, and provided that the marriage should be undone. The *shu-i* commentary adds by way of justification that the husband is 'the wife's heaven and she ought not to remarry'.[71]

A conflict of duty might arise where a woman lost her husband. She is under a duty to keep her chastity and not remarry. This might be said to be a moral duty for the whole of her life but a legal duty (that is, one whose breach was subject to punishment by the code) only for the duration of the period of mourning. On the other hand she had a duty of filial obedience to her grandparents and parents. Should they desire her to remarry, which duty was she to follow? The T'ang code treated as primary the duty of filial obedience. It enacted where a widow has completed the period of mourning for her husband and still wishes 'to keep his memory' (remain a widow) anyone who is not a paternal grandparent or parent and compels her to marry is to be punished with penal servitude for one year; the marriage is to be dissolved and the widow is to return to the home of her former husband.[72] The formulation predicated upon the 'not' phrase shows that the duty and the right of the widow not to remarry was in principle to be respected. Only where filial obedience required compliance with the instructions of her paternal grandparents or parents were her own wishes to be disregarded.

In the Ming code[73] the same basic position as the T'ang code is taken but the punishments are significantly lighter. A widow who remarries during the period of mourning for her first husband receives a beating of 100 blows with the heavy stick, and those who compel her to marry after the period of mourning has been completed (except the paternal grandparents or parents) are also to receive a beating of 100 blows. The Ch'ing code has the same rule with respect to the widow who remarries during the period of mourning but introduces important modifications to the rule governing a remarriage after completion of the period of mourning. In the first place the exception in favour of the paternal grandparents or parents is removed. The code provides that either the paternal grandparents or parents of the widow or the paternal grandparents or parents of her deceased husband will be punished with a beating of 80 blows with the heavy stick should they forcibly, against her will, give her in marriage. In the second place the legal consequences of the forced marriage are made to depend upon whether it has been completed or not. If it has been completed it is to stand and the widow is to remain with her new husband, but the betrothal presents are forfeit to the state. If it has not been completed the widow is to return to the family of her former husband and the betrothal property is to be returned to the giver.[74] By a sub-statute found in the Ch'ing, though not the Ming code, much heavier punishments are imposed on relatives who put pressure upon a widow to remarry and so drive her to commit suicide.[75]

One may detect in the provisions of the Ch'ing code a less rigid application of the principle of filial obedience in that even the paternal grandparents or parents are to be punished for driving the widow into a marriage against her will. In itself this might suggest, conversely, a strengthening of the principle that a wife should 'keep her chastity' and not remarry after her husband's death. Yet there is the additional factor that the marriage, if completed, is not to be undone even though the widow was forced into it against her own wishes. What is here reflected seems to be a greater value attached to the fact that a marriage once completed should not be undone provided that the parties may competently marry. Having acquired the relationship of husband and wife they should retain it even though compulsion was exercised with respect to the wife. All that the general commentary of the Ch'ing code says on the point is that the wife remains with her husband since she has already 'lost her body'.[76]

So far what has been stressed is the equal standing of the husband and wife; it is the wife's status as equal mate that protects her from being dealt with as though she were an inferior. Yet in other contexts what is stressed is precisely the fact that the wife occupies an inferior status vis-a-vis the husband. The relationship of husband and wife was sometimes likened to that between a senior and a junior relative. Such a statement not only implied a general duty of obedience and submission on the part of the wife but also allowed offences committed by a wife against her husband or vice-versa to be treated in the same way as offences committed by 'junior' against 'senior' relatives and vice versa.

Clear examples in which the wife is treated as a junior, inferior to her husband, are provided by the law on beating, injuring or killing and that on accusations. The T'ang code provides that where a husband beats or injuries his wife he is to be punished two degrees less than if he had beaten or injured an unrelated person; but should the wife die the case is to be treated in the same way as that of the death of an unrelated person.[77] The *shu-i* commentary discounts for the present context the understanding of the wife as the equal of the husband and asserts that, although the husband and wife have the one body, the relationship (*i*) between them is the same as that between a senior and a junior relative. On the other hand, merely for beating the husband (or, it seems, inflicting a trivial injury) the wife is sentenced to penal servitude for one year. If the injury is severe, as where the husband is wounded internally and spits blood, she is punished three degrees more than if she had injured an unrelated person. In both cases the husband himself must lodge an accusation.[78]

Some modifications are introduced by the corresponding articles in the Ming and Ch'ing codes. The position of the husband is improved even further. If he beats his wife there is no liability unless he inflicts an injury at least as serious as the breaking of a bone. If there is such an injury the punishment (as in the T'ang code) is two degrees less than that for injuring an unrelated person; if death ensues he is to be strangled. But - another change - the court (in the case of injury) will first inquire whether the husband and wife wish to separate. If they do not, the appropriate punishment for the husband's offence is determined and redemption by payment of money is allowed. Where the wife beats the husband and either no injury or merely a trivial hurt is inflicted, a punishment of a beating of 100 blows with the heavy stick is imposed (less than the T'ang punishment). Should the husband wish to separate this is to be allowed. If there is serious injury the basic rule (with some variation) of the T'ang code applies.[78]

With respect to accusations the T'ang code places the wife vis-a-vis the husband in the same category as junior vis-a-vis senior relatives for whom the former wear mourning for one year, or a grandchild vis-a-vis maternal grandparents. Thus by article 346 a wife who accuses her husband to the court of having committed an offence incurs a punishment of penal servitude for two years. If the accusation is false then the punishment is three degrees more than that prescribed for the offence falsely accused, with a minimum of two years penal servitude.[80] No punishment appears to have been imposed by the T'ang code on a husband who accuses his wife of an offence where that accusation is true.[81] The only reference I have found in the code is to false accusations made by the husband. The *shu-i* commentary (in a question and answer) to article 347 compares a false accusation of the wife by the husband to that by a senior relative of a junior for whom mourning is worn for one year, where the punishment is two degrees less than that prescribed for the falsely accused offence. The commentary specifies that, although the wife in fact is not a junior relative, her relationship to her husband (*i*) is the same as that of a junior to a senior relative.

In the Ming and Ch'ing codes the standpoint is not the same. The position of the wife is not expressly compared to that of a junior relative, and in fact she is more harshly treated than under T'ang law. The relevant article places the wife in the same category as a son or grandson. Should she accuse her husband of an offence which is true the punishment is penal servitude for three years and a beating of 100 blows with the heavy stick; should it be false the punishment is death by strangulation.[82] The general commentary of the Ch'ing code, in explaining this exceptionally harsh rule, stresses the importance of the affection arising under, and the duty of gratitude imposed by, the relationships of grandparent/grandchild, parent/child and husband/wife. If the 'superior' in the relationship commits an offence it is the duty of the 'inferior' to conceal it. To bring the fault to light and make an accusation is an act destructive of the very nature of social bonds.[83] Affection and gratitude are seen as essentially due from the 'inferior' to the 'superior' (from the wife to the husband) and not from the 'superior' to the 'inferior'. This is further shown by the lenient treatment of the husband who accuses his wife of an offence. A later section of the same article provides that where a husband falsely accuses his wife the punishment is three degrees less than that prescribed for the falsely imputed offence. Nothing is said of the liability of the husband for a (true) accusation of his wife.

(iii) The Ending of the Marriage[84]

A marriage might legitimately end in the lifetime of the parties in one of three ways: the husband might repudiate his wife on a ground recognised by the law, both might agree to separate, or either husband or wife or certain categories of their relatives might commit an act entailing in law the end of the marriage. The first depends upon the choice of the husband,[85] the second upon the consent of both spouses, and the third operates to end the marriage irrespective of the wishes of either spouse. What is not normally possible is for the wife unilaterally of her own volition to end the marriage. Indeed if she attempts to end the marriage by leaving her husband she commits an offence entailing a heavy punishment.[86]

The T'ang code punishes a wife who leaves her husband's home on her own responsibility with penal servitude for two years. Should she leave in order to take another husband, the period of penal servitude is increased to three years.[87] The *shu-i* commentary echoes the injunction expressed in the ritual and moral literature: 'the wife follows her husband; she has no 'way' of herself alone'. However it injects a note of commonsense by adding: 'It is difficult for respect within the home to endure. Within the 'inner apartments' how can there not be anger and strife? If the wife suddenly departs after mutual recriminations she is not liable under this law'.

A different, and in some respects harsher, attitude is taken in the Ming and Ch'ing codes. If the wife leaves of her own accord she is to be punished with a beating of 100 blows with the heavy stick and the husband is given the option of keeping her or marrying or selling her to another. Should she flee her husband's home and marry (formally) another, the punishment is now death by strangulation.[88] The general commentary of the Ch'ing code justifies the death penalty on the ground that a wife who leaves her husband in order to follow another man has destroyed the 'way' that should be followed by humans (*jen tao*).[89]

Repudiation of the wife by the husband in all three codes follows the prescriptions found in the ritual and moral books. Indeed the relevant articles take for granted the existence of the seven grounds of repudiation and are framed in the form: should the husband repudiate his wife for a reason that does not fall within one of the seven grounds a punishment is to be imposed upon him.[90] The difference between the codes lies in the punishments, the husband being treated more favourably in the later codes. Under the T'ang the punishment for unauthorised repudiation is penal servitude for 1 1/2 years, and the Ming/Ch'ing 80 blows with the heavy stick. The seven grounds are listed in the commentaries to the articles, viz: lacking a son, shameless behaviour, not serving husband's parents, talking too much, theft, jealousy and incurable illness (? leprosy).

One can say generally that a wife proves herself unworthy and so deserving repudiation if she fails to provide for the continuance of the family line through the birth of a male heir (she has until the age of 50 to do her duty in this respect), if she is unfilial in her treatment of her husband's parents, if she causes trouble within the family, or indulges in certain flagrant kinds of misconduct.

However the codes also strictly follow the 'law' of the ritual books in giving effect to the protection accorded the wife by the 'three exceptions'. Even though one of the grounds permitting repudiation is present the wife still may not be sent away if she has completed the period of mourning for her husband's father or mother, or if at the time of the marriage the husband's family was poor and humble but afterwards became rich and honourable, or if she has no family of her own to whom she could return. The punishment for repudiation of the wife where she is entitled to invoke one of the 'three exceptions' is somewhat less than that for unjustified repudiation, 100 blows with the heavy stick under the T'ang and 60 blows under the Ming/Ch'ing codes, all providing that the wife was to return to her husband's family.[91] There is an important point concealed here. The codes provide that the divorce is void only where the wife is within one of the 'three exceptions'. If she is not, the divorce, although unauthorised, still takes effect and the wife returns to her own family; the husband remains legally liable to punishment but in practice might well escape it should the wife's family lodge no complaint.

Mutual consent is not presented in the codes as a distinct ground of separation. The three codes introduce it in the context of 'the breaking of the bond (*chüeh i*)'. After providing the punishment for failure to separate in the event of an act 'breaking the bond' the codes specify that if a husband and wife cannot live in harmony and agree to separate there is no liability.[92] The very formulation suggests that separation even by mutual consent was not a course of action to be encouraged; it still exhibited a case in which the wife did not 'follow her husband'. Nevertheless as a concession to the realities of the situation a separation desired by both sides was not actually to be penalised.

The 'breaking of the bond' brought into being a state of affairs quite distinct from that entailed by the presence of one of the seven grounds of repudiation. For the latter separation was not compulsory; the husband has a choice whether to renounce his wife or retain her. But where an act constituting 'breaking the bond' occurred separation in principle was compulsory. The T'ang code adopted a strict standpoint. It provided that where an offence destructive of the marital relationship ('breaking the bond') was committed the parties were to separate. A punishment of penal servitude for one year was imposed on either party who disobeyed (article 190). In the *shu-i* commentary it is made clear that the court must first determine whether an act in breach of the marital bond has occurred. Once this determination has been made the parties must separate. Whichever spouse was responsible for a failure to separate incurred the statutory penalty; and separation was enforced. The acts constituting breach of the marital bond are set out in the commentary to article 189. These are:

(i) beating by the husband of a paternal grandparent or parent of the wife;

(ii) killing by the husband of any of the following persons: a maternal grandparent of the wife, a brother (or his wife) of the wife's father, a brother or sister of the wife, or a sister of her father;

(iii) the husband's and the wife's paternal grandparents, parents, maternal grandparents, father's brothers or their wives, brothers, father's sisters, sisters kill each other;

(iv) the wife beats or curses the husband's paternal grandparents or parents;

(v) the wife kills or wounds any of the following: a maternal grandparent of the husband, a brother (or his wife) of the husband's father, a brother or sister of the husband, or a sister of his father;

(vi) the wife commits adultery with relatives of the husband of three months mourning or closer;

(vii) the husband comments adultery with the wife's mother;

(viii) the wife wishes (attempts) to harm the husband.[93]

This list suggests several reflections. All grounds except one are committed personally by the husband or wife. The exception derives from hostility between close relatives of the husband and wife leading to killing and possibly a feud. It is easier for the wife to commit an act 'breaking the bond' than for the husband. If one compares grounds (i), (ii) and (vii) with (iv), (v) and (vi) one notes that the wife commits such an act in a wider range of circumstances than the husband. Finally ground (viii), relating only to the wife, appears to be exceptionally broad.

Fundamentally the position in Ming and Ch'ing law was the same.[94] The punishment for failing to separate on the 'breaking of the bond' was lighter, being a beating of 80 blows with the heavy stick. Acts constituting 'breaking the bond' were more numerous, especially on the part of the husband or his family. For example where a husband pledged or hired out his wife to another to be the latter's wife, or allowed her to commit adultery, or where his grandparents or parents without reason beat and severely injured the wife, the act was held to 'break the bond'.[95] The most important change is that the 'breaking of the bond' did not in all cases make separation necessary. In some cases the party injured was given a choice as to whether the marriage was to continue or not. The 'upper commentary' of the Ch'ing code distinguished two classes of act by which the marital bond was broken: those which permitted but did not require separation, as where the wife beat and injured the husband or the husband beat and injured the wife,[96] and those which required separation as where she is permitted to commit adultery or is given in pledge as wife to another.[97]

As has already been stressed the traditional law, from at least the time of the T'ang dynasty, to a very considerable extent attached penal sanctions to rules found in Han works on ritual and morals. However both the moral and legal rules enjoined behaviour that was not always observed in practice and in fact not enforced by the authorities. As already noted above not only would there have been in different parts of China and among different sections of the population diverse conceptions of what was the (morally) proper relationship of husband and wife, but the legal rules themselves, in theory applicable throughout the empire, were not always enforced. Two examples may be given. The codes, following what is said in the ritual books, strictly prohibit marriage between persons of the same surname.[98] Yet it is known that in fact persons with the same surname did marry with impunity.[99] The divorce law, also, remained something of a dead letter throughout China and probably in all dynasties. Husbands might well escape punishment if they repudiated their wives for a reason not recognised as a legal ground since the wife's family was seldom prepared to take the matter to court.'[100] One may speculate that the enforcement of the law requiring separation on the 'breaking of the bond' would have occasioned severe practical difficulties, except in notorious cases where someone had been killed. The spouses and their families may often have patched up a quarrel and continued to operate the marriage even though technically an act requiring separation had taken place.

Notes

1. Cf. especially McAleavy, Chinese Law, 112ff, and Certain Aspects of Chinese Customary Law in the Light of Japanese Scholarship, 535f.
2. For examples of such differences see Doolittle, Social Life of the Chinese I, 101, 107; Oyamatsu, Laws and Customs in the Island of Formosa, Appendix, v, xif.

3. See further below at note 99.

4. Examples can be found in Hu, The Common Descent Group in China and its Functions, 134ff; Liu, The Traditional Chinese Clan Rules, 68ff.

5. Shiga, Family Property and the Law of Inheritance in Traditional China, 125.

6. See also, apart from Shiga's comments (id), Chikusa, Succession to Ancestral Sacrifices and Adoption of Heirs to the Sacrifices, 153f; McAleavy, Varieties of Hu'o'ng-Hoa: A Problem of Vietnamese Law, 609f.

7. On Tang/Sung law see generally Burns, Private Law in Traditional China; Ebrey, Family and Property in Sung China, 106ff.

8. See Chikusa, op.cit., 154.

9. *Contra* Burns, op.cit., 255, who takes this part of the commentary as referring only to adopted children other than the legal successor. The latter, he holds, cannot be sent away by the adopting parents, any more than the father can dismiss his eldest son.

10. See Burns, op.cit., 202, 216, 221.

11. See also on the T'ang rules Chikusa, op.cit., 161f.

12. Cf. Lê Code, 292; Deloustal, 291.

13. This also applied to the wrongful giving in adoption of a son or grandson, that is, where someone who should have been the legal successor to his own father or grandfather is given in adoption.

14. Interestingly the strict Confucian principle requiring sons to live with their parents during the latter's lifetime was not maintained in Yüan law (Ratchnevsky, Code des Yüan II 97ff), although re-established in Ming/Ch'ing law.

15. For this material and the T'ang/Sung position in general see Burns, op.cit., 115, 130, 174, 176, 238, 240f, 260. Succession is discussed in detail at 192ff.

16. The text speaks also of 'concubine' but this may be an interpolation (Burns, op.cit., 240f).

17. Under the Sung their position seems to have improved since they were entitled to half a son's portion. See Ebrey, op.cit., 118; Burns, op.cit., 263, 274f.

18. This is from the section of the Statutes headed 'Death and Burial'.

19. Probably the T'ang law was similar.

20. For further details on the position of women as heirs see Burns, op.cit.,159ff; Ebrey, 116ff.

21. Shiga, op.cit., 134f.

22. Generally see Jamieson, Chinese Family and Commercial Law, chapter 2; Mading, Chinesisches traditionelles Erbrecht.

23. Ming 2.4 (MLCCFL, 394); Ch'ing article 46, Philastre I, 284; Boulais, 205; Staunton, 49.

24. On this point see Philastre I, 290 where the Ch'ing 'upper commentary' explains the complexities of the law relating to nephews and younger brothers. Philastre is to be followed here in preference to Boulais or Staunton.

25. See, however, Waltner, Widows and Remarriage in Ming and Early Qing

China, 133 and n20, noting that in practice a younger brother might on occasion be appointed legal successor.

26. See the Ch'ing general commentary, Philastre I, 369, and Philastre's fifth decree (371, and Boulais, 400).

27. Ming 4.4 (op.cit., 553); Ch'ing article 76, Philastre I, 367; Boulais, 387f; Staunton 84.

28. See especially decrees I, III, IV in Philastre I, 369f, and Boulais, 396, 401. On the possibility of one person succeeding by adoption to two families and the consequent problem with respect to marriage see McAleavy, Chinese Law, 112ff.

29. The clan rules also tend to prescribe that the person adopted as legal successor should be from the same clan (Liu, Traditional Chinese Clan Rules, 70f). Yet there is some doubt whether the rule, so strictly insisted upon in theory, was in fact enforced. For the varying practices current in Ch'ing times see Oyamatsu, op.cit., Appendix, xif; Leong and Tao, Village and Town Life in China, 14 f; Wolf and Huang, Marriage and Adoption in China, 108ff, 202ff.

30. Ming 4.14 (op.cit., 588); Ch'ing article 83, Philastre I, 391; Boulais, 414 Staunton, 92.

31. Philastre I, 392, decrees I and II; Boulais, 415,6.

32. See Philastre I, 392, decrees I (Boulais, 396), III, and V (Boulais, 400).

33. Cf. the discussion in Mading, op.cit., 76ff, leaving open the possibility that other clan members and even non-agnatic relatives might in fact have had a claim preferred to that of the state (as a matter of custom).

34. Boulais, 398, preferable to Philastre I, 390 decree II.

35. *Contra* Shiga, op.cit., 144 who states that the T'ang rules survived into the later law.

36. See Boulais, p.202 ff; Mading, op.cit., 81f, 98ff, Shiga, op.cit., 143.

37. Generally see Ch'ü, Law and Society in Traditional China, chapter II. For Ch'ing law see Jamieson, op.cit., chapter III; Hoang, Le mariage chinois au point de vue légal.

38. See on this MacCormack, Ethical Principles and the Traditional Chinese Law of Marriage 248 ff, giving references to the literature.I have drawn on this article in what follows.

39. Exceptionally, as where a family had only daughters, a son-in-law might be brought to live in the house of the bride.

40. Sons appointed to official positions were required to move and live within the area of their jurisdictions, but their family home remained that of their parents.

41. Cf. MacCormack, Hausgemeinshaft und Consortium, 4 where (in a different context) a distinction is made between an 'extended family' (where sons on marriage continue to live with their parents) and a 'joint family' (where brothers and their families remain together even after the death of the father).

42. See on these (for example) Chiu, Some Notes on Chinese Customary Marriage, 45f; Doolittle, Social Life of the Chinese I, 65ff.

43. This appears in the oldest of the surviving clan rules. See Yen, Family Instructions for the Yen Clan, 18.Cf. Liu, Traditional Chinese Clan Rules,

84ff.

44. Chan, Reflections on Things at Hand, 177; another of the great neo-Confucian scholars, Chu Hsi, was more realistic and admitted that so strict an approach could not always be followed (op.cit., 179).

45. For Ch'ing rules and practice see Boulais, p.304 f; Doolittle, op.cit., 110f; de Groot, The Religious System of China II, 750ff. See also generally, Waltner, Widows and Remarriage in Ming and Early Qing China; Elvin, Female virtue and the State in China; Mann, Widows in the Kinship, Clan and Community Structures of Qing Dynasty China; T'ien, Male Anxiety and Female Chastity.

46. See especially Wilhelm, Li Gi, 248.

47. This is so for T'ang and later law. In Han times there appears to have been a less close correlation between the moral and the legal rules. See Dull, Marriage and Divorce in Han China.

48. Article 175. Cf. Lê Code, 315; Deloustal, 314.

49. For the Yüan rules see Ratchnevsky, Code des Yüan II, 122.

50. This article establishes who is liable where marriages have been concluded which infringe the code, and then states that where the marriage has been arranged but has not yet been completed, the appropriate punishments are to be decreased by five degrees.

51. Ming 6.1 (op.cit., 639); Ch'ing article 94, Philastre I, 491; Boulais, 539f; Staunton, 107f.

52. Philastre I, 496; Boulais p. 259 nl.

53. Shen's 'upper commentary' adds the further explanation that the first fiancé is only allowed to refuse to take her back where the second marriage has been completed; if it has not gone beyond the mere engagement then she is to return to the first fiancé (Philastre I 497).

54. Philastre I, 495 who has: 'si la fille ne peut pas contracter un autre mariage, on doit de même ne pas casser le mariage'. The text (TCLLHCPL, 1614) simply says 'if the girl does not wish...' The reason for the exception in favour of the girl (not the boy) is that she is the person most prejudiced by completion of the marriage since she has 'lost her body'.

55. Cf. for the general commentary, Philastre I, 494, and see the additional explanation given by Shen's 'upper commentary' 497.

56. See the Ming 'incorporated commentary', MLCCFL, 695-6.

57. It is said that the wife is *ch'i* (of the husband). This is explained in a Han work entitled Po Hu T'ung (The Comprehensive Discussions in the White Tiger Hall) I, 261 as meaning that the wife and the husband are a single whole, they are one body. But it also carries the implication that husband and wife, being halves of the whole, are equal.

58. See below at note 90.

59. Article 177. Cf. Deloustal 314 n4.

60. Ming 6.3 (op.cit., 655); Ch'ing article 96, Philastre I, 504; Boulais, 563; Staunton, 111.

61. Philastre 1, 504.

62. See chapter 10 at note 61 for the offence of hiring out or pledging one's wife to be another's wife.

63. Article 178, Cf. Lê Code 309; Deloustal, 308.
64. Cf. also Ch'ü, Law and Society in Traditional China, 158.
65. Ming 6.3 and Ch'ing article 96, cited note 60.
66. Pilastre I, 504.
67. Ming 6.15 (op.cit. 704); Ch'ing article 107, Philastre 1, 535, Boulais, 621; Staunton, 119. This is virtually the same as T'ang article 191, although the punishments imposed are considerably lighter in the Ming Ch'ing version.
68. Staunton, 118; Philastre I, 533-4
69. Op.cit., 161.
70. This corrects the over general statement made in Ethical Principles and the Traditional Chinese Law of Marriage, 258.
71. Article 179. Cf. Lê Code, 317; Deloustal, 316.
72. Article 184. Cf. Lê Code, 320; Deloustal, 319. The text has 'return to her previous family'; the reference appears to be to her former husband's family as is made explicit in the text of the Ming and Ch'ing articles (below).
73. Article 6.5, op.cit., 660.
74. Article 98, Philastre I, 507f; Boulais, 573; Staunton, 113.
75. Philastre I, 509f (at 510); Boulais, 574. This sub-statute regulates generally the position of the widow forced to remarry and, *inter alia,* increases the punishments imposed on relatives (other than her own ascendants or those of her deceased husband) who exercise force. See T'ien, Male Anxiety and Female Chastity, 23f.
76. Philastre I, 509. This is the same point of view as that shown in the rule applied where she marries a groom other than the one to whom she was first engaged. Cf. also the remarks of Waltner, op.cit., 138. For Ch'ing practice on the remarriage of widows see T'ien, op.cit., 31f, 138.
77. Article 325. Cf. Lê Code, 482; Deloustal, 481.
78. Article 326. Cf. Lê Code, 481; Deloustal, 480.
79. Ming 20.14 (op.cit., 1597); Ch'ing article 284, Philastre II, 327; Boulais, 1401f; Staunton, 341.
80. For the working of the rules see chapter 7, 167f.
81. There is some doubt on the question. See MacCormack, op.cit., 263.
82. Ming 22.5 (op.cit., 1666); Ch'ing article 306, Philastre II, 429; Boulais, 1495; Staunton, 371.
83. Philastre II, 432.
84. Generally see Tai, Divorce in Traditional Chinese Law.
85. In practice this might mean the choice of his parents or paternal grandparents.
86. Under limited circumstances a wife might take the initiative in effecting a divorce, namely where the husband had 'disappeared' for a certain period of time or had been banished for certain crimes. For details see Tai, op.cit., 98f.
87. Article 190. Cf. Lê Code, 310; Deloustal, 309.
88. Ming 6.17 (op.cit., 712); Ch'ing article 108, Philastre I, 537; Boulais, 637; Staunton, 120.
89. Philastre I, 538.

90. T'ang article 189; Ming 6.17; Ch'ing article 108 (cited note 88).
91. The T'ang article further provides that where the wife has committed adultery or has an incurable disease (?leprosy) she is not entitled to the protection of the 'three exceptions'. Of these only adultery survives into the Ming/Ch'ing law (Philastre I, 540; Boulais, 641).
92. T'ang article 190; Ming 6.17; Ch'ing article 108 (cited note 88).
93. This is not an exhaustive list of the grounds entailing 'breaking the bond'. Under the articles of the code an act of the husband could be construed as 'breaking the bond' requiring separation, for example, the sale of the wife as a slave or the giving her in marriage to someone else. Cf. Tai, op.cit., 93.
94. Articles cited note 88.
95. For a fuller list see Tai, op.cit., 94.
96. The latter appears to have been introduced in Yüan law as an act 'breaking the bond' (Tai, op.cit., 93).
97. Boulais, 645.
98. T'ang article 182; Ming 6.7 (op.cit., 669); Ch'ing article 102, Philastre I, 518; Boulais, 582; Staunton, 114.
99. Cf. Ch'ü, op.cit., 92f; Oyamatsu, however, states that the Formosan authorities enforced the rule prohibiting marriage between persons of the same name (op.cit., Appendix, VI).
100. Cf. Tai, op.cit., 90f.

12

Concluding Reflections of a Theoretical Nature

On reading through the codes even in a fairly cursory fashion one already obtains certain impressions with respect to the content and form of the rules which they contain. These impressions are to some extent already conditioned by the training in, or knowledge of, Western systems of law which the reader may have. Thus one is struck with the fact that, by comparison, for example, with what is understood as law in Britain, the traditional Chinese codes deal with a highly restricted subject matter. Essentially they focus upon matters of concern to the emperor and the state and the maintenance of the national rites, the preservation of law and order through the control of the most disruptive acts (such as killing, physical injury, theft and damage to property), the proper conduct of their duties by officials, and the enforcement of the fundamental Confucian values bearing upon the regulation of the family and the conduct of relatives towards each other. Matters of contract, entitlement to property and succession are touched upon only in a fragmentary and isolated fashion.

Such an impression, although reliable with respect to what may be termed criminal law, will be misleading if one assumes that the content of the penal codes exhausts the field of the traditional law. One has to remember that the state produced not only a body of criminal law but also a complex and sophisticated set of rules on the definition and performance of the duties imposed on officials. Hence to the criminal law one has to add what may be termed administrative law, highly developed in traditional China, but very little remarked upon or studied. In addition there are important areas of non-state law operated by clans, villages and guilds, especially relevant for the determination of contractual and property rights. Hence concentration on the penal law, although perhaps the most striking and dramatic section of the traditional law, should not be allowed to obscure the existence of its other components.

Another dominant impression, implicit in what has just been said, is the thoroughly penal character of the rules. Broadly speaking each rule of the code establishes an offence and may be represented in the form: if X commits behaviour Y, Z punishment is to be imposed. The only large block of rules in the codes which cannot be so represented is that entitled the 'General Principles'. These, however, are designed to establish general conditions governing the imposition of punishments (for example the range of possible privileges and exemptions), and hence also possesses a strictly penal relevance.

Reflection upon the penal character of the rules brings out the existence of some interesting differences between the kind of behaviour that would be regarded as suitable for criminal enforcement in the West and that made the subject of sanction in the traditional Chinese codes. Whereas one might expect any centralised society to provide punishments for acts of killing, physical injury or theft, it is unusual to find matters such as breach of the requirements of mourning or failure to honour the terms of a betrothal punished. The explanation for such differences between criminally sanctioned behaviour lies in the scheme of values adopted by each particular society. In the case of traditional China it was the particular set of values associated with the family that led to the introduction into the penal codes of the detailed rules on the observance of mourning or the terms of a betrothal.

Further one cannot help noticing the highly specific content of the rules and the obvious attempt by the legislators, in many areas (not all), to cover every eventuality. Two influences may have been at work here. One is the old legalist insistence on precision and clarity and the need for exact formulation of the circumstances under which the punishment is to apply, so leaving the judge no opportunity to inject extra-legal standards or considerations into his assessment of the case. The other – politically perhaps the more important – is the reluctance of the emperor and his advisers to leave any substantial discretion to the officials charged with the investigation and sentencing of offences. No doubt one factor in the determination of this policy was the desire to retain all legislative power (including that exercised in the establishment of criminal offences) firmly in the hands of the central authorities. But one should not discount entirely the influence of a more altruistic factor, namely the conviction shared – probably in all dynasties – by those concerned with the implementation of criminal policy that a proper correspondence should be observed between the gravity of the offence and the severity of the punishment. To leave officials with judicial responsibilities a free hand in the determination of punishments would, it was thought, have led to serious imbalances occurring in the relationship between the punishment and the crime. One may recall the observations of the early Ch'ing emperors on the matter in their prefatory edicts to the penal codes.[1] Underlying this insistence on ascribing to each offence its proper proportion of punishment is a dominantly retributive conception of punishment, although undoubtedly considerations as to the utility of inflicting pain in order to deter or reform also influenced the legislators.

Another factor highlighted by even a cursory reading of the codes is the importance of status as a determinant of punishment. It becomes transparently clear that the traditional codes do not enshrine a doctrine of equality before the law. One notes the privileged position of officials who by virtue of their office may escape the full punishment that would be imposed on a non-official who had committed the same offence, the fact that 'senior' relatives who commit offences against 'juniors' receive less severe punishments than 'juniors' who commit the like offence against 'seniors', and the disadvantaged position of people falling within one of the 'mean' or servile categories vis-a-vis free persons. Various reasons can be advanced for the grant of privilege to officials.[2] The reason for the differential treatment of relatives or persons belonging to different social classes may fundamentally be the fact that offences by 'junior' relatives against 'seniors' or by 'mean' people against free were simply regarded as intrinsically more wicked and therefore as meriting greater punishment than offences committed by 'senior' relatives against 'juniors' or by free people against 'mean'.

A more thorough study of the codes and their background allows one to establish further conclusions. A comparison of the content of the main penal codes from the T'ang to the Ch'ing reveals the remarkable fact that not only is the substance of many provisions identical (apart possibly from the actual level of punishment) but even the formulation is virtually the same. What from a Western perspective is remarkable is the maintenance of such consistency over so long a period of time, from the seventh until the twentieth century. One can think of several possible explanations (not necessarily mutually exclusive) for this phenomenon. Obviously relevant is the fact, to be touched on further below, that the codes to some extent implement a moral orthodoxy that itself was maintained through the various dynasties in essentially the same form by the Confucian literati. In many cases – and this applies not only to the substance of an offence but especially to the technical quality of the drafting – emperors and their advisers must simply have accepted the merits of the formulation found in the T'ang code and been prepared to adopt it with very little change. One thinks here particularly of the rules on homicide, physical injury and theft. Not entirely unrelated to this point are the considerations that later dynasties had an inherent respect for the achievements of earlier and that within particular dynasties succeeding rulers were reluctant to discard what had been established at the outset by the founder. It is these considerations which may account for the fact that even rules which were clearly obsolete were retained not only in the code of the dynasty in which they were introduced and during which they had become obsolete but even in that of the succeeding dynasty. The most conspicuous example is the T'ang rules in effect forbidding the alienation of land, which reappeared intact in the Sung code even though they had not been applied during the latter part of the T'ang.

Comparison between the content of the codes and the prescriptions found in the Confucian moral and ritual writings shows that in significant areas of behaviour, especially as pertaining to family life, the codes provided punishments for behaviour that contravened the moral prescriptions. At the risk of a certain degree of over-simplification and without regard to the precise differences between the Confucianism of Han, Ming or Ch'ing times, one may say that these moral prescriptions in fundamentals did not change throughout the period of imperial history. Hence they may be regarded as constituting an absolute morality (one asserted by its practitioners to be in effect the social ordering determined by nature and so to hold good irrespective of time or place) and the codes themselves, in so far as they implement and enforce such a morality, as constituting a natural law. But one should refrain from taking the further step and holding that in so far as the codes constitute a natural law, they (and their proper application) were believed by the Chinese governing class or the ordinary people to be part of the mechanism by which the physical fabric of the universe was maintained in balance, a point developed below.

In viewing the codes as a natural law one has to remember the very important circumstance that the morality which they were intended to enforce is that asserted by the small group of Confucian literati and accepted by and large as the official morality of the state. At least some of the prescriptions enjoined by Confucian morality are unlikely to have been accepted or followed by the large mass of the people. This is particularly so in the -case of what may be termed the more ritualistic rules as, for example, those governing the conduct of mourning, the relationship of husband and wife, and the appointment of legal successors (all related to the conduct of family rites).

The rules of the codes are phrased in strongly imperative terms; from the wording one would infer that the legislators intended that they be obeyed and were prepared to enforce them where necessary. Yet one knows in some cases and suspects in others that rules were not enforced and that the actual conduct of affairs, tolerated by the authorities, was in contravention of them. This appears to have been particularly the case in the area of 'civil law', that is, property, contract, succession and marriage. Various reasons, again, can be advanced for this. One, already mentioned, is the reluctance on occasion to delete from the codes rules which had become obsolete, out of respect, it seems, for the emperor or dynasty which had first enacted them. Another, perhaps, is the desire of those responsible for the production of the penal code to include within it a statement of the official position with regard to certain matters, even though the authorities were aware that in practice either the rule was disregarded altogether or that bodies other than the official courts were concerned with the matter in question and did not necessarily insist on observation of the codified rules. One may go further. Even the official courts themselves left certain questions to be determined by other bodies despite the fact that the penal code may have contained relevant rules. One thinks particularly of family, property or commercial matters left effectively to the jurisdiction of the clans or guilds or to determination and resolution by local (village) custom. It could also be thought that the very detail with which the rules establishing particular offences were elaborated may sometimes have militated against their effective enforcement (for example, those concerned with the imposition of collegiate liability on officials).

The various characteristics of the penal codes, some of which have been identified above, give rise to a number of theoretical issues. By focusing upon one or other of them modern Western writers have been led to formulate certain general theories concerning the nature of traditional Chinese law. It is worth saying something about three such theories, in addition to the remarks already made in previous chapters,[3] in order to determine whether there is in fact any evidence by which they can be sustained. According to these theories the penal law is to be regarded primarily as a mechanism for the maintenance of cosmic harmony, as a set of 'models' or guidelines lacking prescriptive or imperative force, or as a set of administrative rules lacking the characteristics of rules of law proper. Interestingly these theories have all been advanced by French sinologists.

The first takes as its basis a supposed relationship between the codes and 'nature', asserting that the rules enacted by the emperor for the behaviour of his subjects 'correspond' to, and reinforce, the regularities to be observed in the manifestation of natural phenomena. Its most sustained exposition has been in Escarra's influential work on Chinese law. Escarra argues that the rules found in the penal codes are designed fundamentally to ensure the continuance of the 'universal order', in the sense of ensuring that the cycle of the seasons continues in its normal way. From this it follows that the notion of 'legal responsibility' bears a sense different from that current in the West. In the Chinese conception one is 'responsible', not in the sense that one has merely failed to observed the behaviour required by a legal rule but in the sense that one has failed to observe such behaviour (enjoined by the codes) as is necessary to secure the maintenance of the 'universal order'.[4] This thesis has been adopted in an even more extreme form by G Padoux who contributed the preface to a translation by Escarra and Germain of a Chinese work on legal theory. Padoux described the positive law as nothing more than the translation into written formulae of the natural order. Violation of positive law, even where it concerned purely civil matters, attracted punishment on the ground that it was a breach of the established order of nature and so damaged the country.[5]

Whether or not one calls the law of the penal codes 'positive laws' one is, according to theses of the kind just described, asserting that the prime function of the rules is not to regulate human behaviour as such but to ensure that nature continues to behave in its regular and customary fashion. Criticism of the general doctrine of cosmic harmony in its application to law has already been advanced. Here it is sufficient to emphasise two points. The main textual support for this view of the traditional law is said to be found in early writings, some allegedly dating from the time of the Chou conquest around 1100 B.C. The statements in these texts are capable of a number of interpretations; it is dangerous to extract from them evidence for some such proposition as 'the positive law is a set of formulae designed to ensure the maintenance of the natural order'.

An illustration may be taken from a passage in a text from the Book of Documents (*Shu-ching*) cited by Escarra.[6] This is the 'Great Plan' (*Hung Fan*) which purports to be a document from the time of the founding of the Chou dynasty, but in fact appears to have been written much later during the Warring States period.[7] The passage in question, referring to what are described as the 'verifications' (that is rain, sunshine, heat, cold, wind and other seasonal occurrences), states:

> Some are called the lucky verifications. Gravity – seasonable rain responds to it; orderliness – seasonable sunshine reponds to it; wisdom – seasonable heat responds to it; deliberation – seasonable cold responds to it; sageness – seasonable wind responds to it. Some are called unlucky verifications. Wildness – constant rain responds to it; incorrectness – constant sunshine responds to it; rashness – constant cold responds to it; (blindness =) stupidity – constant wind responds to it.[8]

Although one may assume that some correlation is being drawn between the weather and the character and deportment of the ruler, it is dangerous to infer from such vague and general statements conclusions as to the precise way in which the penal codes of the great imperial dynsaties, promulgated many centuries after the *Hung Fan* was written, were understood. Whatever beliefs may have been held at the time of the Warring States or earlier epochs by the writers of the texts cited as evidence cannot, without a great risk of distortion, be applied to the elucidation of Ming and Ch'ing (or even T'ang and Sung) institutions. No satisfactory proof has yet been brought to show that the penal codes of the imperial dynasties were regarded, either by the ruling elite who framed and applied them or by the ordinary people subject to them, as mechanisms primarily intended to facilitate the process by which the seasons (each with its appropriate weather) regularly succeeded each other.

The only relationship between the codes and 'nature' which one may legitimately defend is that which treats the codes as constituting a natural law in the sense of the putting into effect of an absolute morality (a morality based, as it were, on 'nature'). There is the possible argument that maintenance of moral standards was itself necessary for the successful functioning of the universe, that is, that grossly immoral behaviour on the part of the ruler and/or his subjects was sufficient to disturb the balance of the universe and so bring about natural disasters and the like. Hence, it might be inferred that the penal codes in so far as they are designed to enforce moral standards are similarly to be looked upon as instruments for the maintenance of cosmic harmony. However one has to reiterate that it is difficult to find evidence to show that the maintenance of moral standards was consistently thought, throughout the ages, the views of some individuals apart, to be causally connected with the proper functioning of natural phenomena, or, that the penal codes themselves were explicity acknowledged as being causally linked in this way with the natural universe.

The second theory according to which the penal rules of the codes are mere 'models' or guidelines is also associated with Escarra who on this point was considerably influenced by the work of Marcel Granet, a sociologist and sinologist belonging to the intellectual circle inspired by Emile Durkheim.[9] Granet had argued that, prior to the process of legal codification beginning in some states in the 6th century B. C. through the inscription of bronze cauldrons with the text of the laws, the rules stipulating punishments promulgated by the Chou kings or rulers of independent states are to be understood only in the sense of 'models'. The punishments enacted in the rules were not intended to be applied; they were merely to inspire fear and so encourage the behaviour desired by the ruler. It is only the rise of the 6th century tyrannies and (a little later) the popularity with rulers of legalist doctrines that led to the framing of penal laws where the punishments were intended to be applied, and where one could speak of obligatory conduct prescribed by the ruler.'[10]

Taking his inspiration from Granet, Escarra has gone much further than his mentor and treated the whole legal history of traditional China in terms of the application of a 'model'. The rules enacted in the penal codes are not to be understood as establishing duties in the sense of prescribing behaviour and generating an obligation to conform. They merely set a standard of behaviour which is to be emulated as far as possible. The punishments themselves have an 'ideal' or 'theoretical' character. This appears to mean, again, that they are intended to provide an incentive for the performance of the behaviour desired but are not in fact applied, at least in any consistent or rigorous fashion. Once one has understood the character of the penal rules as 'models', Escarra asserts, one ceases to be surprised by the fact that so many of them are not applied. Some rules are inserted in the code although there has never been a serious intention on the part of the legislators that they should be applied; others have been inherited from earlier reigns or even dynasties and retained despite the fact that changed social conditions have made them completely obsolete.[11]

The only conclusion one can reach is that such a view of the penal law as no more than a 'model' is a very considerable exaggeration. Of course it is correct to say that in many cases the rules found in the traditional Chinese codes were restatements of, or statements predicated upon, the rules found in Confucian writings. In this sense they can legitimately be represented as establishing the right way to behave and as providing models for the guidance of the emperor's subjects. However the very fact that they are equipped with punishments shows that they are more than just 'models' or 'guidelines'. They also possess an imperative character in that obligations are created by the rules breach of which entails the imposition of a sanction.[12] There is no good reason for thinking that even in the time of the early Chou rulers references to punishment were incorporated in the rules merely to inspire fear and that the punishments described were never applied. No doubt the mention of punishment was intended to inspire fear. But it would succeed in its object only if the punishments were in fact applied. As for the great imperial codes from the T'ang to the Ch'ing it is perfectly clear that the intention of the legislators in many, though not necessarily in all, cases was that the punishment prescribed for breach of a rule should be applied to an offender. So much is evidenced (for the Ch'ing) by the collection of criminal cases decided by the Board of Punishments in the 18th and 19th centuries.[13]

Nevertheless it remains true both that some rules in the codes appear to be obsolete survivals from the past and that others were rarely, if ever, applied. Yet it would be a mistake to conclude from these facts that the penal codes as a whole were 'models' and not laws. The legal systems of many countries contain examples of obsolete or never-applied rules; one does not conclude that these systems lack the character of 'law'. Perhaps the traditional Chinese system possessed a higher proportion of such non-applied rules than is normally found. It may be true both that the Chinese legislators were reluctant to discard rules established by the founder of the dynasty or inherited from previous dynasties even where they had in practice become obsolete, and that they sometimes introduced (for a variety of reasons) rules which they had no intention of enforcing (or no real expectancy that enforcement was possible). It still by no means follows that the penal law as a whole is to be designated a 'model' and held to be deprived of imperative or obligatory force.

The view that the penal codes constitute 'models' rather than law probably derives from an over-emphasis by modern scholars on the early Confucian approach to the task of the ruler. This stressed that the ruler should as far as possible lead the people into the right path by example and moral guidance and that punishments should be imposed only as a last resort in the case of those who proved to be incorrigibly wicked. Whereas this view of the relative importance in government of moral guidance and punishment never altogether lost its appeal, it is clear that in practice the Confucian state from Han times onwards made considerable use of rules imposing punishments. Neither those who framed the penal codes nor those subject to them looked upon the rules and punishments merely as injunctions providing moral guidance.

A third theory has been propounded by L. Vandermeersch.[14] This distinguishes not between law and model but between law and administrative regulation or pseudo-law. Vandermeersch's assumption is that true or proper law comprises a set of rules of universal application, the prime purpose of which is to guarantee to an individual his rights and at the same time ensure that they are not exercised to the detriment of the rights of others. He holds that early China instead of adopting a legal system of this kind (a 'juridical order') relied upon a 'ritual order', the essence of which was that compliance with the forms of behaviour thought in the Confucian scheme to be correct *spontaneously* ensured the harmonious functioning of the universe. Vandermeersch thus takes the same starting point as Granet and Escarra on the relationship between human behaviour and natural phenomena, but comes to a different conclusion as to the nature of the rules, emanating from the sovereign, which impose punishments. He argues that the 'ritual order' come to be supplanted in China by a 'juridical-type order', that is, by a system of obligations imposed and enforced through the apparatus of state power. The role of such a system of administration or pseudo-law, although directed at the repression of wrongdoing, 'was much rather to keep public order from the point of view of the state than to protect the security of the person and of property from the point of view of individual citizens'.[15]

One issue raised by Vandermeersch's thesis may be considered relatively unimportant. This turns upon a question of terminology. It might be thought to be of no great significance whether one applies the label 'law' to certain kinds of rules or not. Vandermeersch chooses to reserve the term 'law' for a set of rules emanating from a country's governing body, concerned primarily to regulate the rights of individuals *inter se* and to protect the liberty of the subject. One may either accept his definition or argue that it is too narrow and restrictive. Thus it may be thought that there is no compelling reason to refuse the label 'law' to systems of rules that conform to the Austinian model, that is, to commands addressed by a political superior to political inferiors and backed up by a threat of force, irrespective of the content of the commands.

Perhaps a more important issue is the extent to which Vandermeersch is correct in his characterisation of the purpose and content of the codified penal rules. Are they no more than public order measures issued for the convenience of the sovereign and having no relation to the rights of the individual? Certainly one might agree that the sovereign was concerned with the maintenance of public order and that many of the rules contained in the code have no specific concern with the grant of rights to individuals or the protection of the liberty of the individual, at least from interference by the state. However it is less certain that one should exclude altogether from the penal codes the theme of protection of rights enjoyed by individuals. The rules which impose punishments on those who kill or injure others or take their property may not be concerned just with the preservation of public order. Although the rules do not articulate as such the rights to preservation of one's body or one's property, they may well indirectly stem from, and reflect recognition on the part of the emperor, of the right of an individual not to be arbitrarily killed, injured or deprived of his property. It is obvious from the reasons sometimes given by the Board of Punishments in the Ch'ing period for its decisions in cases of homicide that the Board was concerned where an individual through no fault of his own was deprived of his life; such concern stemmed not from considerations of public order but from an appreciation of the fact that an individual was normally entitled to expect that he would live for a reasonable span of years and that his life would not be cut short through the act of another.

Neither the fact that the rules of the codes are primarily concerned with the stipulation of punishments nor the fact that in all cases the rules were to be applied by officials should mislead one into thinking that the codes as a whole can be analysed as mere administrative instructions to officials. As is often the case in the formulation of rules of criminal law the legislature makes only a partial statement of the position. It takes for granted the fact that certain conduct is prohibited, that there exists a duty resting on all members of the society to refrain from it, and concentrates on the specific question of punishment. Hence the rule is not drafted in the form 'let no-one commit murder; if he does the officials are to impose a certain punishment' but in the form 'if anyone commits murder, a certain punishment is to be imposed on him'.

Nor is the latter formulation the same as the statement 'if anyone commits murder, the officials are to impose a certain punishment on him'. The point of the statement in the form 'if anyone commits murder, a certain punishment is to be imposed on him' is to show that an intrinsic connection is deemed to exist between the act and the punishment. To kill another in itself entails the liability to punishment; whether the offender is caught or, if caught, successfully punished, does not affect the presence of this liability. To say 'the officials are to impose the punishment' places the emphasis on the particular duty of the officials to pass sentence and see to the carrying out of the punishment. It does not presuppose, or at any rate advert to, the necessary connection between commission of the act and liability on the part of the actor to punishment. Although in the traditional Chinese legal system it is the officials who in fact investigated criminal cases, passed sentence, and ultimately saw to the execution of the appropriate punishment, it is significant that the rules are not formulated as directives to officials but are conceived in the more abstract form 'if act X is committed, punishment Y is to be imposed'.

Notes

1. See chapter 1 at note 77.
2. See chapter 6 at note 87.
3. See chapter 2 at note 39, chapter 3 at note 2.
4. Le droit chinois, 7f, 77f. Cf also the account given in Law: Chinese.
5. Leang, La conception de la loi et les théories des légistes à la veille des Ts'in, VIII, X.
6. Op. cit. 9 n7.
7. Creel, The Origins of Statecraft in China, 456f.
8. Karlgren, Book of Documents, 33 (para 28). Cf. Legge, The Chinese Classics 3, 240f; Couvreur, Chou king, 206f.
9. On Granet see the introductory essay by Freedman in Granet, The Religion of the Chinese People.
10. Granet, La pensée chinoise, 376f.
11. See esp. op. cit. 70, 74f. Cf also his remarks in Law: Chinese, 250.
12. The punishments are evidence of the imperative nature of the rules; they are not constituent of that element.
13. Cf. the sections of the Ch'ing penal code on which there are decided cases in Bodde and Morris, Law in Imperial China, 203f.
14. An Enquiry into the Chinese Conception of the Law.
15. Op. cit. , 14-15.

Bibliography

(See also List of Abbreviations)

Alabaster, E., Notes and Commentaries on Chinese Criminal Law. Ch'eng
Wen Publishing Co. Taipei. 1968 (reprint of 1899 edition).

Alford, W. P., Of Arsenic and Old Lace: Looking Anew at Criminal Justice
in Late Imperial China, California Law Review 72 (1984), 1180-1256.

Baker, H. D. R., Chinese Family and Kinship. MacMillan. London. 1979

Balazs, E, Le traité juridique du 'Souei-chou'. Brill. Leiden. 1954.

Biot, E, Le Tcheou-li ou Rites des Tcheou, 3 vols. Ch'eng Wen Publishing
Co. Taipei. 1975 (reprint of 1851 edition).

Bodde, D, Age, Youth and Infirmity in the Law of Ch'ing China, in Cohen,
J. A, Edwards R. R. and Chen, F. C. (eds.), Essays on China's Legal
Tradition, pp 137-169. Princeton U. P. Princeton. 1980.

__ The State and Empire of Ch'in, in The Cambridge History of China I.
The Ch'in and Han Empires 221 B. C. − A. D. 200, 20-102. Cambridge
U. P. Cambridge. 1986.

Bodde, D. and Morris, C. Law in Imperial China. Exemplified by 190
Ch'ing Dynasty Cases. With Historical, Social and Juridical
Commentaries. University of Pennsylvannia Press. Philadelphia. 1967.

Brockman, R. H, Commercial Contract Law in Late Nineteenth-Century
Taiwan, in Cohen, J. A, Edwards, R. R. and Chen, F. C. (eds), Essays
on China's Legal Tradition, 76-136. Princeton U. P. Princeton. 1980.

Bünger, K, Quellen zur Rechtsgeschichte der T'ang-Zeit. Catholic
University. Peiping. 1946.

__ Uber die Verantwortlichkeit der Beamtem nach klassischen chinesischen
Recht, Studia Serica 6 (1947), 159-191.

__ The Punishment of Lunatics and Negligents according to Classical Chinese
Law, Studia Serica 9 (1950), 1-16.

Burgess, J. G, The Guilds of Peking. Ch'eng Wen Publishing Co. Taipei.
1976 (reprint of 1928 edition).

Burns, I. R, Private Law in Traditional China (Sung dynasty). Unpublished
D.Phil thesis. University of Oxford, 1972.

Buxbaum, D. C, Some Aspects of Civil Procedure and Practice at the Trial Level in Tanshui and Hsinchu from 1789 to 1895, Journal of Asian Studies 30 (1970-1), 255-279.

Chan, W. T, Reflections on Things at Hand. The Neo-Confucian Anthology Compiled by Chu Hsi and Lu Tsu-ch'en. Columbia U. P. New York. 1967.

Chen, F. C, On Analogy in Ch'ing Law. Harvard Journal of Asiatic Studies 30 (1970), 212-224.

—, The Influence of Shen Chih-ch'i's *Chi-chu* Commentary upon Ch'ing Judicial Decisions, in Cohen, J. A, Edwards, R. R. and Chen, F. C. (eds), Essays on China's Legal Tradition, 170-221. Princeton U. P. Princeton. 1980.

Ch'en P, Chinese Legal Tradition under the Mongols. The Code of 1291 as Reconstructed. Princeton U. P. Princeton. 1979.

—, Disloyalty to the State in Late Imperial China, in Ekemeier, D. and Franke, H. (eds), State and Law in East Asia. Festschrift Karl Bünger, 159-183. Harrassowitz. Wiesbaden. 1981.

Chikusa, I, Succession to Ancestral Sacrifices and Adoption of Heirs to the Sacrifices: As Seen from an Inquiry into Customary Institutions in Manchuria, in Buxbaum, D. C. (ed), Chinese Family Law and Social Change, 150-175. University of Washington Press. Seattle and London. 1978.

Chiu, V. Y, Some Notes on Chinese Customary Marriage, in Buxbaum D. C. (ed.), Family Law and Customary Law in Asia: A Contemporary Legal Perspective, 45-49. Nijhoff. The Hague. 1968.

Ch'ü, T'ung-tsu, Law and Society in Traditional China. Hyperion Press. Westport, Connecticut. 1980 (reprint of 1961 edition).

Cohen, J. A, Chinese Mediation on the Eve of Modernization, California Law Review 54 (1966), 1201-1226.

Couvreur, S, Chou king. Ch'eng Wen Publishing Co. Taipei. 1971 (reprint of 1897 edition).

—, La chronique de la principaute de Lou, 3 vols. Cathasis. Paris. 1951.

Creel, H. G, The Origins of Statecraft in China I: The Western Chou Empire. University of Chicago Press, Chicago and London. 1970.

—, Legal Institutions and Procedures during the Chou Dynasty, in Cohen J. A, Edwards, R. R. and Chen, F. C. (eds), Essays on China's Legal Tradition, 26-55. Princeton U. P, Princeton. 1980.

—, The Beginnings of Bureaucracy in China: The Origin of the *Hsien*, in Creel, H. G, What is Taoism? and Other Studies in Chinese Cultural History, 121-159. The University of Chicago Press. Chicago and London. 1982.

—, The *Fa-chia*: 'Legalists' or 'Administrators'?, in Creel, H. G, What is Taoism? and Other Studies in Chinese Cultural History, 92-120. The University of Chicago Press. Chicago and London. 1982.

Dardess, J. W, The Cheng Communal Family: Social Organisation and Neo-Confucianism in Yüan and Early Ming China, Harvard Journal of Asiatic Studies 334 (1974), 7-52.

De Groot, J. J. M, The Religious System of China, 6 vols. Southern Materials Center. Taipei. 1982 (reprint of 1892 edition).

Doolittle, J, Social Life of the Chinese, 2 vols. Ch'eng Wen Publishing Co. Taipei. 1966 (reprint of 1865 edition).

Dubs, H. H, The History of the Former Han Dynasty by P'an Ku, 3 vols. Waverley Press. Baltimore. 1938-55.

_, The Works of Hsuntze. Ch'eng Wen Publishing Co. Taipei. 1973 (reprint of 1928 edition).

Dull, J. L, Marriage and Divorce in Han China: A Glimpse at 'Pre-Confucian' Society, in Buxbaum, D. C. (ed), Chinese Family Law and Social Change, 23-74. University of Washington Press. Seattle and London. 1978.

Duyvendak, J. J. L, The Book of Lord Shang. Probsthain. London. 1963.

Ebrey, P. B, Family Property in Sung China. Yüan Ts'ai's Precepts for Social Life. Princeton U. P. Princeton. 1984.

Eichhorn, W, Bemerkungen über einige nicht amnestierbare Verbrechen in Sung-Rechtswesen, Oriens Extremus 8 (1961), 166-176

_, Die alte chinesische Religion und das Staatskultwesen. Brill. Leiden. 1976.

Elvin, M, Female Virtue and the State in China, Past and Present 104 (1984), 111-152.

Escarra, J, Law: Chinese, in Encyclopaedia of Social Sciences 9, 249-254. MacMillan and Co. London. 1933.

_, Le droit chinois. Conception et evolution. Institutions legislatives et judicaires. Science et enseignement. Vetch. Peking. Sirey. Paris. 1936.

Feng, H. Y. and Shyrock, J. K, The Black Magic in China Known as Ku, Journal of the American Oriental Society 55 (1935),-1-30.

Franke, H, Jurchen Customary Law and the Chinese Law of the Chin Dynasty, in Eikemeier, D. and Franke, H. (eds), State and Law in East Asia. Festschrift Karl Bünger, 215-233. Harrassowitz. Wiesbaden. 1981

Freedman, M, Lineage Organisation in Southeastern China. Athlone Press. London. 1965.

Fung, Yu-lan,, A History of Chinese Philosophy, 2 vols tr. D. Bodde. Princeton U. P. Princeton. 1952-3.

Gernet, J, La Vente en Chine d'après les contrats de Touen-Houang (ixe-xe siècles), T'oung Pao XLV (1957), 295-391.

_, A History of Chinese Civilization, tr. J. R. Foster. Cambridge U. P. Cambridge. 1982.

Golas, P. J, Early Ch'ing Guilds, in Skinner G. W. (ed), The City in Late Imperial China, 555-580. Stanford University Press. Stanford. 1977.

Granet, M, La pensée chinoise. Albin Michel. Paris. 1968 (reprint of 1934 edition).

Haas, O, Gewohnheitsrechtliche Verträgstypen in China, Archiv für Ostasien I (1948), 43-59.

Harrison, J. F, Wrongful Treatment of Prisoners: A Case Study of Ch'ing Legal Practice, Journal of Asian Studies 23 (1964), 227-244.

Heuser, R, Das Rechtskapiteln im Jin-Shu. Ein Beitrag zur Kenntnis des Rechts im frühen chinesischen Kaiserreich. Schweitzer. Munchen. 1987.

Hoang, P, Notions techniques sur la propriété en Chine avec un choix d'actes et de documents officiels. Mission Catholique. Chang-hai. 1897.

_, Le mariage chinois au point de vue legal. Mission Catholique. Chang-hai. 1898

Hsiao, Kung-chuan, Rural China. Imperial Control in the Nineteenth _ Century. University of Washington Press. Seattle and London. 1967.

A History of Chinese Political Thought I: From the Beginnings to the 8ixth Century A. D, tr. F. W. Mote. Princeton U. P. Princeton. 1979.

Hu, H. C, The Common Descent Group in China and its Function. Southern Materials Center. Taipei. Reprint of 1948 edition.

Huang, Liu-hung, A Complete Book Concerning Happiness and Benevolence, ed and tr. Djang Chu. University of Arizona Press. Tuscon, Arizona. 1984.

Hucker, C. O, The Censorial System of Ming China. Stanford U. P. Stanford. 1966.

Hulsewé, A. F. P, Remnants of Han Law I. Introductory Studies and an Annotated Translation of Chapters 22 and 23 of the History of the Former Han Dynasty. Brill. Leiden. 1955.

_, 'Contracts' of the Han Period, In Lanciotti, L. (ed), Il diritto in Cina, 11-38. Olschki. Firenze. 1978.

_, The Legalists and the Laws of Ch'in, in Idema W. L. (ed), Leyden Studies in Sinology. Brill. Leiden. 1981.

_, Remnants of Ch'in Law. An Annotated Translation of the Ch'in Legal andAdministrative Rules of the 3rd Century B. C. Discovered in Yun-meng Prefecture, Hu-pei Province in 1975. Brill. Leiden. 1985.

_, Ch'in and Han Law, in The Cambridge History of China I. The Ch'in and Han Empries 221 B. C. - A. D. 200, 520-544. Cambridge U. P. Cambridge. 1986.

_, Han China - A Proto 'Welfare State'?, T'oung Pao LXXIII (1987), 265-285.

_, The Wide Scope of Tao 'Theft' in Ch'in-Han Law, Early China 13 (1988), 166-200.

Ichiko, C, Political and Institutional Reform 1901-11, in The Cambridge History of China 11. Late Ch'ing 1800-1911. Part 2, 375-415. Cambridge U. P. Cambridge 1980.

Jamieson, G, Chinese Family and Commercial Law. Vetch and Lee. Hong Kong. 1970 (reprint of 1921 edition).

Johnson, W, Group Criminal Liability in the T'ang Code, in Eikemeier, D.

and Franke, H. (eds), State and Law in East Asia. Festschrift Karl
Bünger, 145-158. Harrassowitz. Wiesbaden. 1981.

—, The Concept of Doubt in T'ang Criminal Law, in Le Blanc, C and
Blader, S. (eds), Chinese Ideas about Nature and Society. Studies in
Honour of Derk Bodde, Hong Kong University Press. Hong Kong. 1987.

Jones, W. C, Studying the Ch'ing Code - The Ta Ch'ing Lü Li, The
American Journal of Comparative Law 22 (1974), 330-364.

—, Theft in the Qing Code, The American Journal of Comparative Law 30
(1982), 499-521.

Karlgren, B, Glosses on the Book of Documents, Bulletin of the Museum of
Far Eastern Antiquities 20 (1948), 39-315.

—, The Book of Documents, Bulletin of the Museum of Far Eastern
Antiquities 22 (1950), 1-81.

Kennedy, G. A, Die Rolle des Geständnisses im chinesischen Gesetz.
Inaugural-Dissertation. Berlin. 1939.

Kroker, E, Dienst - und Werkverträge im chinesischen Gewohnheitsrecht,
Zeitschrift für deutschen Morgenländischen Gesellschaft 107 (1957), 130-
160.

—, The Concept of Property in Chinese Customary Law, Transactions of the
Asiatic Society of Japan, 3rd Series 7 (1959) 123-146.

Langlois, J. D, 'Living Law' in Sung and Yuan Jurisprudence, Harvard
Journal of Asiatic Studies 41 (1981), 165-217.

—, Authority in Family Legislation: The Cheng Family Rules, in Eikemeier,
D. and Franke, H. (eds), State and Law in East Asia. Festschrift Karl
Bünger. 272-299. Harrassowitz. Wiesbaden. 1981.

Lau, D. C, Mencius. Penguin Books. Harmondsworth. Middlesex. 1970.

Lee, K. W, The Legalist School and Legal Positivism, Journal of Chinese
Philosophy 3 (1975), 23-56.

Legge, J, The Annals of the Bamboo Books, in The Chinese Classics III.
Prolegomena, 108-176. Ch'eng Wen Publishing Co. Taipei. Undated
reprint of O.U.P. edition.

—, The Shoo King, in The Chinese Classics III, 15-630. Ch'eng Wen
Publishing Co. Taipei. Undated reprint of O.U.P. edition.

—, The Ch'un Ts'ew with the Tso Chuen, The Chinese Classics V. Ch'eng
Wen Publishing Co. Taipei. Undated reprint of O.U.P. edition.

—, Li Chi. Book of Rites, 2 vols, ed C. and W. Chai. University Books.
New York. 1967 (reprint of 1885 edition).

Leong, Y. K. and Tao, L. K, Village and Town Life in China. Ch'eng Wen
Publishing Co. Taipei. 1974 (reprint of 1915, edition).

Liao, W. K, The Complete Works of Han Fei Tzu. A Classic of Chinese
Political Science, 2 vols. Probsthain. London. 1939-59.

Lin, Pen-tien, Vergeiselung and dingliche Sicherungsrechte im chinesischen
traditionell en Privatrecht. Inaugural-Dissertation. München. 1976.

Liu, Hui-chen, The Traditional Chinese Clan Rules. Augustin. New York.

1959.

—, An Analysis of Chinese Clan Rules: Confucian Theories in Action, in Nivison, D. S. and Wright, A. F. (eds), Confucianism in Action, 63-96. Stanford U. P. Stanford. 1959.

Liu, J. T. C. Y, Ou-yang Hsiu. An Eleventh-Century Neo Confucianist. Stanford U. P. Stanford 1967.

Liu, Shih-shun, Chinese Classical Prose. The Eight Masters of the T'ang-Sung Period. The Chinese University Press. Hong Kong. 1979.

McAleavy, H, Certain Aspects of Chinese Customary Law in the Light of Japanese Scholarship, Bulletin of the School of Oriental Studies 17 (1955), 535-547.

—, Dien in China and Vietnam, Journal of Asian Studies 17 (1958), 403-415.

—, Varieties of Hu 'o' ng - Hoa: A Problem of Vietnamese Law, Bulletin of the School of Oriental and African Studies 21 (1958), 608-619.

—, Chinese Law, in Derrett, J. D. M. (ed), An Introduction to Legal Systems, 105-130. Sweet and Maxwell. London. 1968.

MacCormack, G. D, Hausgemeinshaft and Consortium, Zeitschrift für vergleichende Rechtswissenschaft 76 (1977), 10-17.

—, The T'ang Code: Early Chinese Law, The Irish Jurist xviii (1983), 132-150.

—, Mental States as Criteria of Liability in the T'ang Code, Revue internationale des droits de l'antiquité xxxi (1984), 41-74.

—, The Law of Contract in China under the T'ang and Sung Dynasties, Revue internationale des droits de l'antiquité, xxxii (1965), 17-68.

—, Law and Punishment in the Earliest Chinese Thought, The Irish Jurist xx (1985), 334-351.

—, Rectification of Names in Early Chinese Legal and Political Thought, Archiv für Rechts- und Sozialphilosophie lxii (1986), 378-396. Law and Punishment: The Western and the Traditional Legal Mind, in MacCormick, N. and Birks, P. (eds), The Legal Mind. Essays for Tony Honoré, 235-51. Clarendon Press. Oxford. 1986.

—, The Concept of *Tsang* in the T'ang Code, Revue internationale des droits de l'antiquité xxxiii (1986), 25-44.

—, Ethical Principles and the Traditional Chinese Law of Marriage, The Irish Jurist xxi (1986), 247-271.

—, Liability of Officials under the T'ang Code, Hong Kong Law Journal 17 (1987), 142-162.

—, Natural Law and Chinese Philosophy, Codicillus xxix (1988), 24-34.

—, The T'ang and Ming Law of Homicide, Revue internationale des droits de l'antiquité xxxv (1988), 27-78.

—, The Lü Hsing: Problems of Legal Interpretation, Monumenta Serica 37 (1986-87), 35-47.

—, Natural Law and Cosmic Harmony in Traditional Chinese Legal Thought, Ratio Iuris 2 (1989), 254-73.

Liability for Animals in Traditional Chinese Law, The Juridical Review, forthcoming.

MacGowan, D. J, Chinese Guilds or Chambers of Commerce and Trade Unions, Journal of the North China Branch, Royal Asiatic Society xxi (1886), 134-192.

McKnight, B. E, The Quality of Mercy. Amnesties and Traditional Chinese Justice. University Press of Hawaii. Honolulu. 1981.

— Song Legal Privileges, Journal of the American Oriental Society 105 (1985), 95-106.

— From Statute to Precedent: An Introduction to Sung Law and its Transformation, in McKnight, B. E. (ed), Law and the State in traditional East Asia. Six Studies on the Sources of East Asian Law, 111-131. University of Hawaii Press, Honolulu. 1987.

Mäding, K, Chinesisches traditionelles Erbrecht. De Gruyter. Berlin. 1966.

Mann, S., Widows in the Kinship, Class, and Community Structures of Qing Dynasty China, Journal of Asian Studies 46 (1987), 37-56.

Meijer, M. J, The Introduction of Modern Criminal Law in China. University Publications of America. Arlington, Virginia. 1976 (reprint of 1950 edition).

— The Concept of *Ku-sha* in the Ch'ing Code, in Lanciotti, L. (ed), Il diritto in Cina,. 85-114. Olschki. Firenze. 1978.

— An Aspect of Retribution in Traditional Chinese Law, T'oung Pao LXVI (1980), 199-216.

— Review of Nakamura Shigeo, Studies in Ch'ing Law, T'oung Pao LXVI (1980) 348-353.

— The Price of a P'ai-lou, T'oung Pao LXVII (1981), 288-304.

— Abuse of Power and Coercion, in Eikemeiger, D. and Franke, H. (eds), State and Law in East Asia. Festschrift Karl Bünger, 184-203. Harrassowitz. Wiesbaden. 1981.

— Criminal responsibility for the Suicide of Parents in Ch'ing Law, in Idema, W. L. (ed), Leyden Studies in Sinology, 109-137. Brill. Leiden. 1981.

— The Autumn Assizes in Ch'ing Law, T'oung Pao LXX (1984), 1-17.

— Homosexual Offences in Ch'ing Law, T'oung Pao LXXI (1985), 109-133.

Metzger, T. A, The Internal Organization of Ch'ing Bureaucracy. Legal, Normative, and Communication Aspects. Harvard U. P. Cambridge, Mass. 1973.

Miyazaki, I, The Administration of Justice during the Sung Dynasty, in Cohen, J. A, Edwards, R. R. and Chen, F. C. (eds), Essays in China's Legal Tradition , 56-75. Princeton U. P. Princeton. 1980.

Munzel, F, Strafrecht im alten China nach den Strafrechtskapiteln in den Ming-Annalen. Harrassowitz. Wiesbaden. 1968.

Needham, J, Science and Civilization in China II. History of Scientific Thought. Cambridge U. P. Cambridge. 1956.

Ng, V. W, Ideology and Sexuality: Rape Laws in Qing China, Journal of Asian Studies 46 (1987), 57-70.

Ocko, J. K, I'll Take It All the Way to Beijing: Capital Appeals in the Qing, Journal of Asian Studies 47 (1988), 291-315.

Okamatzu, S, Provisional Report on Investigations of Laws and Customs in the Island of Formosa. Ch'eng Wen Publishing Co. Taipei. 1971 (reprint of 1900 edition).

Ou, Koei-hing,, La peine d'après le code des T'ang. Sirey. Paris. 1935.

Palmer, M. J. E, The Surface-Subsoil Form of Divided Ownership in Late Imperial China: Some Examples from the New Territories of Hong Kong, Modern Asian Studies 21 (1987), 1-119.

Pelliot, P, Notes de bibliographie chinoise, Bulletin de l'école français d'extrême orient 9 (1909), 123-152.

Po Hu T'ung, The Comprehensive Discourses in the White Tiger Hall, tr. Tjan Tjoe Som, 2 vols. Brill. Leiden. 1949.

Pokora, T, The Canon of Laws by Li K'uei - A Double Falsification?, Archiv Orientalni 27 (1959), 96-121.

Ratchnevsky, P, Un code des Yüan. Leroux, Paris. 1937.

_, Un code des Yüan II. Presses universitaires de France. Paris. 1972.

_, Un code des Yüan IV. College de France. Institut de hautes études chinoises. Paris. 1985.

Rosner, E, Die 'Zehn schimpliflichen Delikte' im chinesischen Recht der Yüan-Zeit. Inaugural-Dissertation. München. 1964.

Schurmann, H. F, Traditional Property Concepts in China, Far Eastern Quarterly 15 (1956), 507-516.

Seidel, P, Die Sanktion der ungerechtfertigten Bereicherung im chinesischen Recht der T'ang Zeit, Oriens Extremus (1975), 137-159.

_, Das Zurücktreten des Gesetzesbuches zugunsten der Erlasse im Recht der Sung Zeit, in Eikemeier, D. and Franke, H. (eds), State and Law in East Asia. Festschrift Karl Bünger, 207-214. Harrassowitz. Wiesbaden. 1981.

_, Studien zur Rechtsgeschichte der Sung-Zeit. Übersetzung und Kommentierung des ersten Strafrechtskapitelns aus den Sung-Annalen. Haag und Herchen. Frankfurt/Main. 1983.

von Senger, H, Kaufverträge im traditionellen China. Schulthess and Co. Zurich. 1970.

_, Chinesische Bodeninstitutionen im Taiho-Verwaltungskodex. Harrassowitz. Wiesbaden. 1983.

Shiga, S, Some Remarks on the Judicial System in China: Historical Development and Characteristics, in Buxbaum, D. C. (ed), Traditional and Modern Legal Institutions in Asia and Africa, 44-53. Brill. Leiden. 1967.

_, Criminal Procedure in the Ch'ing Dynasty - with Emphasis on its Administrative Character and Some Allusion to its Historical Antecedents I, Memoirs of the Research Department of the Toyo Bunko 32 (1974),

1-45; II,33 (1975), 115-138.

—, Family Property and the Law of Inheritance in Traditional China, in Buxbaum, D. C. (ed), Chinese Family Law and Social Change, 109-150. University of Washington Press. Seattle and London. 1978.

Soothill, W. E, The Analects of Confucius. O. U. P. London 1937.

van der Sprenkel, S, Legal Institutions in Manchu China. A Sociological Analysis. Athlone Press. London. 1966.

—, Urban Social Control, in Skinner G. W. (ed), The City in Late Imperial China, 609-632. Stanford U. P. Stanford. 1977.

Tai, Yen-hui, Divorce in Traditional Chinese Law, in Buxbaum D. C. (ed), Chinese Family Law and Social Change. 75-106. University of Washington Press. Seattle and London. 1978.

T'ien, Ju-k'ang, Male Anxiety and Female Chastity. A Comparative Study of Chinese Ethical Values in Ming-Ch'ing Times. Brill. Leiden. 1988.

Twitchett, D. C, The Fragment of the T'ang Ordinances of the Department of Waterways Discovered at Tun-huang, Asia Major 6 (1957), 23-79.

—, The Fan Clan's Charitable Estate, 1050-1760, in Nivision, D. S. and Wright, A. E. (eds), Confucianism in Action, 97-133. Stanford U. P. Stanford. 1959.

—, The T'ang Market System, Asia Major xii (1966), 202-248

—, Financial Administration under the T'ang Dynasty, 2nd ed. Cambridge U. P. Cambridge. 1970.

—, Varied Patterns of Provincial Autonomy in the T'ang Dynasty, in Perry, J. C. and Smith, B. C. (eds), Essays on T'ang Society, 90-109. Brill. Leiden. 1976.

—, The Implementation of Law in Early T'ang China, in Lanciotti, L. (ed), Il diritto in Cina, 57-84. Olschki. Firenze. 1978.

van der Valk, M. H, Voluntary Surrender in Chinese Law, in Szirma Z, (ed), Law in Eastern Europe. Miscellanea II, 359-394. Sijthoff. Leiden. 1967.

Vandermeersch, L, An Enquiry into the Chinese Conception of the Law, in Schram, S. R. (ed), The Scope of State Power in China, 3-25. School of Oriental and African Studies, University of London and the Chinese University of Hong Kong. London and Hong Kong. 1985.

Wallacker, B. E, The Poet as Jurist: Po Chü-i and a Case of Conjugal Homicide, Harvard Journal of Asiatic Studies 41 (1981), 507-526.

—, The Chinese Offence of Homicide through Horseplay, Chinese Studies 1 (1983), 259-316.

Waltner, A, Widows and Remarriage in Ming and Early Qing China, Historical Reflections 8 (1981), 129-146.

Wang, Yeh-chien,, Land Taxation in Imperial China 1750-1911. Harvard U. P. Cambridge, Mass. 1973.

Watson, B, Record of the Grand Historian of China, 2 vols. Columbia U. P. New York and London. 1961.

___ Hsün Tzu. Basic Writings. Columbia U. P. New York. 1963.

Weggel, O, Chinesische Rechtsgeschichte. Brill. Leiden/Koln. 1980.

Wilhelm, R, Li Gi. Das Buch der Sitte. Diederichs. Jena. 1930.

Frühling und Herbst des Lü Bu We. Eugen Diederichs. Düsseldorf/Koln. 1979.

Williams, G. W, The Middle Kingdom, 2 vols. Paragon. New York. 1966 (reprint of 1895 edition).

Wilkinson, E, Landlord and Labor in Late Imperial China. Case Studies from Shandong by Jing Su and Luo Lun. Harvard U. P. Cambridge, Mass. 1978.

Wolf, A. P. and Huang, C. S, Marriage and Adoption in China, 1845-1945. Stanford U. P. Stanford 1980.

Yang, Lien-sheng, Money and Credit in China. A Short History. Harvard U. P. Cambridge, Mass. 1952.

___ Excursions in Sinology. Harvard U. P. Cambridge, Mass. 1969.

Yen, Chih-t'ui, Family Instructions for the Yen Clan. Yen-shih Chia-hsun. An Annotated Translation by Teng Ssu-yu. Brill. Leiden, 1968.

Zelin, M, The Magistrate's Tael. Rationalizing Fiscal Reform in Eighteenth Century Ch'ing China. University of California Press. Berkeley. 1984.

___, The Rights of Tenants in Mid-Qing Sichuan: A Study of Land-Related Lawsuits in the Baxian Archives, Journal of Asian Studies xlv (1986), 499-526.

Index